Introduction to Management

Introduction to
Management

by Tony Dawson MA., IPFA.

TUDOR

© T. Dawson 1998

Published in Great Britain by Tudor Business Publishing Limited.

First Published 1998

A CIP catalogue for this book is available from the British Library

ISBN 1 872807 03 8

Typeset by Deltatype Ltd, Birkenhead, Merseyside
Printed and bound by Athenaeum Press Ltd, Newcastle upon Tyne

Contents

To George and Simon

New Management Standards

The new standards are more flexible allowing individuals to choose options which meet the functional requirements of their parallel organisational roles.

Under the new standards NVQ levels 3, 4 and 5 include three types of Unit.

Mandatory – core competencies required by all candidates.

Optional – competencies which add breadth and flexibility.

Additional – career specified competencies or professional specialisms namely quality and energy.

There are also two qualifications after NVQ Level 5 – Strategic and Operational.

The qualifications are set out in the panel below:

MANAGEMENT LEVEL 3

For practising managers or supervisors with tightly defined areas of responsibility, some limited opportunity for taking decisions and managing budgets: responsibility for achieving specific results by using resources effectively: and responsibility for the allocation of work to team members, colleagues or contractors.

Seven units required – five mandatory plus two out of a choice of eight optional units.

Mandatory units

A1   Maintain activities to meet requirements
B1   Support the efficient use of resources
C1   Manage yourself
C4   Create effective working relationships
D1   Management information for action

Optional units

C7   Contribute to the selection of personnel for activities
C9   Contribute to the development of teams and individuals
C12   Lead the work of teams and individuals to achieve their objectives
C15   Respond to poor performance in your team
E5   Identify improvements to energy efficiency
E8   Provide advice and support for improving energy efficiency

F5   Provide advice and support for the development and implementation of quality systems
F7   Carry out quality audits

MANAGEMENT LEVEL 4

For practising managers with responsibility for allocating work to others, achieving specific results by using resources effectively, carrying out policy in defined areas of authority contolling limited financial budgets and contributing to broader activities such as change programmes and recruitment.

Nine units required – five mandatory plus *either B2 or B3 and three from the choice of 17 optional units (including B2 or B3 if not taken mandatory)*

Mandatory units

A2   Manage activities to meet requirements
A4   Contribute to improvements at work
C2   Develop your own resources
C5   Develop productive working relationships
D4   Provide information to support decision making
B2   Manage the use of physical resources
B3   Manage the use of financial resources

Optional units

C8   Select personnel for activities
C10   Develop teams and individuals to enhance performance
C13   Manage the performance of teams or individuals
C15   Respond to poor performance in your team
D2   Facilitate meetings
E3   Promote energy efficiency
E5   Identify improvements to energy efficiency
E6   Provide advice and support for the development of energy efficient practices
E8   Provide advice and support for improving energy efficiency
F2   Provide advice and support for the development and implementation
F4   Implement quality assurance systems
F6   Monitor compliance with quality systems
F7   Carry out quality audits
G1   Contribute to project planning and preparation
G2   Coordinate the running of projects
G3   Contribute to project closure

OPERATIONAL MANAGEMENT LEVEL 5

For practising managers who have operational responsibility for substantial programmes and resources: have a broad span of control: proactively identify and implement change and quality improvements: negotiate budgets and contracts and lead high level meetings.

Ten units required – six mandatory plus four out of a choice of 17 optional units.

Mandatory units

A3 Manage activities to meet customer requirements
A5 Manage change in organisational activities
B4 Determine the effective use of resources
C3 Enhance your own performance
C6 Enhance productive working relationships
D6 Use information to take critical decisions

Optional units

B5 Secure financial resources for your organisation's plans
C8 Select personnel for activities
C10 Develop teams and individuals to enhance performance
C13 Manage the performance of teams and individuals
C16 Deal with poor performance in your team
C17 Redeploy personnel and make redundancies
D3 Chair and participate in meetings
D5 Establish information management and communication systems
E1 Identify the scope for improvement in the way the organisation manages energy
E3 Promote energy efficiency
F1 Promote the importance and benefits of quality
F3 Manage continuous quality improvement
F4 Implement quality assurance systems
F6 Monitor compliance with quality systems
G4 Plan and prepare projects
G5 Manage the running of projects
G6 Complete projects

STRATEGIC MANAGEMENT LEVEL 5

For practising managers who: who have responsibility for substantial programmes and resources, have responsibility for the strategic development of their organisation, have a broad span of control, proactively identify and implement change and quality improvements: negotiate budgets and contracts and lead high level meetings.

All ten units are mandatory

A6 Review external and internal operating environments
A7 Establish strategies to guide the work of your organisation
A8 Evaluate and improve organisational performance
B5 Secure financial resources for your organisation's plans
C3 Enhance your own performance
C6 Enhance productive working relationships
C11 Develop management teams
C14 Delegate work to others
D3 Chair and participate in meetings
D6 Use information to take critical decisions

ENERGY MANAGEMENT LEVEL 4

The NVQ covers the full range of activities expected to be carried out by an energy manager and is for either a specialist manager with full or partial responsibility for energy in an organisation or a consultant helping the organisation to improve its energy efficiency.

Nine units required – six mandatory plus three out of a choice of ten optional units.

Mandatory units

C2 Develop your own resources
E2 Provide advice on the development and implementation of energy policies
E4 Monitor and evaluate energy efficiency
E6 Provide advice and support for the development of energy efficient practices
E7 Provide advice and support for the development and implementation of systems to measure energy usage
E8 Provide advice and support for improving energy efficiency

Optional units

A2 Manage activities to meet requirements
B4 Determine the effective use of resources
C5 Develop productive working relationships
C10 Develop teams and individuals to enhance performance
D2 Facilitate meetings
E1 Identify the scope for improvement in the way the organisation manages energy
E3 Promote energy efficiency
E5 Identify improvements to energy efficiency
E9 Determine conditions in the market for suppliers (PSLB 019)
F3 Manage continuous quality improvement

QUALITY MANAGEMENT LEVEL 4

The NVQ is for either a specialist manager with responsibility for quality in an organisation or a consultant helping the organisation to improve its quality performance.

Nine units required – six mandatory plus three out of a choice of nine optional units.

Mandatory units

C2   Develop you own resources
F2   Provide advice and support for the development implementation of quality policies
F3   Manage continuous quality impovement
F4   Implement quality assurance systems
F5   Provide advice and support for the development and implementation of quality systems
F6   Monitor compliance with quality systems

Optional units

A2   Manage activities to meet requirements
B4   Determine the effective use of resources
C5   Develop productive working relationships
C10 Develop teams and individuals to enhance performance
C13 Manage the performance of teams and individuals
D2   Facilitate meetings
D4   Provide information to support decision making
F1   Promote the importance and benefits of quality
F7   Carry out quality audits

Foreword

As chief executive of the Management Charter Initiative, I can recommend this book which covers in depth all of the issues addressed in the Charter.

The Charter emphasises the interrelationship between all areas of management and this text, with its many cross-references to related issues, fully reflects the complexity of the modern organisation and how it relates, both internally and externally, to all aspects of management.

This comprehensive coverage need not deter students of management who wish to study a particular topic, since the text covers specific issues in separate chapters, each self-contained and addressing both the theory and practice of modern management.

Professor Tom Cannon

Introduction

In many texts the subject of management is examined in a theoretical context, somewhat remote from the day-to-day world of the practising manager. Management theory is useful in that, by researching areas in depth and attempting to make general conclusions, it helps codify and organise the various duties of the manager. However theory in isolation can appear to be obscure and distant from the practical, and often changing and difficult, world of the professional manager. This text tries to retain the undoubted benefits of examining management theories whilst trying to link these theories to practical scenarios. Most academic and professional courses are moving towards examining through real life situations, so whenever management theory is introduced I have attempted to accompany it with practical illustrations of its real life applicability.

Each chapter is preceded by a number of learning outcomes which the reader should consider in his or her examination of the chapter. At the end of each chapter there is an exercise, based on the content of the chapter, which the reader may wish to undertake

In researching and writing this book I have been greatly helped by the Management Charter Initiative which has conveniently outlined and categorised the management standards and competences that organisations and practising managers should acquire. The integrated structure of the Management Standards is shown following this introduction.

I have deliberately constructed a large number of chapters; this segmentation allows the reader to focus on separate aspects of the total management environment. However the sectionalisation of the book facilitates the linkage of these separate chapters. within individual chapters reference will be made to other chapters in the book. The text is divided into eight sections. Each section examines part of the managerial environment of the practising manager.

The first section examines the subject from an overall perspective. The second assesses the importance of managers effectively managing themselves. The third section extends the duty of the manger to managing other people. The fourth appraises the specialist area of human resource management. The fifth section examines the organisational dimensions of management. The sixth concentrates on the processes involved in managing an organisation. The seventh section focuses on the management of important functional areas. The final section examines management in the environment of small, entrepreneurial organisations. Unique features of this environment are outlined but the general conclusion is that much of this special environment is reflective of management principles which should be applied to all organisations regardless of their size.

I am grateful to the help given to me by my colleague Neil Fuller and by Mike Green of the International Business and Management Centre, Wirral Metropolitan College. Finally my thanks are accorded to Professor Tom Cannon for his role in creating and developing the Management Charter Initiative and for his foreword to this book.

Tony Dawson 1998

Defining the Subject Area

OBJECTIVES

This section seeks to examine the breadth of issues and perspectives included in the topic area of management. Difficulties in finding a comprehensive yet workable definition of the management task will be acknowledged. The commonly accepted sub divisions of approaches to management will be critically examined. The section will provide a framework from which the remaining sections in the text can be viewed. After reading this section the wide variety of duties of the manager and approaches to management should be better understood.

INTRODUCTION

Before a detailed examination of the subject area of management and its component parts can be made it is necessary to define the term 'management', to prescribe the boundaries of the subject area, to state the perspectives from which the subject will be examined. Hence, in this section, an attempt will be made to define these parameters and perspectives.

Chapter one

The Problem of Management

LEARNING OBJECTIVES

- **Understand the main theoretical approaches to the subject of management**

- **Understand the application of these theories**

- **Understand the extent to which they embrace real life management action**

- **Understand the dynamic nature of this subject**

- **Examine the parameters in organisations with which the reader is familiar**

- **Identify areas for more research**

Management as a formal discipline emerged only towards the end of the nineteenth century. Yet it must be acknowledged that management has been in existence since mankind became organised into formal groups. Consequently it would be unwise to confine any study of management to those people who have studied the topic of management as a formal discipline. It is undoubtedly the case that any study of mankind either in literature, other artistic enterprises, or in philosophical works, contributes as much to the store of knowledge on the subject of management as do the more formal studies of the discipline. Thus any comprehensive catalogue of written management thought must embrace those writings which examine the complexities of human existence and not just those texts which contain the word 'management'. It must be stressed that this comment is not intended to disparage formal writings on management but there is a vital need to draw attention to the immensely wide variety of literature on the topic and the breadth of human knowledge of the subject area.

If we direct our attention towards formal writings on the subject of management we will find that it is surprisingly difficult to produce a definition of management which would completely satisfy all practitioners of management or, more particularly, all management theorists. The reality is that the views of different practitioners and different writers would vary in that they would place different emphases on the different tasks of management. As will be seen in the following chapters of this text the subject of management covers a wide variety of issues. Naturally some managers will develop special skills, aptitudes or interests in some areas, whereas the skills, aptitudes or interests of other managers will be evidenced in other areas of this widely varying subject area. Paralleling this diversity of interest we find that different attempts to establish general principles about the academic discipline of management, through formal writing on the subject, will exhibit similar diversity of emphasis. However any definition of management must attempt to embrace all or, more realistically, as many as possible of those tasks which practising managers undertake. In attempting to establish a comprehensive, acceptable definition of management it might prove useful to examine the history of management thought through the twentieth century. Such an historical analysis will illustrate the benefits and deficiencies of certain types of approach to the problem of defining and examining the concept of management.

Scientific/Classical Approach

This was the prevailing attitude towards the task or duty of management for approximately the first 30 years of the twentieth century. The main concentration of such an approach to the examination of management is on the establishment of order and rationality within the structure and design of an organisation; the duty of the manager would be to create order, rationality and direction in a situation which would otherwise be unordered, and lacking in rationality and direction. Examples of such approaches are the works of F.W. Taylor and Weber but within the broad confines of this approach perhaps the most comprehensive examination of the management task is the work of Henri Fayol. Most of Fayol's research was conducted in the French Armed Forces and, with the benefit of post-Fayol management thought, in many ways his theories can be seen to be well rooted in the special culture of a military environment.

Henri Fayol

Fayol concentrates his attention on the management and administrative requirements of an effective organisation. This effectiveness he argues will be achieved only when certain principles are adopted.

a) Division of work into separate skill areas or functional specialisms. Such specialisation will afford to the organisation the benefits of familiarity and practice. An example of this arrangement would be the type of organisation which creates a separate finance department to deal with all financial matters, a separate research and development department to assume all responsibility for research and development and a separate marketing department to execute all marketing responsibilities.

b) Clear definition of levels and areas of responsibility. Such a clear division will help eliminate any uncertainty in the organisation. Such management arrangements should result in one employee having only one manager. Under such an organisation each manager will have duties and responsibilities carefully defined in such a way that in no circumstances would that manager's authority be usurped by anyone else nor would that manager usurp any other person's authority.

c) The objectives of the organisation should be clearly specified and it should be recognised that individual objectives are subordinate to such organisational objectives. In the establishing of such objectives there should be strong central direction from the senior management of the organisation. This creates a situation where all those working in the organisation will be able to readily determine its purpose and direction.

d) Communication should be effected through vertical structures – that is, the primary channel of communication should be seen to be between the employee and the manager. More detail on this and other channels of communication is found in a later section of this text. Under such an arrangement little opportunity would be afforded for lateral communication (between people of the same level within the organisation) or for informal discussion.

e) To ensure that organisational objectives are achieved, clearly understood, powerful and permanent procedures should be established. The organisation should strive for stability in its workforce to reinforce this emphasis on order and certainty. Such an organisation would be 'driven' by its formal rules and regulations. Perhaps a good example of this arrangement in practice would be the armed forces or the police service.

f) To fulfil human needs within the organisation the management of the organisation should be seen to treat all its employees with fairness, kindliness and understanding when required. An 'esprit de corps' should be developed within the organisation – that is, the employees should perceive a common and mutually rewarding purpose and mission in working within the organisation. An example of this arrangement would be the workings of an effective sporting team where all individual action is willingly directed towards achieving the common goal – victory.

This theory of organisational design can be seen to concentrate its attention on order and certainty. It must be acknowledged that there is some emphasis on the fulfilment of human needs in the work of the organisation – typically in the last desired feature of organisational design (the primary feature of the Human Relations Approach) but undoubtedly the fundamental principles of the work of Fayol firmly establish him in the Scientific or Classical School of management thought.

Such an approach to the management of an organisation has certain attractive features; however, as will be seen later in this chapter, it does have some deficiencies or weaknesses. The main advantages are as follows.

a) It emphasises a rational approach to the management of an organisation. Undoubtedly if subjective judgement is kept to a minimum the emphases should be placed on the provable or proven. Inevitably the management and activity of an organisation should be directed as much as possible towards those areas where success should best obtain. In many circumstances the organisation can learn from the mistakes of the past by ensuring that controls are exerted to 'guide' the organisation in the best direction. Perhaps the best analogy is the parent guiding the child towards successful or acceptable behaviour patterns.

b) It enables the organisation to codify and continue best practice for the application of procedures within the organisation. As will be seen throughout this text many management problems will occur in a typical organisation and anything which provides a clear route through these difficulties is to be welcomed.

c) It can be seen to be particularly appropriate in an organisation with a standard product. The certainty conveyed by such established practices is best suited to circumstances where experimentation is not needed. Indeed in such circumstances experimentation results in wasted effort.

d) It is best practised in an environment of certainty. Such an approach will work best when those defined procedures and practices which are established are seen to be proven. Clearly such benefits of this approach which do exist will not obtain if there is no logical basis in emphasising the tried and tested. For instance when a routine activity is undertaken the tried and tested 'off the shelf' approach is ideal. However if something new is needed the library of proven responses simply does not exist.

There are several problems to this scientific approach.

a) The emphasis on certainty and established activities is not as immediately suited to an environment of change. As will be seen throughout this text many organisations are increasingly subject to such environmental change. Such change demands new ideas be generated and the rigid discipline of this approach is not suited to the more creative environment of 'ideas generation' in that many valuable sources of advice and expertise would be ignored. A particular example of this would be the experience of those closest to client needs who are usually not senior managers (who have the primary authority under this approach) but line operatives.

b) The emphasis on fixed practices is less well justified where there are non-standard production requirements. There will be a necessity to develop individual procedures for separate product designs. The documenting of this wider variety of procedures will be more complex and probably more confusing than would be the case in circumstances of more standardised production. In such circumstances the emphasis on order and rationality might not be as cost effective.

c) The emphasis on rigid procedures may hinder the much needed initiative required in organisations facing a dynamic environment. It is unlikely that all eventualities would be addressed in a work manual and emphasising the supremacy of this inevitably flawed document may inhibit flexibility by those most familiar with task demands. These are most commonly not senior managers but, again, line operatives.

d) The tendency in this approach is to treat the employee as just another resource of the organisation. Later in this chapter and elsewhere in this book, this assumption of machine-like characteristics for mankind will be seen to be incomplete, naive and potentially dangerous.

The Human Relations Approach

This approach assumed supremacy in management thought during the middle decades of the twentieth century. It emphasises the complexities of mankind and devotes much more attention to the satisfaction of human needs within the organisation. It stresses the need for the organisation to obtain co-operation from its employees; it highlights the importance of harmonising organisational and human needs and objectives. According to this approach, only when such human needs are satisfied will the organisation function to maximum effect. This school of thought first emerged from the work of Elton Mayo's Hawthorne Electrical studies between 1924 and 1936. One of his major findings was the importance of group pressures which are placed upon individual employees in the work environment – this will be examined in more detail in a later section. Other examples of such an approach will be found in the work of the Human Relations Motivational Theorists such as Maslow, and Herzberg (examined in detail in the chapter on Human Motivation). This emphasis on human activity within organisations affords the benefits of much more information being generated on this very important dimension of the management task. This can be seen to be particularly important in that, in many cases, employees are the most expensive resource within an organisation. Furthermore, as will be seen in the chapter on Human Motivation, the motivation and co-operation of employees is by no means guaranteed; rather the organisation needs to carefully cultivate and nurture this co-operation. Finally it can be seen that the employee is the most flexible resource available to an organisation and certainly the only resource which is capable of 'taking the initiative' in adapting to changing circumstances. The importance of this will be examined throughout the rest of this text.

However, the undue concentration on this human-centred approach can result in the need to manage other resources being ignored. Furthermore, in its purest form, it will not result in management attention being directed towards the need to co-ordinate the use of human resources with the other resources of the organisation. As, in many cases, the number of people employed by the organisation declines the need to devote exclusive attention to this aspect of management can be seen to be less crucial. However it must be acknowledged that developments in management thought over the past few decades have built on, rather than rejected, the human relations approach. The more thorough attention devoted to the special needs of employees is probably the most important achievement of the formal discipline of management.

Systems Approach

As computer-related technology was introduced into organisations a new style of approach which became known as the 'Systems Approach' began to emerge. This approach likens an organisation to a system similar to that used in computers. The primary aim of the Systems Approach is to model the ideal organisational design. A good example of this approach can be found in the work of Katz and Kahn in 1966.

This theory claims that an organisation consists of a number of sub-systems. Examples of such sub-systems are:

a) production/technical – this sub-system provides the primary function or purpose of the organisation. Examples would be the production lines of industrial enterprises or, in the public service context, social services homes or hospitals.

b) supportive – this sub-system supports the production sub-system. For instance it procures inputs and resources (eg personnel functions) or disposes of products (eg sales or despatch functions).

c) adaptive – this sub-system ensures that the organisation adapts to changing circumstances. An example would be the research function.

This approach has advantages in that it embraces the strengths of the previous two approaches by providing the structure of the Scientific Approach and also accommodating the human dimensions of the Human Relations Approach. However its major limitation is that it seeks to define the ideal and general design for an organisation. Much recent evidence points to the importance of differences between and within organisations – this will be examined in more detail in the section on the Organisational Domain. It has been generally replaced by the Contingency Approach which ceases to seek universal solutions and instead considers an organisational design to be a product of a variety of inter–related factors.

Contingency Approach

This approach has gained prominence as the importance of the special features of an organisation have become recognised. It has assumed more importance as organisations have become increasingly exposed, and have had to adapt to, more rapidly changing environments. It is an approach which is illustrated in coverage of many of the specialist subjects in this text. A good example of this approach is the work of Lawrence and Lorsch.

In their analysis they claim that the desired design of an individual organisation is a product of a number of inter-related factors; these factors will change from organisation to organisation and from time to time within any given organisation.

Thus there will be no one type of design which will necessarily suit all organisations or, indeed, all parts of any one organisation. Examples of these factors are:

a) the environment – the organisation faced with a stable environment might find centralised decision-making structures to be most suited to its needs; alternatively an organisation with a varied environment might find decentralised structures more applicable.

b) size – the small organisation might be better organised through strong central control; the larger organisation might find decentralised structures more suitable.

c) personnel – the organisation with a well educated and trained workforce might find that centralised structures are resisted by its employees; whereas less well educated and trained workers might be more satisfied with centralised management structures.

More detailed analyses and applications of this type of approach are found at various parts of the book – particularly in the future section on the Organisational Domain.

The Work of the Manager

After discussing these different or varied approaches to the work of the manager, it might be useful to adopt a slightly different stance to defining the topic of management. It might be helpful to briefly list the variety of tasks which may be expected from a manager and, as such, the term 'management' can be defined in terms of what practising managers actually do. One of the more comprehensive of such lists is that afforded by the work of Mintzberg, 1983: management consists of the operation of these widely varied roles. These roles are examined in more detail later in the text.

a) Entrepreneur – sometimes the manager must assume the role of risk taker. Organisations sometimes have to deal with unexpected events and in such circumstances there will be little factual evidence upon which to evaluate a possible response. In such situations it is the duty of the manager to at least participate in or, more likely, take the lead in the generation of an acceptable reaction.

b) Resource allocator – the manager is the person charged with the distribution and allocation of resources.

c) Leader – the primary duty of leadership in an organisation lies with the manager. This is not to claim that the leader need necessarily adopt high profile styles of leadership.

d) Communicator – one of the more important roles of the manager is that of acting as the primary disseminator and receiver of information.

e) Monitor and controller – one of the tasks of the manager is to ensure that the organisation is working in ways which are consistent with the achievement of its objectives.

f) Disturbance handler – occasionally the organisation will not function as smoothly as it might and disturbances or disagreements may emerge. In such circumstances it is the duty of the manager to deal with these problems in such a way as to minimise the negative impact on the organisation.

g) Spokesperson – one of the major duties of the manager is to ensure that the interests of those who are managed are properly recognised. In such circumstances it may be necessary to ensure that the group's views are known.

Distinction Between Management and Administration

A useful way of illustrating the variety and diversity of management activity is to draw a distinction between 'management' and 'administration'. The former embraces a wide variety of duties – ranging from planning activity to producing, from motivating to controlling. The latter concentrates upon the production function. Administration can be seen to be a narrow activity. Management can be seen to be a much more wide-ranging activity.

Future Domains of Management

The variety of approaches to management have just been addressed but the analysis would be incomplete if we did not examine future concerns or trends in management. Many of these concerns will be more specifically addressed later in the text.

THE NEED TO ADAPT TO A CHANGING ENVIRONMENT

The analysis so far has addressed the issue of management as if organisations and management existed within a static environment. Since the late 1980s this thesis has been outdated. The environment faced by organisations is rapidly changing. Competition is becoming more robust in all areas of economic activity and is no longer restricted to the national economy in which the organisation might operate. The European Union has, for instance, ensured that organisations operating within its boundaries will have much more immediate access to the whole European market and not just the nations operating within that market. Technology is rapidly changing with increasing access to information from international as well as national sources. Organisations, in these more competitive circumstances, have to be increasingly mindful of changes in customer preferences. Thus all organisations must be capable of reacting to their more rapidly changing environments and the study of management must focus more clearly and specifically on the management of change.

GLOBAL INTERDEPENDENCE

Since the late 1980s many organisations have been operating in an external environment where economic conditions in one economy are increasingly reflective of and influenced by economic conditions in other economies. Financial markets are more rigorously reflecting this global interdependence. Reinforcing this economic interdependence has been the growth in strategic alliances between organisations on a global rather than national scale. Thus, for instance, it has become increasingly common for British companies to operate in other economies and own enterprises operating in foreign markets.

QUALITY

The regulatory framework of many economies has focused more robustly on quality. Consumer organisations have begun to more vigorously demand quality in the economic exchange. Under such economic and social circumstances there has been a major growth in the focus on quality in the products, services, processes and management of organisations.

These three additional features can be seen to expand the domain of management and increase the range of duties and vigilance of managers within organisations.

Summary

The subject of management is wide ranging in its nature. It is not easy to find a definition which is both easy to understand and yet is sufficiently comprehensive in nature to embrace all the tasks of the manager. Different definitions or approaches to the tasks of management focus attention on certain aspects of the work of the manager. In many ways it is probably more productive to define management in terms of those things which managers do, either routinely or exceptionally, in the course of their duties.

During the rest of this text the variety of management tasks and scenarios as afforded by the contingency viewpoint of management and by the views of Mintzberg in particular will be examined. The text will be divided into separate sections, each one representing a subdivision of the total management task. This subdivision must not be seen as claiming that the total and highly complex task of management can be completely subdivided into discrete sections of activity. In the 'live' management exercise it will be found that each claimed separate section of the management task, as hypothesised, will be seen to be somewhat arbitrary. For instance, later in the book the topic of The Manager's Role in Solving Problems will be examined (in the section on Managing Ourselves). An examination of this topic will reveal that it involves elements of self management, elements of managing others, and elements of the Organisational Domain. However, a sensitive reading of this text will show that the sections are introduced as a way of succinctly codifying the subject area of management so that each individual activity area can be investigated in the context of the management issues and perspectives with which it is most directly connected.

Exercise

In the context of an organisation with which you are familiar describe the features of management which you consider to be important.

Further Reading

Argyris, C. (1964) *Integrating the Individual and the Organisation*, Wiley

Beer, S. (1981) *The Heart of the Enterprise*, Wiley

Burns, T. and Stalker, G.M. (1966) *The Management of Innovation*, Tavistock

Child, J. (1984) *Organisations: a Guide to Problems and Practice*, Harper and Row

Connock, S. (1991): *HR Vision: Managing a Quality Workforce*, Institute of Personnel Management

Cummings, T. G. and Worley, C. G. (1993) *Organization Management and Change*, West Publishing

Drucker, P. (1977) *Management*, Pan

Goss, D. (1994) *Principles of Human Resource Management*, Routledge

Katz & Kahn (1966) *Social Psychology of Organisations*, Wiley

Mintzberg, H. (1983) *Power in and Around Organisations*, Prentice Hall

Morden, T. (1996), *Principles of Management*, McGraw-Hill

Schien, E.H. (1980) *Organisational Psychology*, Prentice Hall

Weber, M. (1947) *Theory of Social and Economic Organisation*, Free Press

Managing Ourselves

OBJECTIVES

The purpose of this section is to examine those elements of the management task which relate to a manager's understanding of himself or herself – his or her values, perspectives, management style, personality, and use of time. Thus by the end of this section the reader should understand those elements of managerial success which are directly related to the manager's own actions and over which the manager has direct control.

INTRODUCTION

There are many factors which influence the management environment. Many of those factors are difficult for the individual manager to control. However there are elements of the management environment which are intrinsic to the manager himself or herself. Examples of these features are the values and perspectives which managers introduce into their decision making, the way they perceive others, their enthusiasm for the management challenges they face, their efficiency and the way in which they relate to others. These 'internal' characteristics are a very important part of the total management challenge. In many ways deficiencies in these features of the managerial environment are perhaps the most commonly found, most easily altered and yet, strangely, the most difficult for managers themselves to detect. It is essential, therefore, that the manager understands thoroughly those elements of the total management task which are most directly under his or her control.

Relating to
Others

L E A R N I N G   O B J E C T I V E S

- Be aware of the importance of the subject in the total management environment

- Identify mistakes the manager can make when he or she relates to other people in the management environment

- Assess the causes of such mistakes

- Identify how such mistakes could be avoided

- Create a managerial environment where such mistakes are kept to a minimum

- Illustrate the application of the content of the chapter to real life situations

- Identify areas where more research might be desirable

Perceiving Others

In our lives we are bombarded with stimuli. We hear sounds from other people and from surrounding objects, we see light and colours, we use our sense of smell. Psychologists consider that these varieties of stimuli are too wide for humans to accept; rather it is considered that we interpret these stimuli and organise them into 'perceptions'. This interpretation and organisation requires some judgement to be made. These judgements are subjective rather than objective in nature. Whenever these subjective judgements are made it is possible that mistakes are made.

   These perceptions are perhaps best illustrated by the study of the following optical illusions. Figure 2.1 provides an example of a mistake we may make in our perception of visual stimuli.

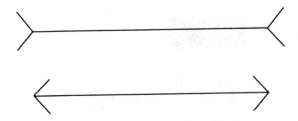

FIGURE 2.1

The two horizontal lines are in fact the same length yet we perceive the bottom line, with its inward facing arrows, as being substantially longer than the upper line.

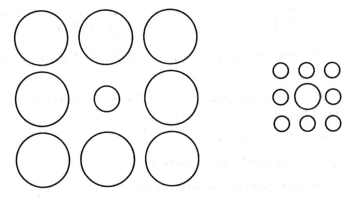

FIGURE 2.2

Similarly in Figure 2.2 the two central circles are of equal diameter and yet our perception is that the right hand central circle considerably exceeds the left hand circle in diameter.

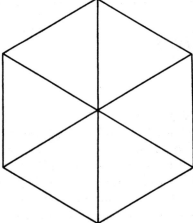

FIGURE 2.3 *Projection of a Cube*

The precise causes of these perceptual errors are not yet fully explained. They are best examined, in this context, as mistakes we can make when surrounding environments complicate our perceptions. The study of the 'Necker Cube' (Figure 2.3) might help us to explain this phenomenon. Our viewing of this cube shows quite starkly our brain imposing three dimensions on a two dimensional drawing – that is, it displays quite vividly the dynamic and interpretative nature of perception.

Figure 2.4 presents us with a drawing which is either seen as an old or a young

FIGURE 2.4 *Young Girl - Old Woman* (source: W.E. Hill)

lady. The same objective stimulus can be seen by two different people as different visions or perceptions. Although it is a mere drawing it helps illustrate that our perceptions of objective phenomena can vary from person to person.

The transposition to the more complex world of management might suggest that it might be seen to illustrate the fact that one person's view of the world can very easily differ quite radically from that of another person.

Figure 2.5 affords an excellent visual exposition of the fact that our perceptions are influenced by surrounding stimuli. The top left hand drawing and the bottom right hand drawing are complete versions of a man and a naked woman. The other drawings are less complete versions of the same drawings. The likelihood of our judging the top right hand or bottom left hand drawings as either a man or a woman can be seen to be substantially influenced by which of the two complete drawings we have previously seen.

FIGURE 2.5 *Girl Figures* (source: G. Fisher)

Extended into the managerial situation, this may provide us with a visual illustration of the extent to which surrounding or preceding stimuli can alter our perceptions of objective events.

Such mistakes made in perception of visual stimuli could be mirrored in mistakes in our perceptions of other people. It might be interesting if we could isolate potential mistakes we might make in our judgement of social or managerial situations or in our judgements of others. If such mistakes are made it is essential that the manager is aware of them and eliminates them from the judgement of management situations.

It must be stressed that the potential mistakes made are merely predisposed tendencies to judge situations or other people. They take the form of subtle rather than crude mistakes and as such they are not easy to detect. In the judgement of another person, the manager will not necessarily totally misjudge the person, but the judgement may be clouded by these perceptual errors.

The managerial situation is one of objective facts and events but the duty of the manager is to impose a subjective judgement to try to isolate reasons for these events or to try to impose a direction on future action. These judgements are subjective in nature and, as such, prone to potential error. The skilled manager should be aware of these subjective features of judgements and should ensure that the subjective element has not caused him or her to misjudge the situation faced.

COMMON MISTAKES IN THE MANAGER'S PERCEPTION OF THE MANAGEMENT SITUATION

a) Halo effect – we have a tendency to judge situations and other people as static. The reality is that situations change and other people are capable of change. This is illustrated by the manager who identifies poor performance in an employee: once this poor performance has been identified it will require great effort on the part of the employee to convince the manager that he or she has changed. It must be stated that the manager's judgement is not totally affected by the halo effect; excellent performance should be detected readily. The problem is that significant, but not startling, improvements in performance may not be detected easily or immediately by the manager.

b) Stereotyping – we have a tendency to judge complex situations in simple ways. We make universal assumptions from isolated experiences. It is evidenced in racial situations and also in general managerial situations. It might be characterised by clinicians not trusting accountants, or by managers judging all social workers as managerially incompetent. The claim is not that all people are bigots but that, on the basis of limited evidence, there is a tendency to prejudge others by classifying them into a particular category, and then making universal assumptions about individual behaviour and motives on the basis of this classification.

c) Projection – we have a tendency to project our feelings onto other people. This is best illustrated by the fact that, often, we assume that everyone must be as enthusiastic as we are about our favoured project. We seem surprised and disappointed when others do not respond as enthusiastically as we expect. Thus the accountant tends to assume that everyone should automatically be conscious of the cost of a particular proposal: the reality is that the operational manager is more concerned with the benefits rather than the cost of a proposal. Again it must be stressed that this is not simple issue; rather each manager is capable of understanding both points of view but enters the managerial situation with different priorities.

d) Selective perception/attribution – we have a tendency to extract from a complex situation only certain elements. Thus in a complex management problem different managers will focus on different aspects of the problem. Hence, if an engineering company has managerial problems of a wide-ranging nature, the engineer may focus on the engineering problems encountered (eg poor machinery), whilst the finance director may focus on financial aspects of the problem (for example resource allocation). This can be extended into the situation where the causes of the problem are identified (this causal relationship is known as attribution).

WHAT THIS MEANS FOR THE MANAGER

When managers examine a managerial problem they are capable of making mistakes. Some of the mistakes they might make are caused by perceptual errors. Thus it is essential that the manager is aware of the possibility of making such mistakes.

The good manager must realise that immediate judgements may be wrong or incomplete and should never assume that others judge the world in the same way or that he or she has a monopoly of wisdom. It should never be assumed that everyone shares enthusiasm for a particular idea or solution to a managerial problem.

The good manager must consider every managerial problem from the widest possible perspective and must make judgements only after rigorous analysis of the problem. He must understand that other people's views are important and that other people need convincing of the validity of ideas. However, as is seen in the section on Managing Others, such convincing may be very difficult.

SUMMARY

Every person is capable of making mistakes in the perception or judgement of events or people. It is possible to identify the more important perceptual errors which can be made. It is essential that managers eradicate or minimise these mistakes. The first step in the elimination of such mistakes is to acknowledge their existence. Managers can best avoid these mistakes by 'placing themselves in the other person's shoes'. The management situation is further complicated by the fact that other participants also make judgements about situations and events which can be as imperfect, partial or flawed as the manager's; in such circumstances it is essential that the manager attempts to anticipate the views, values and perceptions of the other participants in the 'management equation'.

Non-Verbal Communication

In most circumstances concerning the management of other people there is a substantial element of 'face-to-face contact'. For instance many management scenarios are conducted in meetings. Most management situations demand communication directly with others. In such an environment the successful manager must appreciate that, in any inter-personal communication exercise, messages beyond the words used exist. These non-verbal elements of the communication exercise complicate the management task – that is, they add a new dimension to the manager's communication duties. As will be seen in the chapter on Communication most successful managers carefully plan the words used in, and the method of delivery of, the communication; however quite commonly managers fail to appreciate or fail to plan for the more sophisticated elements of the communication – the non-verbal elements.

Successful communicators will reinforce the verbal content of the message with appropriate non-verbal cues. These non-verbal cues are used commonly in our social or non-work communications but frequently managers fail to translate these habits into the occupational environment.

Some of the more important non-verbal cues follow.

i) Facial expression – we can frown, we can smile. These facial expressions can be used to reinforce or maybe confuse the communication. We can criticise but if we smile whilst doing so a degree of co-operation might be obtained which would be difficult to obtain if our expression displayed anger or displeasure.

ii) Gestures – we can shake our fist, we can open our arms. The first is a gesture of hostility, the second a gesture of friendship. We can reinforce a criticism by fist waving; we can assuage criticism by indicating friendship.

iii) Tone of voice – we can shout, which will reinforce criticism. We can use a milder tone of voice, which will temper words of criticism.

iv) We can stand over someone, which conveys an element of hostility. We can sit alongside someone, which conveys cooperation.

v) We can encourage others' contributions by showing interest by eye contact; alternatively we can show a degree of disinterest or even insecurity by avoiding eye contact.

vi) We can present psychological barriers to a communication by imposing physical barriers (eg a desk or table) or by imposing the barrier of distance; speaking to someone from a distance of 15 metres will not be conducive to obtaining their co-operation but the same words spoken from a distance of only one metre will usually be perceived by the recipient as less threatening.

These factors can be well illustrated by reference to Figure 2.6.

It might be best if we did not treat this as a rigorous academic exercise but simply an exercise in spontaneous reaction. We may ask what is untrustworthy about the person in the photograph. There is no formal indication that the person is untrustworthy – he could be a charity worker selling lottery tickets for his charity – and yet the 'messages' the photograph sends are ones which would cause the observer to suspect the motives or integrity of the individual.

i) The camera angle is such that the person is above us – this is seen as threatening.

ii) His fist is prominently displayed – this is seen as a threatening gesture.

iii) His eyes are hidden by dark spectacles – he appears to be avoiding eye contact. This removes the 'human element' from the communication.

iv) His dress is 'loud' – this would cause us to attach to him a casual manner. The word that springs to mind is 'spiv'.

v) He appears to be whistling – this conveys a degree of disinterest in the communication.

FIGURE 2.6

The question which must be asked is whether these 'snap judgements' are truly representative of our feelings when we actually meet others. The conclusion might be that the messages of Figure 2.6 are perhaps rather too simplistic: it affords an experience which is rather unrealistic in that, in the management situation, the manager or the recipient of the manager's message would be capable of more sophistication in the interpretation of the communication; but it may be that Figure 2.6 helps convince us that these features of the communication exercise have some validity and that non-verbal elements of a communication are an important part of the total exercise.

Summary

It is important that the implications of non-verbal communication in management are fully understood. The manager must prepare and plan for non-verbal as well as verbal elements in the communication exercise. If a meeting is being held, seating arrangements are important. If the two parties to the communication exercise face each other across a table there will be a tendency to develop adversarial stances. However if the two parties meet side by side, without the barrier of a table, co-operation will be facilitated. Similarly the manager should try to arrange seats of equal size for communication exercises where co-operation is sought. Conciliatory messages should be accompanied by conciliatory gestures.

Exercise

Describe three occasions in your working life where you have misjudged a situation or the motives of other people. What, if anything, have you learnt from these mistakes?

Further Reading

Baron R.A. and Greenberg, J. (1990) *Behaviour in Organisations*, Allyn and Bacon
Mitchell, T. (1985) *People in Organisations*, McGraw Hill
Pierce, J. and Newstrom J. (1990) *The Manager's Bookshelf*, Harper and Row
Welsh, A.N. (1982) *The Skills of Management*, Gower
Woodcock, M. & Francis, D. (1989) *The Unblocked Manager*, Gower

Self-Management

L E A R N I N G   O B J E C T I V E S

- Understand the importance of time management in the work of the manager

- Analyse the constituent features of time management

- Identify areas where time management may be poor

- Assess ways of rectifying poor time management

- Apply the concepts studied to real life situations

- Identify areas of research in time management where more research might be necessary

- Examine the theoretical underpinning of stress management

- Understand the importance of stress in the managerial environment

- Identify the positive and negative consequences of stress

- Examine ways in which the negative effects of stress could be reduced or, more importantly, avoided

- Create a managerial environment which reduces stress to an optimal level

- Identify areas of stress management where more research is necessary

---

The Management of Time

One of the most common difficulties a manager will encounter in practice is that of ensuring that there is sufficient time each day to do all that is expected. Many times managers seem to make the following comments.

'I get more to do every day!'

'It seems like I have to rush everything! I don't get time to do anything as well as I should.'

'I've no time to spare, I'm rushed off my feet! I wish I could get someone to help me.'

It must be acknowledged that, even though these comments are made, most managers seem to cope with these problems. However there is a distinction between coping and being in control. Unfortunately such comments tend to have predictable longer term consequences:

a) slow deterioration in the quality of management afforded;
b) demotivation;
c) tiredness and sickness;
d) stress.

It must be noted that the task of management is indeed onerous and time consuming; however a skilful manager has to devote attention to the effective management of time. There are a number of loosely linked strategies which can be adopted in managing time and if a manager is to be effective it is essential that he or she is in a position to effectively deploy time or ensure that there is enough time available to devote due attention to all the wide-ranging management responsibilities.

a) Prioritise work – not everything is of equal importance; the problem is that everything which appears on a manager's desk is important to the person putting it there. The manager has to attach a priority to every task that is given. It must be acknowledged that such prioritisation can result in mistakes being made. In such circumstances all the manager can do is learn by the mistakes made. However a skilled or experienced manager should be easily able to prioritise work.
b) Examine current use of time – most people do not spend all their time working productively. There are certain times in the day or week when each of us tends to work best. Equally there are certain times when we tend to work to least effect. It must be admitted that this time varies with each individual; furthermore it must be admitted that these are merely tendencies and are capable of a certain degree of variation day by day and week by week. However it might prove a useful strategy to examine our current use of time and allocate the more challenging tasks to those times where we have achieved most success in the past. Similarly we might allocate the more routine tasks to those times where we have worked to less effect in the past. In conducting this investigation it would be useful to formally map the progress of work over a number of days. This can be achieved by the reorganisation of the typical contents of a diary. This minor alteration will constitute a quick but useful depiction of the current use of time which can be used for critical examination. An example of this document can be found in Figure 3.1. This shows the breakdown of a typical day into convenient time periods and an assessment of the use of these time periods through simple self-observation.
c) Build time for contingencies into the time plan – it is difficult or perhaps impossible to predict all possible events. Hence it is necessary to allocate time slots

where no work is envisaged. If nothing occurs this time can be spent either in rest, reflecting on past mistakes, motivating subordinates or in planning for the future. At worst it will provide a period to deal with unexpected events. The careful analysis of time, or the diary just suggested, will usually show the manager that time already exists to deal with contingencies and that the problem is that this time is not used efficiently.

Time Period	Work Done	Work Interrup-tions	1. Inessential	2. Somebody else could do	3. Wasting others time	Notes
8.30 8.45 9.00 9.15 9.30 9.45 10.00 10.00 10.00 10.00 10.00 5.30 5.45 6.00 Evening	Enter number against time whenever activities change.	Enter a '1' for each, e.g. 1,11	Record impressions, if any, at the time		Record impressions, if any, at the time	Note anything unusual or 'special'

FIGURE 3.1 *Date: Time Use Diary*

d) Carefully control meetings – there is a danger of most meetings taking longer than is necessary. Most meetings are called so everyone can contribute in some way to the discussion and very often people take full advantage of this opportunity. The problem is that this is often at the expense of the busiest person in the meeting – who is usually the manager. Thus the manager should call a meeting only when it is essential: there are more time efficient ways to make most decisions which are made in meetings. Every item on the agenda should be carefully justified. Meetings can be scheduled at times during the day where people have a stake in finishing on time (for example, due to finish at lunch time) . Every item on the agenda should have a time allocated to it. Meetings should begin on time – those who are not there at the beginning will have to suffer the consequences. Finally the most important time saver at meetings is having all the people necessary, and only such people, in attendance and ensuring that they are properly briefed.

e) Never handle a piece of paper without doing something with it – there is a tendency to examine a piece of paper and then simply put it to one side without doing anything about its contents. Every time a piece of paper is scrutinised this scrutiny should contribute something to the resolution of the problem the paper poses. Thus an effective filing system can save time which can be devoted to production. It is often said that 'procrastination is the thief of time'.

f) Delegate – most things which managers do can be more than adequately handled by their subordinates. In fact theories of motivation would suggest that delegation does not merely save the time of managers but also enhances the motivation of those people to whom the work is delegated. It must be acknowledged, however, that delegation sometimes, in the short term, does not save the time of the manager – rather it reallocates the time of the manager. That is, the manager tends to spend less time doing but more time teaching, supporting and monitoring. However it is likely that the good delegator will, in the long term, create more time to devote to other issues.

g) Learn to say 'no!' – much time is taken because people are too polite to say 'No!' It must be acknowledged that a simple rejection is not the desired outcome; rather the manager must politely direct the person making the request to someone else who can help. In many ways this is linked to the issue of Assertiveness dealt with in the next chapter

SUMMARY

In situations of rapid change managers find increasing demands being placed on their time. These increasing demands can result in managers not devoting sufficient attention to the important issues which affect them. If managers do not carefully allocate their time they may feel stressed and less effective managers. It is imperative, therefore, that managers devote attention to the careful management of their time. Such management demands flexibility and adaptability.

The Management of Stress

One of the inevitabilities of life that the practising manager will encounter almost immediately is the existence of stress. This stress is likely to affect everyone in the organisation, both managers and their subordinates. The following analysis will reveal that, although stress is a consequence of human existence, the duties of management are likely to introduce further stress into the life – both personal and occupational – of the manager.

The acknowledgement of the existence of stress is an important skill of the successful manager; the manager must learn to detect signs of stress in others since not to so do would lead, at best, to a misinterpretation of their motives and, at worst, to a loss of their services through sickness or leaving.

However, perhaps more importantly, it is essential that the manager learns to detect signs of stress in himself or herself. As will be seen later stress may result in poor decision making, poor management of others or sickness. The main theme of this text is that the successful and astute manager is one of the most important assets of an organisation and anything which detracts from good management should be avoided at all costs.

Signs of Stress

Stress is sometimes very difficult to detect and yet good management demands prompt detection of stress. It cannot be claimed that stress is something which has been detected only in the past 20 years. However it is a topic which has received more attention over the past 20 years than it has in the past. If the topic has been highlighted by research and, if it falls within the responsibility area of the manager, its effective control and management forms part of the duties of that manager.

EVENT	RELATIVE STRESSFULNESS
Death of a Spouse	100
Divorce	73
Marital Separation	65
Jail Term	63
Death of a Close Family Member	63
Personal Injury or Illness	53
Marriage	50
Fired from Job	47
Retirement	45
Pregnancy	40
Death of a Close Friend	37
Son or Daughter Leaving Home	29
Trouble with In-Laws	28
Trouble with Boss	23
Change in Residence	20
Vacation	13
Christmas	12
Minor Violations of the Law	11

(Source: Based on data from Holmes & Masuda, 1974.)
FIGURE 3.2 *Causes of Stress*

Some of the signs of stress will be medically manifested, some will be more behaviourially manifested, others will be attitudinally manifested. In many ways this topic emphasises more than does any other the immensely complicated task of the manager. In some ways the ability to diagnose behaviour and attitudes might be accepted as the duty of management but the ability to diagnose medical manifestations is not something which immediately springs to mind in the required skills repertoire of the manager.

Fortunately for the manager, signs of stress, although difficult to detect in isolation, are likely to occur in combinations or patterns. Nevertheless it must be accepted that most practising managers can point to times in their career when they failed to either diagnose or successfully deal with signs of stress in themselves or in others.

a) Medical signs – palpitations, chest pains, indigestion, muscle tension, headaches, tiredness. These are signs which a manager can detect within himself or herself but inevitably they will be very difficult to detect in others. Furthermore the mere detection of these signs is not necessarily a symptom of stress. Obviously chest pains and headaches, for instance, can have causes other than stress. Perhaps the technique in self-diagnosis is to detect combinations of such signs coincident with stress situations. The diagnosis of others is much more problematic. Such signs will be detected only by the vigilant and approachable manager and connecting them with non-work related stress may be very difficult without infringing upon people's privacy.

b) Behavioural signs – uncooperative actions, arguments, anxious behaviour, irritability. These should be signs which are easier to diagnose in oneself and easier to detect in others. Clearly there may be causes of such behaviour other than stress. Again, however, the skill might be to look for combinations or patterns of such behaviour.

Household hassles	Preparing Meals
	Shopping
Time Pressure Hassles	Too Many Things to Do
	Too Many Responsibilities
Inner Concern Hassles	Being Lonely
	Fear of Confrontation
Environmental Hassles	Neighbourhood Deterioration
	Noise
	Crime
Financial Responsibility	Concerns about Owing Money
Financial Responsibility for	Someone Who Doesn't Live
	with You

Source: based on information in Lazarus et al., 1985.)
FIGURE 3.3 *Everyday Life and Stress*

c) Attitudinal signs – lack of interest, indecisiveness, accidents. These are again signs which might be most successfully diagnosed in patterns rather than in isolation. It is less likely that the diagnosis of such signs could be attributed to other causes. It must, however, be admitted that this aspect of the subject more readily forms part of the recognised repertoire of skills of the manager than does the ability to diagnose medical signs; managers have been long expected to analyse the attitudes of their subordinates.

Causes of Stress

Having analysed signs of stress it is important that the causes of such stress are analysed before any effective ways of minimising stress are examined. Figures 3.2 and 3.3 illustrate the wide-ranging causes of stress in people's personal lives.

However what these tables ignore is the additional complication of stress within the work environment. In the following analysis the more common causes of stress both from personal life and from occupational life will be examined. Although these are conveniently divided into the two sub-categories, this is not to claim that the two subdivisions are entirely divorced; rather the reality is that both subdivisions are likely to inter play and reinforce each other. Hence a person stressed outside the work environment may behave in work in ways which reinforce his or her level of stress. Similarly a person stressed in work will 'bring the problems home' and add to stress by disrupting the home environment.

NON-WORK-RELATED STRESS

a) personal circumstances, eg bereavement, divorce, marriage, birth of child
b) ill health
c) travel difficulties
d) trouble with family, close friends.

WORK-RELATED STRESS

a) difficult job
b) failure to achieve objectives
c) difficult work colleagues
d) job insecurity
e) lack of career development
f) organisational environment, eg too rapid organisational change, excessively demanding superiors.

A factor which frequently strongly reinforces the stress of the work environment is the feeling of helplessness by those suffering the stress. Often, because of the way in which jobs are structured or allocated, there is nothing they can do to alleviate the problems they are facing and the stress they are suffering. Hence, anything which returns to the employee some feeling of 'control' over the work situation will be seen to be an important help in the management of stress. This is a very important point to note since the manager and the organisation does have some control over the way in which jobs are allocated and designed and this affords to the manager some power or influence in the control or minimisation of work-related stress.

The successful manager must be prepared to examine all these possible causes upon detecting signs of stress in him or herself and in others. Clearly good observation, awareness and communication skills are required on the part of the manager.

Coping with Stress

The fact that the manager's duties in this area involve a responsibility for himself or herself and for others has already been acknowledged. If stress has been detected it is the duty of the manager to ensure that all steps possible are taken to deal with this stress. This involves two separate sets of activity – dealing with manifested stress and stress avoidance or minimisation.

DEALING WITH STRESS AS MANIFESTED

It must be noted that this is probably one of the most serious and difficult tasks facing management. It may well be that in this duty the management has to rely on the help of others more skilled in this area, such as medical experts, and counsellors.

If managers have detected signs of stress within themselves they are well placed to deal with this stress. They could try to reflect upon the experiences they encountered which have caused this stress. They could decide to afford time by 'walking away' from the causes of the stress, by literally taking a walk or taking a holiday. They could find someone to talk to who would provide the opportunity to listen whilst self-examination takes place or who might offer an alternative perspective on the problems faced. Naturally they can act in ways to minimise the causes of the stress. Physical exercise is an acknowledged method of stress reduction. Finally they could attend a course on, and subsequently practise, relaxation techniques, such as sitting down in a quiet room, breathing through the nose, reflecting upon pleasant past experiences .

Such strategies, difficult to put into practice by managers on themselves, are much more difficult to impose on other people. Perhaps managers could at best act as facilitators in stress handling. Awareness of opportunities available – both medical and other – will help make managers good handlers of the stress of others. Successful managers must be sympathetic to the needs of stressed persons. Most certainly managers can seek ways, if deemed appropriate, to act as listeners or counsellors. It is essential, however, that managers realise that such skills are not necessarily within their repertoire and as such require the help of others or the undertaking of training.

MINIMISING STRESS

This is something which is a much more achievable management task. The recognition of the need to minimise stress in self and others is the first step in the task of stress minimisation. Such realisation will cause management to appreciate that stress minimisation becomes part of work objectives. If new work objectives are undertaken, time and resources will be afforded to these newly assumed objectives to allow the acquisition of any skills which may be required. The managers should themselves acquire some skills in relaxation for stress minimisation. In addition such knowledge may help afford a degree of awareness in others of the techniques of relaxation.

Managers must be able to try to minimise the stress placed on all subordinates. This will require an appreciation of the fact that stress is a person-related characteristic – two people placed in the same situation will not necessarily react to stress in the same way. This, in its turn, demands an appreciation by the managers of personality types. There are many theories which attempt to explain personality and personality differences. Perhaps the best for this purpose is the distinction between Type A and Type B people.

Type A people are said to be highly competitive, capable of setting objectives. They take work home, are motivated by achievement, push themselves and find difficulty in relaxing.

Type B people are not driven by time, are capable of leaving work at work, and are driven by outside interests.

It can be seen therefore that Type A people are likely to be more prone to stress – or more particularly work-related stress.

Managers should have acquired knowledge about subordinates and their likely weaknesses or susceptibilities to stress. Assuming that managers fully understand their staff, their motives, their fears and their problems, they can then begin to prepare a strategy to minimise stress in the longer term. This will involve minimisation of stress as a priority in the planning of tasks and the planning of time. The role of effective time management as a way of stress minimisation has already been examined earlier in this chapter.

Managers must understand themselves, and encourage others to understand themselves and what causes stress in their lives. They should be encouraged to plan their time and their life in such a way that stress is minimised. A major help in this is awareness of the possible need for exercise, for work breaks and for holidays.

Managers should ensure that positive attitudes are the most predominant in all working in the organisation – this will be examined later in the chapters on Human Motivation and Communication.

Unless needed for other reasons 'stress inducing persons' should not be employed in the work group. It must be acknowledged that removing someone from the work group may not be easy but if they are shown to be a major source of stress, techniques such as redeployment can be used. It must be emphasised that this should not be, nor should not be seen to be, a 'Witch Hunt' for guilty parties and indeed managers must realise that often they themselves will have either been the guilty party or will have been seen to be the guilty party.

Finally the attitude of openness and freedom of speech will have a major role to play in stress minimisation. An 'open door' policy where all issues are seen to be debatable is desirable in any attempt to minimise stress. This culture of openness can be translated into the strategy of using organisational and job design as a way of affording to individuals more control over their own destiny and hence helping alleviate stress. Organisations and jobs can be designed in such a way that individuals working in organisations and in individual jobs within those organisations are afforded more control over the events which impact on their work performance. These design factors are considered in more detail later in this text but their connection to stress minimisation is now briefly mentioned.

a) Decentralisation – under this strategy employees should have more decision-making power, and the stress induced by feeling frustrated by others' inaction should be eliminated.

b) The appraisal of performance – whereby individuals feel that their contribution to organisational success is fairly and openly recognised. The feeling that no matter how hard employees work their success will be attributed only to management, is a source of considerable frustration and hence stress.

c) Making jobs bigger or more challenging – research and theories of motivation which will be examined later in this text suggest that boredom and frustrated ambition are as likely to be sources of frustration, and hence stress, as are too challenging a job and too rapid promotion. Strategies which enhance the creative and intellectually challenging elements of the job should help overcome these feelings of frustration.

d) All employees should be adequately trained and developed to undertake with success all tasks which are expected of them – this is examined in detail in a later section of the book

e) Special training and development techniques, such as Coaching and Mentoring, examined later in the text, can help minimise stress in the workplace. Briefly they involve dealing with any problems the employee may have in a positive, non-threatening environment

COUNSELLING

Many organisations have found that the facility of counselling is a major asset in the resolution of stress in the workplace. If an employee has encountered the negative consequences of stress it may help if this stress related problem were explored in a non-threatening environment. Counselling affords this non-threatening environment. The facility might be best illustrated by examining its constituent features.

a) The organisation should afford its full support to the facility. Employees must be aware of the facility – thus many United Kingdom police forces inform their employees through widely distributed leaflets and through their wage packets of the facility. This information must be positively communicated referring to Counselling as a facility which should be used wherever necessary and it must be emphasised that its use does not convey any sign of weakness by the user.

b) It should be viewed as a confidential activity. In many organisations such counselling is undertaken by trained personnel who are not employees of the organisation. Irrespective of who conducts the exercise there should be an acceptance of the fact that information revealed will be kept confidential.

c) It should be conducted by trained people – the exercise will explore areas where the employee will feel vulnerable and hence the person facilitating the process should be capable of positively handling the emotions involved.

d) As part of the organisation's commitment to counselling there should be a public commitment to the organisation's willingness to resolve any problems revealed to the best of its ability.

e) It should be perceived by all constituents as a positive, sincere, activity and not merely as an attempt to avoid, for instance, legal responsibility for work-induced stress.

f) It should be equally available for work or non-work induced stress as both are likely to negatively affected the future work of the employee and particularly as both forms of stress tend to interact to exacerbate problems in the workplace.

g) The counselling should attempt to explore problems as objectively as possible. Care must be taken to differentiate between causes and effects of stress.

h) The counsellor should have empathy with the position of the person undertaking the counselling.

i) The counsellor should be able to afford enough time to explore the problems being encountered and equally should have sufficient skills to determine when to halt a session and rearrange a new session.

j) Every session should end with an agreed course of action to be pursued before the next session. All sessions should be finished with an attempt to agree a positive outcome from the session.

k) The counsellor should have listening as well as other communication skills – these are explored in a later section of this text. The counsellor should be aware of what is not being said as well as what is being said. The counsellor should be aware of the necessity for the person being counselled to talk and hence he or she should be prepared to be silent or nearly silent for long periods.

l) The counsellor must be aware of all sources of support that can be afforded to the person being counselled.

m) The counsellor should, where confidentiality allows, ensure that the employee's work stress is kept to a minimum for the duration of the counselling.

n) The counsellor should be skilled enough to agree with the person being counselled when the purpose of the counselling has ended – that is when success has been achieved.

o) The counsellor should, where confidentiality allows, monitor the progress of the person being counselled for a period after the counselling has finished.

p) The counsellor should ensure that the person being counselled feels that there is a ready source of access back into counselling if required even when the counselling has deemed to have finished.

q) Finally and undoubtedly most importantly, the causes of the stress should be eliminated; this can be achieved by preparing the person to handle the stress in future or by eradicating the causes of the stress.

The facility of counselling has been explored as a separate identifiable facility; without wishing to question this facet of counselling it must be admitted that sometimes the need for counselling can be avoided if management adopted the techniques of Coaching and Mentoring just mentioned and explored in greater depth in a later section of this book.

UTILITY OF STRESS/STIMULATION

Up to now the assumption has been that all stress is negative in its impact on people and on the work environment. However it must be recognised that in some ways stress is something which people actively seek. People can become bored very easily and need the challenge of a change in environment or routine to stimulate motivation. This is best illustrated by the levels of medical stress suffered by newly-unemployed people. The reality is that people can perform quite adequately in routinely stressful jobs (eg the surgeon, or the soldier in war).

A possible relationship between stress and performance is shown in Figure 3.4; however the actual relationship is shown in Figure 3.5.

There is a level of stress which produces optimal performance and this level of stress can be under achieved as well as over achieved. It may be that there is an important distinction to be made between 'stress' and 'stimulation'. Stimulation – as exhibited in recreational pursuits, or an interesting job – is something which is desired and indeed actively sought by people. It may be that stimulation becomes stress once this optimal level has been exceeded. It must be noted that this is a very important final observation since experience shows that what causes stress in individuals is not necessarily a particular problem or challenge but the fact that their particular circumstances at that time cause this problem or challenge to be perceived as stressful.

Equally, this illustrates the fact that individual differences in stress tolerance exist and the acknowledgement of Type A and Type B personalities will be useful in explaining these individual differences.

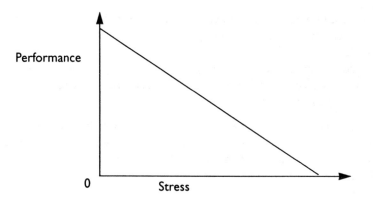

FIGURE 3.4 *Possible Relationship between Stress and Performance*

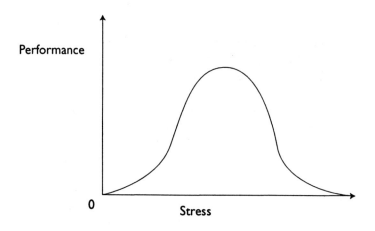

FIGURE 3.5 *Actual Relationship between Stress and Performance*

Summary

Stress as a concept should be carefully distinguished from stimulation. Stress, as latterly defined, is detrimental to work and organisational performance. It is the duty of managers to detect stress in themselves and others. Once this stress has been detected it is the duty of managers to try to eradicate this stress. In the longer term managers must ensure that stress minimisation is an important work priority. Even though the assumption of stress-management responsibilities further complicates and extends the duties of the manager, the manager can make use of people trained in stress minimisation to help eradicate the problem as detected.

Exercise

Describe three occasions in your working life where you have badly managed your time. What might you have done to avoid these problems?

Further Reading

Humphrey, J. and Smith, P. (1991) *Looking After Corporate Health,* Pitman
Newell, S. (1995) *The Healthy Organization,* Routledge
Treacy, D. (1995) *Successful Time Management,* TSB/Headway
Welsh, A.N. (1982) *The Skills of Management,* Gower
Woodcock, M and Francis, D. (1989) *The Unblocked Manager,* Gower

Chapter four

Assertiveness

L E A R N I N G   O B J E C T I V E S

- Understand the theoretical research in the area of assertiveness

- Identify the constituent features of assertiveness

- Distinguish between assertiveness and aggression

- Assess ways in which individuals might enhance their assertiveness

- Advise an organisation on a strategy it might pursue to encourage assertiveness

- Identify areas where more research might be welcome

One significant skill required of managers is the ability to achieve stated objectives. In many large, multi-purpose organisations, different activities and different objectives compete with each other for the allocation of organisational attention and resources. Under such circumstances, in many ways, successful managers can be seen to be those who ensure that their particular responsibility area and objectives receive due attention in the prioritisation process within a multi-purpose organisation. Hence, no matter how sophisticated managers are in the handling of other people, if they fail to obtain organisational commitment to their responsibility area, they will palpably be seen as failures and hence bad managers.

Thus one of the major skills required of a manager is the ability to 'fight his corner'. This ability to 'deliver' may be to some extent a product of certain personality traits. However, as will be seen in a future section, this seeking of desired personality traits in managers will be productive only if the organisation can ensure that people with a ready supply of these traits will be available for employment in managerial positions. Such a strategy removes from the organisation the ability to control its environment and, as such, is not the strategy upon which an organisation should embark. Rather the assumption must be that most managers can be taught or trained to acquire these skills.

If this is the case it is important that the desired skills are carefully defined. To some extent it must be acknowledged that the skills required are organisationally specific – that is, what is required is a product of the particular situation within the particular organisation. However, as a workable exercise it is possible to identify certain general behaviour patterns which would be suitable in most cases to achieve success as just defined. These behaviour patterns are generally known as 'assertiveness'. Perhaps the most productive definition of the term is that used by Kelley (1979) in *Assertiveness Training* where he defined assertiveness as 'self-expression through which one stands up for one's basic human rights without violating the basic human rights of others'.

This definition, in some ways, is limited in that it focuses on general not organisationally specific behaviour. However its undoubted strength is its crucial qualification of not infringing others' rights. There is a major difference between 'assertiveness' and 'aggression'. Perhaps assertiveness is most closely connected with the abilities to persuade and persevere. Aggression involves implications of socially unacceptable or undesirable behaviour; it is a behaviour pattern which is likely to provoke a negative or defensive response from those to whom it is directed.

Equally, assertiveness must not be confused with diffidence or lack of self-confidence. Clearly, in a competitive environment where different actions or projects are competing one with another for prominence, such behaviour patterns are unlikely to produce the desired outcome of 'getting things done'.

Figure 4.1 concisely and in a very practical context distinguishes between the three concepts. In many ways an examination of this Table would suggest that assertiveness is the 'middle ground' between the two extremes of diffidence and aggression.

	Diffidence	Assertion	Aggression
Stance	Moving from one foot to another	Firm, comfortable stand	Leaning forward stiffly
Hands	Wringing hands	Hands relaxed	Clenched fists
Eyes	Eyes averted	Eye contact with other person	Glaring
Voice	Voice hesitant	Voice steady and clear	Voice overbearing
Verbal			
Asking	Tentative statements: I wonder/would you mind/ maybe	Firm Statements: I will/ I feel/I know/I want	Threats: I'm warning you/ you'd better
Responses	Negative statements: It doesn't matter/ never mind	Emphatic: What do you think/ Can you help	Critical statements: This won't do/ it's not good enough

FIGURE 4.1 *Behavioural signs of Diffidence, Assertion and Aggression*

Such behaviour is facilitated if management has a clear idea of what its mission is and why this mission has been assumed. It would be further facilitated if the manager had some firm proposals about how this mission should be fulfilled. However, a distinction must be made between a firm and a rigid proposal, since assertiveness patently demands an appreciation of the views, interests and fears of others.

A further aid to assertive behaviour is the ability to clearly communicate the 'desired future state' (see section on the Organisational Domain). A poor communicator will be a poor persuader. Poor persuasion will result either in rejection or the assumption of hostile stances to impose authority. Neither of these outcomes can be characterised as 'assertive'.

Another characteristic of assertiveness is the ability to understand that, in many cases, it is unrealistic to assume that those who need to be convinced will necessarily enter the negotiations with the same degree of enthusiasm for a particular project which you have. Rather the successful manager needs an appreciation of other people's perspectives, values and priorities, and an understanding of the perceptual errors to which humans are prone, which have been examined earlier in this section, would be of immense assistance.

Finally it must be recognised that such persuasion may take time to achieve fruition. Thus the ability to persevere and not too easily become discouraged is desirable. It must be acknowledged that this 'convincing period' needs to be included in any time plan and the manager with time management skills is much more likely to be categorised as assertive than is a manager who lacks them.

Part of the skill of assertiveness is the appreciation that, in the real world, the individual manager is not always likely to get what he or she wants. This is not necessarily a negative perspective since it is perfectly possible for a manager to achieve more than is thought possible as well as to 'undershoot'. This 'undershooting' is a situation which is likely to exist in many cases and in such circumstances the successful manager is required to enter into a negotiation. As such, in the real world, assertiveness may imply the ability to negotiate.

The ability to negotiate implies an understanding on the part of the manager of what would be deemed to be a successful outcome. This demands an appreciation of what is and what is not negotiable. It requires the ability to distinguish between a compromise and an accommodation. The former will be a positive solution in the long as well as the short term. The latter will be at best an acceptable solution in the short term only and, at worst, a procrastination, which may mean that the problem will reoccur in a more extreme form in the future.

Finally successful negotiation demands an appreciation of timing in the negotiation process. Under most situations some time for reflection needs to be built into the time plan of the successful negotiator. There will usually be a need to reflect upon the situation and consider the benefits of the negotiation exercise by all parties to the negotiation.

Assertive Behaviour

It might be useful to summarise the features of assertive behaviour. It might be characterised by the following features:

a) not being excessively concerned with the approval of others;
b) not feeling guilty if you sometimes consider your own needs as well as those of others;
c) being confident enough to receive and give constructive criticism;
d) being able to articulate your own values, feelings and opinions without fear;
e) making clear what you want from life.

Assertiveness Training

The benefits of assertiveness have been examined but the analysis would be incomplete if we did not examine how unassertive people could be trained to develop more assertiveness. The aim must be to facilitate the development of assertive behaviour.

Although the possibility of facilitating assertiveness on the job cannot be excluded, it is usual for such training to take place off the job in circumstances where experimentation can take place without immediately threatening productive endeavour.

Typically, role play exercises will be used where the individual's natural reactions to circumstances are examined and critically assessed. Such circumstances allow the individual to develop assertive approaches in an unthreatening environment. This form of training could be facilitated by the concepts of Coaching and Mentoring which are considered in a later section of this book.

Neuro-linguistic Programming (NLP): is a technique, first developed in the USA in the 1970s, which:

a) identifies behaviour patterns in high level performers;
b) coaches these patterns in others who wish to improve their performance;
c) overcomes restricted thinking processes and limiting self-beliefs which have contributed to limited performance.

In this technique people will be allowed to monitor their behaviour and motives in a detached fashion. They will be coached in ways in which they can modify their behaviour to become more effective. They will be encouraged to view problems from the perspective of other people and they will be encouraged to mentally rehearse their reaction to events.

Summary

Assertive behaviour allows an individual and manager to gain more control over their work environment. It should not be confused with aggression and similarly it should be contrasted with diffidence. In many ways it can be seen to be synonymous with ensuring that the individual's viewpoint is duly considered. It is probable that some people either from innate characteristics or from early learning acquire assertiveness but equally many people may consider that they could benefit from increased assertiveness. Under such circumstances assertive behaviour can be coached into people.

Exercise

Consider three times in your working life when you feel you might have acted in a more assertive fashion. What might you have done to have increased your level of assertiveness on those occasions?

Further Reading

Baron, R.A. Greenberg, J. (1990) *Behaviour in Organisations*, Allen and Bacon
Humphrey, J. and Smith, P. (1991) *Looking After Corporate Health*, Pitman
Levinson, H. (1970) *Executive Stress*, Harper and Row
Mitchell, T. (1985) *People in Organisations*, McGraw Hill
Newell, S. (1995) *The Healthy Organization*, Routledge
Pedler, M. Burgoyne, J, Boydell, T. (1986) *A Manager's Guide to Self Development*, McGraw Hill
Pettigrew, A. (1972) *Managing Under Stress*, Management Today
Pierce, J and Newstrom J. (1990) *The Manager's Bookshelf*, Harper and Row
Treacy, D. (1995) *Successful Time Management*, TSB/Headway
Welsh, A.N. (1982) *The Skills of Management*, Gower

Chapter five

The Manager's Role in Solving Problems

LEARNING OBJECTIVES

- Understand the theoretical approach to problem solving

- Examine the various approaches which could be used in solving problems

- Identify the strengths and weaknesses of the various approaches

- Assess the factors which need to be considered when a particular strategy is chosen

- Create a strategy for problem solving in an organisation

- Identify areas where you consider more research is necessary

In the real world many negotiations will be quite short in nature. However some negotiations will be somewhat more protracted. In this text the issues surrounding these protracted negotiations will be addressed as 'problem solving'. It must not be claimed that the distinction between what we have called negotiation and problem solving will always be easy or pleasant. However a sensible approach to the issue should make the distinction a workable one. In the following discourse the procedures, tactics and strategies involved in such problem solving will be examined.

Any organisation or any manager will encounter problems. The more an organisation's environment changes the more likely it is to encounter such problems. The problems may be caused by employee difficulties, production difficulties or by market difficulties. This problem demands certain features of managers themselves as well as their management of others – that is the ability to appreciate the range of options available and the ability to select the most appropriate option from that range.

There will be a set procedure which any organisation should adopt to overcome these difficulties.

a) To identify the nature of the problem – the problem can never be solved until there is a realisation that the problem exists. This requires, of a manager in particular, and the organisation in general, good systems of internal and external communication, as the reality is that in many situations problems exist for some time before there is a recognition of them.

   The management of the organisation need to monitor carefully customer complaints and employee complaints to be able to react quickly to the development of any problem.

b) To identify the extent of the problem – not all problems are of equal importance and the minor, single-incident problem needs to be distinguished from the major, recurrent problem. This, in its turn, necessitates a sophisticated and subtle management information and intelligence gathering system.

c) To generate a solution – this is where the manager and the organisation are presented with a number of options. Not all organisations will generate solutions in the same way; similarly not all solutions will emerge in the same way within the one organisation. This variation will be examined later in the chapter.

d) To effect the solution – this requires much more management attention than it may appear to need at first glance. Any change will need to receive the co-operation of all involved in the implementation of that change. This may necessitate consultation with those affected. Equally, consideration needs to be given to the design of the appropriate controls for this new approach. If problems have occurred in the past they can easily emerge in the future; thus consideration has to be given to ensuring that the solution is durable in the medium term by the application of systems of controls.

e) To monitor and review the solution – clearly the mere design of a control system is no guarantee of its success. To determine the success of any alterations to current activity, regular monitoring and review will be necessary. Thus an astute manager has to appreciate that any problem resolution must be carefully monitored for a period of time to ensure that the solution selected was entirely appropriate.

Generating Solutions

As has already been stated, the actual generation of solutions can vary within and between organisations and from manager to manager. The method chosen to solve one problem within an organisation can vary from the method chosen to solve another problem within that organisation. Similarly the methods chosen in one organisation may differ from those chosen in another organisation – even if the nature of the problems in the two organisations appear to be similar. Finally it must be recognised that managers have substantial control over the generation of solutions and, as such, it should be acknowledged that much of the evaluation of the factors involved will be undertaken by the individual manager. There are a number of strategies which can be deployed to effect ideas which may generate solutions.

a) Go alone – that is the manager determines to solve the problem with no help from anyone else. This strategy has the advantage of speed; there will be no need to explain the problem to others. There will be no need to train anyone else in problem-solving techniques. The manager should be more familiar than many others with the nature of the problem – thus the problem will be addressed by someone with substantial, detailed knowledge. However there are several difficulties with this strategy.

   i) In its purest form the knowledge of others is completely ignored even though the rest of those involved in the problem (eg employees) will probably feel that they have something to contribute to the resolution of the problem. The experience of those with knowledge of the resolution of similar problems in other organisations will not be accessed.

   ii) The manager may approach the problem with preconceived ideas as to the nature of the problem and its resolution. If, for instance, the manager is partly to blame in the emergence of the problem, it is unlikely that too much self-blame will be attached to this occurrence.

b) The use of others within the organisation – this strategy will be adopted where it is felt that the manager does not have a monopoly of wisdom on the resolution of the problem. It is useful in that it accesses the opinions and knowledge of all of those affected internally by the problem; the one obvious exception is the customer (if indeed the customer is involved in this problem) but under this approach the customer can be involved in the problem solving exercise. However this strategy has certain problems.

   i) It could be seen as an abrogation of management responsibility. It may well be that those asked to contribute to the resolution of the problem may feel resentful if they feel that the resolution of such problems is the duty of management.

   ii) It is a time-consuming way of solving the problem. Thus care must be taken to ensure that the nature of this difficulty is such that the involvement of all those affected is absolutely necessary. This is particularly important since the manager will not wish to consume too many resources in problem solving at the expense of production activity. An example would be that, desirable though it may be to hold problem-solving meetings with car production workers, the ultimate success of the enterprise depends upon those charged with managing the enterprise.

   iii) This strategy is particularly prone to the evolution of a compromise solution. This does not mean that a compromise is always undesirable; however there is the danger that compromise solutions could merely effectively avoid the addressing of the problem area – attempting to 'paper over the cracks'.

Another statement which might be illustrative is 'a camel is a horse designed by a committee'.

c) The use of externals – under this strategy the resolution of the problem will be left to people from outside the organisation. In its purest form it would be these people who would make the decision; in its less pure form these people would merely advise as to required action. This distinction is not of major importance in this discussion. It has the ready advantage of the use of a more objective approach to the resolution of the problem. These people will also afford the advantage of external knowledge; they will be familiar with solutions to similar problems outside the organisation. However, as a problem-solving strategy, this presents some potential difficulties.

　i)　It may be seen as an unwarranted intrusion into the decision making of the organisation. The external participant is not always welcomed. Given that resolutions will embrace the inconvenience of having to change, it is usually best to ensure that everyone involved should be content with the way in which the decision was reached.

　ii)　The solution may not be fully workable in the unique circumstances of that organisation. The benefits of internal knowledge are sometimes considerable.

　iii)　The external participants will have to be paid to solve the problem. Therefore it is essential that full benefits are obtained from this expenditure. However when claiming this disadvantage it must not be forgotten that any attempt to solve a problem internally will involve the time and resources of the organisation, which might have been better utilised on other tasks – there is an opportunity cost of evolving an internal approach to problem resolution.

Meetings as a Way of Solving Problems

For major problems the most common form of problem solving is seen to be the meeting. However the meeting, as a method or strategy of problem solving, is, in reality, a number of separate approaches to problem solving in that the meeting can be used in different ways. The successful manager must make the appropriate choice from the available range of options and, as such, the control of meetings is as much an exercise in self-management as it is in the management of others.

a) Command – with this approach the meeting is used as a way of merely informing the attenders of a decision taken elsewhere. This approach will afford the benefit of communication of the solution but all the benefits of participation previously claimed will quite obviously not apply.

b) Advisory – in this circumstance the meeting is called merely as a medium for information exchange. The meeting will be followed by a separate attempt to evolve a solution. This attempt may involve a meeting or it may involve a more individual approach to the resolution of the problem. This can be seen to be a particularly useful strategy to adopt where the various participants in the meeting are of different levels in the organisation. It is a sensible strategy to use when there are seen to be clearly different stages involved in the decision making. An example might be the brainstorming of idea evolution and the 'cold weather' evaluation stage, which might be undertaken in a different meeting or by a separate individual.

c) A decision-making meeting by different levels or different groups in the organisation – this is the purest form of problem solving by a meeting/committee. It is particularly useful when there is no monopoly of wisdom or judgement and when different levels, disciplines or groupings within the organisation each have an equal amount to contribute to the decision. It is a powerful way of obtaining commitment to the change or solution.

d) A collegiate meeting – this varies subtly, but materially, from that form of meeting just examined. It is a meeting, not of different groupings or disciplines or different levels, but of colleagues. That is, it is a meeting of those of equal status, with a truly shared experience and interest. It may well be the meeting which precedes that just mentioned in that, at the meeting of different disciplines, the collegiate may be represented by one individual; this individual will need to seek the ideas of the collegiate before that collegiate's views can be represented and presented in the meeting. If the problem is a serious one, both forms of meeting may be needed to ensure that all areas of expertise are involved and to ensure that the solution is one which will be 'owned' by all those involved.

An alternative classification of problem-solving meetings would focus on the way in which that meeting examines the problem and evolves a solution. Some can be seen to be more imaginative than others and hence perhaps more suited to creative thinking; however it might be that the more imaginative are also more problematical and prone to failure. Again the precise choice of activity will be that of the manager. These forms of alternative problem examination can be classified as follows.

Synectics

Under this approach the problem itself is not presented for solution; in its place a problem with similar characteristics, but substantially different in precise scenario, is presented for group evaluation. An example would be the implementation of a no-smoking policy in an organisation by examining the case of the introduction of flexible working hours. The point would be that the two issues would have substantially similar features in their impact on different members of the group but the precise scenario would be different. It would be hoped that under this arrangement the members of the group would learn to appreciate, for instance, the need to sacrifice long held and cherished self-freedoms for the benefit of a more pleasant collective working environment; the removal of the precise 'stake holdings' of the real issue under investigation, it is claimed, would facilitate group co-operation and participation. There are a number of potential difficulties with this approach.

a) The transfer of knowledge and awareness acquired from the two issues is not assured and it is a further duty of the manager to facilitate this transfer. This will be a time-consuming exercise; thus before embarking on this approach the manager must ensure that time is available to effect this transfer.
b) The group members may resent the fact that the true purpose of the discussion was withheld from them.
c) The alternative is to explain the fact that this exercise is merely a 'Case Study'. However in such circumstances the manager needs to ensure that he or she has the immediate and full co-operation of the group in this exercise.

Dialectics

The individual members of the group initially prepare their own problem evaluation and solution. These individual solutions are then examined and evaluated by the whole group. This approach has the benefit of highlighting to each member of the group the importance of assumptions and perceptions in the analysis of a problem. However there are difficulties with this approach.

a) It can be seen as threatening to the individual. This reaction can be overcome by careful and sensitive preparation and counselling by the manager. However it must be acknowledged that this counselling will consume valuable managerial time.
b) The evolution of a consensus approach from such widely different contributions may be difficult or take time.

Search Conference

This is suited to most groups or meetings but particularly to a multi-disciplinary group or meeting. It involves the pooling of expertise on the problem presented with a view to evolving a common perception of the problem and its resolution. This, in many ways, is the most conservative and 'safe' method of managing group activity in that it should result in a thorough examination of the problem. All perceived solutions should receive equal treatment. However it, in its turn, presents one major difficulty: its very conservative nature may prevent the evolution of radical solutions and, in the resolution of some problems, it may be that the seeking of 'safe bets' merely assuages symptoms and avoids the elimination of the real cause of the problem.

Brainstorming

Figure 5.1 briefly explains the process involved in a brainstorming exercise. It involves the generation of a large number of unconventional ideas whilst eliminating the usual tendencies to criticise or prematurely reject these unusual ideas.

The brainstorming process

1 *Selection*

Selection of a topic for brainstorming and the members of the group.

2 *The Problem*

The group is given advance notice of the problem in the form of a brief description of one or two sentences. The group facilitator discusses with the group a limited amount of background information relating to the problem.

3 *Warm-up session*

Members are introduced to the concepts of brainstorming in a relaxed manner. Group discussion tries to identify the barriers to creative thinking and shows how they can be overcome. The actual brainstorming process is explained, together with the four rules of brainstorming: free association, elaboration, suspension of judgement, and speed. A short practice-run demonstrates how little time it takes to produce 50 to 100 ideas.

At the end of the warm-up session, the original problem is restated in as many ways as possible. For example, the problem of reduced profit could be redefined as how to beat competitors, or how to improve marketing. All restatements are written down by the leader.

It should develop a lighthearted, easy-going atmosphere.

4 *Brainstorm*

The facilitator reads out the restatements and calls for ideas. As they flow, they are numbered and written up on a large flipchart with a large felt-tip pen. Each sheet is torn off when full and displayed elsewhere in the room. Freedom of expression should be encouraged. The ideas may number from 150 to 600, or more. There should be no pre-set timescale for this session.

FIGURE 5.1 *The Brainstorming Process*

Problem–Solving Behaviour

The various problem-solving strategies will be accompanied by certain forms of behaviour. Certain forms of behaviour are suited to certain strategies; other strategies can embrace a variety of possible behaviour patterns. It is important to note that much of this behaviour will be that of the manager and, if others are involved, it is the duty of the manager to control their behaviour.

SOLUTION-CENTRED BEHAVIOUR

This indicates that there is some idea about the desired solution. However this form of behaviour can be exhibited in different ways.

a) Directive behaviour – the idea will be that those affected are simply told what the solution will be. This is obviously suited to the Go Alone Strategy previously examined.
b) Prescriptive behaviour – in such a situation the solution is sold to those affected. It will embrace the circumstances where the leader states what the solution will be but then devotes real attention to explaining why the decision has been taken. This is useful when speed is needed but, when conducted with care, it should ensure that there is no resentment encountered from those affected.
c) Negotiative behaviour – this involves a desire to solve a problem in a particular way but also a willingness to discuss and negotiate around the proposed solution. Inevitably there will be different degrees of willingness to negotiate and, in reality, this form of behaviour is a collection of many separate behaviour patterns. It is a good way of obtaining agreement but it needs careful thought about what is and what is not subject to negotiation. If this form of behaviour is adopted the manager must retain some control over the proceedings.

PROBLEM-CENTRED BEHAVIOUR

This will be a different form of behaviour from those just described in that much more attention will be given to a rigorous examination of the problem before any attempt is made to generate a solution. It can be seen that much more time will need to be devoted to problem examination under this form of behaviour. As such, care must be taken to ensure that the benefits of full discussion are really needed. If the problem is serious and there is no monopoly of wisdom or judgement, such a form of behaviour is particularly suitable.

Techniques of Reflection

Assuming that there is to be full discussion, this discussion can be developed in different ways.

LOGICAL OR ANALYTICAL APPROACH

This will involve a structured approach to the problem-solving exercise. It is particularly suited to circumstances where the problem is minor in nature or in situations where there is previous experience of the type of problem encountered. It can be seen to be a structured, controlled response by management to the discovery of a problem. It might be useful where the precise applications of solutions need to be discovered quickly. However it is less suited to situations where substantial change has taken place.

CREATIVE, LESS LOGICAL APPROACHES

Examples might be brainstorming, or the development of lateral thinking techniques. This is an ambitious approach; it may be frustrating to those involved in that the generation of solutions may take some time. It can be judged to be a less organised, less structured approach. As such it is ill suited to situations where the organisation has limited time to evolve and implement a solution. However, it may have uses where the problem is severe in nature; it may be applied with some success where there is no previous experience of the type of problem encountered; it might be of use where the potential solution involves radical change within the organisation. When handled in a sensitive fashion it can obtain real commitment to the preferred solution. It is a technique which is particularly associated with creativity and innovation, the possible uses of which are examined elsewhere in the text. If this technique is chosen, the senior management of an organisation might be well advised to ensure that there is a strong likelihood that some practical solutions will emerge; lengthy, unstructured discussions which produce no obvious results can be extremely dispiriting to those involved.

An alterative classification of the techniques of reflection would be to make a distinction between convergent, divergent and integrative thinking.

CONVERGENT

This is the view where the thinker examines the problem with a microscope. It is most commonly encountered when people feel they have great familiarity with the type of problem being investigated. It is typically found in the thinking of the 'professional expert' who is trained to examine problems from the perspective of a narrow set of values and assumptions. Thus, for instance, in the problems evidenced by the collection of a particular tax, the accountant or tax collector would examine from the perspective of deficiencies in the process of the tax collection. An alternative perspective might well be that the tax itself was ill conceived.

DIVERGENT

In this type of thinking the view is that the 'world should be examined with a telescope'. The precept would be that the solution to the problem is best addressed from as wide a viewpoint as possible. Clearly this is a creative strategy and, as such, is somewhat more difficult to control than the concept of convergent thinking. This approach would tend to encourage the conclusion that the tax was ill conceived. However this type of thinking is not without its problems; it may tend to radical solution when minor technical alteration was what was required. Another difficulty with this approach is that it may result in impractical solutions being evolved.

INTEGRATIVE

It may be that in the examination of a particular problem there is a need for both types of thinking at different stages of the exercise. This would be classified as 'integrative thinking'. It is pictorially depicted in Figure 5.2.

This type of thinking would necessitate initial divergent thinking and finally the techniques of convergent thinking. The problem would be subject to wide-ranging examination followed by the more narrow investigation to enable the chosen solution to be workable. Essentially, in many ways, this type of thinking is 'hot weather ideas generation' followed by 'cold weather evaluation'.

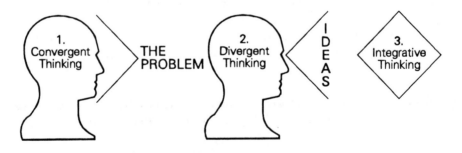

FIGURE 5.2 *The Manager's Role in Problem Solving*

The Organisation and Problem Solving

The various approaches to the manager's role in problem solving have just been examined but it is now necessary to examine problem solving in a wider organisational context. Figure 5.3 shows the process which is involved when an organisation undertakes resolutions to its problems.

DEFINING THE PROBLEM

The organisation must analyse the cause of the problem. In this context, as has been acknowledged in an earlier part of this chapter, it is important to distinguish between symptoms and underlying causes. The nature of the problem needs to be thoroughly examined:

i) Where did it occur?

ii) Who or what was responsible?

iii) Is it an isolated incident or is it likely to reoccur?

iv) Is it a problem, and hence a solution, which impacts on a wider constituency than that at the level it has been detected?

v) What are the consequences of ignoring the problem?

vi) Is it a sign of a future, more severe problem?

Having answered these questions the organisation is then able to assess the nature of the decision which needs to be taken.

RANGES OF DECISION

Problem solving is based upon the making of a decision to eradicate the problem. Thus it is necessary to examine the nature of decisions and who makes decisions in organisations. Decisions can be categorised in a number of ways.

a) Programmed or non-programmed decisions – programmed decisions are those which are considered routine, repetitive or covered by an established procedure. Non-programmed decisions are those where no clear procedure exists. Non-programmed decisions will require the assembling of new routines or procedures and may require the organisation to acknowledge a limited control. Programmed decisions acknowledge a degree of organisational preparedness.

It could, therefore, be seen that the aim of the well managed organisation is to minimise the number of non-programmed decisions it might have to make. Thus

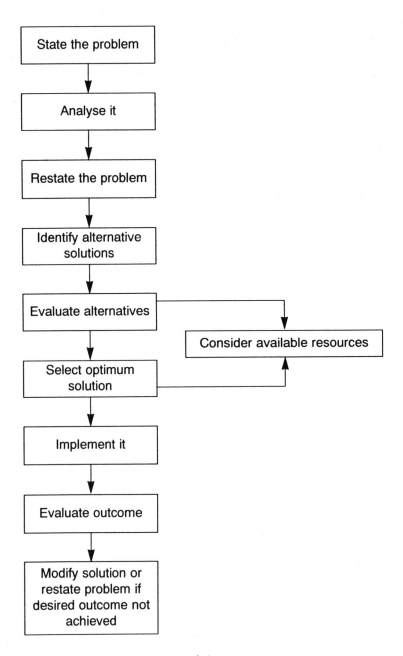

FIGURE 5.3 *Selecting an appropriate solution*

since the late 1980s there has been seen to be an increase in the range of decisions for which an organisation assumes control and preparedness. For instance, many organisations are laying down established, powerful procedures to be adopted even in crisis situations.

Under this approach the trend in organisational management is for organisations to prepare set procedures to be followed in the resolution of problems. However, this should not be seen to infer that the organisation, in this enhanced level of preparedness, would wish to exclude creative solutions to the resolution of problems; the reality is that the organisation would establish a clear procedure within which the solution, creative or otherwise, would be pursued.

b) Levels of decision making – an alternative classification is one which focuses on the level of the decision as to whether it is strategic, system or operational. Strategic decisions are those which are focused on the organisation's achievement of its corporate objectives. System decisions are concerned with how the organisation devises systems to enable it to achieve its objectives. Operational decisions are those whaich are concerned with the proper administration of its systems.

Under this approach the organisation will have to examine who are the stakeholders in each level of decision and ensure that in the making of the decision all legitimate stakeholders are involved.

FINDING THE SOLUTION

Having examined the nature of the problem and identified the nature of the decision to take, it is now necessary to evaluate the likely solutions. It is unlikely for a problem to have merely one solution. Rather the organisation must establish systems which enable it to access the range of solutions available and to evaluate those range of solutions. The more severe the problem the more likely group activity or brainstorming are to be considered useful. In evalulating the solutions it is necessary to examine a number of factors:

a) Risk – the relationship between risk and benefit needs to be assessed. Naturally a low risk/high benefit solution would be desirable; however in the real world there may have to be a choice made between high risk solutions where there is a major payoff and lower risk solutions with a lower payoff.

b) Resources – when a solution is evaluated its likely impact on scarce resources needs to be considered. An maximum payoff solution will not be an optimum solution if it requires the consumption of excessive staff time and attention, money, space, raw materials, and I.T. resources.

c) Time – there will have to be an assessment made of the time available to introduce the solution. A major improvement may require long time periods to implement; however a lower impact solution may require less time. Hence the organisation has to determine the time it has available to solve the problem. A common feature which can be evidenced is for the organisation to 'buy time' by adopting a 'quick fix' solution to enable it to evolve a longer term, more effective solution.

d) The degree of disruption – an excellent theoretical solution may cause too much disruption within the organisation. Hence the organisation must appraise the consequences of implementing various solutions. Only when the benefits exceed the disruption costs should the solution be pursued.

Organisations can be aided in the choice of solutions by quantitative and I.T.-based modelling techniques such as 'decision trees'.

Despite these techniques there are still important management decisions to be taken which can embellish the information provided by these techniques.

Summary

The solution to problems presents a serious challenge to the manager and to the organisation itself. The management of the organisation can adopt a high-profile, leading role in the generation of the solution; sometimes lower profile, more participative approaches may be required. Care must be taken to ensure that the solution emerges before the problem has caused the manager and the organisation too much damage. However, the manager is also obliged to ensure that the solutions which emerge are accepted by all those involved in their implementation. In evolving the appropriate response the management must be prepared to be flexible and adaptable. It is highly likely that certain responses would be desirable in some circumstances and other responses might seem more attractive in different circumstances. The manager has several strategies which can be adopted and several techniques which can be used in the problem-solving task. The selection of the solution will require of the manager a thorough understanding of himself, others, the organisation and the particular problem.

Exercise

Examine the ways in which you solve problems in your working life. In what ways, if any, do you consider you might improve your skills in this area by utilising different problem solving strategies?

Further Reading

Adair, J. (1984) *The Skills of Leadership*, Gower
Leavitt, H.J. (1978) *Managerial Psychology*, University of Chicago Press
Pfeffer, J. (1981) *Power in Organisations*, Pitman
Snape, E., Redman, T. and Bamber, G. J. (1994) *Managing Managers*, Blackwell
Welsh, A.N. (1982) *The Skills of Management*, Gower
Woodcock, M. and Francis, D. (1989) *The Unblocked Manager*, Gower

Managing
People

OBJECTIVES

The purpose of this section is to examine those aspects of the total management task which are directly connected with the difficulties inherent in managing other people: ensuring high levels of motivation, ensuring good communication, appreciating the nature of group activity, choosing the appropriate leadership strategy. After reading this chapter the student should be able to appreciate the difficulties which are inherent in the management of other people and be aware of actions which the manager can take to ensure the co-operation of those he or she is responsible for managing.

This should be seen as a separate aspect from the next section, The Management of Human Resources. The latter is connected with institutional responses to the challenge of managing human beings, for example personnel management systems, whereas this section addresses issues more directly connected with individual or small group management.

INTRODUCTION

When managers approach their duties they will soon be aware of difficulties inherent in the management of those with whom they have direct contact. They will quickly discover that subordinates do not necessarily feel favourably disposed towards the organisation. They will find that the task of communication is fraught with practical problems. They will need to be mindful of group activity, norms and pressures. They will soon be aware of the importance of their chosen leadership style. Successful managers need to understand the problems inherent in managing other people. They need to appreciate that all these problems can be overcome; however they must understand that the elimination of such difficulties is an immense managerial task, which is based upon a full appreciation of the needs, motives, desires and values of the people who are to be managed.

Chapter six

Human
Motivation

L E A R N I N G   O B J E C T I V E S

- **Understand the major theoretical approaches to human motivation**

- **Interlink these various theories of motivation**

- **Identify areas where these approaches would be reflected in real life**

- **Assess the importance of individual differences in motivation**

- **Appraise the importance of variation in levels of motivation within individual employees**

- **Construct an organisational environment which will optimise motivation**

- **Identify areas where further research is necessary**

It is an axiom of management that a manager cannot possibly fulfil every production task within the organisation for which he or she is responsible. Only by delegating duties to others can the manager possibly afford productive activity to the organisation. However, such delegation demands or necessitates the effective management of those people to whom the various productive tasks have been entrusted.

One of the most important responsibilities of managers is obtaining maximum co-operation and productivity from those people they have empowered to work on their behalf. This, and indeed any duty of management, is far from easy to achieve. The behaviour and attitudes of those supervised will not necessarily be wholly co-operative nor indeed reflect maximum motivation. In this context motivation can be defined in terms of the extent to which the employee works to full capabilities and the extent to which the employee acknowledges the legitimacy of and seeks to achieve and co-operate with organisational objectives and interests.

The primary herer is to assess the various elements of employee motivation; it is necessary to examine the potency of different elements of human motivation in the workplace. It might be that this examination reveals that motivation in the occupational environment is best studied from the perspective of human motivation in the personal and social as well as occupational environment. This examination reveals that employees can be motivated by various characteristics of their total life experience. These sources of motivation, in all aspects of life, are seen to be economic, social, status and self-growth – all of which will be examined in greater detail in the chapter. The main premise and the main conclusions from these investigations will be that the human being has powerful sources of motivation other than money which can be evidenced in the non-occupational aspects of his or her life; and that these sources of motivation can be introduced into the work environment to produce a more motivated group of employees.

The variety of sources of motivation are well illustrated by an examination of some prominent theories of human motivation. In examining this subject area a number of theories of human motivation will be assessed from a practical perspective, with a view to constructing a comprehensive model which explains the complexities of human motivation in the work environment. Fortunately the theories of human motivation which will be examined can be linked together to provide a view of human motivation which will enable the practising managers to anticipate and facilitate types and levels of motivation which will aid the achievement of their organisations' objectives.

McGregor's Theory

Douglas McGregor states that, in assessing the desired style of leadership to be adopted in an organisation, the managers of that organisation can make two starkly contrasting sets of assumptions about the nature of human motivation.

a) Theory X:
   i)   people are lazy;
   ii) employees will need constant supervision;
   iii) these people will work only when supervised;
   iv) the primary way to induce motivation is to pay the employee.

This set of assumptions he directly contrasts with another set of assumptions which could be made.

b) Theory Y:
   i)   far from being lazy, people are, by nature, highly active;

ii)   people do not need constant supervision;

iii) people will act voluntarily;

iv)   people have powerful sources of motivation other than money.

His argument is that it is the assumptions which managers make about human motivation which determines their approach to design of leadership strategies within the organisation.

Under Theory X assumptions, leadership behaviour will be directed towards forceful, high profile, authoritarian styles of leadership. If Theory Y is assumed then chosen leadership styles will be more directed towards involving the subordinates in the decision making of the organisation. Furthermore his theory is that observed human behaviour in the workplace is a product of the chosen leadership style. The assumption is that people in organisations which allow them little autonomy and freedom will show types and levels of motivation which are consistent with the leadership actions to which they are subjected.

It is necessary to test this theory against practical observations. This examination of behaviour in the work environment would show that these are rather crudely presented assumptions but that it is possible to find people within most organisations who seem to behave generally in accordance with Theory X and Theory Y principles. Some people will do nothing unless they are closely supervised will appear to have extremely mercenary attitudes towards work and only those actions which are directly financially rewarded will be afforded to the management of the organisation; others will appear to act by showing initiative and working when not closely supervised, and will co-operate by working longer hours than normal even when not being paid to do so.

A further examination would suggest that many of those who display Theory X behaviour in the work environment, behave in Theory Y ways outside the work environment; they may have social interests which they pursue with great vigour for no financial reward – examples might be membership of quiz teams or sports organisations. Unless we assume that these two groups of people have radically contrasting sources of motivation and life priorities and that, furthermore, the Theory Y social life and Theory X occupational life people have 'split personalities' the only explanation of these quite startling variations is that they must be caused by differences in the environment within which the two sets of behaviour patterns are conducted.

A closer examination reveals that there is a tendency for Theory X people to have different types of job than Theory Y people; Theory X people tend to be found in jobs where little status is attached or where little job challenge is afforded, whereas Theory Y people tend to work in jobs where status is afforded to the holder of that job or where there is significant challenge or creativity. Examples of Theory Y people would be found often in management occupations where status is afforded, where job content is challenging and where the holder of the post has a substantial degree of control over job content.

Thus it could be concluded that, if the co-operation of the worker is to be sought or if maximum motivation is to be achieved, the work environment in general and jobs in particular must be designed in such a way as to attract Theory Y behaviour.

Maslow's Theory

The theories of Maslow (1943) have attracted great attention and, in many ways, could be seen to be the origin of many of the other theories. He claims that mankind has a number of different levels of need. The assumption is that these levels of need can be arranged into a Hierarchy of Needs. These are portrayed in Figure 6.1.

FIGURE 6.1 *Maslow's Hierarchy of Needs*

People need to satisfy one level of need before they will progress to attempting to satisfy the next level of need. An examination of Figure 6.1 shows that these different levels of need are constructed in the following ascending order.

a) Physiological – these are assumed to be the most basic and fundamental of all needs; examples would be hunger and thirst. If people are hungry or thirsty their only need will be to satisfy these needs and, in such circumstances, the assumption of the desire by such an individual to fulfil higher level needs is either redundant or naive. Having satisfied this, most basic, level of need the individual will then progress to attempting to satisfy the next level of need.

b) Safety – when the individual has satisfied the physiological needs and only when these are satisfied, that individual will seek safety or will then assume safety needs. This need will then assume priority and only when this need to feel safe has been satisfied will the individual then progress to trying to satisfy the next level of need.

c) Love – Maslow states that eventually the individual will feel the need to be accepted as a member of a social grouping, for example a sports team, a theatrical society. Furthermore if the individual is not satisfying this level of need and does not feel an accepted member of the group, he or she will be greatly distressed and all behaviour can be seen to be directed towards being given such group membership.

d) Esteem – in Maslow's theory once the person has been accorded group membership that person will no longer be content and the desire to fulfil a higher level of need will emerge – esteem within the group. The person will need to be seen as a valued and important member of the group or team. Once the individual has satisfied these needs of esteem, and only when these needs have been satisfied, might he or she progress to the final, and most controversial, level of need.

e) Self-Actualisation – this is the level of need concerned with the fulfilment of full human potential, the need to constantly improve upon current activity levels or improve intellectually or increase skills acquired. In such circumstances, the person who does well no longer has the desperate need to be praised (esteem). The knowledge that the job was done well is a reward in itself. According to Maslow most adults are capable of progressing to this level of need. It will be only when this level of need is fully met that all sources of motivation will have been tapped.

An examination of the practicality of this theory reveals that it holds many attractions. An examination of human behaviour would support the existence of the first four levels of need and, most importantly, suggests the potency of the need for love and esteem cannot be doubted. However, there are certainly some doubts about the practical evidence surrounding some of its contents; for instance the precise order of these needs can be questioned. It is distinctly possible that individual actions might be seen as supporting the satisfaction of more than one level of need at any one time. Secondly, the existence of self-actualising needs in all people can be questioned. There are certainly some people who seem to be perfectly content with team membership as a major, and final, goal in life. However, it must be stressed that the existence of the fifth level of need in many people cannot be questioned. Most people will acknowledge that they gain significant satisfaction from doing a challenging job well.

To conclude the examination of this theory and focusing attention on McGregor's Theory X behaviour, it can be seen that some jobs do not afford the fulfilment of the last three levels of need. Sometimes people are not allowed to communicate with others during the period of work; some jobs are not such that great status or esteem is attached. Some jobs are so mundane that fulfilment of self-actualising needs does not exist. If Maslow's theory is legitimate and if these needs are not satisfied then not all sources of human motivation will have been accessed.

Argyris' Theory

The theorist Argyris claims that people naturally progress from immaturity into maturity. This move from immaturity to maturity is characterised by a number of changes. The nature of such changes is expressed in simple terms in Figure 6.2.

IMMATURITY	⟶	MATURITY

Dependence ....Relative Independence
Short Time Perspective ....Long Time Perspective
Subordinate Position..............................Equal or Superior Position
Internal Rewards ....External Rewards

FIGURE 6.2 *Immaturity - Maturity Theory (source: Argyris)*

The most important changes are described by Argyris in his theory.

a) The growth or progression from subordinate status to status of equality or superiority – the child is treated as the subordinate member of the family group. In adulthood the individual is treated as an equal, or even a superior, by other members of the family group.
b) The move from short term goals to longer term goals – young children are generally considered to behave in ways which suggest short term goals (the next feed, the next play period) whereas adulthood is characterised by the assumption of longer term goals (undergoing the sacrifice of leisure time to study for examinations as the price to be paid for better rewards in the future).
c) The move from external rewards to internal rewards – children are rewarded in external ways; the granting by others of explicit praise such as a pat on the head, a gift in return for socially acceptable behaviour patterns. As the child matures there is less emphasis on external rewards, and the values of good behaviour and good citizenship become accepted as worthy in their own right. These can be seen to be internally driven rewards.

Argyris claims that when mature people are placed in a work environment consistent with these mature characteristics, all their needs will be satisfied and they will behave at work in ways which are consistent with their behaviour and values in their social lives. However, when they are placed in work situations which display immature features, they will behave in ways which are consistent with such an environment; that is, they will behave in immature ways.

An examination of the practicality of this theory would suggest that it has some practical applicability. Certainly the examples of mature and immature behaviours and values can be observed to be well documented. If this theory is to be accepted it would both explain the mature behaviour patterns of Theory Y people and the apparently immature or unco-operative behaviour of Theory X people; human behaviour and human motivation in the work environment is driven by the characteristics of that work environment.

Herzberg's Theory

Herzberg's theory of hygiene and motivating factors in the work environment is one which has received much approval by practising managers. It can be seen to be consistent with the major themes of the theories just examined. Herzberg claims that those elements of the working environment which actually cause dissatisfaction are different in nature or character from those environmental elements which will produce real satisfaction. Those elements of the work environment which produce dissatisfaction he entitles 'hygiene' factors; those which cause satisfaction he entitles 'motivating' factors. Figure 6.3 provides a illustration of his categorisations.

Motivators	Hygiene Factors
❑ Achievements	❑ Company Policy and Administration
❑ Recognition	❑ Supervision - the technical aspects
❑ Work Itself	❑ Salary
❑ Responsibility	❑ Interpersonal Relations - supervision
❑ Advancement	❑ Working Conditions

FIGURE 6.3 *Herzberg's Motivation – Hygiene Theory*

According to his theory, hygiene factors are those which are related to the environment within which the job is carried out; examples would be the salary it attracts, the working conditions, the quality of supervision.

In contrast, motivating factors are those which are actually part of the job itself; examples would be advancement, the job content, responsibility, the achievement afforded by doing the job.

According to Herzberg's theory the removal of the dissatisfying parts of the work environment will not actually produce satisfaction with the job; all that will result is a feeling of mere acceptability, perhaps illustrated by statements such as 'My job is OK; it pays the mortgage'. The introduction of real satisfaction into the job will demand those features categorised as 'motivating'. Only if these elements are included will statements like 'I really like my job, in fact I cannot wait to get into work in a morning!' be expressed.

Herzberg claims that to introduce motivation into the work environment, techniques such as job enrichment need to be introduced; this involves the introduction of richer or intellectually more challenging elements into the content or specifications of the job.

When Herzberg's theory is tested against real-life experiences it can be seen that the technical precision of the distinction between dissatisfaction and satisfaction is, at best, a nice distinction or, at worst, tortuous. The claim that 'dissatisfaction' and 'satisfaction' are not at two ends of one continuum is certainly difficult to understand and certainly contrary to established semantics. However, the theory is useful in that it presents real, practical options for the manager to introduce into the work content of employees.

For the purposes of the assessment of the practicalities of Herzberg's theory it might be best to view hygiene factors as sources of motivation only in the short term and to view motivators as sources of motivation in the longer term; in fact this is consistent with one way in which Herzberg himself has interpreted his theory. If this interpretation is adopted, the distinction between the two becomes a little clearer. If managers attempt to motivate their dissatisfied employees by paying them more, it may well be that the employees are thankful for this increase in remuneration but their thanks will be short-lived; their new, more positive, attitudes to work will soon disappear. They will soon forget that they have received a pay rise. There is evidence to suggest that the introduction of job enrichment procedures does improve long-term productivity in that fewer mistakes are made, absenteeism is reduced. This might be seen as indicating the longer-term potency of 'motivators'. Examples of these applications are the job enrichment programmes conducted in the Volvo factories in Sweden and the Phillips factories in the Netherlands.

However there are some problems which have been encountered in the application of the theories of Herzberg.

a) It proves very difficult to change the technology of some jobs so that enriching factors are introduced. For instance, the available technology in many manual occupations does not readily afford many obvious options to increase the challenge of the job. The work of many manual workers is soon learned and to describe any element of their work as 'challenging' might be deemed to be unrealistic. Under such circumstances the manager has to find substitutes for enrichment. One alternative might be job rotation whereby the individual does not have the technology of the job changed but rather is moved around from job to job to introduce some variety into the work environment. This is useful in that such rotation can be easily introduced. However problems are found in that the challenge is short-lived; the individual may soon become familiar with all the requirements of all the jobs and boredom re-emerges.

Another alternative is job enlargement; under such circumstances the technology of the job is not changed but the individual is made responsible for a larger section of the overall production task. An example would be dismantling the production line in a motor car factory and creating small work teams responsible for a large section of the construction of the motor car. This has the advantage of being easy to introduce (but not as easy as that of job rotation); its 'shelf life' as a source of motivation may exceed that of rotation in that the challenge of a bigger job will endure for longer. However, after some time has elapsed a bigger, but routine, job may cease to be a challenge to the worker.   Finally, some of the duties which would normally be seen as the prerogative of the manager can be given to the extended job. For instance, the employees could become more involved in the design of the product they are producing; they could be involved in the planning of the quantity and quality of work they have to produce. Perhaps, more ambitiously, they could be afforded more contact with the customer (this, they may see as a major change). Suddenly they are deemed more trustworthy and the theories of motivation so far examined would suggest that this, in its own right, will be a major source of motivation. These alterations to the content of the job are not really enrichment in its purest form but they may be seen to be acceptable alternatives; in many ways they could be seen to be a compromise between enrichment and enlargement.

b) The benefits to be obtained tend to be long-term in nature since improvements will be found only in the longer term and, in the short term, actual deterioration in performance might be encountered. A more challenging job is one where more mistakes can be made. Thus during the training period productivity problems will probably be detected. As has already been stated, many of the durable benefits surround better productivity through fewer disputes, through less absenteeism, rather than by simple day-to-day productivity improvements. Even though there are probable benefits to be obtained in the longer term, all organisations need to continue to exist in the shorter term; in fact for many organisations in competitive situations a poor short-term performance will threaten the longer-term existence of the organisation – the organisation may lose its market position.

Stress or Stimulation and Performance

All the theories examined up to now have assumed that all people are equal. The reality is that individuals vary in all their characteristics, including the extent to which they can be challenged. Furthermore, an analysis of stress in the workplace reveals that the extent to which individuals welcome a challenge can vary from time to time. The reality is that most people will sometimes find that the challenges which work presents are rather greater than they would welcome and hence a cause of stress. There is an optimal level of challenge beyond which performance begins to deteriorate. This has already been examined in the previous section of this text. The theory of Berlyne (The Optimal Level of Arousal, 1969) acknowledges the existence of this variation from individual to individual, the variation within one individual from time to time, and the existence of an upper limit on the acceptability of a challenging job. This term 'arousal' can be interpreted as a psychological feeling of challenge. He argues that the relationship between arousal and job performance is not one of ascending performance as challenge increases (as predicted by the previous theories) but one approaching a normal curve; that is, there is an optimal level of arousal beyond which performance deteriorates. (Figure 6.4).

Berlyne states that it is not just the job content which contributes to arousal; rather people vary in their personalities. The distinction between Type A and Type B personalities has been mentioned in the previous section. People have different tolerance levels to stress. Thus he would predict that people with Type A personalities will be less disposed to welcome challenging jobs than would be those with Type B personalities. To an extent it can be seen practice in that people who suffer from nervous disorders often seek less challenging jobs. Secondly, people's personal circumstances vary from time to time. People encounter periods of stress during their personal lives and according to Berlyne these contribute towards their total level of arousal. People under stress are less likely to seek or welcome a challenge in their jobs than will people under less personal stress. Again to an extent this can be evidenced in reality in that, for instance, a person about to sit an afternoon examination would prefer to undertake an unchallenging job the morning before the examination.

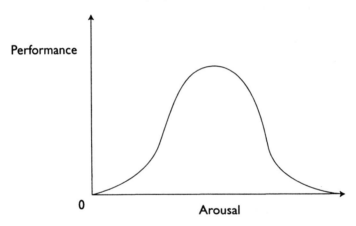

FIGURE 6.4 *Theory of Arousal (source: Berlyne)*

Equity Theory and Cognitive Dissonance

It is necessary to acknowledge the role played in the motivation process by individual judgements or cognitions. When people judge their commitment to their job they make judgements about the fairness of the way they are treated. According to equity theory and the theory of cognitive dissonance, in the making of these judgements, people make comparisons. According to these theories they make both internal and external comparisons and as a result of making such comparisons they will make conscious decisions about their workplace behaviour and observed level of motivation. Figure 6.5 shows the judgements they make and the consequent actions they can take.

| Type of Inequity | Type of Reaction | |
	Behavioural Action	Cognitive Judgement
Overpayment Inequity	Raise your inputs (eg work harder)	Convince yourself that your outcomes are deserved based on your inputs (eg believe that you work harder than others so you deserve more pay)
Underpayment Inequity	Lower your inputs (eg reduce effort)	Convince yourself that others' inputs are higher than your own (eg rationalise that the comparator is really more qualified, and so deserves higher outcomes)

FIGURE 6.5 *Equity Theory*

INTERNAL COMPARISONS

Workers make a comparison between what they feel they put into a job (their inputs) and what they feel they get out of a job (their outputs). According to these theories individuals feel the need for their inputs to equal their outputs. It must be stressed that it is harmony, equality or sonance which is sought and if individuals feel they are getting more out of a job than they are putting into it they will feel as dissatisfied as they would be if the reverse situation applied. This is a statement which needs to be tested against reality in that, upon first examination, it is more easy to conceive of a situation where people would express satisfaction when their outputs exceed their inputs. The assessment of both inputs and outputs is a complex task involving more than a judgement about physical effort or monetary reward. Examples of the variety of these judgements are now analysed.

a) Inputs – according to these theories the individuals judge many things to constitute part of their assessments of these inputs.
   i) They will make judgements about the level of education and training brought to the job. For instance, they may feel that they are highly trained and that this is justification in itself for a certain level of reward. This can be observed in practice when skilled workers point to their skills as justifications for their receiving higher pay than unskilled workers.
   ii) They will make judgements about the amount of effort they expend in doing the job. This again is encountered in practice in that workers very often justify

their higher pay by referring to the hours they work or the physical effort they expend.

   iii) They will make judgements about their status. Again this can be seen in practice in that the statements of skilled workers are not confined solely to those surrounding their skills but also refer to their having higher status than the unskilled worker.

b) Outputs.

   i) Quite obviously individuals will evaluate their financial or monetary rewards.

   ii) They will also make judgements about the status they are accorded by the job. Thus it can be seen in practice that people justify remaining in relatively poorly paid jobs by emphasising the status of their job. The secretary to the managing director might often quote this as one of the major rewards of the job.

   iii) Employees will make judgements about the working conditions attached to the job. If pay is poor they may console themselves by emphasising the convenience of working hours or the cleanliness of the work environment.

According to these theories the worker will make judgements about all the inputs and all the outputs. If the total of the inputs does not equal the total of the outputs then dissatisfaction will be created in the mind of the worker. If inputs are seen to exceed outputs, a state of 'cognitive dissonance' exists. That is, there is an absence of harmony or equality in judgements of the input–output equation. Under such circumstances workers will strive for harmony or equality in these judgements, or 'cognitive sonance'. The most obvious action is to work less hard; however according to these theories any other part of the equation can be altered and examples of such changes in judgement are now examined.

a) Workers can make a decision to downgrade their assessment of the worth of their inputs. For instance, they can reassess their judgement of their level of training and conclude that perhaps they are not as well-trained as they first thought.

b) They can reassess their judgement of the working conditions surrounding the job. For example, they might decide to place a higher value on their pleasant working conditions.

Thus it can be seen that any side of the equation can be altered to achieve harmony or equality.

EXTERNAL COMPARISONS

Equity theory extends beyond the making of internal comparisons; in addition to the internal comparisons just examined it extends into the making of comparisons with other workers. According to this part of the theory, workers compare their position with some other workers whose general inputs they consider to be equivalent to their own (known as the comparator or other). Thus, for instance, the civil engineer may compare himself or herself with the mechanical engineer. The workers will be content only when their outputs are judged to be comparable with those achieved by their comparator or other. If true equality is not achieved, according to this theory, discontentment will result and the person making this comparison will strive for equality in judgement. If, for instance, the civil engineer discovers that the mechanical engineer receives more pay, he or she might reassess the working conditions in both circumstances and judge his or hers to be better than that of the mechanical engineer. Alternatively he or she might reassess the level of training both have undergone and conclude that the mechanical engineer is the better trained. At the extreme, he or she might decide that the comparator is no longer legitimate and seek another comparator (eg the mining engineer). The final solution is to leave the job for one with better pay ('leave the field').

When this theory is tested against behaviour, in practice it proves difficult to reach a conclusive assessment as to its legitimacy. Certainly people do make comparisons of their total rewards from work compared to that of others. Certainly it can be seen that all the factors involved in the assessment of inputs and outputs do constitute a more complex total remuneration package which more closely reflects reality than does the simple financial model. As has been seen in the previous analysis, many of the actions predicted by an assessment of poor relative remuneration can be seen in practice.

The circumstances which are meant to obtain when perceived remuneration exceeds perceived inputs present a much more difficult problem from the perspective of practical evaluation. As has already been stated, if this obtains, according to this theory, the individual will not be content with this lack of harmony and will do something to produce a more harmonious judgement. This action may involve working harder as a result of a feeling of unease: 'I must work harder to justify this level of pay!' Alternatively it may result in the individual reassessing other inputs by, for instance, upgrading the perception of his or her own skills. Another action which might be predicted is a downgrading of some aspect of perceived outputs. For instance it might be that the employee reassesses the working hours as more anti-social than originally thought.

This test of the full legitimacy and practicality of equity theory is more problematical. It is possible to detect situations where the individual may work harder to eliminate feelings of unease. However, it is possible to detect situations where the worker does nothing and willingly accepts this disharmony. This situation may be compounded by the individual making longer term judgements such about receiving rewards now from past, poorly rewarded efforts as well as present efforts.

In conclusion the practical assessment of equity theory is inconclusive but certainly it does have some legitimate features. Perhaps its major use is its illustration of the importance of subjective judgements and cognitions in the motivation process and hence the active mental involvement of the worker in the judgement of fairness.

Expectancy Theory

There have been several theorists who have written emphasising the role of anticipation or expectancy in the motivation process (for example Vroom, 1964; Porter and Lawler, 1968). The theory is presented in Figure 6.6. All these theories state that motivation is the result of three separate judgements that people make.

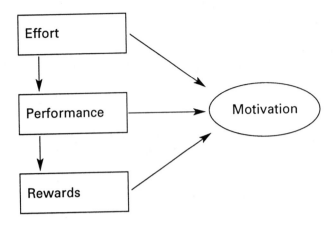

FIGURE 6.6   *Expectancy Theory - The Basic Model*

a) Expectancy – the judgement that effort will result in performance.
b) Instrumentality – the belief that these results will be rewarded.
c) Valence – the recipient's judgement of the attraction of these rewards.

Under such circumstances the individual will work hardest only when it is believed that such efforts will produce results and when these efforts are accompanied by attractive rewards. Even if the individual obtains attractive rewards, he or she will only work to maximum capacity if it is believed that efforts will produce results. This will explain the circumstances where an individual feels that no matter how hard he works there is nothing he can do to improve the situation. Similarly, if an individual is paid by results and those results were under his or her control, only if the individual judges the rewards as attractive will he or she be impelled to maximum effort. Finally, the importance of reward itself is emphasised.

This approach broadly accords with those previously examined in that it recognises that motivation and reward are intimately linked. Furthermore rewards are seen to span wider issues than mere financial remuneration. The practical implications of an Expectancy Approach to motivation is shown in Figure 6.7. Depending on where the motivational weakness in the linkages occur, different management responses are required to improve these linkages. The more comprehensive theories in this category also stress the involvement of features other than motivation in job performance. Figure 6.8 explains this more complex relationship between motivation and performance.

The worker's individual abilities and skills will limit the performance of even the most motivated worker. Similarly, a poorly motivated employee may work satisfactorily simply through using his or her high abilities and skills to moderate effect.

Individuals will be limited in what they do by their perception of their role in the

Problem	Solution
1 Working hard does not improve performance	Design jobs so that hard work produces results
2 High levels of performance do not receive rewards	Introduce payment by results

FIGURE 6.7

organisation. Thus, no matter how motivated a worker and no matter how impressive his abilities and skills, it is unlikely that he will fulfil work obligations which are seen as the duty of someone else. This is a very important point to note since it may well be in the interests of the organisation that the individual actually showed initiative and acted in ways beyond 'role perception'. The importance of role flexibility in achieving organisational success will be examined later in this text.

Finally, even the most motivated individual will perform badly if there is no opportunity to perform well. A good example of this would be the field surgeon operating on the battlefield – motivated though he or she might be – performance would be considerably enhanced by the equipment available in peacetime.

Wider expectancy theory holds many attractions in its testing against real world experiences. The linkage of ability to perform with motivation is a particular aid to our understanding of the nature of motivation and work performance.

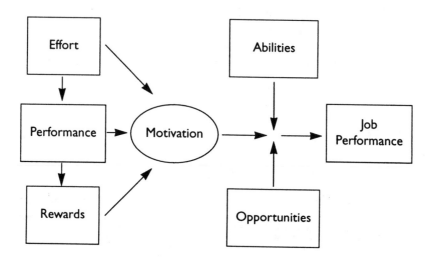

FIGURE 6.8 *Expectancy Theory: An Overview*

Hackman (1975) has tried to elaborate within his expectancy theory upon the higher-level needs hypothesised by Maslow and Herzberg. According to Hackman an individual's desire for personal growth and development is served by five separate features of job content:

a) skill variety – the ability to use different skills and abilities;
b) task identity – a complete and meaningful piece of work;
c) task significance – a job of real importance within the organisation;
d) autonomy – the facility to work with a significant degree of independence;
e) feedback – adequate and timely feedback about the perceived level of performance.

In Hackman's opinion, if all five constituent features are present then the desire for personal growth will be strongly evidenced and hence motivation will ensue. If one or more features are absent the extent to which the others are evidenced will dictate the extent to which motivation will result. With only a small number present there will be a very limited chance of motivation.

Summary

All the theories examined have been tested against situations where they might be said to exist in practice and they have been seen to have at least some practical uses and legitimacy. Perhaps the most important conclusion which can be reached from an examination of all these theories is the existence of powerful sources of motivation other than that of money. However, this must never be interpreted as a conclusion that money is unimportant. Money is both a reward in itself, a payment for the absence of other sources of reward and, to some extent, a measure or reflection of other rewards (for example status).

Finally motivation is only part, albeit an important one, of the individual's willingness or ability to perform his or her allocated work tasks well.

Exercise

Contrast the ways in which you are motivated in your private and public life. What, if anything, could happen to your working life to bring the two sources of motivation closer together?

Further Reading

Aronson, E. (1976) *The Social Animal*, Freeman

Berlyne, D. (1969) *Arousal and Performance*, University of Toronto

Brehm, J.W. and Cohen, A.R. (1962) *Explorations in Cognitive Dissonance*, Wiley

Connock, S. (1991) *HR Vision: Managing a Quality Workforce*, Institute of Personnel Management

Herzberg, F. (1966) *Work and the Nature of Man*, World Publishing Co.

Hunt, J. (1981) *Managing People at Work*, Pan

Litwin, G.H. and Stringer, R.A. (1968) *Motivation and Organisational Climate*, Harvard University Press

Maslow, A. (1954) *Motivation and Personality*, Harper and Row

McClelland, D.C. (1961) *The Achieving Society*, Van Nostrand

McGregor, D. (1960) *The Human Side of Enterprise*, McGraw Hill

Molander, C. and Winterton, J. (1994) *Managing Human Resources*, Routledge

Schermerhorn, J.R., Hunt, J.G., and Osborn, R.N. (1995) *Basic Organizational Behaviour*, John Wiley

Wigley, D. (Dec 1989) Performance Review, *Motivation and Organisational Culture*, Health Services Management

Communication

Chapter seven

L E A R N I N G   O B J E C T I V E S

- **Understand the wide-ranging nature of communication in an organisational context**
- **Understand the theoretical analysis in the area of communication**
- **Identify the differences between formal and informal communication**
- **Understand the importance of patterning of communication**
- **Assess circumstances where communication within an organisation has been ineffective**
- **Create a strategy for controlling communication within an organisation**
- **Identify areas where you consider more research is necessary**

It is estimated that managers spend 75 to 80 per cent of their time communicating. If this is so, presumably the need to ensure effective communication is one of the most important duties of the manager. Unfortunately in the real world examples of poor communication are legion.

Definition

It is often assumed that communication takes the form of telling someone to do something. However, communication is a much more extended, complex and subtle process, embracing careful examination of what is to be transmitted, how it is to be transmitted, ensuring the existence of an environment conducive to full understanding of the message sent, ensuring that the message received has been identical to that sent, and finally that the communication has been accepted and acted upon by its recipient.

This comprehensive list views communication from the perspective of the sender of the message. It must be further recognised that the act of communication could be viewed from the perspective of the recipient of the message. As such it must be emphasised that communication is a two-way process, involving the sending and the receipt of a message and that one major criterion in the judgement of the success of a communication exercise is whether the receiver actually receives what the transmitter thinks he or she has transmitted. In many ways this list of duties could be seen as a near exhaustive list of the duties of management itself.

Figure 7.1 shows the breadth of constituent features of communication and some of the more important duties of the manager at each stage. An alternative classification which might be useful is that communication takes the form of:

a) creating;
b) transmitting;
c) receiving;
d) interpreting.

some or all of the following:

i) ideas;
ii) facts;
iii) opinions;
iv) instructions.

Thus communication extends from sending to receiving and involves much more than the sending of facts. It embraces the creation and sending of a wide variety of messages, the choice of mode of transmission, the interpretation of these messages and the obligation to ensure accurate interpretation and acceptability. Undoubtedly it is one of the most complex and challenging tasks facing the manager.

Forms of Communication

Communication can take many forms and embrace a variety of media. In many ways the sender of a message has considerable freedom in its mode of delivery; each of these modes of delivery has strengths and weaknesses and it is essential, therefore, that the mode of communication is consistent with the particular communication and its purposes. This variety of media will be presented in a form which shows the various alternatives available to the manager in the choice of mode of delivery.

	SENDING		RECEIVING	
Problem:	What do I want from the communication?	How do I want to communicate?	Problem:	What is being said?
Stage:	ENCODING	TRANSMISSION	Stage:	INTERPRETATION
Solution:	Select precise wording and format	Choice of Method	Solution:	Careful scrutiny of words, timing, tones and related actions

FIGURE 7.1 *The Communication Exercise*

a) Written/word of mouth – the communication may be written down on paper, on a computer screen or facsimile machine; alternatively it may be the spoken word. The written version tends to convey more authority as it is consistent with the more traditional scientific approaches to management. The written version stands as a record of the communication and might be referred back to in the case of confusion. The spoken word tends to be seen as less formal and may be more suited to communication attempting to persuade in that it more readily evokes a reply. This is consistent with a more human relations oriented approach to the management task.

b) By telephone/face-to-face – the spoken word need not be conveyed in the direct presence of all parties to the communication. Telephonic communication is suited to situations where the parties to the communication are distant and the only alternative is the rather more formal mode of written communication. It is particularly suited to urgent communication where an element of persuasion is involved – this is because it is generally seen to be less formal than the other machine forms of communication and more immediately responsive to the needs of the two-way demands of such a communication. However, in situations where face-to-face communication is possible and persuasion is needed, telephonic communication should be kept to a minimum. Face-to-face communication is deemed to be more friendly than the more remote telephonic communication. As has been seen in an earlier section, such persuasion conducted on a face-to-face basis can be reinforced by strong non-verbal cues.

c) Verbal/non-verbal – when face-to-face communication takes place, some commentators have suggested that the least important element of the communication is the words used. We reinforce words with certain non-verbal cues. The nature and importance of this element of the communication exercise has been examined in a previous section of this text.

d) Formal/informal – here the sender of the message has less latitude than in other classifications in that the nature of the message will tend to place the communication in one of these categories. However, it is important that this distinction is made since both categories will necessitate that certain choices as to the mode of delivery are made. A formal communication is intended to convey a degree of authority; it is an official communication. Alternatively the communication could be more informal in nature; an unofficial/semi-official communication. Persuasion is best undertaken through an informal mode of communication since the desired co-operative response might be more readily afforded by the recipient of the message; it will be seen to be less threatening. Instruction is better conducted through formal media since the required environment of authority is more immediately conveyed to the recipient of the message. Formal communication is particularly suited to written forms since a permanent authoritative record of the communication will exist.

e) Vertical/horizontal – the communication can be between superiors and subordinates (vertical) or between equals (horizontal). It is the vertical form of communication which is emphasised in traditional or scientific approaches to management. A common form of horizontal communication is that between different disciplines within the organisation. Horizontal communication is likely to take an informal form; whereas vertical communication is likely to be formal in nature.

f) Upwards/downwards – vertical communication can come from subordinates to superiors (upwards) or it can come from superiors to subordinates (downwards). Again, under traditional approaches to the management task it is the downwards communication which receives emphasis. Under human relations approaches to management the need for upwards communication is emphasised.

g) One-way/more-than-one-way – although all communication consists of both sending and receiving something, some communications are intended to evoke a reply whereas others are intended to evoke a response. One-way communication is intended to evoke a response or act, whereas more-than-one-way is intended to evoke a reply. One way communication must not be dismissed but inevitably most inter-personal communication within an organisation will necessitate a two-way element.

h) Internal/external – up to now the assumption has been that the communication takes place within an organisation; however the communication might be between the organisation and the outside world. In such circumstances the communication is likely to have formal characteristics. An example might be a press release or advertisement. A common form of external communication in the public service is the public meeting. As many organisations have increasingly assumed firm responsibilities to meet consumer needs or satisfy customer demands such external communication becomes increasingly Important.

i) Traditional/electronic media – a distinction can be made between those communication media which rely upon traditional facilities or technology (e.g. face-to-face, telephonic, written) and those which rely upon new technology. Since the 1990s there has been a rapid expansion in those organisations which, to supplement traditional communication media, use facilities provided by more recent technology such as video/remote meetings through satellite media, Email and Internet communication. These new technologies are exciting additions to the traditional communication media. They constitute quicker access, more extended access to information and, particularly, access to new market opportunities.

Given this wide variety of modes of communication each with its special strengths and weaknesses, it is essential that when the communication takes place the best form or mode is chosen. For instance, if persuasion is needed, written, downwards communication may not be wholly appropriate.

None of these forms of communication will necessarily be easy or guarantee success; it is essential that careful choice of communication takes place and that the available alternatives are carefully considered.

Communication Problems

Despite the available options just considered and despite the fact that in most situations a prepared manager should be in a good position to effect successful communication, it must be accepted that problems in communication are found in most organisations. It is essential that any communication is understood in all its parts; that is the receiver fully understands what the sender intended, including opinions and attitudes. As has already been mentioned, unfortunately this is not always the case. To further stress the importance of good communication it may help to examine the most common causes of communication difficulties within an organisation.

a) Incorrect choice of medium – the form of the communication was inappropriate to its purpose. An example might be written communication when the primary intention was to persuade; under such circumstances face-to-face communication might have been more suitable.

b) The content of communication – very often, in practice, communication may be hindered by the recipient not having the ability to understand the communication. This commonly is not a result of the ignorance of the recipient but of the way in which the communication is phrased. An example of this is when a member of one professional discipline communicates with a member of another discipline in the accepted language of the former rather than the latter. A more pejorative definition of this problem would be the use of 'jargon'. Another example would be the distribution of marketing surveys which contain questions which are difficult to understand as currently phrased.

c) The communication may be too 'big' to be fully assimilated in the time available. An example would be a qualified worker, who has no 'feeling' for the needs of trainees, attempting to explain too much of a complex task. The result of this may be confusion or, at worst, exasperation.

d) The communication may contain too little information to be fully understood by the recipient. An example would be a communication quoting the location of a meeting without any instruction how to find that location.

e) Poor or inappropriate timing – the same message can be successfully received at one time but not at another. The recipient may be overwhelmed with work and, in such cases, may not have time to devote to the communication. This is a problem encountered especially when messages are sent at the end of the working day. This problem introduces a new dimension into the communication task. Achieving success in this area is very difficult. It necessitates a significant degree of preparation by the author of the communication, which is usually the manager. Clearly a manager who knows the work patterns and preferences of the workforce will be better placed to more effectively communicate.

f) To the wrong person – not all messages are intended to be sent to all people. Messages should be sent to those who need to receive them. An obvious mistake which can be made is sending the message to the wrong person. If the person who receives the message is the wrong person the required response will not be evoked. This may appear to be so obvious a point as to not warrant making; however, an examination of the real world would suggest that there are many examples of instances where a person who should have been told something was not; equally there are many examples of instances where communication has been made with people who need not have been 'bothered' with it. Both mistakes are equally serious since, in the former case, the production task will be effected with poorly or inadequately informed persons and, in the latter case, the problem is not just that of being seen to waste the time of the recipients – a further and more serious danger is that the environment might be created where future relevant communication is ignored.

g) Problems 'spilling over' from past experiences – many communications break down not because of the communication in question but because the two or more parties to the communication do not trust each other. Trust may have been broken by past failures in communication. Thus it is essential that particular managerial attention should be directed to those communications which take place in areas where failure has previously occurred. This problem, in its turn, further complicates the communication task since it must be acknowledged that any communication exercise does not take place in a historical vacuum. Receivers of messages decode these messages with all kinds of predispositions and pre-judgements about the motives of the sender.

h) Confusing non-verbal signals – sometimes communication can break down if the non-verbal signals used are not appropriate to the purpose of the communication. Thus an intended friendly communication delivered in a hostile tone of voice may not be received as friendly. The importance of this problem has been examined in a previous section of this text.

i) Wrong communication pattern – this is the topic area of the next part of the chapter. As will be seen, each communication has an appropriate pattern and it is essential that the appropriate pattern is chosen.

Communication Patterns or Networks

Communication can be networked or patterned; that is, it can be examined and plotted from its source or sources to its destination or destinations. This networking/patterning is very useful in that the particular pattern chosen can be assessed as to its appropriateness; in addition the occasions and places of any break-down or distortion in the communication can be isolated and remedial action taken. Before the importance of patterns or networks can be understood it will be necessary to examine some of the more common networks or patterns.

THE CHAIN

In these circumstances the communication passes from one person to the next in a fixed direction – either upwards, downwards or sideways. (Figure 7.2) Its major use is where speed is essential and where the communication is simple in nature. It is particularly suited where the organisation has accepted, and understood, levels of authority. It is suited to more stable environments; the importance of this point will be examined in the future section on the Organisational Domain but, briefly, the suitability relies heavily on the utility of tried and tested solutions.

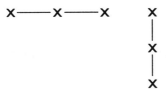

FIGURE 7.2

THE CIRCLE

The communication is passed around a number of people and returns to the originator. (Figure 7.3) An example would be the sending of a memo. It is particularly useful where one person has a monopoly of information on the topic under discussion but where all the persons involved in the communication are of

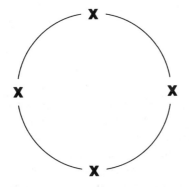

FIGURE 7.3

equal status. In addition it is appropriate for simple messages. An important point to note is that, in its purest form, this communication would not be altered by any of the recipients. However, it must be recognised that this can be adapted to embrace the possibility of, for instance, written responses on the memo which was distributed, affording to the sender the brief responses of the recipients. Under such circumstances it must be acknowledged that a pure communication circle does not exist; however, it is probably true to claim that such a communication pattern would more closely resemble that of a circle than it would any other pattern.

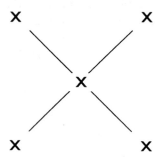

FIGURE 7.4

THE WHEEL

There is a central giver or receiver of information. (Figure 7.4) An example might be a committee with a strong chairman. It is a particularly useful pattern of communication where different disciplines are involved, for instance the corporate issues of a company or a public service organisation. Given that there is a central giver or receiver, it is useful where speed is essential and where there is a central source of power such as chief executive, general manager, prime minister or president. In many ways it can be seen to be little more in character than an extension or elaboration of the communication chain and it must be accepted that the circumstances where both patterns of communication are desirable are very similar but not identical.

ALL CHANNEL

In these circumstances everyone communicates directly with everyone else. (Figure 7.5) An example might be a free-flowing discussion in a committee of equals. Another example might be a quality circle – a group of equals charged with discussing issues of product quality which impact upon their particular part of the production process (the quality circle will be examined in more detail later in this text). It is particularly applicable where debate or interchange of ideas is important; it is of further use where communication in general is being encouraged, that is, communication beyond the purposes of the present task may be encouraged. Organisations making difficult decisions might find it a useful pattern of communication in that an input from a variety of sources of expertise can be made. However, it must be stressed that it is a potentially slow way of communicating.

It can be concluded, therefore, that the technique of patterning of communication is a very useful aid to the manager. It can be used when reviewing the success of a particular communication: alternatively the manager can deliberately construct a pattern which will best suit the particular purpose or purposes of the communication exercise in question.

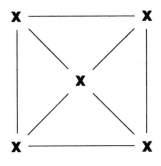

FIGURE 7.5

Committees

The use of committees or meetings as an aid to the total management process overlaps many of the separate elements of the total management task. However, given that the major benefit afforded by such committees or meetings is the facility they afford to access a wider source of expertise through interpersonal exchanges, they are probably best examined in the context of this rather than any other chapter. The committee as a communication and decision-making entity is of particular importance in the public service in the United Kingdom. Organisations in the public service often have to make very difficult decisions affecting a wide variety of interest groups, for instance the decision about whether to build a large housing estate impacts upon such specialisms as housing, policing, shopping, transport, social services and education. Similarly, in many instances private sector organisations have to make decisions with similarly wide-ranging impact. Under such circumstances these organisations can and, in the case of many public service organisations, have evolved the committee as an important form of communication and decision making. The use of committees affords certain advantages and certain problems.

ADVANTAGES

a) More work can be done – given that the committee consists of more than one person, the formation of a committee increases the resources available to the making of the decision. Similarly the breaking up of a large decision-making body into a number of committees affords to the organisation more time to devote to its various duties.

b) More representative – if the item being discussed has an impact on a wide variety of interest groups, it is desirable that each one of these interest groups has some say in the communication and subsequent decision. The committee provides a good mechanism for increasing representation. The more representative the decision the more it is likely to be accepted by all interested parties.

c) Pools expertise – not only does a committee increase the numbers of people making the decision, it also broadens or increases the expertise used in making the decision. If the decision is one where the expertise of a number of different disciplines is needed, the committee is an ideal vehicle for the making of such a decision. It is often said that 'two heads are better than one'.

d) Facilitates communication – clearly in the context of this chapter this advantage must be seen as a major contribution to the total management task. Furthermore, the communication (particularly between disciplines) developed during the committee's proceedings can be extended beyond the boundaries of the committee.

e) Co-ordinates the activities of the constituent members or develops a shared perception or perspective – the committee should ensure compatibility of actions amongst its constituent members. The committee decision has forced them to agree upon a particular course of action. If the committee had not existed the various interest groups may have acted in dissimilar ways. This advantage assumes more importance if the shared experience develops shared future perspectives on future problems.

f) Reinforces the authority of individual decisions – when a decision of significant importance has to be taken there is a tendency for individuals to be fearful of making such a decision or feel the need for collective ratification of such a decision. Under such circumstances the formation of a committee will help the various members to afford to each other mutual support.

g) Smaller than the parent body – in cases where the parent body is large the environment within such a body inhibits speedy decision making, co-operation and individual contribution. The tendency will be to debate, posture and delay. If a representative, but smaller, body can be created, this smaller body should facilitate co-operation, speed and individual commitment to the taking of a decision.

PROBLEMS

a) Compromise of decision – it may be that the act of compromise facilitated by a committee results in a poor decision; it is sometimes said that 'the camel is a horse designed by a committee'.

b) It can be dominated by one person – under such circumstances many of the advantages claimed for a committee are rendered redundant. However, if the primary purpose of the creation of the committee was the need to afford support for a difficult individual decision this factor should not necessarily be viewed as disadvantageous.

c) Difficulties in establishing full representation – in many cases, if all interested parties were to be represented, the committee would be so large that it would cease to function properly. However, often complaints are made to managers that the composition of a committee is inadequately representative of all legitimate interest groups.

d) May become self-indulgent – the committee may begin to take decisions which, although they may be in the interests of the committee, are not really in the interests of the parent body. This can, to an extent, be overcome by ensuring that all committees have a fixed life and have to prove their right to exist beyond this period or purpose. The tendency for committees to exist beyond their useful lives has been documented in, for instance, the Bains Report on the Management of Local Government in England and Wales (1972). The traditionally more commercial environment of the private sector makes this problem less likely but nevertheless it must be seen to be a potential problem in all sectors of economic activity.

e) People outside the committee need to be convinced – the mere act of creating a committee does not in itself mean that the decisions will automatically be acceptable to everyone. The reality is that in many cases people outside the committee will need to be convinced of the appropriateness of the decision. This will tend to extend the decision-making period and complicate the problem of evolving an acceptable decision.

f) Co-ordination of the decisions of related committees – the tendency for a committee to 'develop a life of its own' has already been acknowledged and as such there may be a need to co-ordinate the activities of the various committees working within an organisation. This problem may be overcome by the appointment of a policy or co-ordinating committee. However the appointment of such a committee itself introduces new problems:

   i) ensuring representation of this committee;
   ii) determining the boundaries for freedom of action for each committee;
   iii) extending the time taken to make a decision;
   iv) resentment caused if the decision of the original committee is altered.

Communication in Specific Managerial Environments

It might be useful to illustrate the principles discussed in this chapter by examining communication medium in three specific situations.

Instruction

Instruction is a form of communication where the primary purpose is for the author of the communication to guide others, commonly subordinates, in behaviour which is expected. This form of communication is noted by the fact that very limited input is required of the recipients in that the content of the message has already been decided and their contribution is deemed to be limited; naturally, as with any communication exercise, this does not mean that their contribution is non-existent. It must be noted that instruction can be a varied phenomenon – ranging from military orders through to semi-informal information exchange – and, as such, there will be a wide range of characteristics from which the author can chose. In this situation the communication is best illustrated by dissecting it into its constituent features.

a) The author must clarify to his or her own satisfaction why the communication is necessary. For instance is the instruction being given because the recipients have behaved badly; is it because the recipients are unsure as to what is expected of them; is it because a new situation is about to be encountered; is it to improve a very minor fashion an already impressive behaviour? All these are legitimate areas where instruction may be given but the tone of the instruction will vary radically from one reason to another. In the case of poor behaviour the tone must be forceful, in the case of improving already excellent behaviour the tone should be much more conciliatory.

b) The author must clarify what is expected of the recipients. For instance if the message is complicated more time will have to be provided to ensure they have fully understood the message. Alternatively if there needs to be a change in commitment and not just in behaviour the author will have to specifically check for this change in commitment as well as mere change in behaviour.

c) The author must decide when to instruct. The circumstances of the case will dictate when the instruction takes place. If there is a need for a training period the communication will have to allow time for this training to take place. If there is a need for confidentiality the author may need to delay the communication as long as possible.

d) The author should make an appropriate choice of medium. Oral instruction may be useful if co-operation is expected or if some form of immediate feedback is required. Alternatively written instruction may be required if there is a need for a record of the communication. It is recognised that many instruction situations make use of both media.

e) Throughout the instruction the author must be mindful of the recipients' attitudes and needs. For instance, if they will be initially negatively predisposed to the instruction the author might have to devote time to explanation and persuasion. Similarly, if the recipients are likely to be disturbed by the instruction the author will have to devote attention to dealing with the consequences of this disturbance. The author should always check that his or her assumptions as to the recipients' attitudes and needs is correct and as such it must be noted that any communication is effective only when it is viewed from the perception of the recipients not the perception of the author.

f) Throughout the exercise the author should give maximum attention to the need to explain. This is not to state that the explanation is required in every case but that the author should never asume that explanation is not necessary. Simply it is another illustration of communication having to be viewed from the perspective of the recipient not the author.

g) The author will have to check for understanding. It is a maxim of communication that it is effective only when it has been understood by the recipient.

h) The author should monitor and review every instruction exercise. The author must be constantly mindful of the need to change approach during the instruction if the present approach is not working. Similarly every communication exercise should be viewed by authors as a learning exercise. If the author thinks carefully about what happened during the instruction it is likely that he or she will find something to improve upon in the future.

Public Speaking

An increasingly important skill required in the repertoire of the manager is the ability to speak in public or convince an audience. As organisations become more mindful of the need to interact with their external environments such public interaction between the organisation and its external constituents is increasingly evidenced. If this communication is undertaken, one very important medium is oral communication. This is a skill which has, historically, been required of very few managers and one where most people approach the task with an understandable trepidation. This communication can be illustrated by dissecting it into its constituent features.

a) The author must be trained in this new, potentially stressful, experience.

b) The author should be prepared − there will be little chance to rectify a misunderstanding as the recipients will assume that their perception of the speech is the final, authoritative, version of the communication. Unlike one-to-one communication there will be little facility for checking for full understanding.

c) It is very hard to assume behaviour which is inconsistent with one's personality. Thus any training on public speaking tries to emphasise the need to be 'natural' so that the author can at least appear to be comfortable with his or her delivery.

d) The author must be prepared to keep the attention of the audience. The author should not assume that the audience will approach the communication with as much enthusiasm as he or she does. To this end the author must, at least, appear enthusiastic and appreciate the importance of non-verbal communication; there will be a need to maintain eye contact but it must be accepted that this is difficult if the author is nervous. This, again, reinforces the need for training in public speaking. It is a fact of life that most people have natural distracting mannerisms, particularly when they are nervous. Examples would be to brush one's hair with one's hand, to wave one's hands about uncontrollably. These mannerisms must be coached out of any public speaker.

e) The author must carefully chose the words used in the exercise. If the audience is unfamiliar with the issue being addressed, technical language should be avoided. This is another example of a communication being successful only if it is understood by the recipients.

f) The author must progress the speech at a speed which the audience can follow. It may be that the same point needs stating several times, admittedly in different language, to ensure that the message is received.

g) The author should be aware of the dangers of communicating too much and should consider the key messages to communicate and concentrate on these issues. If the speech is to be filmed and repeated in shortened version the author should insert into the speech so called 'Sound Bites' which will convey the major message of the speech in a few words when it is repeated in shortened form.

h) Experience suggests that variety helps keep the audience's attention. Thus, wherever possible, particularly if technical issues are being addressed, the author should think about using visual aids – such as slides or overhead projector slides – to reinforce, illustrate and add variety to the message.

i) Wherever possible the speaker should try to allow a period for checking understanding – for instance by a question and answer session at the end of the speech. Experience suggests that, if this facility is available and is useful, it may prove counter productive to allow too short a period of time for such clarification.

Team Briefing

The more organisations focus on team activity, the more communication within a team environment assumes importance. One important facet of team communication is the team briefing which is defined by the Industrial Society as: 'A systematic, flexible drill which ensures that, at every level, employees are kept informed about issues which affect them and their jobs, through their own managers and supervisors'. This definition highlights certain features of the team briefing:

a) It is a drill – which indicates that there are certain features which will be commonly used.

b) It is intended to embrace employees at all levels not just those at the highest level.

c) It is concerned with issues which affect employees' working lives and hence it operates in a high-stake environment.

d) It is conduced by the team leader or an appointed deputy.

As with the other communication exercises the team briefing can be illustrated by dissecting it into its constituent features:

a) Usually it should be conducted at a predictable time and in a predictable place. It is a regular and frequent form of communication and, if there needs to be a change of time or venue, all constituents need to be informed. A common time for briefing is at the beginning of the work period affected by the briefing. Commonly such briefing take place on work territory but sometimes the tradition of the team might be to undertake the briefing on 'neutral' territory such as a refreshment area.

b) Although it is a formal exercise it should be conducted in as informal an atmosphere as possible and, as such, it should be face to face and the reliance on the written medium should be kept to a minimum. It should be perceived as a participatory exercise and adequate time should be given.

c) Its very regularity can present a problem in that it might be held when there is no purpose. Every team briefing should have an agenda which is relevant to the challenges of the work period covered. This is not to claim that managers should hold irregular team briefings; their regularity is a very important positive quality. As such managers should strive to hold regular briefings but should equally strive to determine an agenda for each briefing; it must be noted that in the rapidly changing environment faced by most teams the production of a legitimate agenda should not present too much difficulty.

d) A briefing should be, by its very title, as brief as possible. If the briefing is to be regular the team should ensure that productive endeavour is disrupted as little as possible by the briefing. It must be admitted that this does conflict to an extent with point b) but, no doubt, a happy compromise on duration can be accomplished.

e) Its very regularity can engender a degree of complacency on the part of the team leader; thus it is essential that the team leader carefully monitors all briefings to ensure that they are having maximum positive impact. Similarly every such exercise should be viewed as a learning experience to facilitate the progress of future briefings.

Summary

Good communication is an essential prerequisite of any well-managed organisation. However, good, and consistently good, communication is difficult to achieve. The communication problems of organisations can be overcome, either wholly or in substantial part, by proper planning and control by the authors of the communications. Ensuring good communication is probably the most important duty of the manager. Good communication will overcome many potential management problems; however, poor communication will introduce further complications or difficulties into the management of the organisation. The barriers to good communication can be identified and managerial action to eliminate them can be taken.

Finally, in public service organisations and in larger private sector organisations, committees offer a useful means of communication and decision making. The introduction of a committee into the communication system of an organisation can bring problems but these problems can be minimised if the use of committees is restricted to those areas where they have certain benefits and if their membership is chosen carefully.

Exercise

Critically appraise the communication patterns in an organisation or a section of an organisation with which you are familiar. What would you do to improve the communication in that environment?

Further Reading

Argyris, C. (1964) *Integrating the Individual and the Organisation*, Wiley

Curson, C. (ed) (1986) *Flexible Patterns of Work*, IPM

Etzioni, A. (1971) *A Comparative Analysis of Complex Organisations*, Free Press

Harvey-Jones, J. (1990) *Making It Happen*, Guild

Kanter, R. M. (1990) *When Giants Learn to Dance*, Routledge

Kay, J. (1993) *Foundations of Corporate Success*, Oxford University Press

Mintzberg, H. (1983) *Power In and Around the Organisation*, Prentice Hall

Richards, S. (Autumn 1989) Managing People in the Civil Service, *Public Money and Management*

Schermerhorn, J.R., Hunt J.G., and Osborn, R.N., (1995), *Basic Organizational Behaviour*, John Wiley

Taylor, F.W. (1947) *Scientific Management*, Harper and Row

Toffler, A. (1981) *The Third Wave*, Pan

Chapter eight

The Management of Working Groups

L E A R N I N G   O B J E C T I V E S

- **Understand the importance and application of research in the analysis of working groups**

- **Appreciate the importance of group norms and group dynamics**

- **Assess the importance of the organisational management of group environments**

- **Understand the importance of theoretical knowledge in team building**

- **Appraise this research in real life contexts**

- **Appreciate the need for organisations to manage team building and team dynamics**

- **Identify areas where more research may be necessary**

A working group can be defined as a collection of individuals, with a sense of identity, with a collective purpose and, particularly in the case of permanent working groups, with a loyalty to or conformity to norms of behaviour and attitudes. Any study of the management of large organisations must recognise the importance such groups play in the life of the organisation. They can be seen to develop, facilitate or satisfy social or affiliation needs (see chapter on Human Motivation). They can help individuals share the burden of the many difficult decisions which need to be made in any organisation. In the case of groups deliberately created by the management of the organisation, they help afford more expertise to the decision making than would be afforded by the abilities of the individual employee working alone.

A thorough understanding of the human aspects of management demands a study not just of individual behaviour and motives, but of the behaviour of an individual within a group, an examination of the impact of group pressures on the individual, and a study of the behaviour of the group collectively.

Features of a Group

Groups are an inevitable feature of organisational activity. Sometimes the nature of the production process necessitates that workers are aggregated into working groups (eg a team of workers building a house). Sometimes impermanent groups are created by management to fulfil a particular task (eg project group or a working party). Indeed this intrinsic nature of group work can be seen to intrude into the designs of most jobs.

The examples introduced thus far are examples of formal groups; their existence is recognised in the formal design of the organisation's activities. However, even if management of the organisation or the nature of the job does not specifically create groups, the very existence of social activity within an organisation will cause groups to emerge. If the production process does not revolve around groups, such groups will form during non-production periods such as lunchtime, breaks, out-of-work meetings. It is necessary to examine some major characteristics of working groups.

a) They develop attitudes towards work – Elton Mayo in his studies in the Hawthorne Electrical Plants between 1924 and 1936 recorded the importance of the formation of such group attitudes. If group members deviate in any way from these norms, they are subject to enormous group pressure to conform to these group attitudes or norms. Such pressure may take the form of physical coercion; however, it is more likely that the pressure will be psychological in nature, embracing such actions as denial of social interaction and/or rewarding when attitudes conform with group norms.

b) Such group attitudes extend into judgements about the management of an organisation. Some groups develop positive attitudes towards the management of the organisation, whereas others develop negative attitudes.

c) Groups develop collectively acceptable productivity levels. This can be seen to be an extension of group attitudes towards work and towards management. Given that individual productivity is one of the more obvious manifestations of the individual's attitude to work or attitude towards management, it is those who deviate from these accepted levels of production who are immediately subjected to the group or peer pressure. This is a very important point to note since in the real world such group norms may not necessarily be harmful to organisational needs and, indeed, as will be seen later in this chapter, these norms can demand a quality of work above that which would be expected by the management of the organisation.

d) The feeling of group identity can cause the group to become hostile to other groups who, even in a very remote sense, are seen to be threatening to the group.

This problem can be exacerbated when this group loyalty can be reinforced by professional loyalties. This is a very important point to note since in most complex, multi-purpose organisations there is a need for different groups to liaise and work with each other. Thus, for instance, in case conferences relating to designated 'problem families' there will be a need for social workers, health visitors, general practitioners, police and teachers to work closely together.

Alternatively, in the private sector the development of a new product will require joint input from the different disciplines of production, finance, sales, marketing, and the joint working of these disparate groups is essential to organisational success. Similarly, in a more permanent context, the board of the organisation is collectively charged with working towards organisational not professional goals.

e) Even if there is no deliberate attempt to work against the interests of the organisation, this loyalty to the organisation can cause groups to become too reliant upon fulfilling internal group objectives. For instance, there may be immense pressure from the human resource function to develop systems which, although precise and perhaps desirable in professional terms, are unnecessarily refined for organisational purposes.

This counterproductive group behaviour is also examined in the concept of 'Groupthink' suggested by Janis in 1968 which is characterised by:

a) a sense of invulnerability – the fact that pet schemes contain no risk;
b) moral blindness – what we do is right;
c) tendencies to negatively stereotype 'outsiders';
d) strong group pressure to quell dissent;
e) self-censorship by members – 'do not rock the boat';
f) secrecy.

These are generalisations about the nature of group behaviour and attitudes. They are probably best evidenced in the case of long-established groups. The more negative elements of these characteristics will not usually be seen in groups of senior employees such as the board of the organisation. Figure 8.1, reflecting the work of Tuckman and Jensen in 1977, shows that the strong group pressures which have been mentioned are characteristic of the 'norming' and 'performing' stages of group development.

What this Means for the Manager

There can be little doubt that group or peer pressure is very powerful. Hence any attempt to form group norms will be very difficult and complex. Any attempt to change established group norms will be even more difficult since the protective actions of the group will be even more powerful. It is essential that the manager recognises the existence of and attempts to assess the nature of these group norms.

This is necessary since it is only by examining such norms that managers can access full and comprehensive information about the nature of the work process.

However, this is not to claim that the manager should deem such groups norms as fixed. If, upon examination, the manager finds that group norms and objectives are harmful to those of the organisation, it is vital that he or she strives to harmonise group and organisational norms and objectives.

Stage	What happens
1 Forming	Members get to know each other and seek to establish ground rules
2 Storming	Members come to resist control of group leaders and show hostility
3 Norming	Members work together, developing close relationships and feeling of camaraderie
4 Performing	Group members work together getting their job done
5 Adjourning	Groups may disband after either meeting their goals, or because members leave

FIGURE 8.1 *The Five Stages of Group Development*
(Source: Tuckman and Jensen 1977)

What the Manager Can Do

As has already been acknowledged, such remedial action will be one of the most difficult tasks facing the manager. Inevitably the required action will vary from organisation to organisation and from circumstance to circumstance. Some group norms will be more firmly entrenched than others. Sometimes the manager will be helped by the fact that on occasions the continued existence of negative group norms will be clear to all concerned, including the members of the group itself. For instance, if the organisation is threatened with closure the manager will be unlikely to find serious resistance to changes in work practices which are seen to have contributed to organisational difficulties. It must be stressed, however, that such a situation will rarely obtain and that the need to change group norms may be less obvious to the members of the group. Furthermore, any manager who assumes that serious work difficulties would automatically limit resistance would be naive.

Despite the variety of circumstances which can exist there are a number of actions which can be identified which should facilitate changes in norms, objectives and behaviour.

a) There must be a free and open recognition of the group and, within limits, its right to exist and furthermore have an impact on its members. Admittedly there may be extreme circumstances where a more confrontational approach may be necessary but nevertheless this more politic strategy should be adopted in the overwhelming majority of cases. Persuasion is usually preferable to confrontation.

b) The precise nature of group norms needs to be assessed. In practice this may not be easy since a successful group may present its norms in the public arena as the inevitable consequence, not of group norms, but of the production process itself. Sometimes it is difficult to distinguish between those elements of production which are limited by external pressures and those which are limited by group pressure. Very often it is only by comparing the group production levels with that of a similar group, possibly outside the organisation, that this distinction can be made. Hence a manager may need to access information from outside the organisation. Such information may be of further utility in that it may provide guidance as to suggested improvements.

c) The manager needs to discover the group's view of the rationality of any norms which exist. This is essential since in most cases the group itself is the only institution within the organisation with complete information about the reasons for group attitudes and the practicality of suggested improvements.

It can be seen, therefore, that any attempt to change group norms will, in the vast majority of cases, necessitate effective and sophisticated communication by the manager. The importance and applicability of such communication has been examined in the immediately preceding chapter. Briefly, the communication should be two way, be through such a medium as to obtain co-operation and afford sufficient time for all information to be fully digested. Finally, time must be allocated to allow the group itself to fully reflect upon the changed circumstances. Usually an unforced change will elicit the best response from all those affected.

Forming a Group or Building a Team

Up to now the emphasis in the discussion has focused on existing groups with existing norms and attitudes. However, on occasions, management of an organisation has a much more positive role to play in that they themselves may create or develop a group or a team. It may be the intention that the group will be of a long lasting nature; it may be that the intention is for the group to be short lived. These differences are not material to this discussion.

Under these circumstances the management of the organisation should be better able to control the emergence of organisationally dysfunctional group norms. There are certain actions which management can take to try to encourage organisationally functional groups or teams.

a) Wherever possible, care should be taken to ensure that only those whose skills or attitudes are in harmony with the needs of the task and the needs of the organisation be appointed to the team. The importance of harmonising team skills and the importance this plays in ensuring organisational success will be examined later in the chapter. However, stated briefly, team co-operation is best ensured when success rather than failure has been achieved.

b) The team should be carefully chosen so that the constituent members evolve happy working relationships one with another. This is not to say that all members of the group need have identical outlooks on the task or have identical motivations. This again will be examined later in the chapter. Such harmony can be achieved only by a diligent and knowledgeable team creator. However, a happy working team is an important element in maintaining group co-operation.

c) The group or team should be given objectives which match organisational needs. Clearly, care has to be taken to ensure that the group's internally generated objectives accord with those afforded by management but certainly, if sufficient thought is given at the objective-setting stage, this harmony of objectives should be more easily achieved. Equally, care must be taken to ensure that the group or team does not feel that its objectives have been imposed unreasonably by management. Under such circumstances the 'ownership' of the objectives will be a matter of debate and hence maximum co-operation might not be obtained. This ownership is probably best achieved by involving group members in the evolution of their terms of reference and objectives.

d) The group or team should be given the training necessary to achieve success; the importance of success in helping to ensure future co-operation has already been examined. In addition, the group should be afforded maximum support to ensure it achieves its objectives. This may involve the manager in giving to the group maximum help in removing barriers to information.

e) The group should be granted optimum freedom to pursue its objectives, whilst at the same time ensuring that help is afforded when problems are encountered. This may involve high-profile guidance or alternatively it may involve little more than reassurance. The particular circumstances of the case should dictate the most appropriate action. In most cases an 'open door' policy should be adopted to help reassure the group that advice and assistance is available where needed; that is the group should be encouraged to seek advice whenever real problems are encountered. The importance of this will be emphasised in the next chapter.

f) Techniques such as coaching may help the group achieve its objectives to best effect. Minor mistakes should not be the cause of criticism. Careful attention will need to be directed to differentiate between serious and minor mistakes. The members of the group should not be allowed to become dispirited at any stage. It may be that, if the problem was perceived to be of sufficient importance to be given to a group in the first place, minor mistakes will be inevitable. If this is the case then this fact must be freely and widely recognised. The technique of coaching will be examined in more detail in the next section of the text.

g) The final responsibility of management is to determine when the group or team needs to be disbanded. Naturally this will obtain only if the group is seen to be temporary in nature. The disbanding of a group is a bold act in that the members of the group may have developed suchloyalties one with another that to actually disband it would be demotivating. Under such circumstances the astute manager

Stage 1	Stage 2	Stage 3	Stage 4
Prework	**Create performance conditions**	**Form and build team**	**Provide ongoing assistance**
☐ What work needs to be done?	☐ Provide all resources	☐ Establish boundaries - who is, is not in the group?	☐ Intervene to eliminate group problems (eg problem members)
☐ Is a group necessary?	☐ Provide all needed personnel	☐ Arrive at agreement regarding tasks to be performed	☐ Replenish or upgrade material resources
☐ What authority should group have?		☐ Clarify expected behaviours	☐ Replace members who leave the group
☐ What are group goals?			

FIGURE 8.2 *Hackman's Stages of Group Formation*

may be able to extend its responsibilities. However, on many occasions this extension of responsibilities is impossible and actual disbanding may need to be managed; in many ways this can be seen to be a separate management task in itself.

Figure 8.2 portrays the work of Hackman (1987) on the responsibilities of the manager in creating an effective working team.

Differences Within the Group

Given that the major reason for the creation of any working group is to widen the expertise available to the organisation in either the making of a decision or the execution of a particular task, it can be seen that one of the most important contributions to group success is the choice and roles of its constituent members. Belbin, 1981, has examined the importance of personality type and the balancing of personalities within teams in the achieving of team success. His work was conducted in the context of managerial teams. His findings are shown in Figure 8.3.

Chairman/Team Leader

Stable, dominant, extrovert
Concentrates on objectives
Does not originate ideas
Focuses people on what they do best

Plant

Dominant, high IQ, introvert.
'A scatterer of seeds'
Originates ideas
Misses out on detail
Thrustful but easily offended

Resource Investigator

Stable, dominant, extrovert
Sociable
Contacts with outside world
Salesman/diplomat/liaison officer
Not original thinker

Shaper

Anxious, dominant, extrovert
Emotional, impulsive
Quick to challenge and respond to
    challenge
Unites ideas, objectives and possibilities
Competitive
Intolerant of wooliness and vagueness

Company Worker

Stable, controlled
Practical organiser
Can be inflexible but likely to
    adapt to established systems
Not an innovator

Monitor Evaluation

High IQ, stable, introvert
Measured analysis not innovation
Unambitious and lacking
    enthusiasm
Solid, dependable

Team Worker

Stable, extrovert, low dominance
Concerned with individual's
    needs
Builds on others' ideas
Cools things down

Finisher

Anxious, introvert
Worries over what will go wrong
Permanent sense of urgency
Preoccupied with order
Concerned with 'follow-through'

FIGURE 8.3 *Personality Mixes in Teams (source: R.M. Belbin 1981)*

According to Belbin's classifications the successful team will need people to play complementary, not identical, roles. For instance, there will need to be someone who tries to initiate ideas; someone who will develop these ideas into concrete suggestions; someone who will attempt to develop these ideas within established organisational priorities; someone who will nurture the team through its difficulties; someone who will be able to finish or tidy up the loose ends; and someone who will co-ordinate.

It must be stressed that his findings are firmly rooted in the particular circumstances of the groups and organisations he examined. However, the importance of his findings lies not in the precise conclusions he reached regarding personality and balance of personality requirements, but in his observation that successful groups may require different personalities from their constituent members and that many of the skills of good team creation lie in the careful planning of their composition.

Intra-Group Conflict

It must not be claimed that the unanimity of purpose and collective ideals will be evidenced in all groups or teams. The reality is that groups or teams can exhibit disharmony. This intra-group conflict can emerge from a number of causes:

a) inability of the group or team to define a collective purpose;
b) differing perceptions within the group or team as to its collective purpose;
c) members being required to fulfil a role which is at odds with his or her personality or aspirations;
d) individual members resenting compromise on issues they feel strongly about or over which they feel they have some expertise;
e) individuals feeling that their creative abilities are being compromised;
f) the group or team has served its purpose and should now be disbanded.

Inter-Group Conflict

This issue has been examined elsewhere in this chapter but it is worth repeating that counterproductive conflict between groups or teams can very easily emerge; this is not to claim that all such conflict is organisationally dysfunctional but that such conflict can work to the organisation's detriment. If such conflict creates debate and the consideration of alternative perspectives then the conflict can be seen to be organisationally functional. However, if the conflict is seen to deteriorate into suspicion, jealousy and the unnecessary withholding of information then dysfunctional inter-group or team behaviour will be evidenced. Thus it is essential that the organisation carefully monitors such conflict and ensures that its more negative consequences are avoided.

The Successful Team

It might be useful to summarise the factors just considered in team formation and assess the qualities of a good or effective team:

a) each individual will have the trust and support of all other members of the team;
b) each individual within the team will be perceived to be of equal status and importance;
c) each individual will use his or her unique abilities to team benefit;
d) there will be a collective, owned purpose and agreement on objectives;
e) there will be open channels of communication and discussion within the team and between the team and other interested parties.

Summary

One of the most important responsibilities of the manager is to ensure that those norms of attitudes, values and behaviour which emerge in groups are consistent with the needs of the organisation. When an organisation actually creates groups, such management control should be more easily achieved and the task of the manager should be a little easier. However, even in such circumstances the successful manager or team creator will be the one who appreciates the nature of the task demands and the importance of group dynamics.

Exercise

Critically examine the techniques used to build and sustain a team with which you are familiar in either your working or social life. To what extent do you consider the team dynamics described in management theory are realised in real life?

Further Reading

Adair, J. (1986) *Effective Teambuilding*, Gower
Aronson, E. (1976) *The Social Animal*, Freeman
Belbin, R.M. (1981) *Management Teams*, Heinemann
Connock, S. (1991) *HR Vision: Managing a Quality Workforce*, Institute of
  Personnel Management
Drucker, P. (1977) *Management*, Pan
Harvey-Jones, J. (1990) *Making It Happen*, Guild
Janis, I.L. and Mann, L (1977) *Decision Making*, Free Press
Kanter, R. M. (1990) *When Giants Learn to Dance*, Routledge
Kay, J. (1993) *Foundations of Corporate Success*, Oxford University Press
Molander, C. and Winterton, J. (1994) *Managing Human Resources*, Routledge
Schermerhorn, J.R., Hunt, J.G., and Osborn, R.N., (1995), *Basic Organizational
  Behaviour*, John Wiley
Zander, A. (1983) *Making Groups Effective*, Jossey Bass

Chapter nine

Leadership and Delegation Within Organisations

LEARNING OBJECTIVES

- Identify the main theoretical approaches to leadership

- Assess circumstances in which such approaches might be useful in the exploration of real life issues

- Appreciate the importance of behaviour in leadership situations

- Appraise the factors which contribute to the acceptability of various styles of leadership

- Identify areas where more research might be necessary

- Examine the importance of delegation in the managerial environment

- Appraise situations where delegation may be difficult

- Advise on the environment necessary for the effective use of delegation

- Identify areas of delegation where more research might be useful

In colloquial terms the two words 'management' and 'leadership' could be deemed to be synonymous; the interested lay person would see the act of managing as that of leading. In reality the act of management can be seen to be very similar to the act of leading. In direct or subtle ways the main duty of the manager could be said to be leading. However, this linkage demands a reassessment of the definition of the word 'leading'. In colloquial terms leadership acquires high profile and ordering qualities. If this reassessment embraces the requirement to develop, support and motivate individuals or groups to achieve stated tasks, the act of leadership can be seen as fundamental to the act of management.

An examination of reality suggests that the leadership task is extremely varied. If the assumption is that 'Leadership is what leaders do', many widely differing types of leader can be found. World history has provided thousands of examples of successful leaders such as Ghengis Khan, Lenin, Churchill, Montgomery and Margaret Thatcher. A detailed examination of the leadership qualities of these widely varying leaders might produce a huge list of seemingly contradictory features. This list might embrace such varying quantities as 'physical bravery', 'astute behaviour', 'cunning' and 'fairness'. Any examination of the topic of leadership should, at worst, acknowledge and, at best, explain such variety of features.

Furthermore an examination of the types of leadership used in organisations would often suggest that in most organisations there are different layers of leader and each leader may exhibit his or her own desired type of leadership.

Leadership and Management

Despite the immediately preceding analysis which linked leadership and management it is necessary to distinguish between the two related but differing concepts. Leadership can be linked to change whereas management is more closely connected with stability. Leadership can be seen to be a concept which facilitates change and management a concept which consolidates and embeds the changes once they have been developed. This is not to be seen as a precise distinction since part of the duty of facilitating change is to develop its acceptability and part of the duty of the manager is to identify redundant activity. Nor should it be claimed that leaders and managers need to be different people; rather the list of management qualities examined in the first chapter of this book can be seen to embrace many aspects of leadership. Management might be seen as the shorter-term, routine activities of the manager whereas leadership constitutes the innovatory, longer-term duties of the manager.

Perhaps the most productive conclusion to this debate would be to state that commonly leadership is a constituent feature of management but one which requires separate skills from those which the manager will usually utilise. However in certain, rare, circumstances leadership and management may need to be undertaken by different people.

Theories of Leadership

As with many aspects of the total management task it is impossible to find unanimously accepted theoretical expressions of the requirements of good leadership. An examination of these theories allows a classification of them into three main types.

TRAIT THEORIES

These theories focus on the personality requirements of the good leader. They would suggest that it is the personality of the leader which defines the ability to lead. Such theories may well be characterised by statements such as 'leaders are born not made'. However, a rigorous assessment of the wide variety of tasks required of a leader would suggest that personality is only one, albeit important, requirement of a good manager. An examination of the legitimacy of these theories can be assessed by the fact that by 1950 over 100 studies attempting to define traits required of managers suggested that traits common to these studies accounted for only five percent of the total. (The other features will be examined under the heading of Contingency Theories).

STYLE THEORIES

These theories attempted to accommodate such apparently wide variety in leadership traits and instead focused on the required behaviour of successful leaders. This behaviour could be defined in terms of the style of leadership, that is, how a leader should lead. One of the most comprehensive of such theories is that of Tannenbaum and Schmidt (1957) hypothesising a continuum of leadership styles, ranging from authoritarian at one end to democratic at the other. The major conclusion of this theory is that the desired leadership style is democratic. This is shown in Figure 9.1.

CONTINGENCY THEORIES

Such theories can be seen to be an extension of the style theories. Observations of managers practising successfully in the real world suggest that different styles can be, and are, used to equal effect in different circumstances. The point at issue is what causes different styles of behaviour to be appropriate at different times and in different circumstances. A good example of this type of theory is Charles Handy's 'Theory of Best Fit'. This theory states that the required leadership approach depends upon or is contingent upon the inter-relationship between the following factors.

a) The personality of the leader – any leader has to lead within the constraints of his or her personality. Acting in a way which is inconsistent with one's personality is very difficult. In many ways if the leader has a dominant personality, that leader, if he or she finds acting in ways which are contradictory to his or her personality too difficult, may well be advised not to try to adopt participative leadership styles; rather such a leader would be advised to act in ways consistent with autocratic leadership styles. This is not to claim that leaders with dominant personalities should always act in autocratic ways. However, what this theory does do is acknowledge the importance of the leader's own preferences in the adoption of the most appropriate style of leadership behaviour.

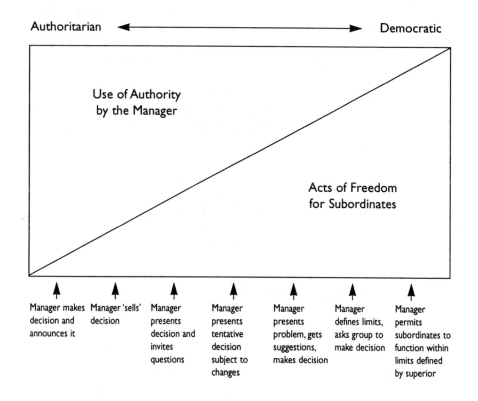

FIGURE 9.1   *A Continuum of Leadership Styles*
(adapted from Tannenbaum and Schmidt, Harvard Business Review, 1957)

b) The personalities of the subordinates – any statement which claims that all people like to be involved to a maximum extent in the making of decisions can be seen to be untrue. The reality is that some people prefer an environment where little, if any, initiative is expected of them. It may be that some people would prefer participative styles of management whereas others would prefer more autocratic styles.

c) Extent of perceived wisdom – if the leader is seen to be highly knowledgeable about a particular subject area, a leadership style which affords to the leader great power will be tend to be accepted by all involved as realistic and acceptable. However, if knowledge is widely diffused throughout the organisation, more participative styles might be more appropriate.

d) The need for speed – if a speedy decision is needed, then any style of decision making which prolongs that decision will be deemed to be undesirable. However, if an organisation works properly most decisions it needs to take should not be of this crisis nature and the extent to which autocratic leadership styles, justified on the grounds of speed will be needed, is limited.

e) Requirements of the task – a complex task may involve accessing the knowledge of many people and necessitate a democratic style of leadership. On the other hand, a task might acquire its complexity because of the expert knowledge needed; in such circumstances a high-profile form of leadership may be required.

f) Organisational culture – a major determinant of the desired style of leadership is the prevailing culture of the organisation. This is examined in more detail in a later chapter. For instance, if the prevailing culture is one of power, an autocratic style of decision making and leadership might be desirable.

g) Past events – the mere fact that a particular style of leadership has worked in the past may indicate that it is the preferred style in the future. This factor may outweigh the more rationally-based contingent features.

According to Handy's theory the optimum style of leadership is determined by the interplay between all these factors and their respective importance in the circumstance being examined. If any problems are encountered, one element in the equation should be changed to produce harmony. This change will usually be the style of leadership but it could be other elements such as 'Organisational Culture'.

The Creative Leader

Over the past few years some attention has been directed towards seeking a contingency theory of leadership which focuses on those qualities which will usually be required of a leader when the organisation itself is entering a period of uncertainty. Such an environment will be the subject of more detailed examination in a later section of this text. At the moment it would suffice to conclude that most organisations work in increasingly uncertain environments. In such situations it might be that the leader needs to have some abilities which will enable him or her to guide the organisation through this period of uncertainty. One theory which addresses this particular issue is that of Turrell, 1986. This theory is outlined in Figure 9.2.

A distinction between two separate leadership styles is made – transformational and transactional. The former type of leadership style promotes leadership qualities which challenge the accepted approaches within the organisation; put simply they 'lead from the front'. The latter style of leadership produces behaviour patterns which seek consensus approaches to problem resolution. The former is more creative in its philosophy. The required thinking patterns are more strategic in nature. The latter is more tactical in its approach. Using the language of planning, addressed in more detail in a later section of this text, the former evokes a rational approach to the planning exercise, the latter a more incremental approach to this exercise. The desirability and applicability of this approach to leadership will be examined more fully in the chapter which addresses the Management of Change.

A technique which has been used to develop such wide-ranging and creative leaders is that of action learning. This technique will be examined in the next section of this text.

Transformational	Transactional
Empowers	Bargains
Inspires by vision, ideals	Is task centred
Mixes home and work	Separates home and work
Has a long term focus	Has a short-/medium-term focus
Challenges	Coaches sheltered learning
Rewards, informally, personally	Rewards formally
Is emotional, turbulent	Is comfortable, orderly
Simplifies	Complicates

FIGURE 9.2 *The Transformational/Transactional Leader* (Source: Turrell, 1986)

Requirements of Good Leadership

In addition to the theories just examined it will be helpful to explore those characteristics of the leader which would normally be expected for the achievement of success.

a) A good leader must be positive – the leader should focus not on problems but on the resolution of those problems. A positive attitude is needed to serve as a good example to subordinates and as a strategy for successful action. This must not be interpreted as appearing over-confident. On the contrary, one of the signs of a good leader is identifying whether to seek external help in the conduct of his or her duties.

b) A good leader must be consistent – such consistency is a source of certainty and comfort to subordinates. Subordinates, even if they do not like the style of leadership to which they are subjected, can at least adjust their actions to harmonise with the demands of their leader. This harmonisation can be achieved successfully only when they can predict the reactions of their leader. It is often quoted that 'better the devil you know than that you do not know!' This must not be interpreted to mean that the leader should not adapt behaviour to suit the varying needs of varying tasks. However, it does emphasise the importance of the need for those being led to anticipate the values and actions of the leader.

c) A good leader should be aware of and responsive to the needs and expectations of the subordinates. Only when a leader has assessed these needs and expectations will he or she be in a position to adopt an effective style of leadership. As has already been emphasised, the expectations of those being led are of massive importance in the success of any leadership enterprise.

d) Good leadership demands self-knowledge – only when a leader has analysed all his strengths and weaknesses will he be able to manage all the diversity of tasks which is demanded. The good leader is one who 'plays to his strengths' and acknowledges his weaknesses.

e) Good leaders tend to be those who can argue their case effectively – particularly about resource availability. Often good leaders are those who are seen to protect the interests of those they lead. Thus an effective leader is one who ensures that the group being led has resources sufficient to succeed in its tasks. This is particularly emphasised by Mintzberg in his review of the duties of the manager.

f) Sometimes leadership needs to be high profile, sometimes it needs to be lower in profile. The effective leader is the one who can distinguish between those occasions which demand stronger leadership and those which require a 'hands off' approach.

g) Good leaders are those who are not seen to be unduly critical of their staff. Wherever justified, a leader should be seen to publicly praise staff and the occasions where public criticism is made should be kept to a minimum. This is not to underplay the role of negative criticism in that any leader should be aware of the need to change unsuccessful action. However, it does, quite starkly, indicate that any failure is, to an extent, attributable to poor management. The role of negative criticism in demotivation has been examined in the chapter on Human Motivation.

h) A good leader should be prepared, wherever circumstances allow, to delegate work to subordinates. This feature of leadership is examined in more detail later in this chapter.

i) A good leader should be an effective communicator. This has been examined in more detail in the chapter on Communication. The importance of this characteristic of leadership cannot be underestimated.

j) Good leadership requires effective management of time. This has been addressed in more detail in the chapter on Self-Management.

k) A good leader is one who acknowledges the importance of, and actually deals with, the training and development needs of subordinates. This, in its turn, is examined in greater detail in the next section of this text. This training and development not only affords a more capable workforce to the leader but it also affords one which is more effectively motivated to support the leader in varied tasks and duties.

l) In the changing environment of most organisations, good leaders are those who can adapt their behaviour to meet the changing and varied demands of the situations they will encounter. Some leadership tasks may demand autocratic styles, some democratic styles, and some laissez-faire styles. This adaptability and flexibility can be seen to be an increasingly important requirement of the effective leader.

Action–Centered Leadership

One of the most important practical impacts of the contingency approach to leadership has been the emergence and practice of the concept of action–centered leadership. This concept has been developed by Professor John Adair and is based on the assumption that the leader has three sets of equally important duties or functions:

  i) achieving the task;
 ii) building a team;
iii) developing individuals.

This must not be seen as claiming that in all cases, and at all times, the leader must assume that all three duties are of equal importance; the reality will be that over a period of time and in most, but not all, cases these three duties or functions should be viewed as of equal importance. This assumption is diagrammatically shown in Figure 9.3.

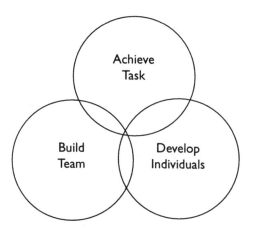

FIGURE 9.3 *Action-Centred Leadership*
(AFTER JOHN ADAIR)

ACHIEVING THE TASK

It is almost a truism to state that the leader has the duty to achieve results. No matter how well developed a leader's inter-personal skills, if that leader fails to deliver the task assigned he or she will be judged poorly.

Building a team

One of the important determinants of task success is developing a successful and co-operative team; this is attested elsewhere in this section of the text. The leader should be concerned not just with ensuring success in the task in hand but also in developing an environment for successful task completion in the future. This will normally involve team co-operation, and team building can be seen to be of significant importance.

Developing individuals

Finally, one of the most important determinants of task and team success is the quality and motivation of the people doing that task and working in that team; this again has been examined in more detail earlier in this text. As such, particularly in the long term, the primary requirement of the leader — achieving task completion — demands that the leader devotes time to developing the individuals under his or her control.

Excessive Task Orientation

As has already been mentioned, on some occasions the leader may have to give primacy to the duty of achieving the success of the task in hand. However, the point at issue here, and in the other points to be examined, is not a minor but a major imbalance; where the concentration on the one seriously impinges on the other duties of the leader. This is diagrammatically shown in Figure 9.4. With this scenario the leader will strive at any costs to achieve task success and, in such circumstances, the need to achieve an environment for longer-term success will be sacrificed. The team and the individuals within the team may be resentful and simply bide their time to exact revenge.

Excessive Team Orientation

This problem is typically exhibited by the leader who has an apparently obsessive desire to be seen as one of the team. It is diagrammatically show in Figure 9.5. The problem with this stance is that, on occasions, the leader may have to take decisions which, although unpopular at the time, are required in the short term and are also in the long-term interests of the team. This imbalance can be found commonly where the leader has been promoted to that position from the ranks of the team team which he or she presently leads.

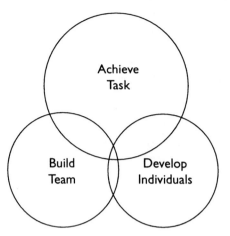

FIGURE 9.4 *Task Orientation*
(Source: C. Chase, 1990)

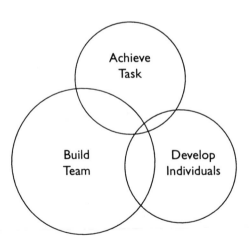

FIGURE 9.5 *Team Orientation*
(Source: C. Chase, 1990)

Excessive Individual Orientation

In many ways this is a fault which is difficult to avoid since, in most cases, task and team success is built on firm appreciation of the needs of the individual member of the team. The problem is that, in practice, often the concentration on individuals will not be equally distributed throughout all members of the team (Figure 9.6). For instance when a leader, understandably in his or her own eyes, concentrates attention on someone in a group of a different sex, religion, colour or age, there may come a time when this is resented by the rest of the group.

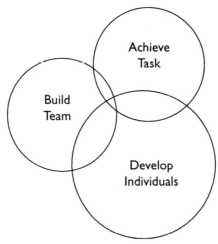

FIGURE 9.6 *Individual Orientation*
(Source: C. Chase, 1990)

How to Achieve Balance in Duties and Functions

The concept of action-centred leadership can and has been applied with success in organisations. A model of the various processes involved in leadership is shown in Figure 9.7. The detail of the various parts of these processes is examined in more detail in a later section of this book. However, a brief synopsis reveals that the leader will be charged with the duty of defining or setting the objectives to be achieved. Once the objectives have been set the leader will then have to evolve a plan which, when executed, will achieve the specified objectives. This plan will then have to be explained to the team members charged with its execution. During their execution of the plan, the team members will have to be monitored in their actions and supported

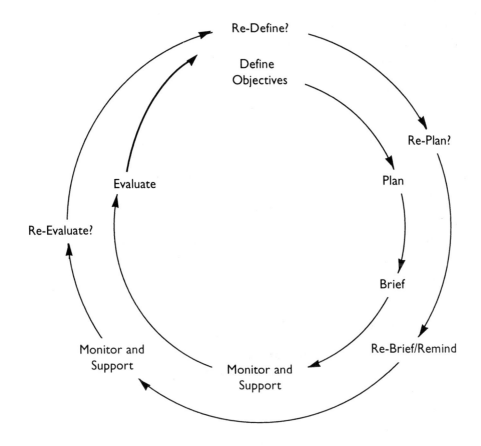

FIGURE 9.7 *The Leadership Cycle*
(Source: C. Chase, 1990)

in their attempts to achieve the desired organisational goals or objectives. Once plans have been executed, the extent to which activity has satisfied organisational objectives needs to be determined. The final element in the leadership process or circle is the redefinition of objectives based on experience gained during the first leadership or planning cycle.

It has been found that a 'check list' of key actions can be usefully employed by the leader in every aspect of leadership duties. The following analysis will examine the more important of these key actions in the context of the primary duties of the leader: achieving the task, building a team and developing individuals.

ACHIEVING THE TASK

a) Being constantly mindful of the requirements of the task.
b) Understanding how the task fits into the overall organisational objectives.
c) Trying to ensure harmony of task requirements with organisational structures.
d) Carefully explaining to all concerned the requirements of the task in hand.

e) Careful planning of the task.
f) Vigilant monitoring of performance.
g) Evaluating the success of the task.

BUILDING A TEAM

a) Involving the team as a whole in the setting of objectives and plans.
b) Carefully coaching the team in the achievement of its designated tasks.
c) Ensuring effective communication with and within the team.
d) Careful choice of team membership.
e) Regularly consulting the team on the desirability and progress of day-to-day activity.
f) Involving the team in the monitoring of progress and the evaluation of activity.
g) Diligently explaining to the team of any changes in the requirements of its designated task.

DEVELOPING INDIVIDUALS

a) Consulting individuals before targets are set.
b) Ensuring that each individual has the training necessary to execute the tasks required.
c) Ensuring that each individual has the resources necessary to achieve success.
d) Ensuring that the design of jobs best matches the skills and aspirations of individuals.
e) Striving to know and understand each individual's fears, circumstances and aspirations.
f) Striving to remember the name of each individual.
g) Ensuring that he or she, as a leader, is approachable and sympathetic to the particular circumstances of each individual.
h) Praising and thanking each individual for any success achieved – this praise and thanks must be given on a regular basis.
i) Counselling and coaching each individual to achieve maximum potential.

CONCLUSION

The concept of action-centred leadership, which has been quite widely implemented, requires that the successful leader simultaneously pays attention to:

a) the need to achieve the task set;
b) building and developing an effective team to carry out this and future tasks;
c) ensuring that each individual in the team receives sufficient attention and support to feel and be an effective and valued member of that team.

At any time, one of these duties may assume primacy but in the long term the successful leader must ensure that all three duties receive adequate and generally equal attention.

Path-Goal Model

This is a contingency model of leadership, developed by Robert House and Terrence Mitchell (1977), which is reflective of the expectancy theory of motivation. It suggests that the primary duties of the leader are:

a) to establish valued or desired rewards in the workplace;
b) to explain to subordinates the kinds of behaviour which will lead to goal accomplishment and the achievement of these valued or desired rewards.

The theory suggests that four kinds of leadership behaviour are possible contingent on the circumstances applying.

a) Directive – where the leader assumes high-profile behaviour through prescriptive behaviour, guidance, direction and rescheduling work.
b) Supportive – where the leader assumes much less prescriptive behaviour and concentrates more on supporting individuals and the team.
c) Participative – this is focused more on change than the previous behaviour pattern. However, it is distinguished from the first category in that the leader relies much more on team participation in achieving the desired objective.
d) Achievement oriented – this is a style of behaviour which is focused on the need to effect regular, ongoing change in productive activity. The leader will set challenging goals and then encourage team members to achieve these goals.

The precise style adopted is deemed to be contingent upon:

a) the personal characteristics of the subordinates;
b) the environment external to the team – such as the system of authority in the organisation, the speed with which change needs to be effected.

Leadership and Participation

Vroom, Yetton and Jago (1988) produced a model of leadership which examines in some detail the various levels of participation which the leader may wish to invoke in making decisions. They suggest that there are five levels of participation:

a) AI – the leader makes the decision personally using information available;

b) AII – the leader seeks information from the group but then takes the decision personally;
c) CI – the leader consults individuals within the group, but not the group as a whole, then makes the decision personally;
d) CII – the leader consults the group collectively and then makes the decision personally;
e) G – the leader involves the group in all aspects including full participation in the decision.

The choice of level of participation is contingent upon a number of factors surrounding the decision to be made. Key factors are:

a) the quality required of the decision;
b) the availability and location of information;
c) the commitment needed for followthrough;
d) the amount of time available.

The model is complex and provides as very useful guide which the leader can use in deciding upon desired levels of participation.

Leading in a Less Deferential Society

Since the 1950s advanced economic societies have commonly experienced a movement towards less deference. In such circumstances people are less willing to cede authority to others simply because of their position. Perhaps the more traditional command and control style of leadership might be seen as reflective of the more traditional deferential societies of the earlier half of the twentieth century. Indeed, as has already been acknowledged, the command and control style still has positive value. However, from this perspective, it could be that, where the command and control style still exists, it is reflective of organisational cultures which still facilitate deference. As such the command and control style will still be found, for instance, in the Armed Forces. However, if leadership is to survive in the sections of economic and managerial activity less willing to accept deference, it must reflect the preferences of these sections.

The United Kingdom Industrial Society in January 1998 published the results of a survey of 1,000 employees. This published research entitled 'Liberating Leadership' suggests that there are two predominant forces advocating a new, more liberating style of leadership. The first is the increasing intolerance of deference in the workplace, reflecting the movement in the rest of society. The second is the increasing preference for flat structures; within such structures the regular contact synonymous with high profile command and control styles is not possible and styles of leadership reflecting these new structures have to emerge. The characteristics of the leader in this less deferential society are shown to be:

a) showing enthusiasm - the leader will be unable to motivate those around unless he or she is clearly committed to and enthusiastic about the work programme;
b) recognising individual effort - if subordinates are to be motivated their efforts should be recognised and receive due praise;
c) supporting subordinates - only when the subordinates feel they are being positively supported by their leader will they show the enthusiasm required to work in the less rigid work environment;
d) trusting work colleagues - if employees are to show flexibility they must feel that they are trusted by those to whom they report: good leaders are shown to be those who genuinely want others to succeed;
e) showing confidence - employees will adapt more positively to those leaders who seem to know where they are going: given that all employees are expected to be flexible in their work programmes they are not likely to feel confident to express such flexibility if their leader is prone to panic;
f) honesty and integrity - those who are seen to lie or knowingly mislead are not likely to engender the trust of their subordinates.

Leadership and Discipline

One very important duty of the leader is to ensure adequate discipline in the organisation. Sometimes the leader or manager will be required to discipline an employee. Under such circumstances the manager must adopt a professional and methodical approach to the disciplinary process. In evolving this approach attention must be directed towards the following features of the exercise:

a) The focus must be on changing the employee's deviant behaviour. Thus attention must be given to encouraging the employee to improve his or her behaviour. Although it must be stressed that inevitably this process must be seen to be formal in nature, emphasis must be given to the exploration and encouragement of improvement.
b) In many economies the legislative process demands certain formats for a disciplinary process. The process must, at all costs, comply with established law and agreed procedure. For instance in the United Kingdom the Advisory, Conciliation and Arbitration Service (ACAS) lays down standard procedures which should be followed. Commonly organisations have procedures which have been negotiated with their employee representatives.
c) The exercise is likely to be painful to the employee. Experience reveals that often deviant behaviour is undertaken without malice to the organisation. In such cases the deviant behaviour might be best addressed informally, before formal disciplinary process is undertaken. An example might be poor timekeeping from a previously excellent employee. Rather than progress formal proceedings the manager might be advised to establish whether the poor timekeeping is due to

temporary personal circumstances (such as family ill health). If so private, temporary, arrangements can be made.

d) The process is a semi judicial one thus justice must be done and be seen to be done. Punishment can be exercised only when the case against the employee is proven. As in all judicial environments the importance of equity is paramount. Thus all employees must be treated equally.

Mindful of these features it might be useful to examine constituent elements which might be expected in a standard disciplinary process.

a) The employee should be allowed to be represented by, for instance, a trade union or association advocate. At the very least the employee should be allowed to have someone to witness the proceedings on his or her behalf.
b) The employee should be advised in writing, prior to the hearing, of the purported offence.
c) The case should be restated at the hearing.
d) The employee should be allowed to state his or her case and examine witnesses or present defence witnesses.
e) All proceedings should be carefully recorded and this record should be available for all parties to scrutinise.
f) The verdict should consider the nature of the offence, the previous history of the employee, previous decisions, the precedent set, the likelihood of improvement, agreed penalties.
g) The employee should be formally informed of the verdict, any improvement expected, time available for such improvement, the consequences of no improvement being afforded, help which might be available, and the appeals process.

The Importance of Delegation

There are three main types of delegation – upwards, sideways and downwards. The majority of this analysis will reflect the last type but it is necessary briefly to examine the first two types.

UPWARDS

This is where a task which would normally be the responsibility of a subordinate is passed by that subordinate to a superior. Inevitably such a form of delegation is not common in that the norm would be for jobs to be allocated to appropriate levels in the organisation. However there are precise circumstances where such action is wholly appropriate. These are shown in Figure 9.8.

- The task is relevant to the superior as it will have an impact on his or her area of responsibility. For example, it may affect strategy, staffing or budgets.
- An assignment delegated to you or a subordinate suddenly goes beyond the agreed framework for action. For example, a task may suddenly assume political sensitivity or attract media attention.
- The superior has authority or information relevant to a situation, which you do not possess, for example, where an issue affects another department, over which the senior has control.
- You become aware of an issue within the internal or external environment which you are not equipped to deal with but which may have escaped senior management attention. For example, a new piece of legislation which has strategic implications for the organisation.
- The scope of a delegated task is wider than was first assumed and you run into problems, perhaps in terms of timescales, budgets or lack of expertise.

FIGURE 9.8

SIDEWAYS

This happens where an individual would pass on authority for a job to someone of his or her own level in the organisation. Again such delegation will not be common since normally individuals will be given responsibility for a job because they have the time and expertise to execute that job. However, there are precise circumstances where such sideways delegation might be desirable:

a) Where the individual who is normally responsible for the job is called away unexpectedly.
b) Where that individual is absent from the workplace through holiday or some other predictable circumstance. It might be expected under these circumstances that the work would be delegated upwards or downwards. However, if the work is too complex to be undertaken by subordinates the latter possibility is excluded. Similarly, if the work is not of sufficient importance to pass upwards the former possibility is excluded.
c) Where the work, to be properly executed, needs the expertise of someone from another section.

DOWNWARDS

Delegation is the transfer of the authority for doing something from a superior to a subordinate. Most of the theories of leadership would suggest that in many, if not all, circumstances the effective leader needs to be an effective delegator. Even if the leader adopts a high-profile stance on leading the organisation through periods of uncertainty, he will be capable of affording enough time to such challenging tasks only if he has delegated the more routine duties to someone else, usually someone beneath him in the organisational hierarchy. In addition, as is emphasised in the chapter on Human Motivation, delegation is said to be one of the keys to effective management of other people. Finally, the importance to the manager affording enough time to deal with all the varied leadership duties has been emphasised in the chapter on Self-Management.

Despite all these forces emphasising the need for effective delegation, the norm in organisations is for delegation to be poorly executed. There are two statements commonly made within organisations. Firstly, the manager who claims that there is no use delegating anything to subordinates because they so frequently interrupt for guidance that it would have been quicker to do the job himself. Secondly, subordinates who complain that their manager is constantly passing down those tasks which are too messy or too boring to do himself.

These problems reflect poor delegation but, although they are commonly encountered, fortunately they can be rectified or, better, avoided by a prepared manager or leader.

Effective delegation is a challenging management task in its own right and one which consequently requires due attention in its own right. The first issue to address is the purpose of delegation. This is a question which many managers do not, or feel they do not, have the time to ask or answer. Unfortunately the answers to this question are fundamental to the proper functioning of the delegation task. Without some thought being given to this question it is easy to see how the delegation problem might not proceed as smoothly as it might. In many ways, after this question has been answered the rules for good delegation are easy to construct and practise.

a) To free management time − if managers spend their time doing themselves all those things for which they are responsible, they will not be able to do those things which managers are supposed to do (such as motivating their subordinates, planning, monitoring and controlling). Thus delegation may allow the manager to concentrate more on management issues.

b) To improve the task decision − in most jobs it is those people who actually do the job who know where its pitfalls lie. In most situations the leader either will have no direct experiential knowledge of the production tasks he or she controls or will have acquired this knowledge so long ago as to be unknowledgeable about the realities of present-day production activity. Therefore, it is essential that managers tap in to this invaluable source of expertise of their subordinates.

c) To train and develop their subordinates − much is written about the need to train and develop employees. This training and development need not require expensive courses; the production process itself often provides the most valuable and relevant source of training and development. When properly controlled, the delegation of responsibility can be seen to be the most relevant and most motivating way of training and developing subordinates.

d) To motivate employees − much is written about the problem of motivating employees. It can be seen that, properly controlled, the delegation of work is one of the best ways to motivate employees; it should extend job content and stimulate involvement by employees in their job content, the importance of which is addressed in the chapter on Human Motivation.

e) To encourage initiative and flexibility – recent approaches to management emphasise the desirability of developing in employees the ability to use initiative and be flexible. When used properly, delegation is a very good way of developing these qualities in employees in that it should place them in situations where the task demands more flexibility and initiative.

Having determined the uses of delegation to the manager, the rules for its implementation must now be examined. Most delegation fails because it is not properly implemented. Managers can eliminate most potential problem areas by following a number of simple rules.

a) Asking not telling – so often the interested observer is told how managers order rather than ask. The most routine of tasks can be seen as worthwhile if the environment surrounding its creation was rooted in socially-accepted human values.

b) Precise instructions – managers can create a feeling of uncertainty by not giving clear instructions. How often have we heard the comment 'Look at last year's files'? How often have we found last year's files to be useful? Even if we can follow someone else's working papers, the situation will have changed from last year. Imprecise instructions will often result in a poor delivery; a poor delivery will result in criticism rather than praise. Criticism provides a particularly poor environment for motivation.

c) Ensuring an atmosphere of helpfulness – the astute manager should realise that the mere act of delegating does not always mean that the individual to whom the task has been delegated will not encounter difficulties in fulfilling this task. These circumstances may have obtained even if the task had not been delegated and hence the request for help should not be seen to imply failure.

d) Giving due thanks – perhaps the art of good management is attention to detail. Sometimes this attention to detail is not easy to achieve. How often have we forgotten to thank others? How often have we noted that others have not thanked us? What is a minor lapse of concentration is seen by others to be a fundamental management flaw. The granting of thanks for a job well done is to afford a human element to the production task. The desire of human beings to be treated as such in the work environment has been emphasised already in this text.

e) Ensuring adequate resources – as has been mentioned previously there is nothing worse than being given a task and then feeling frustrated by not having the resources to do the task and do it well. Only when the task is successfully executed will the necessary or desired motivation be evidenced.

f) Ensuring adequate skills – the skill level of the person to whom the task is entrusted is as important in the success of the enterprise as is the level of resources given. Clearly good delegation implies success and success will obtain only if the individual has all the skills required to achieve success in the task execution.

g) Ensuring the tasks are developmental – the task which was delegated last year may not be sufficiently challenging this year. The manager's task is to be seen by subordinates as enabling them to improve their skills and widen their experience. If this developmental quality is ignored the delegator will never obtain full appreciation and co-operation from the people to whom he or she delegates the work.

h) Ensuring an atmosphere of trust – successful delegation does not begin with giving the task. Rather it must be preceded with the establishment of trust between the two parties. Consequently a poorly performing manager will find that the mere act of increasingly delegating tasks to subordinates, and furthermore adopting all the rules previously mentioned, does not immediately obtain the co-operation and support of these subordinates.

i) Low-profile monitoring and control – naturally the mere act of delegation does not remove from the manager the need to ensure the task is properly executed. Monitoring and control should be conducted in an atmosphere where the person to whom the task has been delegated feels duly trusted in the proper execution of the task.

j) Producing flexible organisational structures and values – this issue is considered in more detail in the section on the Organisational Domain. Delegation is effective only if it elicits the desired response. A manager might fully address all the rules previously listed but find that rigid values in the organisation result in lack of co-operation. This difficulty is illustrated in organisations where the immediate response to a request to do something which is slightly beyond a person's job description is 'Do it yourself – you are paid to do it!'

Thus the creation of an environment suited to effective delegation is often the responsibility of more than the individual manager attempting to delegate. Rather the total organisational environment should be one which affords a positive response to changed circumstances.

Level of Authority Given in Delegation Exercise

In this analysis it might have been assumed that the same degree of delegation or authority was intended in every example of delegation. Inevitably the managerial environment will provide much more variety and complexity. Different examples of delegation will intend different degrees of autonomy to those to whom the task has been delegated.

Figure 9.9 shows the work of Maddux (1990) reflecting the different levels of authority which might be conveyed and the reasons underlying these differing levels of authority. These levels range from mere research powers with no decision-making power through to full decision-making powers without any necessity to specifically report to the person who delegated the task.

Delegating for results		
Level of authority	Assignment	Reason
1	Look into the situation. Get all the facts and report them to me. I'll decide what to do.	The employee is new to the job and the supervisor wants to retain control of the outcome.
2	Identify the problem. Determine alternative solutions and the pluses and minuses of each. Recommend one for my approval.	The employee is being developed and the supervisor wants to see how he or she approaches problems and makes decisions.
3	Examine the issues. Let me Know what you intend to do, but don't take action until you check.	The supevisor has confidence in the employee, but does not want action taken without his or her approval. This may be because of constraints from higher management, or the need to communicate the action to others before it is taken.
4	Solve the problem. Let me know what you intend to do, then do it, unless I say no.	The supervisor has respect for the employee's ability and judgement, and only wants a final check before action is taken.
5	Take action on this matter, and let me know what you did.	The supervisor has full confidence in the employee and has no need to be consulted before action is taken. He or she only wants to know the outcome.
6	Take action. No further contact with me is necessary.	The supervisor has total confidence in the employee. The employee has full authority to act and does not need to report the results back to the supervisor.

FIGURE 9.9. *Source: Maddux, 1990, p 46*

Summary

In most circumstances the tasks required of the leader are extremely varied. The analysis of the variety of such task suggests that there is no one type of leadership behaviour which will achieve success in all circumstances. The study of leadership indicates that any list which attempts to embrace all the requirements of good leadership will be very long and of little use in planning for desired styles of leadership. The effective leader is one who can adapt to the wide variety of situations demanding leadership. Crisis situations demand different qualities of the leader than do routine situations. Any leader must be capable of leading in both types of situation. Sometimes the leader will need to lead the organisation through periods of uncertainty; sometimes the leader will need to consult widely to obtain the full co-operation of others.

In most leadership situations, effective delegation is a major aid to the manager in that it affords an excellent way of motivating, training and developing a subordinate. However, proper delegation is one of the most challenging tasks facing a manager. The practical skills in this situation are probably to anticipate the needs and expectations of those to whom the task is delegated. A manager who can capture these skills will be well placed to be judged a good delegator and hence a good manager.

Exercise

Examine the characteristics of a someone you know who you might categorise as a Leader. To what extent do this issues examined in this chapter accord with your real life experiences?

Further Reading

Adair, J. (1983) *Effective Leadership*, Gower
Adair, J. (1986) *Effective Teambuilding*, Gower
Armstrong, M. (1994) *Performance Management*, Kogan Page
Blake, R. and Mouton, J. (1964) *The Managerial Grid*, Gulf
Chase, L. *The Manager as Leader*, The Industrial Society
Handy, C. (1985) *Understanding Organisations*, Penguin

Handy, C. (1990) *The Age of Unreason*, Hutchinson

Handy, C. (1992) *The Gods of Management*, Century Business

Harvey-Jones, J. (1990) *Making It Happen*, Collins

Hunt, J. (1981) *Managing People at Work*, Pan

Liberating Leadership (1988) – The Industrial Society

Maccoby, M. (1981) *The Leader*, Simon and Schuster

McDonald, S 'Don't boss, lead', First Executive *The Times* January 29th 1998

McGregor, D. (1960) *The Human Side of Enterprise*, McGraw Hill

Schermerhorn, J. R. Hunt, J. G. and Osborn, R. N. (1995), *Basic Organizational Behaviour*, John Wiley

Stewart, R. (1983) *Choices for the Manager*, McGraw Hill

Stewart, R. (1989) *Leading in the NHS*, Macmillan

Vroom, V and Jago, A. G., (1988), *The New Leadership*, Prentice-Hall

The Management of Human Resources

OBJECTIVES

Over the past 50 years most large enterprises have recognised the need to devote special attention to the problem of providing arrangements which afford proper and effective management of the human resource. This need has been more recently recognised in many public service institutions within the United Kingdom. After reading this section the student should appreciate the breadth of responsibility of such management arrangements; furthermore he or she should be aware of the various management techniques which can facilitate the formal management of the human resource.

INTRODUCTION

Large, complex organisations understand that one of the most important duties of the management of their organisation is ensuring that adequate structures and processes exist to properly manage and control their employees. These processes will be concerned with a wide range of activities; the breadth of these will be examined in the first chapter in this section. What these activities have in common is their intimate connection with people-related aspects of management.

Chapter ten

Human Resources Management

L E A R N I N G   O B J E C T I V E S

- Understand the concept of the human resource management function and its distinctiveness from the personnel function

- Assess the range of issues embraced by human resource management

- Identify the various options available for the implementation of the concept

- Identify areas where more research might be useful

As will be seen in the next chapters in this section of the text, the human resources director or manager, commonly afforded the title personnel director or manager, is responsible for a number of personnel-related issues. The emergence of this discipline or professional specialism within organisations is, in many ways, due to the recognition of the importance of human relations issues in the total management task. It must be acknowledged, at this stage, that the areas of responsibility are those where other managers, more directly concerned with production issues, also have a significant responsibility. If we could anticipate points which will be made later in this chapter, it would probably be true to claim that the primary duty of any human relations professional in the enterprise is to promote those elements of the management task which specifically address people-related issues.

Thus, in many ways, some of the responsibility of this person has already been addressed in the two immediately preceding sections. However, this section affords an opportunity to discuss, in some detail, additional management activities where more formal management processes and structures may be involved. The additional areas are listed below; the detailed analysis of most of these will be reserved for the chapters dealing with these particular areas.

a) Human resource planning – that is, ensuring that proper mechanisms exist to plan for future manpower or human resource needs.

b) Industrial relations – that is, the provision of adequate mechanisms to ensure that relationships between the management of the organisation and its workforce are as harmonious as possible; this would include an assessment of the importance of remuneration and discipline in the achieving of this objective.

c) Welfare – the duty of management to promote employees' welfare. This might include the provision of care and facilities for retired employees.

d) Recruitment and selection – the acknowledgement that no enterprise will achieve success unless it has employed the right type of employee.

e) Training, development and induction – employees need to be afforded with the skills and knowledge required of them by the organisation so that they can work to maximum effect.

f) Job evaluation – the ensuring of fairness in the distribution of rewards when different jobs in complex organisations make differing demands on those who hold these jobs.

g) Performance appraisal – the increasing recognition afforded to the role of assessment of individual progress in both the motivation and reward processes.

Again it must not be claimed that these issues are or should be the sole responsibility of the manager specifically charged with developing proper systems to manage these activities. For instance, the operational manager is best placed to determine the skills required of new employees and needs to be intimately involved in the recruitment and selection and training processes. Nor should it be claimed that there is a need for a specialist department or section to promote or co-ordinate these issues. Equally, it may be that the disciplines of human resource management are so firmly entrenched in the operational managers of the organisation that there is no need to employ a specialist in this area; these issues will be addressed specifically in the section on the Organisational Domain. However, to anticipate the points which will be made during that section of the text, as long as the organisation can ensure that due regard is placed on these human resources issues then it can be seen to be satisfactorily accomplishing that element of the total task which we call human resources management.

Human resource or personnel management is a part of management which has been long established in the private sector. However, in many parts of the United Kingdom public service the provision of a specialised management activity known as human resources or personnel management is a relatively recent part of organisational management. Central government together with most local and health authorities introduced personnel management only in the mid 1970s. A brief observation of the ways in which organisations execute their human resource management challenges might suggest that, if the discipline has only just been recognised as one of importance in an enterprise, then there will be a tendency to afford this discipline through central departments; thus in infancy the discipline needs to be nurtured. However, as the discipline receives wider acceptance in the organisation, more decentralised deliveries might be acceptable and, at the extreme, there may be no need to employ any specific human resource professionals.

As has already been acknowledged, all these activities are inherent features of the job of any manager in that all managers have, for instance, to plan their personnel requirements, to train their subordinates, to liaise with employee groups (including trade unions) and to deal with the personal problems of individual employees. Some organisations will ensure that all of the responsibility for these aspects of management lies with the operational manager; some organisations will evolve a prominent role for the human resource expert in the provision of such services. In some organisations the personnel function is afforded by an expert working in a central or corporate department whereas in other organisations the personnel experts are employees, albeit ones with specialised knowledge and specialist responsibilities, of the operational departments.

Personnel Management or Human Resource Management

Human resource management can be seen to have its roots in the more traditional personnel management function of organisations. The personnel manager or directorate was traditionally charged with overseeing the management functions associated with personnel. It embraced functions such as planning the human resource requirements of the organisation, overseeing its industrial relations policies, writing job descriptions, defining training requirements. As will be seen in this section, the traditional personnel function and the human resource management function address similar, if not identical, areas of total management activity.

The distinction between the two concepts is one of their degree of involvement with the corporate objectives and activities of the organisation. Commonly the personnel function is seen as administrative and reactive. For example Nick Georgiades (*Personnel Management*, February 1990) suggested a set of job titles for the personnel manager:

a) The Administrative Handmaiden – writing job descriptions, visiting the sick.
b) The Policeman – ensuring management and staff obey the rules.
c) The Toilet Flusher – administering downsizing.
d) The Sanitary Engineer – ensuring an awareness of poor management practices.

Under this philosophy, the personnel function consists of the core of personnel-related issues and is charged with implementing rather than initiating the organisation's personnel policies.

Human resource management is considered to be a much more proactive, strategic activity. The recent philosophy has been that, particularly in circumstances of rapid and continuous organisational change examined extensively in earlier sections of this text, unless the organisation's human resource policies and activities are considered as an essential part of its strategic planning the organisation will be poorly placed to succeed. The emerging, more powerful human resource management can be seen to embrace:

a) promotion of management policies which will develop maximum organisational success encompasing management of change, cultural, motivation and teambuilding issues;
b) the role of empowerment and motivation in strategic planning;
c) human issues in the corporate management and objectives of the organisation.

Although personnel management and human resource management address many similar issues, it is the stage and extent of, and rationale for, involvement which creates a much more powerful, proactive role for human resource management.

The Special Role of the Human Resources Manager

The need, at some stage in the development of the organisation, for an expert in human resources is emphasised by the specialist nature of the people aspects of management. This specialist nature has already been addressed in, for instance, the chapters on Human Motivation and Communication. Managing people is as much a specialised discipline as the management of finance. This is not to claim that there should not be an input from the non–human resource professional, but rather that there should be some specialist advice or input from a human resources specialist. The reality is that the operational manager and the human resources specialist or personnel manager, at the early stages of the development of the discipline, rely upon each other to a significant extent. The operational manager will need the detailed, people-related, knowledge of the personnel manager; and the personnel manager will need the advice of the operational manager on such issues as training. The particular organisational benefit obtained from the employment of personnel experts is the highlighting of the complexities of the management of people. However, it must be noted that there is a cost attached to the employment of such experts and only if the organisation is of sufficient size to justify the employment of such people should specialist personnel experts be recruited.

Summary

In complex organisations their is a need to ensure that organisational management accords sufficient attention to the need to secure acceptable systems and processes in the management of its more directly related human issues. In some cases, this devolved responsibility will be executed by personnel experts; in other cases the devolved responsibilities will be deemed to be the prerogative of the general management of the operational department. In such cases some system of shared or divided managerial responsibilities is very often implemented; the person working in the personnel function in the operational department has obligations to report to both the operational manager and the corporate personnel manager. The degree of decentralisation of the personnel function is often related to the personnel management maturity of the organisation. In those institutions which are just developing the personnel role, there is usually a highly centralised personnel function whose main duty is to promote the development and growth of this function. However, in organisations where the role is well entrenched, a system of devolved personnel management very often facilitates the ownership and internalisation of the personnel activities.

Exercise

Consider, in the context of an organisation with which you are familiar, the use which could be made of a recognised, formal human resource management function.

Further Reading

Bramham, J. (1995) *Human Resource Planing*, IPD

Connock, S. (1991) *HR Vision: Managing a Quality Workforce*, Institute of Personnel Management

Curson, C. (ed) (1986) *Flexible Patterns of Work*, IPM

Georgiades, Nick (February 1990), Personnel Management

Goss, D. (1994): *Principles of Human Resource Management*, Routledge

Harrison, R. (1995) *Human Resource Management: Issues and Strategies*, Addison-Wesley

Hunt, J. (1981) *Managing People at Work*, Pan

Oldcorn, R. (1985) *Management*, Pan

Richards, S. (Autumn 1989) Managing People in the Civil Service, *Public Money and Management*

Thomason, G.A. (1981) *A Textbook of Personnel Management*, IPM

Torrington, I. and Hall, I . (1987) *Personnel Management – A New Approach*, Prentice Hall

Williams, A.P.O. (ed) (1983) *Using Personnel Research*, Gower

Chapter eleven

Human Resources Planning

LEARNING OBJECTIVES

- Understand the concept of human resource planning

- Appreciate the contribution which the concept can make to the effective management of an organisation

- Identify the factors which should be considered in the construction of the human resource plan

- Appreciate the intimate relationships between the various sections of the plan

- Appreciate the respective contribution and importance of recruitment and selection, training and development and retention

- Assess the factors which need to be considered when an organisation is required to reduce its workforce

- Critically appraise the human resource planning in organisations with which you are familiar

---

The United Kingdom Institute of Personnel Management in 1989 defined human resource planning as the systematic and continuing process of analysing an organisation's human resources needs under changing conditions, and developing personnel policies appropriate to the longer term effectiveness of the organisation. It is an integral part of corporate planning and budgeting procedures since human resource costs and forecasts both affect, and are affected by, longer term corporate plans.

This definition emphasises several important features of the formal human resource planning activity.

a) It is conducted within a dynamic not static environment — it constitutes an on going process or activity. In other words, a human resource plan should be regularly updated to accord with changing circumstances.

b) The plan itself allows the organisation to react to such changing circumstances with some degree of order and control.

c) The human resource plan both affects and is affected by financial considerations.

d) A human resource plan is an aid to longer-term strategic organisational activity.

The Human Resource Planning Process is outlined in Figure 11.1 An examination of this figure shows that the human resource plan is, in the short term at least, a product of the business plan of the enterprise. As such, the organisation's human resource planning is conducted not in a vacuum but in an environment mindful of and responsive to organisational needs.

From these objectives an assessment of the tasks needed to fulfil these needs is made. From the assessment of these required tasks an assessment of the skills required to effectively address these tasks is made. This will necessitate a thorough examination of the numbers of employees required, the timings of such requirements, and the skills required of these employees at the various stages of the operational plan.

The human resource plan then attempts to organise the human resources of the organisation in such a way as to achieve organisational objectives. It can be seen that an organisation which produces a formal plan is well placed to evolve an organisational structure which affords the environment necessary to achieve the organisation's objectives. Alternatively, it could be concluded that any organisational structure which is evolved without examining the problem at the manpower level is likely to be deficient.

The process, then, necessitates an examination of the existing manpower resources within the organisation: the numbers of employees, their existing skills, their age structures, the present way in which those employees are grouped or structured. It may well be that existing employee numbers, skills and structural deployments will not be conducive to the fulfilment of the organisation's objectives and plans. It may be that the organisation needs to examine how it can improve its human resources. This may involve the organisation employing new people. However, a good human resource plan will examine the constraints of the external market. Desirable though it might be to employ a specified number of people with specified skills in the future, the practical feasibility of employing such people needs to be examined. For a typical large organisation this will require the analysis of national, regional and local labour market information and indeed, in certain circumstances, an international dimension may need to be accessed. This will require the determination of the likely actions of other organisations to which future employees might be attracted. This may require an examination of the job content afforded by such likely competitors, the financial

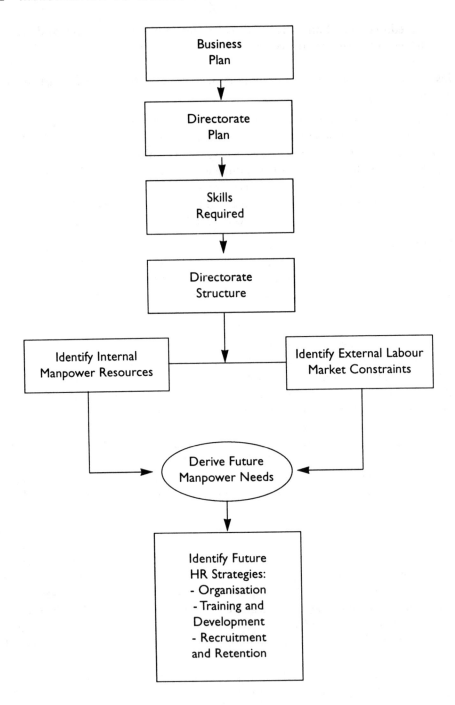

FIGURE 11.1 *Human Resource Planning Process*

benefits likely to be offered, the training and development opportunities and other elements of the job environment, such as attitude to flexible working practices.

So far the human resource plan has allowed an assessment to be made of current employee attitudes, loyalties, skills and a comparison to be made with likely demands at future specified points in time. It has effected this comparison whilst examining the future state of the labour market. The final and most important part of the plan is an assessment of the future training and development, recruitment and retention needs of the organisation; which employees, and in what numbers, require what types of training and development? What new types of employee, and in what numbers, does the organisation need to employ at specified times in the future? Furthermore, the human resource plan necessitates a formal assessment of what employment strategies will be needed to retain those employees for the period required by the operational plan.

The Issue of Retention

It may that the human resource plan reveals that so-called natural wastage is excessively high. During any time period in a large organisation employees will leave for a number of reasons beyond that organisation's control: they or their family may leave the area; they may reach retirement age; they may leave as part of their normal career development; they may become ill; they may leave to look after their family. Indeed it might be claimed that such a natural throughput of labour brings to an organisation much needed new approaches and enthusiasm.

However such a change in the workforce brings with it costs: new employees need to be recruited and selected; new employees need to be inducted; new employees need initial training; new employees involve some disruption of the working group.

An organisation needs regularly to question whether its natural wastage is excessive. Under such circumstances the organisation will be required to scrutinise the reasons for employees leaving; this can be relatively easily achieved by exit interviews whereby employees are questioned as to their reasons for leaving. If the organisation finds that some of the causes are not 'natural' but due to problems emerging in the organisation, it might wish to rectify these problems rather than commit itself to the costs of recruiting, selecting, inducting and training new employees.

Thus, the issue of increasing the retention rate of employees becomes a legitimate managerial project for an organisation. If this excessive wastage is due to low remuneration, the organistion might give consideration to reassessing its remuneration package by maybe rewarding employees for staying in the organisation. If it is caused by limited promotion possibilities it might reconsider its promotion policies. However it must be admitted that, in time of flattening organisational structures, pure promotion may not be readily available. Under such circumstances the organisation might have to direct its attention to wider developmental issues such as job variation, job enlargement, and job enrichment. If the excessive wastage is confined to one section of the organisation, there may be clear signals that some aspect of management is remiss in that section. The organisation should then be obliged to rectify this problem.

Reduction in Staff Numbers

An examination of real life human resource planning reveals that on many occasions the plan demands an actual reduction of staff numbers. This reduction in staffing needs to be professionally and effectively managed. In shedding of staff an organisation will have two objectives:

a) complying with the law;
b) striving to retain the goodwill and motivation of those remaining after the reduction.

THE LEGAL ENVIRONMENT

In the United Kingdom the primary legislation applying to this area is the Trade Union Reform and Employment Rights Act 1993 (TURER). TURER obliges an organisation seeking to reduce to its workforce to undertake certain actions before it institutes compulsory redundancy:

a) It must restrict recruitment in the areas of employment concerned.
b) It must ensure that employees beyond normal retirement age are retired.
c) It must not allow paid overtime in the areas of employment where reductions are taking place.
d) It must institute short-time working.
e) It must strive for transfer or retraining of staff where possible.
f) It must terminate the employment of temporary or contract staff.
g) It must seek early retirement or voluntary redundancy before instituting compulsory redundancy.
h) In all these actions is must seek the co-operation of employee representatives.

ENSURING GOODWILL AND MOTIVATION OF REMAINING STAFF

The goodwill and motivation of remaining workers is extremely important. The established working groups of remaining staff will have been disrupted, previous colleagues will have been seen to have lost their jobs. This is hardly the environment to retain the goodwill and consequent motivation of those remaining.

It could be claimed that many organisations would consider instituting the legal provisions just mentioned even if the legal environment did not prescribe their introduction. Many of the matters introduced by the law can be seen as attempting to limit the harmful consequences of termination. Such actions will at least ensure that remaining workers will feel that the organisation has tried to limit the harm done to its workforce.

However, with this objective assuming primacy, it might be that an employer seeking to reduce the workforce could voluntarily pursue additional activity to mitigate the negative consequences which might ensue. It might be useful to examine what, in addition to the matters just discussed, an employer could voluntarily institute:

a) It could seek to gain new employment for those staff leaving by approaching other employers, by approaching employment agencies, by advertising vacancies in other organisations.
b) It could prepare these staff for future employment by helping them with future career plans; it could help them prepare CV's and application forms for other employment; it could tutor them in the skills required at selection.
c) It could seek to mitigate the financial consequences of loss of employment by advising on entitlement to benefits or by advising on handling personal finances and investment.
d) It could focus on counselling for all those affected, both those no longer employed and those who continue to be employed.

Some Practical Issues which should Be Addressed

The human resource plan, and specifically the examination of external market conditions, will reveal whether the likelihood is that the organisation will need or, more particularly, be able to employ full-time or part-time employees. If the analysis reveals that it is the part-time section of the labour market which is likely to afford the organisation with its required skills, then the organisation might have to reconsider its present employment hours to make it more attractive to potential recruits. The overwhelming majority of part-time employees are women with family responsibilities and it may be that the organisation's present working patterns conflict with the family responsibilities of these future potential recruits. The organisation must then either adjust its working practices or accept the consequences of failing to adjust.

Finally, the concentration of this analysis has been upon human resource planning conducted in situations where the labour market or budgetary constraints are such that the original plans of the organisation are found to be achievable. It must be recognised that the human resource planning exercise can itself highlight unachievable plans; desirable though the operational plan is, the required labour either cannot be provided or the cost of providing it will be prohibitive. It is extremely important to note, therefore, that the human resource planning exercise can be an invaluable tool in assessing the practicality of operational plans.

Who Should Produce the Human Resource Plan?

The production of the human resource plan will be a complex exercise; it will involve inputs from all operational managers, the finance manager and the human resources expert. The operational managers will be responsible for advising what needs doing and upon the skills required of the workforce. The finance manager will need to impose financial discipline on the process – human resource plans can so easily become an expression of the ideal but unachievable. The role of the human resource expert is more problematic; he has the skills to contribute to the assessment of the capabilities of staff. The immense complexities of such judgements are addressed in this and previous sections of this text. The human resource expert can afford more objective advice on the capabilities of staff.

Summary

Human resource planning is a process which allows an organisation to exert more managerial control over its human resources. It enables the organisation to better plan its recruitment and selection, its training, its development and its remuneration policies. It should help to draw attention to areas of poor manpower management. However, effective manpower planning is a major task which involves operational, financial and personnel management. If the organisation's objectives change in any way this should result in a review of the human resource plan. Many of the issues examined in a typical human resource plan are examined in more depth in the rest of this section of the book.

Exercise

Design a human resource plan for an organisation or section with which you are familiar. If you feel you have insufficient information about your work environment choose an organisation from another environment such as a school or a club.

Further Reading

Armstrong, M. (1992) *A Handbook of Personnel Management Practice*, Kogan Page

Bramham, J. (1995) Human Resource Planning, IPD

Curson, C . (ed)' (1986) *Flexible Patterns of Work*, IPM

Hunt, J. (1981) *Managing People at Work*, Pan

NHS Management Executive (1992) *Human Resources Planning for the Finance Function*

NHS Management Executive (1992) *Right First Time*

Thomason, G.A. (1981) *A Textbook of Personnel Management*, IPM

Torrington D. and Hall, L. (1987) *Personnel Management – A New Approach*, Prentice Hall

Williams, A.P.O. (ed) (1983) *Using Personnel Research*, Gower

Chapter twelve

Getting the Right People

L E A R N I N G   O B J E C T I V E S

- **Understand the importance of effective recruitment and selection in achieving organisational success**

- **Identify the constituent features of a recruitment and selection process**

- **Appreciate the various methods of selection which could be used**

- **Assess the utility of methods other than the selection interview**

- **Examine the qualities of an effective selection interview**

- **Appreciate the importance of equal opportunities in recruitment and selection**

- **Critically appraise the recruitment and selection in organisations with which you are familiar**

I t could be argued that the obtaining of the right type of employee is the most fundamental requirement of good organisational management. Without the right type of employee, any organisation cannot even begin to operate. However, the obtaining of the right calibre of employee is so often poorly or inadequately conducted.

Inherent in the obtaining of the right person are two admittedly connected processes: recruitment and selection. The terms are often considered to be synonymous. It must be acknowledged that the terms are linked but certainly not synonymous.

The recruitment process ensures that the organisation obtains the required quantity and quality of potential recruits; it is concerned with selecting, from those potential recruits, those who will best meet the needs of the organisation. The recruitment and selection process can be best examined by initially assuming a number of questions need to be answered. Prime among these is 'Why do Organisations Attempt to Obtain Personnel?' This is not such a simple question as it first appears. The answering of this question evokes several responses and only after the management of an organisation has answered this question is it in a position to effectively recruit and select.

a) To obtain the right people – this is the most obvious answer to the question. As has already been acknowledged, an organisation which attracts the wrong type of person will not achieve its objectives as effectively as it might. For instance, an organisation wishing to employ mechanical engineers would be well advised to seek and employ people with the required mechanical engineering skills. Similarly, a high technology computer software company needs to employ people skilled in computer technology. It must be recognised that this is the most important answer to the question asked; however, there are further important issues to be addressed.

b) Employee satisfaction – a further facet of the exercise is the acknowledgement that the potential employee has a stake in the exercise; he or she will want to be in a position at the end of the process to judge whether this is the organisation for which he or she wishes to work. This is not an act of pure altruism on the part of the organisation since, if the employee proves to be dissatisfied with the organisation, then, as already been examined in a previous section of this book, the organisation will not obtain value for money from this employee. This is an often ignored part of the process.

c) Motivation – the importance of motivating employees has already been discussed in the chapter on Human Motivation. It is often forgotten that the recruitment and selection processes constitute the first occasion on which the organisation meets its potential recruits; this is the first opportunity the organisation has to ensure that it treats the person in ways which will facilitate maximum motivation. High levels of motivation will be hard to achieve if the employee feels badly treated during the recruitment and selection processes, or was unimpressed by these processes. In many ways this point alone emphasises the importance of the need to rigorously analyse ways in which the organisation obtains its employees.

d) Public relations – the need for all organisations to protect their public image will be examined later in this text. If an organisation fails to suitably impress its recruits with its recruitment and selection processes it will find that it might begin to develop a reputation as a poor and ineffective organisation. This is particularly important where the people being recruited come from occupations where there is a scarcity of labour. Under such circumstances the organisation will be heavily reliant on this public image to attract recruits of the required quality.

Thus the obtaining of the right people is a vital part of the total management task. It is a two-sided process; it is essential not just that the organisation wants the people but that the people want the organisation.

The process whereby the organisation seeks to obtain the right type of employee can be examined in a number of inter-linked stages.

a) The person conducting the exercise must establish the existence of a vacancy for the potential recruit to occupy. This will necessitate the examination of an organisational plan; no organisation can have an effective recruitment and selection process unless recruitment and selection are linked to organisational objectives. An organisation cannot establish its human resource needs unless it can establish what its operational intentions are. For instance, a sales organisation cannot employ a salesperson until it knows what it intends to sell. As will be seen in a later section it may be that the organisation does not have a high-profile plan; on occasions the plan could be deemed to be described by what the organisation currently does. Nevertheless it must be stressed that effective recruitment and selection are based upon identified operational needs.

b) Manpower or human resource plan – having established its operational intentions, an organisation can then determine the level and quality of manpower it needs to carry out its tasks effectively. Only by planning its manpower requirements can an organisation have any rational basis for determining the types and numbers of personnel to recruit. Again, as will be seen elsewhere in the book, it must not be claimed that this plan is subject to regular reassessment; nevertheless any recruitment and selection process which fails to base itself on such a plan will be flawed.

c) Assessment of current numbers and skills – when an organisation has established what its manpower needs are, it is then in an position to assess its current manpower resources. Only if its current resources fail to match those required in its manpower plan should an organisation decide to recruit. Even in such cases, the immediate response may not be that recruitment is needed; for instance, if the gap which exists is not a numbers but a skills gap then the required managerial action may well be training of existing staff not recruitment of new staff. In many ways, training would be the most desired option since it may be a more effective way of enhancing levels of motivation within the organisation.

d) Job description – having established the need to fill a vacancy and having decided that this vacancy needs to be filled through recruitment and selection rather than retraining, the organisation needs to prepare a description of the job which the new recruit would be expected to do. Only when this is done is the organisation in a position where it can commence the public part of its recruitment process. The preparation of a job description is not necessarily an easy task. It would consist of an organised list of the essential features of the job. In certain occupations this is not too difficult; the essential features of the job of a machine operator can be described with some ease; the normal job content will adequately describe the job.

In some cases, for instance in times of change or in jobs with wide ranging responsibilities, such as senior management, the various elements of the job content are so varied and changeable that the preparation of a job description becomes far from easy and a simple listing of job content becomes, at best, lengthy and, at worst, incomplete. Under such circumstances the organisation needs to assess certain key features which may indirectly describe the job. An example of such an approach to the construction of a job description is shown in Figure 12.1 The title of the job may give some indication of the work done – for instance the title 'general manager' will describe the job of the general manager in the United Kingdom Health Service. Similarly the term 'managing director' will in itself constitute a reasonable description of the job undertaken by the person holding that post. The salary paid may give an indication of the level of responsibility. The description of the person's immediate superior may give some indication of the level of responsibility required for a particular job. The indication of the number and grades of a person's subordinates may, in its turn, help describe the level of responsibility of the person concerned. Special conditions relating to the job may need to be specified, such as the need to work unsocial hours.

Job Title

To whom responsible?
Number and level of subordinates?
Salary
Key tasks
Location
Conditions of employment

FIGURE 12.1 *A Specimen Job Description*

e) Personnel or person specification – this is a list of the qualities which might be expected of the person who would be best at the job. It is especially important since the aim of the recruitment and selection process is not to match a person against a job description, which may have few human characteristics, but against a description of the type of person who would be best suited to carry out the described job. An example of such a specification is given in Figure 12.2 – here two commonly used sets of criteria are listed. Perhaps the point to note is that if they are chosen they should be used as a starting base and adapted, if needed, to the particular demands of the particular job. It would contain reference to such issues as level of education, past work experience, aptitudes, personality, motivation. The main aim of the personnel specification is to prepare a factual basis for comparing the people applying against the qualities required. It must be acknowledged that there may be problems encountered in judging the required qualities and that a description of people-related qualities is much more difficult than a description of job-related qualities. For instance, the judgement of the required type of personality may be one of little more than speculation; furthermore, issues surrounding the description of a personality type are not the subject of unanimous acceptance within the ranks of personality theorists. Some experts judge personality through 'ink blot tests', others through lengthy, structured lists of questions, others through free flowing essays.

Age Range
Educational Qualifications
Experience
Motivation
Personality
Background eg. Family ties and mobility

FIGURE 12.2 *A Specimen Personnel Specification*

f) Advertisement – before people can be recruited they have to be made aware of the job vacancy. The wording and placing of the advertisement is a further problem which management has to address. Obviously the advertisement must attract people to the job but, as has already been seen, there is a danger in describing only the good features of the job. The wording of the advertisement must be realistic. The placing of the advertisement is an issue which requires further managerial attention. The perfectly worded advertisement will be effective only if it appears in the media which are read, watched or listened to by those types of person which the organisation wishes to attract.

g) Assembly of appropriate documentation – once people have replied to the advertisement, the organisation must assemble documentation which enables the candidates to apply for the job; an application form needs to be designed and distributed. The form must be so designed as to require from the candidate factual information which will be of use in the selection process. In many cases such forms are not ideally suited to the requirements of the task. It is far too easy to seek out the general application form used in other parts of the organisation. It may well be that different forms need to be designed for different vacancies. Every piece of information accessed through this medium must be relevant to the selection process. However, in some cases common organisational application forms might be desirable. This will be examined later in the chapter.

h) Short listing – in most circumstances an organisation will receive far too many applications to be able to allow every applicant to proceed through the full selection procedure. What is usually required is a procedure whereby the more apparently attractive applicants are selected for further investigation. This 'short listing' is a very important management task since the organisation must ensure that those people it is excluding from its further selection procedures are truly not suitable. This is particularly important since such people will not have a chance to convince the organisation of their skills. Often, in practice, short-listing exercises are not afforded the priority by managers in their time planning that they really warrant. In fact the short-listing exercise should be seen to be as integral and important part of the selection process as the final selection itself. This problem is often encountered in organisations where the short listing is carried out by people other than those who actually conduct the final exercise. This is not to say that such division of duties is unacceptable but that if it is used then good communication should exist between the parties to the two parts of the same exercise.

i) Choice of selection method – the variety of selection methods available is examined later in the chapter. The wide range of options demands that the organisation rigorously justifies its chosen method. The reality in most organisations is that the traditional method, the interview, is automatically used as the sole method of selection. This is not to say that this method is not desirable, but that other options should be explored.

j) Conducting the selection process – here again practical difficulties may arise; some examples are examined later in the chapter using the context of the selection interview. Briefly, the major difficulties encountered revolve around using unskilled people or using skilled, but ill-prepared, people. The purpose of this exercise is not just to ask the right questions (in the case of an interview) but to accurately record the answers and then to ensure that the person presented is accurately judged against the personnel specification. The difficulties of judging others in an inter-personal context has been examined in the second section of this book.

k) Offer and acceptance procedures – the selection process should indicate the most suitable applicant. However, before the organisation can employ the successful applicant he or she must have been offered and have accepted the job. This procedure is mainly a clerical one but nevertheless it is one which requires full managerial attention. There are many stories of people failing to be offered a job when they had passed the selection criteria or being expected to start a job when they had in fact rejected the offer. It is particularly important that this part of the procedure is accurate since it may result in the creation of a poor reputation if it is done badly. The importance of first impressions in the future motivation of the employee has already been attested.

l) Monitoring and review – it is essential that the success of the recruitment and selection process is regularly monitored and reviewed. Only when this is done can the organisation claim that its procedures are effective. Such matters as the success of new recruits and/or their length of service need to be ascertained before any procedure can be categorised as successful.

Figure 12.3 outlines eight sets involved in attracting the right person, selecting the right person and retaining that person as an organisational asset.

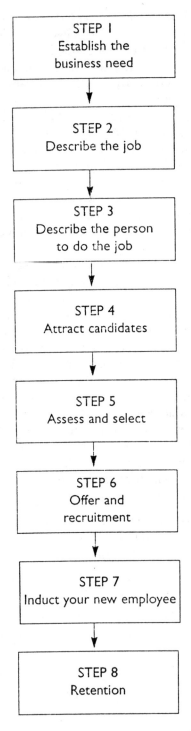

FIGURE 12.3 *How to attract and retain an employee*

Selection Methods

There are a variety of methods of selection. An organisation must chose the option(s) which it feels suits its particular needs. As has already been pointed out, many organisations do not rigorously analyse their chosen method.

a) Employing anyone who applies (possibly with the qualification that they meet simple defined criteria) – it must be acknowledged that in certain occupations at certain times the selection method need not be too sophisticated. For instance, in certain manual jobs in times of full employment the mere physical size and strength of an individual gives sufficient evidence to justify employment. Although this strategy is possible, it should be adopted only after due thought has been given to the possible consequences.

b) Past experience or past education only – sometimes the organisation need not pursue an expensive formal selection process. The application form (properly verified) may constitute sufficient evidence to employ an individual. As long as the person has sufficient experience and/or education he or she may be deemed suitable to do the job. Again before this strategy is adopted due caution should obtain. Written records of an individual's past achievements are notoriously subject to manipulation at worst (telling lies) or editing at best (the creation of a C.V.).

c) Head hunting – there are a limited number of cases where the normal procedure is radically altered. A person may be 'head hunted'. That is, the organisation feel they know not just the type of person to do a job but the very person they think is best suited to do the job. Under such circumstances they may decide to attract that one person to apply for the job. However, an organisation undertaking this policy must be wary of the possible repercussions from the person's existing employers; discussions may need to take place with the appropriate employee representatives before such a bold strategy is adopted. Such a strategy assumes that past actions are a good predictor of future success. This is indeed a high-risk enterprise and should be undertaken only after careful consideration. Nevertheless, it can be seen to have been the most common way of appointing chairmen of public corporations in the United Kingdom. Naturally it must be acknowledged that what appears to be head hunting is a process whereby the 'screening' process has been covertly conducted.

Useful though these three methods might be in some cases it must be acknowledged that a more formal selection exercise will be needed in most cases. The opportunity to make wholly valid judgements from prepared information will be limited. In such cases, the majority, a more formal selection process must be undertaken.

d) I.Q. test – it may be that the intelligence of a person is deemed to be sufficient evidence to justify employment. Under such circumstances an assessment of level of intelligence alone will constitute sufficient authority to employ. It is more likely that this will form only part of the selection method; it is commonly used as a complement to, not a substitute for, other methods. An example of one such element of an intelligence test is shown in Figure 12.4. Useful though this information may be in making judgements about the desirability of employing someone, it is highly likely that important components of the person will be ignored. The number of occasions where pure intelligence composes the sole criterion for job success will be very limited. However I.Q. can be used in a more general context; for instance the organisation may decide that it wants to employ only those people who fall into a particular I.Q. category – for example the top 10%. Much more commonly, however, it might want to exclude candidates on the basis of I.Q. – for example it might not want to employ the bottom 40% of the population as measured by I.Q. Alternatively it might decide that for reasons of team harmony it might want to exclude the top 10%.

I.Q. measurement may be of future use to the organisation providing useful information, for instance, on development strategy. It must be stressed that this strategy is not necessarily advocated but if an organisation does pursue selection on this basis according to duly considered judgements this does afford one extra use of the I.Q. Test.

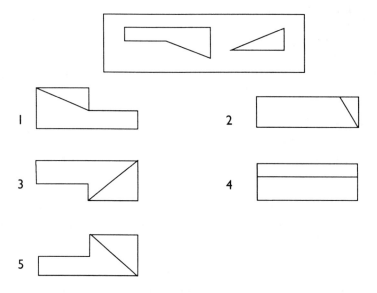

FIGURE 12.4 *Example of Special Aptitude Test Question*

The I.Q. test, the personality test and the aptitude test are collectively known as psychometric tests in that they attempt to measure or assess psychological parameters or characteristics of individuals.

e) Aptitude test – in some cases the successful holder of a job may need certain abilities or aptitudes. For instance, the person working in a computing department may need to have an aptitude for computers. In such cases these aptitudes can be assessed by the use of specifically designed tests. Unfortunately there is no real agreement on the usefulness of some of these tests. Consequently they tend to be used as complements for rather than substitutes for other selection methods.

f) Personality test – in most jobs the personality of the person is a major constituent feature in predicting occupational success. In such cases it will be necessary to assess the personality of the applicant. Formal personality tests may be considered to be a more reliable assessment of an individual's personality than will be judgement by, for instance, an interviewer. Unfortunately there is no one universally accepted authority on the assessment of personality. Most organisations which use personality tests use them as a complement to, rather than a substitute for, other selection methods. Such personality characteristics which are deemed to be important tend to focus on the individual's social skills. An example of such social skills criteria is shown in the work of Riggio, 1986 and is summarised in Figure 12.5.

---

1. **emotional expressivity** - the ability to express emotions nonverbally (e.g. through gestures)

2. **emotional sensitivity** - the ability to 'read' the emotional and nonverbal communications of others

3. **emotional control** - skill in stifling spontaneous expressions when this is necessary or feigning emotions that are not really experienced

4. **social expressivity** - the ability to speak fluently and engage others in social interaction

5. **social sensitivity** - the ability to understand others' verbal statements, plus general knowledge of social norms (knowing what is considered appropriate in various situations

6. **social control** - skill at self-presentation (presenting oneself to others in a favourable light) and at playing various social roles (eg. the respectful subordinate, the caring supervisor).

FIGURE 12.5 *Riggio's Personality Profile*

g) Scenarios – in some cases the work situation can be modelled in some way: an example might be a hypothetical management problem. Individuals can be observed and assessed on their ability to cope with the resolution of these problems. They are often used where group discussion and the ability to communicate with others is being assessed. Such group discussion might be additionally useful since the problem-solving and social skills of a number of candidates for the same job can be compared and assessed. In the case of management selection, there should exist many examples of managerial break-down or deficiency within the organisation and these should be carefully examined to isolate possible uses in such scenarios.

h) Presentations – it might be that, under certain circumstances, the presentation of a topic of concern to the organisation affords some extra source of information as to the qualities of individual, short-listed candidates. This form of selection would help isolate those candidates who have useful ideas which the organisation can use. Similarly, if communication skills are considered to be an important facet of the job, this form of selection provides extra information from which an informed choice can be made.

i) Other methods – there are a number of less frequently used selection methods:

   i) A small number of organisations require candidates to complete application forms in their own handwriting. This could ensure that the candidate appears to have the required standard of literacy; it may also afford the organisation with information as to whether the person's work will be neat enough for others to follow. However, as I.T. limits the amount of handwriting needed in most organisations, the legitimacy of this form of selection might be questioned. It is important to note that such handwritten forms enable the organisation to use graphology as a possible means of determining personality traits.

   i) Some organisations ask for a recent photograph to accompany the application form. This might simply be for recognition purposes; however, it is possible to use such photographs as a shortlisting method which prevents the organisation from selecting people who it considers will not adequately reflect the image of the organisation. This form of selection may be legitimate, but the organisation must ensure that its use is restricted solely to that purpose and in no way should be seen as contravening Equal Opportunities principles.

   iii) 'Trial by Sherry' – the organisation may wish to test the candidates' social skills by placing them in an informal gathering where their inter-personal skills can be assessed. This is quite a common form of selection as part of a battery of tests for more senior posts in organisations.

   iv) In 1996 the concept of the telephone interview emerged in the United Kingdom economy. For a number of years it has afforded a cheap, efficient way of selecting people for low-skill, temporary jobs. Similarly it has been used by recruitment agencies to shortlist or pre-screen candidates; however, in 1996 a small number of large, corporate organisations extended the system into the higher skill, permanent employment market. Examples of such organisations are Standard Life, Nationwide and NatWest. NatWest utilised it as its final shortlisting process for its graduate trainee recruitment programme. In excess of 1,000 were interviewed by telephone and 50 selected for the final selection process. It involves the organisation informing the shortlisted candidates of the process and telephoning them at an agreed time. In addition to the obvious economy it is claimed that it constitutes an extra assessment in jobs where communication by telephone is involved. Clearly fairness issues intrude where an organisation fails to inform the candidate and tries to catch them unawares. It is suggested that this will be a more commonly used method when video telephones are easily available.

j) The selection interview – this is the most commonly used of all selection methods. The interview could be conducted by a panel or it could be conducted by an individual. The candidate might have one, or more than one, interview. It presents one of the most obviously useful ways of assessing an individual's capabilities.

When used properly it can be a useful way of collecting facts, of assessing personality, of assessing communication skills and of assessing level of motivation. An additional facility afforded by such an interview is that the vast majority of candidates might expect this to constitute at least part of their assessment and any assessment which ignores this method might consequently be judged, at best, unusual and, at worst, unfair. Unfortunately, as will be seen in the next section of this chapter, there are several mistakes which can be made in the selection interview. A selection interviewer either has to be well trained or be a naturally gifted interviewer. The fact that virtually everyone in employment has been interviewed for their job and yet only some are successful may say something about the level of ability of some interviewers. This is not to claim that all the possible reasons for performance failure can be detected or predicted by an interview; for instance, an individual's personal circumstances can change quite radically during the period between the interview and the detected poor performance. Nevertheless most poor performances can be predicted within the first few weeks of an individual's employment and hence the general criticism of interviewing skills does have some validity.

Qualities of a Good Selection Interview

Many selection interviews are very poorly conducted and one of the most common complaints found in organisations is the improperly conducted selection interview. In most cases the following characteristics should be strived for.

a) Preparedness – the interviewer must be adequately prepared for the interview. The interviewer should have read and made notes on the application form; sometimes applicants gain the impression that it is only during the interview that the application form is read. The interview must be arranged in such a way as to avoid interruptions; many stories are heard about interviews being interrupted by telephone calls. This is especially important to note since its rectification demands no expensive training of the interviewer but the application of good time-management skills. Any encouragement of good time-management skills in the context of selection interviewing should result in wider ranging benefits to the organisation. Additionally, it is worthy of special mention since it is a fault which will be immediately detected and adversely judged by the interviewee.

b) Stress – in most circumstances the stress involved in a selection interview is not a desirable feature of such an interview and, in most circumstances, one of the major tasks of the interviewer is to try to overcome the candidates' feelings of stress. This might be achieved by a pleasant manner or by asking a few easy questions at the beginning of the interview. Many stories are heard of aggressive behaviour by interviewers. It must be acknowledged that there are some jobs where stress is an integral feature of the job and in such circumstances a certain level of stress in the interview might be desirable; an example of this might be the recruitment of a senior officer in the military services, where the ability to perform under unusual levels of stress is an important feature of the job. Nevertheless, the fact that aggressive questioning is rarely justified cannot be denied. Such questioning will be judged as unfair by the interviewee and many good potential employees may be lost to the organisation, or many employees may enter the work environment with a less than perfect judgement of the quality of the organisation itself.

c) Purposeful questions – the questions must be seen to be fair and related to the circumstances of the interview. The main aim of the interview is to match the person against the personnel specification. Hence it is crucial that irrelevant questions are not asked. It is very difficult to prepare a list of questions all of which are judged by the interviewee to be wholly relevant. Perhaps the point at issue is that all questions must be carefully scrutinised to ensure their complete or partial validity. A good instance of the problems created by such a situation is where the interviewer deliberately asks a very difficult question to see if the candidate appreciates the full impact of the question. The question itself is fair but it may be perceived by the interviewee as unfair or unreasonable. Perhaps a practical way out of this dilemma is for the interviewer to still ask the question but acknowledge at the outset its difficulty.

d) The candidate must be allowed to fully develop an answer; it is necessary that during the interview it is the candidate who does most of the talking. Unfortunately in some cases interviews are dominated by the interviewer. This is not to claim that the interviewer should be silent or should not be in control of the interview; but there is a clear distinction between interviewer control and assertiveness and interviewer dominance. Clearly there will come a time when the interviewer has to interrupt a candidate to progress to another area of the interview. It may well be that, if handled sensitively, such an interruption might be welcomed by the candidate. Perhaps the skill is to briefly mention the reason for the interruption. The skills required by the assertive, as opposed to overbearing, manager have been mentioned previously in this text. Finally it must be admitted that there are acceptable reasons for interviewer contributions to interviews; a part of the interview process is telling the interviewee about the organisation or the job. Despite the qualifications just made, the need to allow the candidate a fair chance to show his or her skills cannot be over-emphasised.

e) Accurate recording – it is sometimes very difficult to remember every response of every candidate. Hence it is necessary to design a form which allows the interviewer to record the appropriate responses of the candidates. Naturally this recording should be done in such a way as to guarantee accuracy whilst not distracting the candidate.

f) Right length – the interview should be of a length which allows the candidates to display all their abilities; however it must not be so long that fatigue sets in. It would normally be assumed that anything less than 30 minutes was too short and anything more than one hour was too stressful and fatiguing. It must be stressed however that the required length of time is judged by the particular circumstances of the particular interview.

g) Control over non-verbal aspects of communication – the importance of non-verbal communication is covered in the chapter on Communication. Wherever possible the candidates must be given chairs of similar size and comfort to those given to the interviewers. The interviewer should never give signs of disapproval or lack of interest; it must be acknowledged that many interviews are conducted by people who do not seem to realise the importance of the non-verbal aspects of the communication.

h) Accurate judgement – most interviewers when questioned would claim that they were good judges of others. Unfortunately, as can be seen in the second section of this book, when one individual judges another several mistakes can be made.

It can be concluded that the successful use of the selection interview is far from easy to achieve. Most managers will have to strive to acquire all the skills required of the good interviewer. Many of the skills required of the good interviewer can be translated into the environment of other selection methods – particularly the need to be prepared.

The Organisational Dimension

Some organisations strive to introduce common practices into their selection processes despite the fact that the jobs undertaken by, and hence the skills required of, their various workers might be widely varied. This might be achieved by common publicity material, the desirability of which is obvious. However, it can be extended to embrace deliberately constructed organisational application forms. It can be further extended into common selection methods and, probably more importantly, common selection criteria. An example might be where the organisation has deliberately decided to seek common personality characteristics in all its employees, be they managers or manual employees, or from widely differing professions. This strategy has been employed by several health authorities in the United Kingdom public service. Such actions by organisations might appear at first glance to be the actions of an unprepared and inattentive management. The initial judgement may be that widely differing jobs require widely differing characteristics. Thus applicants for the post of accountant in a hospital may be puzzled by questions which they consider more appropriate to the job of a nurse.

However, such actions may be a positive reaction to the management's view of the way in which the organisation needs to be run. For instance it may feel the need to develop a corporate image to present to its clients and it may consider too disparate a group of employees a hindrance to this corporate dimension. Alternatively, it may have decided that inter-disciplinary working would constitute a major feature of the work environment and that under such arrangements employee personality or value differences may be undesirable. Finally, it may demand of its employees much more flexibility in work practices than might be suggested by traditional role-based job descriptions. The potential importance of this will be discussed in detail in the section on the Organisational Domain.

The Respective Roles of the Human Resource and Operational Experts

One of the most controversial areas in recruitment and selection is that surrounding the roles of the human resource and operational experts. It is the operational manager who should have the most knowledge concerning the skills and aptitudes required of the successful applicant, particularly where they pertain to technical skills. Thus the operational manager must be involved in the process.

However, the judgement of other people is far from an easy task; it may well be that the person skilled in the personnel aspects of management, which may include, amongst others, the human resource expert, needs to be involved in the process. If the organisation can ensure that its operational managers have all the required skills then the personnel manager may not need to be involved.

Even if this is the case, there may be a need to involve the human resource expert or some other person as well as the operational manager; the organisation might need to ensure that there is consistency across all its sections and departments. In addition it may well be that different people are skilled in enquiring into different aspects of the candidate's suitability for the job. Within reason, the more people involved the less danger there will be of undue bias or unfairness entering into the process. This use of more than one selector may be achieved by more than one person sitting in on one interview; alternatively it might be achieved by more than one interview.

Finally, in the case of the organisation which wishes to introduce an organisational dimension into the selection exercise, for valid reasons which have just been explained, the need for someone with human resource skills becomes all the more necessary. It may well be that such an expert is ideally placed to provide the necessary overview on required people skills. Even here it must be attested that other co-ordinators, typically the managing director, may have a major role to play.

The Role of the Assessment Centre

Some organisations have recently begun to make use of the assessment centre in the selection of staff. A good example of such organisations would be some of the larger health enterprises in the United Kingdom.

Such a centre would typically be composed of a two or three day multiple method mode of selecting the right people. It would commonly be undertaken in an environment removed from the pressures of routine production activity, for example at the organisation's training base. Usually there would be a number of assessors involved in the process charged with the assessment, using a number of modes, of the candidates. Examples of such modes would be: an interview, a group exercise, an individual work exercise, the completion of a personality assessment questionnaire, and ability and aptitude tests.

They have the benefit of affording the opportunity for all candidates to be assessed at the same time (facilitating comparison); furthermore they allow the battery of assessments to be aggregated into an overall judgement. It might well be that the multiplicity of tests helps to overcome the deficiency of any one form of assessment. It allows the different assessors to discuss their different perceptions of each candidate, thus helping overcome the problem of assessor bias. Finally, and a point not to be underestimated, they should help the candidate feel that the organisation has tried to assess the wide range of his or her abilities; as such it might enhance the public profile and positive image of the organisation.

Such a mode of assessment is a costly exercise. All assessors involved need to be trained, but admittedly this could be seen as an advantage. Additionally, the removal of a number of managers from the work environment at any one time may place strains on the normal operational activities of the organisation. The criticism is not that the managers are released from operational activities (this should be seen probably as an advantage) but that several managers are absent from routine management duties at any one time.

The Use of External Agencies

Some organisations decide that the recruitment and selection process is such a specialised process that they would prefer to pass on this responsibility to external recruiting agents. This has the advantage of allowing the organisation to make use of such expertise when, and only when, it needs it. It has the additional benefit of ensuring that the organisation can concentrate its management attention on its core activities. Inevitably under such circumstances the organisation has given over direct control of this process to another agency and it is sensible management practice for the organisation to monitor carefully the actions of such agencies.

The Responsibility of the Organisation in the Recruitment and Selection Process

The wide range of methods of selection available has just be examined. These afford to the organisation potential massive power over the candidate. However, since 1989 in the United Kingdom all organisations, where selection takes place under the control of a member of the Institute of Personnel and Development (IPD), have had to assume certain obligations to candidates. The IPD issued a code of conduct which imposed upon organisations certain obligations:

a) all candidates should have due notice of the method/s of selection chosen;
b) all candidates should have due notice of the approximate length of time of the selection process;
c) all organisations should guarantee to all candidates due confidentiality of any information disclosed during the recruitment and selection process;
d) the organisation must assemble evidence to convince themselves, and potentially the IPD, of the validity of all selection methods chosen;
e) if any part of the recruitment and selection process is given over to external agents, the organisation is still responsible for the acts of these agents.

Equal Opportunities

Equal opportunities is an issue which legitimately appears in many aspects of an organisation's human resource policies. It embraces not just selection but also promotion, termination and development. However, it might be productively illustrated in the context of selection. Equal opportunities tries to ensure that no-one is subject to any discrimination on grounds which are not immediately and legitimately related to the job. A rationale of equal opportunities in the business environment follows.

i) It is a legal requirement in most cases concerning gender, race, and disability and any contravention of the law will be both embarrassing and potentially costly. (See Equal Pay Act 1970, Sex Discrimination Act 1975, Race Relations Act 1976, Disability Discrimination Act 1995). Any organisation must ensure that in its selection policies (including recruitment literature), development and promotion policies, and in its redundancy or termination policies, it does not discriminate on the grounds of gender, race or disability. Any specifications as to race, gender or physical ability must be directly and legitimately related to the decisions made.

The one area which is not covered by legislation in the United Kingdom is discrimination on the grounds of age. Thus any attempt to introduce policies ensuring that age is not used as a reason for excluding someone from a job or from promotion cannot rely upon statutory backing; in this area, and indeed possibly in the other areas, additional and more logical bases for equal opportunities need to be sought. Thus it is useful to seek a logically based justification for equal opportunities as a means of ensuring rigorously analysed management practice.

ii) It might be considered to be good management practice to ensure that only the best people are selected and/or promoted. Unnecessary restrictions need to be eliminated; although the issue is inevitably complex, it is generally considered that most abilities and qualities are not gender or race specific. The issue is not as clear in the area of disability, although it might be seen that in many non-manual jobs all people of a certain intellectual ability, regardless of physical ability, have something to contribute.

In a competitive environment organisations might need to publicly represent and reflect all the constituent parts of their market. Thus, for instance, a public service organisation has clients who are male and female, who come from various racial backgrounds, who have different degrees of disability. Furthermore, it could be argued that having employees who can empathise with all sections of their market will give an organisation an advantage in a competitive environment. In addition, the demographic structure of the population makes it increasingly difficult for any organisation to exclude from the employment market people of both genders and any race.

As has already be acknowledged, the issue of discrimination on the grounds of age cannot be based on legislation. However, the arguments just pursued could be seen to apply as much to age as to the other characteristics. Age discrimination is especially found amongst young and old people. Young people sometimes find themselves excluded from job opportunities because they 'lack maturity'. Older people are sometimes disadvantaged in that they are considered to be too inflexible. Both assertions need to be proven; if a young person who has maturity is denied the opportunity the organisation will not be best served; if an older person with flexibility is excluded again the organisation has lost an opportunity to employ or promote a good employee. Perhaps more importantly it must be recognised that such assertions are far from fully supported in reality. Wisdom and flexibility, it might be argued, are not age specific; there may be as many variations within an age group as between age groups. Even if such assertions are substantiated, imposing age-related criteria might be considered to publicly exclude certain client groups. Equally, organisations will be excluding from their employment base substantial proportions of the available working populations.

Given that organisations which discriminate on the grounds of age are likely to be dominated by those aged 30–45 years, if they continue to so discriminate against young and old people they might root their competitive advantage in a small section of the population; in a potentially rapidly changing environment they might be merely cloning their competitive disadvantages.

It must be repeated that this is an area where research is inconclusive, but perhaps the most telling test an organisation could undertake is whether the bad publicity which might obtain from such a situation has been 'worth it'. The marketing opportunity of being seen to not discriminate on the grounds of age must not be ignored. Perhaps the most public of such statements is that made by the do-it-yourself group, B&Q, who promote the benefits of employing those aged over 50 years, pointing to their high reliability; it might be noted that a large percentage of those using such retail outlets are within the age groups concerned. Under such circumstances, it could be that this empathy with its customers might be noticed and might increase its chances of selling to customers in this age group.

The need to ensure equal opportunities in all aspects of human resource management is, in the overwhelming majority of cases, well founded. In such circumstances organisations should seek to adhere to equal opportunities principles in all their employment practices. It must be admitted that, particularly in large organisations, such a policy may not be easy to introduce. It may be contradictory to long-established practices; longer standing employees may need to be convinced of its legitimacy; it may be contravened without the organisation or indeed the person responsible being aware of such discrimination. Hence, it is a policy which should be fully explained; all those implementing employment policies should be adequately trained and it must be monitored as to its implementation. Many organisations have accommodated these difficulties by formulating equal opportunities statements and written policies which are deemed to be fundamental to their operations; such policies will be explained to all staff responsible for implementing them.

Flexible Career Patterns and Employment Portfolios

The analysis of recruitment and selection would be incomplete if the issue of changing employment patterns were not examined. Since the early 1990s employment patterns in the United Kingdom have begun to change. The tradition in the United Kingdom used to be based upon permanent contracts for those employed; people, working within a permanent contractual framework, could tend to base their careers within certain functional disciplines, for example engineering, accountancy, marketing. Only as people were promoted within corporate organisations did their responsibilities widen to accommodate more general management issues.

However this career path, although it did contain some flexibility, is beginning to be replaced, or at least challenged, by a different pattern of employment and a different career pattern.

1. There is a increased tendency for people to be employed on fixed-term contracts. This mirrors the rapidly changing external environment faced by many organisations.
2. As a consequence of these short-term contracts individuals are experiencing work in a more varied environment. This variety embraces both the range of organisations in which they work and also the work they do within those organisations.
3. The temporary nature of many of these jobs and the increased variety it affords to, or enforces on, employees involves individuals in having more varied experiences but less in-depth experience in any one specialism.
4. Potential employees are having to focus more on building up an employment portfolio in which their varied experiences are contained.

These more flexible employment practices are usually considered to be financially beneficial to organisations and in situations of increasing competition more organisations are switching to such flexible employment patterns. This increasingly flexible employment market has been seen to limit the extent to which pay is based on collective bargaining. More commonly organisations are rewarding employees on short-term individual contracts. An additional benefit for organisations is that they need expend money on employment only when jobs need to be done and the period of the contract lasts only for as long as the task required. The impact of these changes on reward systems is examined in the chapter in this text dealing with remuneration issues.

However, these changes can be seen to impact on employment issues other than finance. The changed market conditions means that, even if the organisation does not wish to to do, the organisation might have to refocus its employment policies around shorter-term contracts. In such circumstances the issue of precision in human resource planning can be seen to assume more importance. If an organisation is forced by market conditions to employ people on short-term contracts it must ensure both that the organisation has work for them to do and also that the work matches with a substantial degree of precision the availability of staff with the required skills.

Similarly the organisation will be faced with an increasing number of candidates with quite varied career experiences. To fulfil the career expectations of these people, the organisation will have to focus more on providing these employees with more variety in the workplace. Finally, the organisation may find that it has to rely more on the employment or career portfolios rather than the traditional use of references from a previous employer.

Summary

The recruitment and selection process serves several purposes. It embraces situations where it is not just the organisation selecting the candidate but the candidate approving the organisation. When done well the process can enhance the level of motivation of its recruits; however, when it is done badly it can be detrimental to motivation. There are several methods which can be used in the selection of employees and, important though it is, the selection interview is only one of those methods. The selection interview requires great skill and judgement on the part of the interviewer. Many people need to acquire these skills and judgement. In many organisations there is a role, be it full or partial, for the human resource expert in this massively important area of management activity. The roles of these two types of person can be effectively married to organisational benefit in an assessment centre.

Exercise

Critically appraise the recruitment and selection process you were required to undertake in obtaining your present job. If you are currently not employed examine the same question in the context of an occasion when you failed to gain employment.

Further Reading

Beardwell, I. and Holden, L. (1994) *Human Resource Management: A Contemporary Perspective*, Pitman

Bramham, J. (1995) *Human Resource Planning*, IPD

Cousey, M. and Jackson, H. (1991) Making Equal Opportunities Work, Pitman

Curson, C.(ed) (1986) *Flexible Patterns of Work*, IPM

Hunt, J. (1981) *Managing People at Work*, Pan

Management Executive, Guidance Notes on Human Resource Management (1992), NHS

NHS Management Executive (1992), *Right First Time*

Thomason, G.A. (1981) *A Textbook of Personnel Management*, IPM

Torrington, D. and Hall, L. (1992) *Personnel Management – A New Approach*, Prentice Hall

Williams, A.P.O. (ed) (1983) *Using Personnel Research*, Gower

Affording the Required Skills

L E A R N I N G   O B J E C T I V E S

- **Understand the importance of effective induction, training and development in the success of any organisation**

- **Appreciate the importance of effective planning and monitoring in any actions which may be taken**

- **Identify the range of options available in training and development**

- **Appraise the contribution which might be made by coaching**

- **Appreciate the role which might be played by mentoring**

- **Critically appraise all concepts examined in the context of an organisation with which you are familiar**

- **Examine areas where further research might be needed**

A ll large organisations and most small organisations need to give considerable attention to the task of ensuring that their employees have the skills necessary to do their present job properly and to be able to fulfil other tasks in the organisation, which they may be required to do at short notice, well. The term which immediately springs to mind in this context is 'training'. However, as will be explained in this analysis, the affording of such skills to employees by management spans areas other than those immediately understood by the use of the word 'training'. This is not to disparage the role played in this exercise by training; indeed in most circumstances it can be seen to address most of the responsibilities of management in this area.

In addition to traditional training, emphasis will be placed on wider development issues and also issues concerning induction. In many ways the skills required of management in these areas are quite similar; for instance, as with most aspects of management, a prepared management is an effective management.

The three topics are of particular importance in the public service since organisations working in the public service give great emphasis to training, development and induction. Similarly, as organisations in the private sector devote more attention to the quality of the product they deliver, the need to employ properly trained personnel becomes more pressing. Furthermore, the traditional distinction that training is for low-level employees and development for higher-level employees is no longer acceptable.

Learning Theory

Training and development are concerned with the acquisition of new skills, new concepts, new approaches, new philosophies. Before a training or development programme can be developed it is necessary to focus on how and why people learn these new skills, concepts, approaches or philosophies.

Firstly, the evidence reveals that only when people are motivated to learn will such learning have maximum impact. To ensure the training has meaning they should have explained to them, to their satisfaction, clear objectives and standards expected from the new skills, concepts, approaches or philosophies. If progress is to be achieved in the striving for these new activities, regular and positive feedback should be given to them. They should be effectively and positively rewarded for achievement. Negative rewards should be reserved only for truly exceptional unco-operative behaviours. Throughout the whole process the people being trained or developed should be involved and own the activities which they are undertaking.

Individual Differences in How People Learn

The creation of a training and development programme might be complicated if it were found that different people learn in different ways. Peter Honey and Alan Mumford suggest that people's learning styles or approaches can be subsumed in four categories:

a) Theorist. This person will learn best by striving to understand concepts before attempting to apply them in practice. This person will benefit from a more remote, conceptual approach to training or development. This person's programme will have to be highly structured. Time will have to be devoted for analysis of learnt activity. For instance such a person will feel frustrated by an approach to I.T. learning which encourages the trainee to experiment with the I.T. facilities provided. This person will be better instructed through the off-the-job facilities examined later in this chapter.

b) Reflector. Such a person wishes to observe phenomena, think about them at his own pace and then act. This person will need to develop learning at his own pace. This person may feel frustrated by being forced to interact in a learning group, preferring to interact primarily through asking questions. It might be that open or distance learning approaches well match the requirements of this person.

c) Activist. This person will strive to learn by becoming involved and will be frustrated by theoretical approaches to learning. This person will be best served by approaches which present him with problems and require the development of solutions.

d) Pragmatist. This person might be seen as a modified form of activist. He needs to see the direct benefit of any training or development before it will achieve any success. The person will be ideally suited to the on-the-job solutions examined later in the chapter. The person will be frustrated by off-the-job approaches but will feel that the open-ended approaches favoured by the activist will lack structure.

The legitimacy of the distinction between the learning styles is supported by the fact that only 20 percent of managers questioned by Honey and Mumford suggested that they had preferences for three learning styles, whereas 35 percent of managers identified with only one style of learning.

The distinction between these four types of person is of immense importance in that a training or development programme may need to be tailored to the particular requirements of each individual participant. It may also be that in the wider, longer-term development of the individual, the programme might wish to facilitate in each individual the learning styles with which they feel most frustrated; however, if this is to be attempted it must be executed in such a fashion that it is not perceived as threatening by the participants. If this development approach is to be adoped, the facility of mentoring, examined later in this chapter, may prove a major asset.

Kolb's Learning Cycle

This approach wishes to promote the concept of active learning or 'learning by doing'. It is a concept which can be particularly applied to the wider development of individuals rather than to specific training issues. It is graphically represented in Figure 13.1.

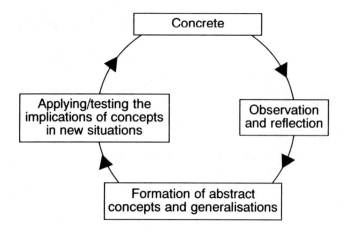

FIGURE 13.1 *Kolb's Learning Cycle*

It can be seen to embrace all four learning styles hypothesised by Honey and Mumford. The cycle begins with a concrete work experience, the individual observes his or her success in this experience, reflects on the experience and ascertains what went right or wrong. From this reflection he or she develops abstract concepts and generalisations linking the reflection to wider environments. Finally, he or she applies these new concepts to generalisations to the next concrete work experience.

Kolb's learning cycle has utility in that it can be used as a working model for planning, monitoring and facilitating learning within an organisation. Again if any problems are encountered by an individual it might be that mentoring will afford an extensive remedial facility.

Training

Before an effective training programme can be prepared the question 'Why train?' needs to be answered. The answer is a little more complex than might be thought initially.

a) Firstly, organisations train so that those doing the jobs can do them successfully. Obviously there is no point in giving someone a job to do if that person does not have the appropriate skills to do that job. If the person is not trained, any money injected into the production process will be money wasted. A construction engineer is of no use to an organisation unless he or she has the appropriate skills to construct buildings which are safe for occupation.

b) Sometimes people are capable of doing the job but they would do the job better if they received some training. The distinction between this and the immediately preceding point is subtle but important. Taken in isolation the first point would assume that required skills are static in nature. This point recognises the fact that in many cases people enter new jobs with some previously acquired relevant skills but that their performance potential might not be as high as it might be with some training. In addition this point acknowledges the circumstances where long-standing employees might need to adjust to changes in production technology; few, if any, jobs have fixed skill content. A final factor to note is that this point introduces the self-growth characteristics admitted in the chapter on Human Motivation; it admits the idea that, even in apparently simple jobs, the need to train is not a one exercise phenomenon.

A good example would be the training of a telephonist/receptionist. The job requires initial training in the proper running of the telephone system. However, as technology progresses more sophisticated technology may become available; for instance, facsimile machines may be introduced into the organisation. A further refinement might be the introduction of electronic mailing systems. Both these developments may require a major input by the traditional telephonists and may require the acquisition of new skills. The organisation may decide to place greater emphasis on serving its customer needs and place more emphasis on the receptionist part of the job description.

c) Sometimes the need to provide a safe work environment may constitute a major consideration in the decision to train an employee. Some jobs are dangerous and to ensure that the job is done well and that all hazards are avoided (to save money, to avoid court proceedings and as a moral obligation) some training may be needed. This factor can be seen to be particularly important when public service employees provide a service where, unless the job is done carefully, the public itself may be in danger (for example, driving a train). Naturally such a public safety obligation is not restricted to the public sector; a driver of a vehicle carrying dangerous chemicals needs to have skills appropriate to the driving of such a vehicle. It must be recognised that this need not be limited to situations of physical danger; the doing of any job badly can seriously endanger the organisation. This is an important point to note since it further reinforces the organisation's stake in ensuring effective training.

d) Finally one factor which is often forgotten is that organisations can use the training vehicle as a method of equipping the employee to deliver a product to the best of his or her ability. The importance of doing a job well is a major part of the employee motivation responsibilities of the manager. The benefits of good training extend beyond the training domain itself into the wider organisational domain.

These factors play a major part in the design of a good training programme. The organisation has a major stake in good training and training is a continuous process.

How To Train

When a decision is made to train an employee there are a number of types of training which can be used. In many ways the choice of the desired method is a product of the reasons why an organisation trains. The environment within which the training is effected should be ideally conducive to the acquisition of new skills, the updating of existing skills and the motivation of the employee.

a) Formal training, for example, educational courses. This formal training has certain advantages.

   i) Mistakes made do not impact upon the production process.

   ii) The trainee can learn in an appropriate, unstressed learning environment taught by qualified trainers. Under such circumstances the fear of making a mistake is removed; the job can be taught in 'digestible chunks' so that the trainee is not overwhelmed with too much detail at any one time.

   iii) The wider environment within which the job is undertaken can be addressed by explaining why a job is done as well as how it is done. The educational course will often focus on issues surrounding the precise job content as well as those intrinsic to the job itself; this advantage is reinforced by the fact that the people who are affording the training, having themselves acquired some training in 'how to train', should appreciate the need to explain the wider or occupational environment issues.

However, this type of training does have one major disadvantage: it may not immediately motivate all trainees; quite frequently comments like 'it's too much like school' are heard. Many trainees enter the training environment with a desire to be thrust immediately into what they perceive to be real life situations.

b) On-the-job training – the trainee learns the job whilst doing it. It must not be claimed that this method necessarily involves the trainee being required to do the whole job immediately; when done properly this form of training can be as structured and as appreciative of trainee needs as off-the-job methods and often the job will be learned in 'small digestible chunks'. It must be equally acknowledged that there is a strong tendency for such training courses to try to progress trainees into trying the whole job fairly quickly. This method of training has certain advantages.

   i) It will appear to the trainee to be more obviously relevant. Comments such as 'that's what I'm here to do' will often be heard. The desire of many trainees to enter the 'real world' must not be underestimated.

   ii) The training process can be conducted whilst introducing the trainee to future work colleagues and this can be seen as reinforcing the perceived relevance of the training. Furthermore, it formally recognises the future importance of such working groups; this has been addressed in an earlier section of this text.

However there are some problems with this form of training.

   i) Mistakes involve loss of production. Thus mistakes can be costly. For instance, it would be foolish to allow a trainee diamond cutter to cut diamonds on the first day of employment. Obviously, in such circumstances, a diamond substitute will need to be used.

   ii) Although this is not a necessity there will be a tendency for the trainer to be less aware of the need to explain the reasons for doing the tasks in the precise way they are done. Only a prepared management will have ensured that the trainer has the all the skills required to train. Despite this comment it must be acknowledged that the traditional apprenticeship training in areas such as joinery and brick laying were generally recognised to afford effective forms of training.

   iii) The making of mistakes in front of future work colleagues can be demotivating. The possible demotivating effects of such mistakes should not be underestimated.

c) Awareness-orientated training – this form of training can be seen to be more closely linked to development. It involves creating an awareness by the individual of the need to develop improvements in certain areas of his or her performance. It can be seen to embrace assertiveness training and neuro-linguistic-programming considered earlier in this book.

The Training Process

The need to afford to trainees an effective training programme embraces both production and motivational issues; any organisation attempting to address training needs would be well advised to ensure that the training programme is as effective as possible. Many training programmes do not rigorously examine the whole of the training process. On many occasions insufficient consideration is given to what is taught or how it is taught. A comprehensive training process will involve a logical examination of the following issues.

a) Business plan – the starting point for what needs teaching is what activities the organisation needs to undertake.

b) Human resource plan – having considered what needs doing, the person in charge of the training process must ask what the personnel requirements of the organisation are in terms of numbers and skills and type of people needed to perform production tasks.

c) Job description and task analysis – the jobs done in the organisation need to be described in sufficient detail to enable a training programme to be prepared. The starting point for this is the job description; however, this is of more use in the recruitment and selection process. For training purposes, a more detailed document, breaking a job down into its constituent tasks, is needed and this is known as a task analysis. No thorough training programme can be prepared without a detailed examination of what a person has to be trained to do. This will provide the basis for decisions about what elements of the task to teach at any one time.

d) Personnel analysis – many training programmes fail to give attention not just to the job but also to the skills required of the person to do the job. It cannot be claimed that the preparation of such an analysis is easy. However, a thorough training programme must try to address these issues.

e) Assessment of the trainee's existing skills – many training programmes fail because they do not give attention to the skill gap. They may assume too much existing knowledge and devote insufficient time to the training process. However, it is equally possible that the organisation may run the risk of boring and demotivating trainees by underestimating their existing knowledge base.

f) Choice of training method – many programmes fail because they choose an inappropriate method of training. Formal training programmes are more suited to some types of job and 'learning on the job' is suited better to others. It is amazing how often training methods are based on historical practice rather than rational analysis. This is not to claim that historical practice should be ignored in this decision since historical practice may well be based on tried and tested methods.

g) Train the trainers – perhaps the most common complaint made by trainees is that those who train them have little skills in training. It must be acknowledged that training trainers is a costly process. However, when all the costs of training are assessed it should be seen as value for money. This is especially important as it should be recognised that affording the skills in training, and the responsibilities of training existing workers, is a potentially important part of addressing their skill growth needs.

h) Monitoring and review – the progress of the training scheme must be regularly assessed. Such questions as 'are the trainees happy or are they leaving the organisation before they are fully trained?' need to be asked. The technique of the exit interview, when people are asked to explain their reasons for leaving the organisation, affords a useful tool in this respect. Many serious problems are avoided by recognising the start of a problem early in any management process.

Development

Organisations have to look beyond the immediate future. They have to plan not just what they intend to do in the future, they have to plan to ensure that they will have staff with the required expertise to do those things. Management cannot guarantee that those people currently holding jobs will continue to do so in the foreseeable future. Things such as sickness do occur; in such circumstances someone will have to be prepared and able to step in at short notice to do those things currently done by the person who is sick. For many reasons, in most circumstances, it is desirable that the job is done by someone currently working for the organisation. These reasons include such things as the development of loyalty to the organisation. The organisation being seen to show loyalty to its staff, the limiting of damage done to established work patterns and established work groups. The importance of these points is examined elsewhere in the text.

The organisation must be seen to develop the skills of its workforce as a important part of the motivation process. An additional extremely important reason for emphasising the role which can be played by development is the contribution it might make in producing a more flexible and adaptable workforce. The need for such adaptability is examined in the section on the Organisational Domain.

In short, for the reasons explained above, management must give its attention to development as well as training. Development can be seen as part of career planning. It must be stressed that, for the full benefits of such development to be afforded to the organisation, it must not be seen as a process reserved for only certain people working in the organisation. Rather it should be seen as a commitment throughout the organisation, available to all. This all-embracing feature of development must be emphasised since in many organisations it is restricted only to senior/middle level management; under such circumstances it can be seen to be a cause of some resentment to those not benefiting and the full benefits of a flexible and adaptable total workforce will not be evidenced.

This does not mean that the task of development is one which is easily achieved. By the very fact that it involves the future not the present, it becomes more difficult to conduct; it is far from easy to predict those skills which will be needed in the future and such things as rapid changes in technology may make such predictions problematical. It is difficult to convince people of their need to develop skills for the future. The reality is that the need for development is something which has to be 'sold' within any organisation. It may be that organisations with task cultures, a topic which will be examined later in this book, might more readily embrace the concept of development. However, the difficulty of a task is as much a reason for doing something as it is avoiding it. The more successful organisations are those which are prepared, to some extent, for all eventualities.

If development is undertaken, a process very similar to that involved in training must be undertaken. The only differences are that the job descriptions, task analyses, and personnel analyses may have to be prepared for future jobs. It must be recognised that such documents are less likely to be wholly accurate predictors of requirements and development exercises which will inevitably lead to more general skills being taught.

Similarly, the development methods which can be used broadly accord with those used for training. However, the very fact that the jobs and existing knowledge may not exist in the organisation at present make it more likely that some formal training becomes more appropriate. This off-the-job development is also more likely to generate the commitment and motivation which is part of the justification for development. People undergoing this development are more likely to feel that the organisation values them if it is prepared to send them away on a course. Additionally, a learning environment removed from the pressures of routine activity will afford the stimulus to acquire such new skills.

Career Development

In the wider organisational development it is essential that the organisation pays attention to developing the careers as well as abilities of its employees. This will demand that the organisation affords in the career plan of its employees:

a) the breadth of experience required to progress the employee through the organisation (e.g. experience in staff and line activities, experience of risk taking and control activities, experience of head office and local activities).
b) a range of role models and guides who will encourage the individual in the acquisition of the wider range of skills;
c) opportunities and challenges to allow the individual to utilise the wider range of experiences gathered.

Such career development can be complemented by the assumption of personal development plans (PDPs) and employee development programmes (EDPs). Personal development plans are constructed by the employee in conjunction with help from the organisation. They commit the individual as well as the organisation to the development programme. EDPs allow, within the work experience and complemented by special courses, individuals a range or menu of development opportunities from which they can plan their development. Since the mid-1990s in the United Kingdom qualifications attached to the accreditation of work based learning have facilitated the concept of PDPs and EDPs. At the managerial level in organisations, recent United Kingdom developments such as the Management Charter Initiative (MCI) has helped reinforce the concept of PDPs and EDPs by outlining ranges of management experiences which might be expected at different levels of management. Finally, the development of organisationally linked Masters of Business Administration (MBAs) have helped consolidate managerial development and PDPs and EDPs in particular.

The Role of Coaching

Over the past few years some organisations have utilised the facility of coaching to help train and develop staff. Coaching allows the individuals to use their day-to-day work as an aid to the learning process. The major aim of the coaching exercise will be to make individuals aware of ways to enhance their abilities and develop their repertoire of skills. It can be used in a wide variety of circumstances ranging from simple training to wider issues of development. The coach would usually be the individual's manager or supervisor.

The coaching exercise is a direct translation from the sporting environment into the wider occupational environment. It is a management style rather than a precise management technique. It requires the adoption of the longer term perspective and develops the repertoire of skills the employee needs now and in the future. The normal work environment is used to facilitate the acquisition or development of these skills. The manager becomes not just a person who orders and controls but one who addresses both organisational and individual needs at one and the same time (just as in football where the player is coached in new techniques and tactics both to enhance ability as a player and usefulness to the team as a whole).

The benefits of coaching are quite varied. Coaching affords the facility of on-the-job training and at the same time it affords the facility of a wider developmental frame. It allows training and development to be executed contemporaneously with production activity. Probably its major benefit is in the creation of an atmosphere between the manager and the employee whereby both are seen by each other in a human and positive light. It creates an environment where both organisational and individual needs are satisfied. In a more general sense the responsibility of coaching encourages managers to apply their mind to the human domain of the management task.

The ability to effectively coach is not one which will be inherently present in all managers; in many cases the attitude of mind in which coaching is nurtured needs to be developed within the individual manager. Coaching will take time and any manager wishing to develop this mode of training and development needs to allocate time to allow it to be undertaken with full effect. All the benefits of employee motivation can only be achieved if the time required to coach an individual properly is allocated.

The Role of Mentoring

Many large organisations are beginning to utilise the facility of mentoring. Under such an arrangement a senior person, not the individual's line manager, is allocated the responsibility of 'looking after' and nurturing a less senior person. Such mentoring may embrace the coaching discipline (perhaps in a less stressful environment), allowing the individual to articulate fears and apprehensions, and to voice preferences for future development; affording guidance to the individual in the undertaking of challenging tasks or assignments; acting as a role model for the individual to follow; and facilitating the individual's network of organisational contacts.

This is an extremely wide range of responsibilities and obviously mentors have to be chosen with care. In many ways such a wide range of skills is hard to teach and organisations may need to discover those people who have the full range of skills already or who would not need much training to develop them. Despite the apparently immense size of this task many organisations have found that it is not too difficult to find individuals who can be developed into good mentors. In fact, the major difficulty encountered has not been discovering such people but allowing them enough time to fully develop their role as mentor.

The benefits of such an approach to training and development are again wide ranging. The support system offered to the individual being mentored is an obvious source of stress avoidance and motivation. Often the mentors, if they are given the time to develop their role, will see the mentoring duties as allowing them to develop the repertoire of their own skills including their people-management skills. When used properly it is an excellent way of facilitating both vertical and horizontal communication channels within the organisation. Finally, it is an extremely effective way of developing, in junior employees, those skills of senior personnel which have been proven of benefit to the organisation. This should be of immense benefit in succession planning and the development of skills within an organisation to allow it to successfully 'ride' the problems of retirement and ill health.

The qualities of the mentor are varied. Whether these are innate or whether they can be introduced with training is not considered in this analysis.

a) The mentor should have empathy with the scheme of mentoring. Clearly a committed mentor is likely to be far more effective than one who has reservations about the concept

b) The person should have empathy with the proteges. If conflicts are found in this area the required degree of mutual trust is likely not to be evidenced.

c) The person should have some experience in the areas they are hoping to develop; this might suggest that the mentor needs to be older than the protege, but age is not always a useful criterion. All this means is that the mentor should have experience within the organisation.

d) The protege should be able to identify with the mentor. This might mean that, far from encouraging wide age ranges, the two parties should have similar age characteristics. An example might be that a useful mentor for a 'career break person' might be someone who has recently undergone the same experiences. It would be helpful if this quality and the immediately preceding one were not seen as competing.

   A more sensitive issue is whether organisations should match people from the same social background in an attempt to establish identification. This is an area which is worth exploring but it should not be construed as automatically meaning that all women proteges should have women mentors or that ethnic minority proteges should have ethnic minority mentors. Perhaps a more sensible interpretation might be that in a large organisation there should be a store of mentors who might fill these categories if the protege requests.

e) The mentors should be successful at their job. As mentors they will be most successful if they can be seen to be overtly good role models.

f) The mentor should have good formal communication skills. Mentoring will involve liaising throughout the organisation and hence the ability to communicate formally to different levels of the organisation can be seen as a desirable quality.

g) Mentors should have good informal communication skills. The most important feature of mentoring is that it should be conducted in an relatively informal, unthreatening environment. As such the mentors have to develop informal communication skills. This quality also applies when the mentor is liaising with other managers about problems faced by the protege. Rarely will such problems be resolved in a formal atmosphere; rather such people-related problems are commonly best resolved through informal meetings.

h) The mentor should have good listening skills. Admittedly this is a quality of communication but given that part of the mentoring process might be concerned with listening to problems without appearing unsympathetic it might warrant special mention.

i) It might help if the mentor were not the protege's line manager. Frequently the mentor might have to try to resolve problems as objectively as possible and it may be that the line manager is not best placed to exercise the required degree of objectivity.

The issue of whether the person should be inside or outside the organisation is also worthy of brief analysis. A carefully chosen person within the organisation will have the required contacts and knowledge to overcome problems. However, a person from outside the organisation is likely to introduce less subjectivity and can more readily afford alternative perspectives. Both choices might be, in the appropriate circumstances, legitimate. If an organisation is to pursue a scheme of mentoring it must make this decision based upon a thorough examination of the circumstances obtaining.

Action Learning

Action learning is an approach to learning, development and leadership which has received attention since the 1980s. It focuses on the increasing pace of change encountered by organisations. This increasing pace of change, it is argued, creates increasing numbers of real life problems where there is no obvious store of knowledge which can be immediately accessed and utilised in their resolution. One of the most prominent workers in this field is RW Revans.

Its extension through domains of learning and development to leadership issues affords to it a wide range of possible applications and/or objectives. It is an attempt to move away from the didactic mode of knowledge acquisition that somewhere there will exist an expert on any particular problem and that once the manager or worker has accessed the taught advice of this person the problem will then be solved.

Rather, this approach focuses on the knowledge and experience of the individual worker in the resolution of problems. Supporting this worker will be both an understanding and involved superior, and interested and involved clients (or co-workers). Action learning involves the creation of an 'action learning set'. This set is shown in Figure 13.2.

It emphasises that learning about some of the more complex matters which affect organisations is best undertaken within a 'learning community'. One participant or member of this community is the problem setter. The problem which is given to the learning community must be a real organisational problem and the setter of the problem will be actively and positively involved in the generation and assessment of the solution. Another member of this community is the person who is directly charged with the problem resolution. The final participants are a small number of fellow workers who have a vested interested in the resolution of the problem (clients).

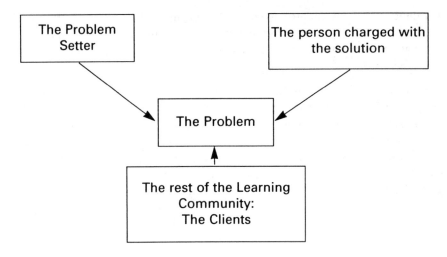

FIGURE 13.2 *The Action Learning Set*

A fundamental assumption of the action learning scenario is that the learners themselves have to isolate the real questions which should be asked. It is assumed that real world problems are so complex that the setting of an assignment or problem to resolve does not, of itself, necessarily predict what the effective questions to be answered are. Essentially the group may be afforded a problem based on symptoms with a view to their evolving both causes and practical resolutions to these causes. All members of the learning set positively support and nurture the action learner in the learning experience. The intention of such scenarios is for this support and nurturing of others to be a learning experience in itself. The typical resolution as outlined by Revans is shown in Figure 13.3.

The aim of such learning experiences is for all participants to learn far more than issues surrounding the problem solved. The intention is that their problem resolution skills in general will be reinforced or considerably enhanced. The thesis would be that they would in future themselves be more confident and hopefully better equipped if they were presented with a problem with no obvious, immediate solution. Finally, they should become more skilled, through observing their own and others' actions in a real life problem resolution exercise, in team building and working with others.

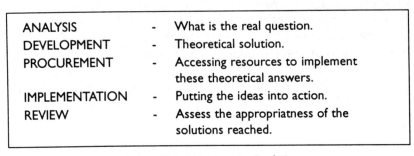

FIGURE 13.3 *Action Learning Resolution*

One immediate possible practical application of this approach to learning is to use the scenario presented as a method of developing and reinforcing managerial skills.

Induction

Induction is the process whereby a new employee is informed of the important features of the organisation other than those which are directly connected with his or her job. It aims to make the employee aware of organisation-wide issues such as organisational culture, needs of internal clients, size of the organisation, structures of departments directly related to his or her own.

Often the induction process will consist of lectures from senior people from different parts of their organisation; often these are complemented with visits to selected sites to see the production process in action. In the case of a local authority, for instance, this may involve lectures from all members of the management team (or their carefully selected substitutes), together with visits to selected schools, old persons' homes, fire stations, etc. Similarly a management trainee in the retailing sector may receive lectures from the sales director, the marketing director, the finance director, together with visits to appropriate sales points.

The major purpose of the induction exercise is to equip the individual with all the knowledge required to fulfil his or her responsibilities to best effect. To properly execute these responsibilities the individual will need to be knowledgeable not just about issues concerned with the production of his or her part in the organisational enterprise but with issues such as the needs and expectations of clients.

However, it must be acknowledged that induction has wider purposes than those concerned with pure productivity enhancement. Allowing an individual to see the wider perspective should be a motivating activity. The full purpose of the job is both explained and, more importantly, often seen. Introducing an individual to the wider organisational perspective early in employment might help provide an environment where, if needed, individuals are able to act in ways which are not rigidly constrained by their precise role definition within the organisation.

Thus induction serves a quite wide variety of purposes. However, as with all such well intentioned exercises it is essential that the task is done well. A common mistake is to chose only those sites which reflect well upon the organisation. New employees are often heard to comment that the 'problem children of the organisation' are never shown on such courses. Any organisation would be unwise to expose new employees to the worst features of the organisation but nevertheless statements identifying the relative excellence of the establishments visited must be made.

Another frequently voiced difficulty in organising induction courses is that of determining the appropriate length. Clearly this is something for the organisation itself to determine. However, care must be taken to ensure that the employee is treated well at each stage of the process; this will demand that at no stage should the employee feel that the lecture or visit is unduly rushed. At the same time lectures and visits can take too long and in such circumstances there is a real danger of boredom setting in.

Finally, it must be stressed that an organisation must ensure that all people involved in the induction process see the process as being of importance to the organisation. An organisation may well be advised to select those involved only from a group of properly trained employees.

Summary

Affording the right skills is an extremely important duty of management. In this exercise, management must be seen to be well intentioned and skilled. The providing of an environment whereby the right skills can be either taught or developed is quite a wide ranging management responsibility. Everyone in the organisation should feel a sense of 'ownership' of and participation in the acquisition of these skills. The benefits of such activity must not be reserved for the selected few. However, mistakes can be made in these processes. It is the job of vigilant management to ensure that these mistakes are avoided. If these mistakes are avoided and all the processes work successfully, the organisation should find itself with a more skilled, more motivated, more flexible workforce. In such circumstances it will find itself better equipped to deal with its tasks.

Exercise

Examine the ways in which you have developed in your social life; compare this development with that you experience in your working life. Critically compare and contrast these two parts of your life.

Further Reading

Armstrong, M. (1992) *A Handbook of Personnel Management Practice*, Kogan Page
Beardwell, I. and Holden, L. (1994) *Human Resource Management: A Contemporary Perspective*, Pitman
Bramham, J. (1995) *Human Resource Planning*, IPD
Bratton, J. and Gold, J. (1994) *Human Resource Management: Theory and Practice*, Macmillan

Connock, S. (1991) *HR Vision: Managing a Quality Workforce*, Institute of Personnel Management

Curson, C. (ed) (1986) *Flexible Patterns of Work*, IPM

Graham, H. and Bennett, R. (1995) *Human Resources Management*, Pitman

Honey, P. and Mumford, M. (1992) *The Manual of Learning Styles*, Peter Honey

Hunt, J. (1981) *Managing People at Work*, Pan

Kolb, D. A. (1984) *Experimental Learning*, Prentice-Hall

Molander, C. and Winterton, J. (1994) *Managing Human Resources*, Routledge

NHS Management Executive (1992) *Guidance Notes on Human Resource Management*

NHS Management Executive (1992) *Right First Time*

Revans, R.W. (1984) *The Sequence of Managerial Achievement*, MCB University Press

Thomason, G.A. (1981) *A Textbook of Personnel Management*, IPM

Torrington D. and Hall, L. (1987) *Personnel Management – A New Approach*, Prentice Hall

Williams, A.P.O. (ed) (1983) *Using Personnel Research*, Gower

Chapter fourteen

Rewarding the Employee

L E A R N I N G   O B J E C T I V E S

- Identify the range of factors which need to be considered in any remuneration exercise

- Examine the contribution which job evaluation might make to the remuneration policy of an organisation

- Appraise the importance of performance appraisal

- Assess the extent to which performance appraisal could be used in the remuneration policy of an organisation

- Examine the importance of the correct management and application of a salaries and wages policy in the achievement of organisational success

---

Job Evaluation

For any organisation to be effectively managed it must have some idea about the nature of each job undertaken within the organisation; furthermore it must have some idea of the relative worth of each one of these jobs. Finally, to an extent, the relative worth of each job should be reasonably reflected in the job rewards systems of the organisation.

Job evaluation is a process which allows an organisation to analyse and assess the content of jobs. Its particular use is the placing of all the jobs in a rank order with the possible purpose of using this rank order as a basis for payment. The aim would be that those jobs identified as high in the order would attract more pay than those identified as low in the order. This is not a technique which enables the precise worth of an individual job to be determined; the relative internal worth of a job is determined since it allows jobs within an organisation to be compared one with another and their relative worth to be assessed. This process should provide a rational basis for the distribution of scarce pay resources. If it is conducted on a regular basis it should ensure that changes in job content are reflected in similar changes in job reward.

The act of placing jobs in an acceptable and accurate rank order is fraught with difficulty. However, as has been attested elsewhere in this text, difficulty should never be used as an excuse for inaction. An examination of the topic reveals that there are a number methods of job evaluation available for an organisation's management to choose. Each one affords both benefits and potential problems to the evaluation task. What all these methods have in common is their reliance upon subjective judgements.

It is important to note that one major feature of any evaluation exercise is its credibility. It must command the support of all, or most, of those working within the organisation. Any attempt to arrange pay in what is perceived to be an arbitrary fashion is naive and undesirable.

RANKING

This method involves the examination of all jobs within an organisation and an assessment of their relative worth. The way in which they are assessed is based upon an evaluation of the whole job and no attempt is made to break up the job into its component parts. Once this process has been completed the relative worth of all jobs will be based upon their place in the rankings.

This technique has the advantage of simplicity but it has a number of potential difficulties. Firstly, it can be seen to be a crude and unscientific way of assessing the worth of the job, in that it places great reliance on subjective judgements about the whole of the job. The judgement of the total content of a job without some attempt to break it up into its constituent parts might be seen to be at best difficult and at worst indefensible. It is possible that a technique which breaks up the job into its component parts would be more easily justified.

Secondly, under this technique widely varying jobs are assessed. It may prove very difficult to compare the job of the managing director with that of the office cleaner. The main problem is that the jobs so vary that any attempt to assess their relative worth may lead to spurious, inaccurate and invalid judgements.

Finally, the results may be impracticable in that they do not recognise established hierarchies or groupings. Thus, no matter how justifiable and accurate the exercise, it might prove difficult to pay the chief executive in a local authority less than the headteacher of a large comprehensive school, or the production line worker more than the production line foreman.

CLASSIFICATION

Under this approach, before any attempt is made to assess the worth of any job, all jobs are placed into groupings or bands based upon established groupings within the organisation. All management jobs will be placed together in one discrete grouping which will be separated from unskilled manual jobs (which in their turn are placed into a separate discrete grouping). Once this grouping has been undertaken the jobs within each grouping are assessed as to their relative worth. The method used to assess this worth is that of the whole job (just as in the ranking method).

This method has the advantage of ease of comparison in that only similar jobs will be compared and assessed. It has the further advantage of not being seen to threaten established hierarchies and groupings.

SKILL
- ☐ Education and training required
- ☐ Experience
- ☐ Initiative and creativity

RESPONSIBILITY/DECISION MAKING
- ☐ Complexity of work
- ☐ Supervising work of others
- ☐ Equipment or process
- ☐ Material or product

EFFORT
- ☐ Mental demands of job
- ☐ Physical demands of job

WORKING CONDITIONS
- ☐ Pressures in the job
- ☐ Difficult or hazardous conditions

FIGURE 14.1 *Factor Comparison for Job Evaluation*

However, it may be that the acceptance of these groupings allows serious anomalies to develop in that established groupings are not subject to questioning even though over time the contents of jobs between groupings may change radically.

Secondly, the method of assessment could be seen to involve the same crude judgements about total job content as would the previous method in that it is difficult to justify the assessment of the worth of a job without breaking it up into its component parts.

FACTOR COMPARISON

In this method a number of qualitative factors concerned with the job are selected such as technical skills necessary to do the job, physical demands of the job, responsibility for subordinates, and responsibility for financial issues. A typical list of such factors is shown in figure 14.1.

The worth of each factor is assessed by the examination of pay in key 'benchmark jobs'. Each factor in the job is then rated against these benchmark values. An example is given in figure 14.2.

A benchmark job is chosen and its constituents parts are assessed. From the total remuneration package attached to that job, the element of remuneration deemed, by subjective judgement, to be afforded to a particular characteristic is determined. An example might be that the finance director's salary is £50,000 and the element connected with his or her responsibility for financial matters is deemed to be £30,000. That is, if the job solely involved responsibility for financial matters he or she would have been paid £30,000. The remaining £20,000 would be deemed to result from other characteristics of the job such as people-management responsibilities. The 'going rate' for this level of financial responsibility would then be judged to be £30,000. If someone spent 50 percent of their time on this level of financial responsibility then for that element of their job they would be paid £15,000. For another job characteristic, such as physical effort required, a separate benchmark job would be subject to similar scrutiny. This technique is more scientific than the previous techniques but it is more difficult to apply; in addition, although it appears to be highly precise, it is nevertheless based upon judgement (both of the job itself and the acceptability of the benchmark jobs). Any accuracy indicated, therefore, may be spurious.

	% of job	pay rate	job value
technical	50%	£10,000	£5,000
physical	25%	£6,000	£1,500
responsible	15%	£30,000	£4,500
finance	10%	£20,000	£2,000
Total Pay			£13,000

FIGURE 14.2

POINTS RATING

This is the most common form of job evaluation found in organisations which use job evaluation techniques. Desired qualities of the job are chosen, similar to the approach of the factor comparison, such as technical skills, financial responsibility, responsibility for other people. Points are allocated to each on the basis of the importance of the characteristic in the particular job and on the assessment of the existence of this characteristic in the job. Thus, for instance, financial responsibility might be weighted double physical effort (that is it receives an automatic doubling of score). A total score is computed and pay is determined on the basis of this score. This technique can be used across all jobs without any attempt to group them, or across jobs already grouped. This technique has the advantage of more apparent accuracy than the first two methods examined but care must be taken to ensure that this accuracy, based as it is on judgement, is not spurious. In addition, it does not involve the difficulty of extracting a benchmark job which was evidenced in the last method examined, but it is still based upon subjective judgement and hence its validity is based entirely upon the validity of these judgements.

Limitations of Job Evaluation

Despite the immense efforts which might be expended on creating and justifying such a scheme and whatever the method or technique of evaluation chosen, the concept of job evaluation can be at best only part, albeit rational, of the financial remuneration within an organisation.

Firstly, it will find resistance if it attempts to depart too radically from existing practice; hence the techniques which permit some grouping of jobs might be more readily accepted. Secondly, individual performance may vary within a given job and the worth of the job to the organisation might be determined not just by the job itself but also by the individual doing the job. This additional complication will be dealt with immediately following this analysis. Thirdly, pay may be affected by market conditions; for instance a job might be valued quite lowly through such evaluation techniques, but, because of scarcity of supply of people with the appropriate skills, the organisation might have to pay high wages to attract people with those skills into the organisation. Finally, the organisation might wish to encourage its workers to be loyal and might wish to pay more on the basis of length of service. This factor is certainly reflected in grade scales in public service organisations where workers start on the bottom of a pay grade and progress through the grade in time.

Introducing a Job Evaluation Scheme

The difficulties or complexities just examined should not be interpreted as suggesting that job evaluation within an organisation is not desirable or indeed, in part, not practicable. However, if an organisation wishes to introduce a scheme of job evaluation it would be advised to adopt certain management procedures.

a) Consult the workforce on the concept and practice – any job evaluation scheme will succeed only if it is accepted by the workforce. If the scheme is imposed upon the employees it is unlikely to be accepted. This consultation should address both the concept itself and the particular method chosen.

b) Training of those evaluating – as has been seen all methods of evaluation demand judgement. Those charged with making these judgements should possess sufficient skills to make, at best, valid or, at worst, defensible judgements. It may be that a pilot scheme may need to be adopted so that any mistakes made are limited in their impact.

c) Establish an acceptable appeals procedure – in a large, varied, multi-purpose organisation, such as many of those operating in the public service, the jobs being evaluated are so varied that any job evaluation exercise is likely to result in anomalies and/or grievances. Under such circumstances the organisation must be seen to deal adequately with these disputes. Organisations may need to provide for a powerful and accepted appeals process to help overcome at least some of the perceived inequities which may result.

It can be concluded, therefore, that the concept of job evaluation affords an organisation one way of establishing a fair basis for remunerating its employees. There are a number of methods or techniques which can be used to evaluate the relative worth of a job. However, a fair system is not necessarily a system which will be accepted readily. The acceptability of remuneration systems is based usually on other factors as well as the worth of the jobs. Thus a scheme of job evaluation, if desired, will not in itself guarantee a readily accepted remuneration system.

Performance Appraisal

The evaluation or the appraisal of an individual's work performance is a topic which has attracted much attention in recent years. It can be seen to be a method of introducing into the remuneration package an element of elegibility which could be built on the rationality afforded by a good job evaluation scheme. Organisations have begun to place much less emphasis on collective remuneration packages and more emphasis on the payment of an individual based upon an evaluation of his or her performance.

It must be recognised that such performance-related pay has long been a major feature of many wage systems but its extension into the area of salaried staff is quite recent. In this context it has become more important to assemble information on individual performance. However, the assessment of the performance of an individual employee has benefits well beyond those affording rational evidence for introducing an element of fairness and flexibility in the remuneration of that individual. These benefits range from motivation enhancement through to improving the observation skills of management and only after assessing the full purposes of performance appraisal can any judgement be made by an organisation regarding its acceptability or its form of delivery.

PURPOSES

a) To determine the level of productivity of the employee and to provide evidence for productivity–linked pay. This feature of the concept will receive further examination later in the chapter.

b) To improve management observation – in organisations where the level of productivity is easily assessed or where the assessment of performance is a stated managerial task, management attention is automatically directed towards workers' performance. It is easy to see why the concept of performance appraisal first became rooted in manual occupations; in many circumstances a manual worker's actual production is relatively easy to measure.

   However in circumstances where the assessment of performance is less easy, for instance in the work of many non-manual workers, particularly those in managerial jobs, it may well be that management observation and attention to performance is not as impressive. The requirement of management to appraise individual performance will improve management observation.

c) To determine current levels of performance – this is really an extension of the previous point in that without the specific incentive to appraise performance it could be that the management of the organisation has incomplete knowledge of the details of current performance levels.

d) To identify areas for improvement – if the management of an organisation improves its observation of employee performance, it should be better placed to determine areas for performance improvement. This should not be seen as a negative approach to the management task since the main aim of an organisation must be to constantly seek improvements in its performance. Appearing to focus on negative aspects of performance can have a detrimental impact on employee motivation; thus any evidence so assembled must be sensitively handled. In most situations such areas for improvement should be used as 'a carrot not a stick'.

e) To appraise the success of the recruitment and selection programme – some organisations spend large amounts of money on their recruitment and selection, but only if they keep a close check on the performance of new recruits will they know that such recruitment and selection has been effective; a poorly performing recruit is a bad recruit.

f) To ascertain the success of the training and development programmes – many organisations spend large amounts of money on training and developing their workers. The utility of these potentially highly expensive programmes can be assessed only after proper examinations of performance improvement have been made.

g) To access the intimate knowledge of the worker – in most management situations either the manager has never done the job he or she is managing, or did the job so long ago that changes in systems, procedures or technology will have substantially changed the job. In such a situation most knowledge about the job lies with the person doing that job. Thus it is highly likely that the individual worker has at least as much, if not more, knowledge than the manager about such issues as to how to improve performance. Certain appraisal methods can be employed which may help 'tap into' this expert knowledge. However, it must be stressed that only certain appraisal methods will access this knowledge and indeed these methods will succeed only if they are handled sensitively.

h) To enhance worker motivation – as has already been acknowledged, appraisal can improve the quality of management observation. If the knowledge so acquired is used in a positive way (eg commending good performance) performance appraisal could be a major aid to the difficult task of motivating employees.

i) To prepare factual evidence for formal reviews/procedures – for instance, it may be that the organisation wishes to pursue disciplinary procedures against an individual employee; in this circumstance it would be advised to have factual evidence to substantiate its claims.

Appraising Performance

Despite the immense benefits to be obtained by measuring employee performance, in many cases such measurement is difficult to undertake; furthermore it will be seen that only when the assessment is handled in a sensitive fashion will all the benefits be obtained. In fact, if handled in an insensitive fashion, performance appraisal can have deleterious consequences for the organisation.

In certain circumstances performance can be assessed easily by simple productivity measures; for instance, if the production process is concerned with manufacturing chocolate bars and the quality of the product is assured by the production process itself, the worker's performance is simply the number of bars of chocolate produced.

However many jobs, particularly those in the public service or managerial jobs in all areas of economic activity, do not afford such easy measures of productivity and more complex and indirect methods of appraisal have to be sought. Each will afford advantages to the appraisal process but it must be admitted that each will attract potential problems which will need to be overcome if the appraisal exercise is to succeed.

a) Judgement by the employee's immediate superior or manager – this is commonly known as 'parent–child' appraisal. This method is the most commonly used. It involves the employee's immediate superior making judgements about the work of that employee. Such an approach has advantages.

   i) It 'gets to the heart' of performance appraisal in that it forces the manager to take more interest in the performance of the worker and should both improve the quality of the manager's observation skills and, if used sensitively, should enhance employee motivation.

   ii) This manager is likely to have more knowledge about the performance of the worker than does any other manager and the judgement will be made on 'firm rock not sand'.

However, there are several disadvantages in this method of appraisal.

i) It may be that the manager concerned has too much of an investment in the production enterprise to judge employee performance on wholly objective criteria.

ii) The manager may be guilty of the 'halo effect' misjudgement of the situation – examined in a previous section of this text. The best example of this would be the circumstance where a previously poorly performing worker will probably have to work extra hard to overcome the manager's pre-judgement of his or her work and motives in the workplace.

b) Appraisal by the manager's immediate superior on the performance of that manager's subordinates – this is commonly known as 'grand-parent–child' appraisal. This method, in its turn, has advantages.

i) The person conducting the appraisal is both less likely to be guilty of the 'halo effect' misjudgment and also is less likely to be seen to be protecting established interests.

ii) It helps the 'grandparent' to identify any managerial weaknesses of the 'parent'. This naturally assumes that these deficiencies are acted upon and as such it may help improve the quality of the information and management throughout the organisation.

iii) When used in a sensitive fashion it can be reassuring and motivating to the employees since they feel that senior management has taken an interest in their performance. As such vertical communication should be facilitated.

These are disadvantages in this method also:

i) The appraisal will be made with less detailed knowledge – the person conducting the appraisal is more removed from operational knowledge and the appraisal may lack both accuracy and credibility.

ii) The workers being appraised feel inhibited in a potentially stressful situation. They may be fearful of criticising production methods to a person of such seniority and the benefit of accessing the expertise of the workers themselves may not be afforded. Only in situations where a proper atmosphere of trust has been established will such an ambitious appraisal method be of full organisational benefit.

c) The appraisal could be undertaken by another line manager at the same level as the employee's superior – this is sometimes referred to as appraisal by 'aunt/uncle'. This has the advantage of providing an objective environment for the appraisal. In addition it can help provide a wider experience for the manager responsible for the appraisal. It can also facilitate better communication within the organisation in that both those being appraised and those appraising are afforded the opportunity to communicate with another department or discipline. However, if the appraisal is conducted in an insensitive manner it could hinder inter-disciplinary communication. This facilitation of communication is of particular importance in large multi-purpose organisations where communication between disciplines can present difficulties.

Finally, it can provide an encouragement to the standardisation of management practices within the organisation. This will only be seen as an advantage if there is a real need to standardise such practices across the organisation; however, if this is slightly altered to suggest that it might publicise and promote best practice, this could be seen as a more certain advantage. It must be stressed that this method is both unusual and ambitious and as such it can result in the appraisal being conducted in an environment of relative ignorance; for instance, the director of social services will have less knowledge about education than will the director of education and the director of marketing will have less knowledge of finance than will the director of finance.

d) Human resource professional/employee – it could be that the people-related problems of appraisal are so difficult to overcome that a manager with specific people-related skills is needed. However, when such a person conducts the appraisal it could be seen to threaten the managerial authority of the operational manager. Similarly, it may be that this person does not have ready access to the facts related to the appraisal.

e) Appraisal of the manager by the employee – this is commonly known as 'child/parent' appraisal – this can be seen to be a particularly unusual and ambitious form of appraisal. However, in certain circumstances it could be argued that the activities of the manager so impact on the subordinates that they have a legitimate right to pass comment on the performance of their manager. If this form of appraisal is used it is essential that the authority of the manager is not seen to be undermined; in addition, assurances must be sought that the appraisal is entirely honest and that employees do not see this as an opportunity to obtain revenge. As with all ambitious ventures, careful managerial control will be necessary to ensure that this type of appraisal is of benefit to the organisation.

f) Peer appraisal – this may be seen as a particularly useful form of appraisal where employees work in groups. In such circumstances employees have a vested interest in ensuring that all members of the group work in such a way as not to hinder the work of the group. However, as is seen in an earlier section, not all groups work in ways which support organisational objectives and the excellent performance of one individual may result in adverse criticism. In such a circumstance the very actions which management wished to encourage would receive adverse commentary.

g) Client evaluation – it could be argued that the performance of an individual impacts most upon the client and that the opinion of the client affords to the organisation an extremely valuable source of information. However, if such a form of appraisal is chosen the organisation must ensure that its employees do not feel unduly threatened and that it is not seen to be abrogating itself from managerial responsibility. If this form of appraisal is chosen it might have most success in an organisation with a client culture (that is in an organisation which sees the serving of clients as its major objective).

h) Self-evaluation – that is the employee evaluates his or her own performance. It could be that this form of appraisal accesses the most detailed knowledge since it is the individual himself or herself who has most knowledge about performance. He or she knows more than anyone where less than full attention and co-operation is given to a job. However, if such a method is chosen an atmosphere of mutual trust and respect must be present. Individuals will be honest only when they feel they can trust those to whom they have given information.

The impression may have been given that only one form of appraisal is possible. However, it may be that there are important advantages in several forms of appraisal and in such circumstances these advantages might be retained only by employing several forms of appraisal. At best these various forms of appraisal will complement each other to provide a more complete impression of performance. At worst they may provide a variety of information, some of which appears to be contradictory, and in such a situation careful assessment of these variations in judgement needs to be made.

Only when the appraisal affords to the employee some facility to participate will full benefit from any form of appraisal be obtained. Any appraisal which does not seek the employee's views will be incomplete and demotivating.

An example of a typical performance appraisal form is shown in Figure 14.3. It shows the sections to be completed by the two parties to the exercise.

Development Centres

A possible way of obtaining both the full advantages of such multiple appraisal and the advantages of employee response is by the use of development centres where employees and appraisers will, removed from the pressures of routine production matters, assess both the present activity of the employee, the areas for potential improvement and developmental needs. Such centres are being used, for instance, by some of the larger health organisations in the United Kingdom public service. An additional advantage of such a centre is that it provides an opportunity for work peers to contribute to each other's assessment. The additional transfer into the area of assessing developmental needs should not be underestimated. Desirable though such an appraisal environment might be, the considerable expense of mounting such a venture must be considered and only if it affords value for money should it be undertaken.

Requirements of the Appraisal Exercise

To succeed an appraisal exercise should have certain features:
a) Careful clarification of objectives - both the appraiser and the appraisee should be aware of exactly what has been agreed.
b) Jobs should be carefully designed to accommodate the new, agreed, objectives.
c) Both parties should feel that the judgements made were fair and objective.
d) Communication should embrace formal, informal and listening elements. If there is agreement on future objectives and standards these objectives and standards

STRICTLY PRIVATE AND CONFIDENTIAL
STAFF PERFORMANCE REPORT

SURNAME .... FIRST NAME(S) ....

Date of Birth ....

DEPARTMENT .... JOB TITLE .... GRADE ....

Length of time in present job .... Date of previous review ....

PART 1   To be completed by Job Holder

i. Have there been any special office or domestic circumstances that have affected your performance of the job during the period under review?
Please answer Yes or No .... If 'Yes', what were they?
....

ii. Are there any ways in which the Company can help you do your job better?
....

iii. Would you like the opportunity to change your job within the Company?
Please answer Yes or No ....

If 'Yes', please explain what jobs you would prefer and why? Are there any abilities which you possess that you feel can be useful to the Company in other work? For example, previous business experience, further education or personal aptitudes.
....

Date ....   Signed ....

PART 2   To be completed by the Job Holder's immediate supervisor

i. What are the member of staff's strong points?

ii. What points need improving?

iii. How are you helping the Job Holder to improve on these points?

iv. How do you intend to develop this member of staff during the next review period?

v. Overall assessment.

vi. Previous overall assessment.

vii. General comments which should include any aspects of the Job Holder's qualities or performance that are not covered above.

FIGURE 14.3 *Specimen Appraisal Form*

should be formally recorded. Such formality will facilitate organisational control over the appraisal process. However, despite this formal dimension to the communication exercise, most communication should be informal in nature. Excessive formality will inhibit the required degree of cooperation. Similarly, emphasis should be placed on the often forgotten dimension of communication - listening. Only when an environment which facilitates listening is created will both parties be able to understand the positions and aspirations of their partner in the appraisal process.

Performance-Related Pay

The concept of paying individuals partly or wholly on their performance is one which has been mentioned previously. Given that it has received much attention in the last few years it is necessary to examine its utility in the total reward process.

a) It helps to reward exceptional performance – it may be that the individual feels unfairly treated by receiving only the same level of pay as that afforded to poorer-performing work colleagues.
b) It helps to ensure that poor performance receives appropriate managerial attention. The mere act of attaching financial rewards to performance assessment should help concentrate the appraiser's attention on the task in hand.
c) It provides a financial incentive for good performance in that the individual can share in the rewards of such good performance.

However, if these benefits are to obtain from such a remuneration system, the system of performance-related pay needs to be managed carefully.

a) The performance being rewarded must be under the control of the individual employee. There is little, if any, point in rewarding someone for a performance which is not under his or her control. At best it will reward unexceptional effort and will not produce the required motivation in the future; at worst it will penalise someone for circumstances outside his or her control. Under this situation the act of introducing performance-related pay can cause resentment and demotivation.
b) Careful consideration needs to be given to the extent of the scheme. Many organisations restrict the scheme to senior management. This restriction may be valid but it can result in the impression being created that either senior management are better treated than 'more humble employees' or that senior management are reaping the financial benefits from the efforts of the rest of the workforce. This is not to claim that such schemes should be used throughout the organisation; however it does mean that the full impact of selective introduction needs to be carefully considered.
c) It is better if there is thorough discussion on the concept of the introduction of the scheme. Such schemes tend to work best when they are not imposed on the organisation's employees. This is of particular importance because it both involves substantial change in the work environment and focuses on probably the most politically sensitive issue in the management environment – pay.

d) There should be some discussion and subsequent agreement on the detail of the scheme – this might be of particular importance in determining what aspects of performance should be measured or appraised. If there is no such agreement then the necessary environment of certainty will not be provided and the necessary commitment to the scheme will not be obtained.

e) There should be sufficient funds available to fairly remunerate exceptional performance. It would be a poor scheme which failed to reward adequately any such performance. This is particularly important because it may be that the motivational effects of the scheme produce immense benefits and, if the promised money is not forthcoming, then massive demotivational effects will follow.

f) The scheme should be seen to possess both horizontal and vertical equity – equal effort should attract equal reward and unequal effort should attract unequal reward. In practice, in widely varying organisations such as those operating in the public service, this equity may be difficult to achieve. However, awareness of the potential problem is at least a step in ensuring its removal.

g) People being appraised must know what is expected of them – they must be given clear objectives and targets against which they will be judged. Again this is not necessarily as easy to achieve as it first appears in organisations which are subject to rapid change. However, if such change does obtain the individuals being appraised must be regularly updated as to what is expected of them.

h) The appraisers must be trained – the difficulties in appraising have been examined previously. This training will take time. Thus care must be taken not to introduce the scheme too quickly.

i) Whilst admitting the existence of confidential information (for instance, individual pay) the system must be operated with optimum openness. If those being appraised feel that important parts of the scheme are shrouded in secrecy the required degree of cooperation may not be obtained.

j) There should be an effective complaints procedure – no matter how well a scheme is planned and operated the nature of the appraisal of performance is so sensitive that complaints will be inevitable. When such complaints are received they must be seen to receive fair treatment.

It can be concluded, therefore, that both the appraisal of performance and its link to financial rewards can be of significant benefit to the effective management of an organisation. This is not to claim that such appraisal is either easy or that performance-related pay is appropriate in all cases.

In the recent past some organisations have abandoned individual performance-related pay. Despite the benefits obtained for the motivation of the individual worker they claim that the scheme is prone to created disharmony in the organisation and in established working groups. This can be seen to particularly apply in environments where individuals' work is interconnected. Under such circumstances it has sometimes proved unpopular to reward these individuals differentially. Rather than continue this disharmony such organisations might want to refocus on group performance-related pay or abandon the pay element entirely. In group performance-related pay it would be the working group and not individuals who would receive the financial reward.

Salaries and Wages

Having examined possible refinements to traditional reward systems, it will be necessary to examine the more traditional aspects of such reward systems. One of the most important, if not the most important, aspect of the management of an organisation's manpower is the way in which it organises its financial remuneration to its employees. It must be acknowledged that the importance of the topic focuses upon only the financial sources of motivation and that the existence of other sources of motivation have been attested previously in this text.

It is necessary to distinguish between the two partly separate reward mechanisms. Salaries are mainly paid to non-manual staff, whereas wages are the main method of financial remuneration afforded to manual workers. However, the distinction between the two types of payment is rooted as much, if not more, in the history and culture of most organisations as it is rooted in rationality. Salaries tend to be paid every month whereas wages tend to be paid more frequently. An examination of practice reveals that the time period for wages payment has increased in many organisations over the last few years. Fortnightly wage periods are now quite common and monthly wage periods are sometimes encountered. In a historical context salaries have tended to be paid through cheques or bank accounts whereas wages have tended to be paid by cash. Again this distinction is disappearing and many organisations pay either few or no wages through the medium of cash.

In a historical context salaried staff used to benefit from more generous conditions of service than did waged employees; an example would be more paid sickness leave. This distinction has become of less importance as, over the last 20 years, the conditions of service enjoyed by the two groups have grown closer together. Finally, the tradition has been for wages to embrace incentive payments whereas salaries have tended to ignore incentive payments. This distinction, in its turn, has become less clear as wages systems not involving incentive payments have developed and as salary systems embracing incentives have begun to emerge. It could be argued, therefore, that it is no longer as necessary to make a distinction between salaries and wages. However, given that the differences between the two systems do exist to some extent this analysis will continue to make the distinction.

SALARIES

There are a number of salary systems which can be used in an organisation. The reality may be that most examples which are found are based upon combinations of systems. For instance, if an employee is paid within a certain salary band but the payment increases every year as he or she progresses through that band, that system could be seen as a compromise between the first two structures which will be examined.

a) A graded structure based on job evaluation – the relative worth of a job is determined through a system of job evaluation. A common variant of this system is that the salary is paid within a certain band and the salaried employee moves through this band as service in the organisation increases. This is the most common form of salary structure. It has the major advantage of ease of calculation and ease of justification. If the job evaluation is deemed to be fair this system should afford the benefit of equity.

b) Rate for length of service under this type of structure — the longer an employee has worked for an organisation the more the employee is paid. The main assumption would be that the longer an employee has worked for an organisation the more worth that employee will be to the organisation. It affords the advantage of rewarding experience; it also rewards organisational loyalty which, in many circumstances, will be of benefit to the organisation in that the longer employees stay with an organisation the less the organisation has to spend money on recruitment and training. It also recognises that the worth of the existing employee is already known whereas that of the new employee is still a matter of speculation. It is an easy system to administer and the importance of ease of administration in a supportive, rather than productive activity, such as salary payments should not be underestimated. The major disadvantage of this type of structure is that it may prove difficult to retain younger and possibly high quality employees since the situation where older, less productive, employees are being rewarded for their efforts can be highly demotivating.

c) Progression curves — in this instance the employee will be paid more when his or her abilities are seen to have improved. One of the more common examples of such a system would be the enhanced payment of an employee upon the gaining of qualifications. This is a common factor in many payment systems in the public service. It could be seen as an increased reward for increased worth. However, it must be admitted that it may be difficult to assess worth and certainly payment by qualification is an imperfect substitute. Nevertheless, it is probable that a qualified employee does afford some increased benefit to the organisation.

d) Performance-related pay — this is examined in more detail earlier in this chapter. It would be commonly seen not as a separate system in its own right but as a useful refinement to a non-performance-based salary level. Care must be taken to ensure equity and accuracy in the judgement of performance; furthermore, such a system should be financed not by increased expenditure but by more efficiency.

e) Profit sharing — this can be used with a wage system as well as with a salary system. This again is likely to be a refinement to a more traditional salary structure rather than a system in its own right. It attracts the particular advantage of granting the employee a direct financial stake in the performance of the organisation. It is an effective, but not the only, way of fostering loyalty to the organisation. The importance of creating common stakes between the organisation and its employees can be seen to be a major contribution to the immense task of developing and facilitating employee motivation within the workplace. It is, however, of more limited use when the performance of the organisation is not reflective of the effort of an individual employee and, as such, these common stakes may seem to lack credibility and acceptability. It is also seen to be a more remote reward than the more immediate incentive payments. However, its main limitation in the context of most of the public service is that it cannot be used as an incentive where the organisation is not one which is expected to make profits.

f) Share option schemes – again this can be used for wages as well as salaries. Under these arrangements employees can be granted the right to buy, or in some circumstances, be given shares in the organisation. It is a facility which has become increasingly used in the United Kingdom private sector. This is very similar in its effect to the profit-sharing option just examined. It has the additional advantage that the common stake is strengthened through the common ownership dimension. Perhaps the main problem is that the extent of the reward obviously depends upon the market price of the share; such a price may not be stable in its worth to the employee and its incentive worth can be doubted. Furthermore, the price of a share is not likely to be reflective of the individual effort of the employee. The major restriction is that in organisations where no shares exist it quite simply cannot be used.

g) Semi-financial rewards – these can also be afforded under a wages system. Examples would be a company car, free medical insurance, cheap or free pension scheme. In many ways such rewards are an attractive proposition to the organisation wishing to use salary as a motivational tool in that the actual financial benefit to the employee could be increased by possible taxation advantages; perhaps more importantly such 'perks' can convey the status or esteem rewards as outlined by the motivational theorist Maslow. However, many of the afforded taxation advantages have been eroded over the past few years through changes in taxation in the United Kingdom.

WAGES

There are a number of wage systems which can be employed in an organisation. Such systems may not exist in their discrete forms in many organisations. It may well be that an individual organisation would make use of a combination of the schemes about to be examined. In fact the tendency has been for organisations to be much more flexible in evolution of their wage systems than in that of their salary systems.

a) Time rate – the employee will be paid a fixed amount irrespective of production levels achieved. This system is particularly appropriate where quality of the product is deemed to be important; there will be no incentive to sacrifice quality for quantity. It has particular uses where effort is not reflected in production levels achieved. It affords to the employee certainty of reward and it is easy to administer. Its main problem is the absence of a financial incentive to perform. In many ways it can be seen that this type of wage system has the characteristic of a traditional salary system; that is, the payment is not based on production levels achieved.

b) Measured day work – under this system of remuneration the employee will be rewarded if a certain level of production is achieved. This constitutes an incentive to perform to a certain level since either no pay or more limited pay will be forthcoming if this level is not achieved. If the level is carefully set the threats to quality, an increasingly important priority of many organisations (see later in the text), offered by many other incentive methods should not be encountered.

c) Piece work – under such an arrangement the employee will be paid according to the amount of production achieved. It is more likely that this will be used as an addition to a time rate system. It has particular uses where the quality of the product can be assured; furthermore, it has particular use where results are reflective of effort. However, care must be taken to ensure that quality is not sacrificed. Such schemes can be dispiriting in that the reward is not certain. They can be administratively complex and the importance of this facet should not be underestimated.

d) Bonus schemes – a bonus scheme is usually associated with an extra payment in excess of time rate payments. It has the benefits of increased incentive to achieve certain levels of production. Its major disadvantage is that it usually proves to be costly to administer. In many ways this can be seen to be the waged equivalent of performance-related pay and as such all the controls which have been suggested for performance-related pay should be introduced into bonus schemes.

e) Group incentive payments. This could be as easily used for salary payment as well as wage payment. It has particular applicability where results depend to a great extent on group effort. A previous section of this book examines the importance of such group productivity. It can prove to be a useful way of reinforcing group spirit. However, if the group feels dissatisfied with the reward achieved it can prove an incentive rather than the intended deterrent to organisationally dysfunctional group activity.

Local Pay Bargaining

The idea of the local institution paying wages and salaries on the basis of local, not national, agreements has attracted increasing attention in the last few years in the United Kingdom. In many parts of the private sector and in most parts of the public service there is a long history and strong culture supporting national pay and conditions of service negotiations. However, in the environment of change which obtains in many parts of United Kingdom and internationally, such practices might be seen to be less relevant and less suited to organisational needs than they once were. This point will be addressed later in the book.

When more competition is introduced it could be argued that the institutions operating in such an environment should be granted substantial freedom and flexibility to operate in these more challenging circumstances. This competition has been seen to have grown in importance within the United Kingdom private sector through the abolition of trade barriers within the European Union. The introduction of competition into the public sector environment has reinforced the need to respond to new and radically different environments.

One response to such change has been the growth in local pay bargaining or partial local pay bargaining within the United Kingdom public service. For instance, the introduction of privatisation creates an environment where more emphasis can be placed on local negotiations in the Water Industry. The National Health Service Trusts have been granted more local flexibility in negotiating the pay and conditions of service of most staff.

These changes acknowledge the need for organisations and their employees to respond more flexibly in their negotiations on remuneration packages in this less certain environment. If organisations in the public service are to be given more freedom in the meeting of business objectives, it might be necessary for them to be afforded more freedom in the examination of the local labour environment. If an organisation is encountering skill shortages in certain areas, it makes little sense to restrict its freedom to pay the rate to attract people into those jobs where those skills are needed. This justification of local negotiations is supported by the fact that in those industries just illustrated such skills shortages tend to be regional rather than national in character. In some senses, then, national negotiations introduce an element of undue rigidity in an environment of substantive change (see chapter on the Management of Change). Local pay bargaining is linked closely with the growth in payment by performance or, more accurately, part payment by performance.

However, when the concept of local negotiations is considered and evaluated, it must be seen to involve extremely politically sensitive arguments. There is little doubt that the concept of local negotiations is based partly on rational argument but also partly on political dogma. If local bargaining and negotiation is to be introduced throughout the public service it should be widely accepted on managerial criteria and not seen to be driven by political considerations. One major problem with the increasing trend towards local pay negotiations within the United Kingdom public service is that a thorough examination of wage and salary negotiations reveals that whether conducted at national, regional or local level these negotiations require special management skills and experiences. It is an undoubted fact that there is a skills shortage of staff with such negotiating ability within most locally or regionally based organisations (including the trade union movement). If this trend is to continue, organisations adopting these changes need to acquire within their ranks such negotiation skills. Such a move can be seen to involve a substantial change and it is difficult to envisage a situation where such a degree of change can be introduced without some controversy and some problems.

The concept of local pay bargaining is not as problematical in the private sector. National agreements are not uncommon in the private sector and changing the basis of remuneration to a more locally determined basis can present problems in organisations with a history of national pay negotiations.

Flexible Employment Patterns and Financial Rewards

As has been acknowledged earlier in this text there is increasing evidence of people being employed on fixed term rather than indefinite contracts. The more flexible employment environment has certain probable impacts on the remuneration of such employees:

a) Individual rather than collective contracts will tend to predominate. As individuals are employed at different times, for different purposes and for different time periods the logic of the collectively bargained contract can be seen to less readily apply.

b) There will tend to be an increased likelihood of an individual performance-related element to be included in the contract.

c) As each contract and job will have its own unique features, remuneration based on established practice will be less immediately relevant; under these changed conditions remuneration based on job evaluation principles will be much more obviously applicable.

Summary

The problems presented to management by employee reward systems are considerable. Financial remuneration constitutes only one element, albeit important, in the total remuneration package. Also included in such rewards are the fulfilling of affiliation and self-actualisation needs as hypothesised by Maslow.

When management attention is directed towards this part of the problem many opportunities are afforded; unfortunately at the same time many potential difficulties are encountered.

A financial remuneration system must be seen as fair by those it purports to serve. The major complication is that of being seen to be fair to all involved. Wherever practicable financial rewards should be related to both the nature of the job and the performance of the individual within that job.

Any attempt by an organisation to introduce significant changes into its remuneration systems should be seen as a major managerial challenge in its own right. Various parties to the negotiations may have well established or even entrenched attitudes. Any attempt to try to effect change in this area may cause these attitudes to be challenged and in many cases resistance to such change can be anticipated. It is the duty of a vigilant management to anticipate all such resistances and to adopt ways of positively responding to them.

Exercise

Produce a job evaluation assessment for a job with which you are familiar. To what extent do you consider job evaluation to be a fair and acceptable system of determining reward?

Further Reading

Anderson, G. (1993) *Performance Appraisal Systems*, Blackwell

Armstrong, M. and Murlis, H. (1988) *Reward Management*, Kogan Page

Bramham, J. (1995) *Human Resource Planning*, IPD

Curson, C. (ed) (1986) *Flexible Patterns of Work*, IPM

Fletcher, C. (1993) *Appraisal: Routes to Improved Performance*, Institute of Personnel Management

Goss, D (1994): *Principles of Human Resource Management*, Routledge

Harrison, R. (1995) *Human Resource Management: Issues and Strategies*, Addison-Wesley

Harvey-Jones, J. (1990) *Making It Happen*, Guild

Hunt, J. (1981) *A Textbook of Personnel Management – A New Approach*, Prentice Hall

NHS Management Executive (1992) *Guidance Notes on Human Resource Management*

Wigley, D. (December 1989) Performance Review, Motivation and Organisational Culture, *Health Services Management*

Williams, A.P.O. (ed) (1983) *Using Personal Research*, Gower

The Organisational Domain

OBJECTIVES

The way in which an organisation is managed is not simply a product of the decisions of individual managers. Rather, in the management of the organisation, individual managers are affected greatly by wider factors such as the organisation's environment, its design, the rate of change to which it is subjected. After reading this chapter the reader should be more aware of the importance of organisation-wide issues as they impact on the way in which the organisation is managed.

INTRODUCTION

When individual managers conduct their management responsibilities they will find that their style is a function partly of their own self-management skills and the ways in which they themselves choose to manage their subordinates. They will find that their freedom of action is substantially affected by wider organisational issues. For instance, they will find that the design of the organisation significantly affects their sphere of managerial influence; they will discover that the established practices and attitudes throughout the organisation will limit the ways in which they can pursue their managerial objectives. In the following section these wider, organisational elements of the management environment will be considered.

Chapter fifteen

The Organisation and its Environment

L E A R N I N G   O B J E C T I V E S

- Understand the concept of the organisational environment

- Identify the constituent features of an organisation's environment

- Examine ways in which this environment can be classified

- Understand the need to examine interrelationships between the constituent features

- Assess the application of this concept as an aid to assessing organisational strength

- Apply the concept in the context of organisations with which you are familiar

- Identify areas where further research might be necessary

Any organisation exists within an environment; that is, it exists within a legislative and moral or ethical framework. Furthermore its range of actions are substantially dictated by the range of employee skills it has available. These factors can be considered to be examples of the environment of the organisation. These and other aspects of the organisation's environment will be examined in this chapter. The major learning aim is to acknowledge that the organisation is constrained in its actions by its environment. That is not to say that this environment is easily determined. Nor does it mean that an environment cannot be changed, particularly in the longer term.

The reality is that it may be difficult on occasions to isolate all elements of an organisation's environment. It may be possible to change individual features of an organisation's environment. For instance, as has already been seen, the people who work in an organisation are an important feature of the environment of that organisation; the people in an organisation can be changed, either in their skills, by training, or by recruiting new people.

Many organisations are so complex that the environment faced in one section will be different to that faced in another. Continuing with the human environment example, the skills and aptitudes of employees in the engineering section may be entirely different from those of the employees in the sales section.

Finally, it must be acknowledged that an organisation's environment will change naturally over time. If a new manager is recruited, this manager will bring different experiences and abilities from his or her predecessor and this environmental change will inevitably alter, to some extent, the way in which the organisation is managed.

It is crucial to our understanding of the nature of organisational environment to appreciate that the various elements of such an environment do not exist in discrete isolation one from another. The reality is that the various elements composing an organisation's environment impact on each other; for instance the manager's views are affected substantially by the skills and attitudes of his or her staff. Consequently when changes are made to one aspect of an organisation's environment, these changes can impact upon other aspects of the environment. A change in legislation (one aspect of environment) impacting upon a health institution can cause greater media attention (another aspect of its environment) to be focused on its activities. Thus the introduction of internal markets in the United Kingdom health service has focused media and public attention on many health issues, not just those concerning the internal market itself.

Environmental Factors

To appreciate fully the nature of an organisation's environment it may be necessary to examine many of the constituent features of this environment. Figure 15.1 shows the nature of these environmental factors as they impact on the organisation. It is important to note at this point that such drawings or environmental maps are a useful facility available to the management of an organisation. One of the major uses of such maps is in planning and organising the reaction to changes in environment. Such diagrammatic presentations afford a practical model which can be used to both plan change and to anticipate areas of resistance to such change.

It is possible to subdivide the environment of an organisation into two main categories: internal and external. It must be noted that the recognition of internal features does not accord with the use of the word 'environment' in common parlance. However, a rigorous examination of all the elements which impose upon an organisation's ability to react to its challenges cannot ignore these internal features.

This is not to say that these two categories are always discrete but it is probable that internal factors will be related more to each other than they will be to external factors.

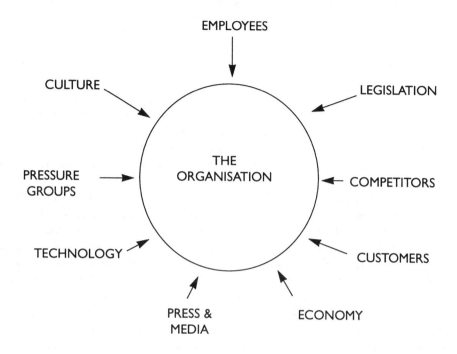

FIGURE 15.1 *The Environmental Map*

INTERNAL FACTORS

a) People – this is one of the more important, if not the most important, elements of an organisation's environment; an organisation will be affected by the skills, the experience, the attitudes, the loyalties and the personalities of its employees. One of the most important contributors to the success of a hospital is the commitment and training of its doctors and nurses. This can be translated into the private sector context. The history of industrial relations in the car industry has been littered with examples of how a disaffected workforce can influence the performance of an organisation.

b) The organisational design – that is one example of an organisation's environment which can be altered. However, in the short term an organisation is constrained in how it meets its challenges by its design. An organisation with tall organisational structures will work in a different way than an organisation with flat organisational structures. Similarly an organisational design based on market segments is likely to behave differently than one whose organisation is based on functions. An organisation whose support services (such as finance and personnel) are provided by central departments is likely to react in a different way to one whose support services are based in operational departments. An organisation which centralises its intelligence gathering activities or learning experiences in a specialist department (such as research and development) will react differently than will an organisation where such intelligence gathering and learning is deemed to be the responsibility of those immediately involved in production activity. The importance of and nature of organisational design will be addressed in the next chapter.

c) Culture – this will be examined in more detail later in this section. An organisation will be affected by the way in which those working in it expect to respond to its challenges. The organisation's workers may expect and accept that its clients will play an important part in the design of its products. Alternatively their view may be that the client has no part to play in its production activities and in fact would be considered to be 'an unwelcome intruder'.

d) Quality of management – in many ways this has been addressed in earlier sections of this text; however, an additional factor to consider is that the emphasis placed on management skills is an organisational issue. Some organisations have skilled managers. Some organisations lay great emphasis upon the development of good management skills. Other organisations tend to promote people on the basis of their technical rather than managerial skills. No matter how well intentioned the manager, his managerial success will be determined to a substantial extent upon whether the organisation deems it appropriate to place him in circumstances where he can utilise management expertise and also whether it affords support to nurture such skills. These variations in standards will impact inevitably on the way in which the organisation operates. The supposed poor quality of management in the United Kingdom public service was the subject of several reports in the 1970s and 1980s, criticising particularly their tendency to promote people on the basis of their technical rather than managerial qualities. The supposed poor quality of management in the British private sector was the subject of several reports in the late 1980s and early 1990s.

e) Group attitudes – the importance of this part of the organisation's environment has been examined earlier in this book. It is important to note that the way in which a manager uses groups is affected substantially by the organisation's policies on group involvement. All people working in organisations are members of a group or, more realistically, more than one group. However, organisations differ in the ways in which they respond to these groups. They can react positively to the existence of group norms, trying to change them by persuasion; alternatively they may refuse to acknowledge the existence of such norms. In short, group activity can be organisationally functional or dysfunctional (it can work for the benefit of or to the detriment of the organisation).

f) Approaches to planning – this aspect of the organisation's environment will be examined later in this text. Some organisations place little emphasis on a formal planning process, concluding that current activity is an acceptable basis for future activity. This has been the traditional approach in the British public service. However, other organisations may consider that future success is ill defined by current activities and may determine to afford a much higher profile to the planning task. Such organisations will tend to be those operating in circumstances of rapid change. The importance attached to a formal planning process, then, can be seen to constitute an important element in how the organisation is managed.

g) Quality of control systems – this, in its turn, will be examined in a later section. Some organisations lay great store by the development of high quality control systems; a good example of this is the great emphasis placed by the police service on its control systems and activities. Similarly, the manufacturing sector places great store by its quality control systems and such systems constitute an extremely important part of the environment of those organisations.

Other organisations do not place such a great emphasis on the control of their activities, preferring to wait until something serious happens before they act. An example might be the more traditional approaches to control of activity exhibited in parts of the British public service where amendments are effected only if serious difficulties are encountered. Such variations in standards will impact materially on the way in which the organisation conducts its business.

EXTERNAL FACTORS

It must be recognised that this aspect of the organisational framework more readily accords with the more common usages of the term 'environment'. External factors constitute the most important aspect of the topic area in that they compose those elements of the organisation's environment which are substantially imposed upon it; alternatively, they constitute areas where the organisation has little, if any, control.

a) Legal constraints – most organisations are restricted by their statutory responsibilities. This can take the form of organisationally specific legislation, for instance many United Kingdom public sector bodies are allowed to do only those things which legislation permits them to do. Or it could be the Memorandum and Articles of Association which restrict the areas of the economic activity of an organisation operating in the private sector. All organisations are affected by more general legislation such as that governing employment regulations. In many ways the most important external constraint on an organisation's management is the restrictions imposed upon its operational activities; the importance of this factor, particularly in the public service, cannot be underestimated.

b) Economic restrictor – all organisations are constrained in their actions or their success by the economic environment within which they operate. This factor can be either the state of the economy generally or the state of the relevant sector of the economy. Organisations working in periods of economic growth in their sector tend to find their activities less onerous than when their sector of the economy is experiencing difficulties. No matter how astute the organisation and its management, if the economic circumstances are such, in the private sector context, that there exists little demand for their products they will, inevitably, be limited in their ability to sell their products and be successful. Equally, in a taxation funded context, if the organisation and its management cannot access sufficient resources to operate effectively, then they will probably be judged as unsuccessful regardless of the skills they apply in their management duties.

c) Social and ethical demands – many social considerations have significant impact upon an organisation's activities. Such factors as threats to the physical environment (Green issues) will place restrictions, over and above legislation, on how an organisation can conduct its activities. If an organisation is examining is waste disposal activities, it may find that it has to address environmental considerations as well as purely economic decisions.

Similarly an organisation may be constrained in its range of options by ethical considerations. These are best characterised in terms of society's ethical standards. For instance, during the Gulf War in 1991 the forces acting for United Nations' interests had imposed upon them, or alternatively themselves assumed, the need to minimise damage inflicted on non-combatants. It may be that the more public environment within which most of the public service operates causes this factor to be of special importance in this sector of economic activity.

d) Customer demands and expectations – it must be recognised that, to some extent, the organisation's actions are driven not by internal decisions but by customer expectations. The precise importance of this factor is impossible to judge universally. The total environment of an individual organisation is to some extent a product of its assumptions about consumer power and the importance of the customer. In many parts of the United Kingdom public sector, the assumption of the importance of meeting customer preferences is quite recent. However, in many parts of the private sector the importance of this aspect of the organisational environment has been long recognised.

e) The actions of competitors – in the real world this is an extremely important feature of the environment of many organisations. The more an organisation is subject to competition the more it is restricted by the actions of its competitors. Organisations need to be mindful of the likely reaction of their competitors before they decide to act in a particular way. For instance, British Telecom will need to be mindful of the market stance of Mercury before it undertakes a particular venture.

f) Influence of suppliers – this, in its own turn, greatly affects the environment of many organisations; an organisation is influenced by the people who supply it with raw materials or component parts. Such factors as response and delivery times need to be considered before new projects can be undertaken.

g) Technology – undoubtedly one of the more important restrictions on an organisation is the nature of available production and information technology. There is no point embarking on a particular project if either the technology prohibits its implementation or if it is impossible to access certain crucial pieces of information relating to its implementation. Also worthy of examination are both the immense opportunities and immense problems afforded by the rapid rate of change of technology improvements. An organisation operating in competitive circumstances will need to be constantly vigilant of opportunities provided by technology to effect a competitive advantage. Here the links between the various elements of the organisation's environment are well illustrated since this point overlaps both technological and competitive features.

h) The activities of pressure groups – this again affords an illustration of an important world environmental issue; many organisations find that they operate in areas where pressure groups are active. In such circumstances the likely reaction of a pressure group to a proposed action is a vital consideration prior to the consideration of a particular course of action. For instance, when deciding to close a school the reaction of parents needs to be considered before action is undertaken.

i) The actions and stances of the press and media – it is important to note that many organisations operate in an open or public environment. These organisations need to be sensitive to press and media reaction to their activities. A hostile press and media reaction is a very important factor to consider before undertaking a necessary but potentially unpopular action. In many cases large organisations ensure that the press and media are courted to try to ensure their favourable reaction. This can be seen to be of particular importance in the public service, although its importance in a competitive private sector context must not be underestimated.

Political, Economic, Social, Technical Environment

If the analysis of the organisation's environment requires, the environmental factors can be categorised not just by their external or itnernal characteristics but also whether they are political (eg legislative environment), economic (eg customer income), social eg relationship with clients), or technical (for example I.T. or manual systems). Figure 15.2 diagrammatically portrays this form of analysis.

	INTERNAL	EXTERNAL
Political	composition, power and influence, culture structure	politics in country, external image
Social	people, teams, groups structures	customers, relationships with local community
Economic	resource costs, funds profitability, roce	market income economic subventions received
Technology	production and I.T./I.S.	production and I.T./I.S. availability

FIGURE 15.2

General, Intermediate, Internal Environment

An alternative classification is one which divides the external environment into those aspects which are intimately connected with the organisation and those which are less intimately connected with it. The more distant category will be known as 'general' and less distant can be classified as 'intermediate'. Figure 15.3 illustrates in more detail this form of classification.

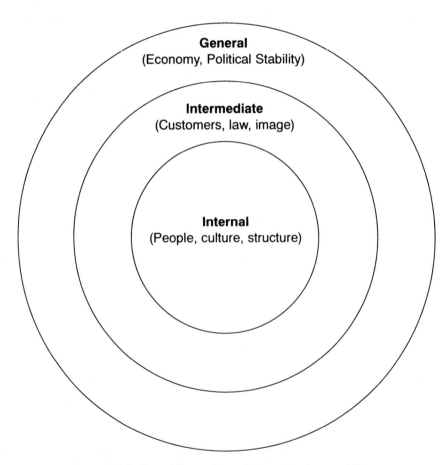

General
(Economy, Political Stability)

Intermediate
(Customers, law, image)

Internal
(People, culture, structure)

FIGURE 15.3 *General, Intermediate and Internal Environmental Factors*

Summary

Undoubtedly organisations are constrained and influenced by the environment within which they operate. An organisation's environment can, on occasions, be changed but such change is very often difficult to control. In many ways the examination of this topic could be considered to be an examination of all aspects of the subject area of management.

It is possible for an organisation to plot or map the environmental influences to which it is subject. Such maps will enable the organisation to be aware of the environmental dimension and fully accommodate all such influences in effecting its management responsibilities and decisions. A more rigorous examination of some of the individual aspects of the organisation's environment will be made in this section and in other relevant sections of the text.

Exercise

Describe and analyse the environment of an organisation or a section of an organisation with which you are familiar.

Further Reading

Beer, S. (1981) *The Heart of the Enterprise*, Wiley
Burns, T. and Stalker, G.M. (1966) *The Management of Innovation*, Tavistock
Etzioni, A. (1971) *A Comparative Analysis of Complex Organisations*, Free Press
Garratt, R. (1987) *The Learning Organisation*, Collins
Kay, J. (1993) *Foundations of Corporate Success*, Oxford University Press
Mintzberg, H. (1983) *Power in and Around Organisations*, Prentice Hall
Mintzberg, H. (1989) *Mintzberg on Management*, Free Press
Morden, T. (1996), *Principles of Management*, McGraw-Hill

Chapter sixteen

International Management

LEARNING OBJECTIVES

- Understand the changes facilitating an emerging international dimension to management

- Appreciate the possible stages involved in the evolution of an international approach to management

- Identify the nature of a global organisation

- Appraise the similarities of and differences between a multinational and a global organisation

- Appreciate the difficulties in establishing a global perspective

- Examine the issues debated in the context of an organisation with which you are familiar

---

The increasing interdependence of world markets has already been examined briefly earlier in this text. The increasing ease of international travel has allowed many organisations and customers to expand their vision beyond their traditional national-based markets into international markets. The increasing access to information, massively facilitated in the late 1990s by the expanding Internet, has allowed organisations greater access to world markets. Information about preferences in all nations is more easily determined. Individuals worldwide have increasing access to products and services throughout the world. Satellite technology has enabled individuals and organisations to experience life in other parts of the world. Financial markets have become increasingly interdependent to the extent that events across the globe can impact on the fortunes of many world economies, not just those immediately geographically proximate. The period of 1980 to the late 1990s can be seen to be the era of the creation of continent-based trade boundaries encompassing the European Union, the North American Trade Agreement and South East Asia Trade Agreements.

All these changes have expanded the market opportunities to many organisations in that, for instance, trade barriers have been reduced and international knowledge transfer has been facilitated. Some commentators have suggested that this international dimension has expanded to create an emerging international culture. All these circumstances allow most organisations opportunities to trade and operate beyond their traditional geographical boundaries. It must be recognised that these opportunities are also available to competitors. Many organisations in this increasingly internationally competitive environment have decided that this global dimension should be addressed positively; to ignore this global dimension would allow competitors to compete in an organisation's own traditional markets. A good example of this global consciousness is the increasing tendency for European and American Higher Education establishments to increase their international presence.

This analysis must not suggest that the natural evolution for all organisations is to expand into international markets. However what it does suggest is that the global market is a legitimate market for many organisations.

Furthermore this analysis should not suggest that this international dimension is entirely a feature of the late twentieth century. Indeed in the United Kingdom the international dimension has long been a feature of the manufacturing sector; the United Kingdom has for at least two centuries been heavily reliant on exporting its manufactured products. Companies such as ICI have long had a global presence. The analysis does however reveal that the changes of the last few years have enabled organisations outside the pure manufacturing sector to increase their global aspirations.

The Development of the Global Organisation

Kreitner (1995) suggests that for many organisations the assumption of a global aspiration is an evolutionary rather than revolutionary phenomenon; over a period of time an expanding organisation develops global dimensions.

DOMESTIC ACTIVITY

In this stage the organisation's operations and perspectives are concentrated on the domestic market. All activities are based on market research based on domestic markets.

INTERNATIONAL ACTIVITY

At this stage the organisation begins to expand its horizons into the international arena. It is characterised simply by the organisation exporting its products or services. Thus, for instance, higher education establishments will seek to enrol overseas students.

MULTINATIONAL ACTIVITY

This stage of development has long been evident in the American automobile industry in that American companies have sought to manufacture their cars in Europe. This has allowed them to dramatically reduce their costs. Indeed the reason for this development many decades ago was that to manufacture cars in the USA and simply export them to foreign markets would have been cost prohibitive. The multinational organisation is characterised by its international operations; it is also characterised by its firm home base for such issues as resource allocation and expansion. In the United Kingdom for many decades concern was expressed about the sizable presence of American companies whose resources were directed from the United States.

THE GLOBAL ORGANISATION

In the 1990s management writers have hypothesised a distinction between the multinational organisation and the global organisation. The former will always retain its national roots whereas the latter is much more globally focused and globally located. The global organisation, if it exists, will have few, if any, national loyalties. It will deploy its resources around the world with the perspective of the world being its market and its natural home base. The global perspective is perhaps best illustrated by the words of Mr Goizueta the Chief Executive Coca Cola in 1996: 'We used to be an American company with a large international business. Now we are a large international company with a sizeable American business.' The global perspective of Coca Cola is shown in Figure 16.1

It is suggested that there are two stages in the development of the global organisation.

THE GLOBAL HIERARCHY

In such a stage the organisation bases its various specialisms in different locations. This is illustrated by automobile companies manufacturing different models in different locations around the world.

THE FULLY GLOBAL ORGANISATION

In such an organisation resources are deployed throughout the world with no rigidity. Thus the organisation could produce all its products or services in all countries. Under such circumstances the organisation will be able to adapt to any local circumstances prevailing in local markets. In the case of McDonalds, for example, if a particular country has unique dietary requirements or preferences these will be readily reflected in the products afforded in the country. In 1996 McDonalds changed its range of products in France to more readily harmonise with French preferences.

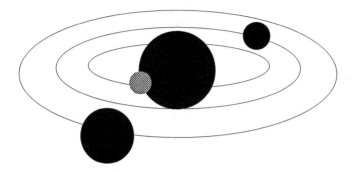

● 1886 Cure for Headaches -1 Shop   ● 21st Century Sales in 195 Countries
● Relationships with 155 Countries   ● More than U.S. Government

● Drunk in Space

FIGURE 16.1 *Coca-Cola - The Global Dimension*

Figure 16.2 showing the range of countries in which Coca Cola is sold might illustrate the global nature of the Coca Cola Corporation.

FIGURE 16.2

Developing the Global Perspective

Naturally the assumption of this perspective may need to be developed and nurtured in the organisation. As is mentioned elsewhere in this text the assumption of the flexible approaches needed in a varied global perspective rather than those based rigidly on national values will be far from easy to effect.

The global organisation will need to develop attitudes and values which reflect the variety of human experience found through the world. The organisation should not inhibit its development by rooting its approaches in one culture. It will need to be appreciative of and responsive to different religions. For instance, McDonalds operating in India might have to understand that products based on beef are unwelcome. Similarly an organisation operating in an Islamic country may well be advised to allow its employees the opportunity to express their religious beliefs by offering regular prayer periods and locations. Indeed such a global organisation might feel it necessary to appreciate that employees of the Islamic faith in non-Islamic countries should be afforded similar facilities.

As much business is transacted face to face, global organisations need to accommodate cultural variations in non-verbal communication. Managers moved around the world will have to be trained in appreciating cultural and national differences in acceptable personal space - that is the area of space which should not be invaded in interpersonal face to face communication.

The global organisation needs to be aware of the distinction between high and low context cultures. In Europe and the United States (low context cultures) communication focuses strongly on the words used in the communication exercise. As such business contracts tend to be effected through carefully and precisely chosen words. However in high context cultures and countries, communication through mechanisms other than words can assume supremacy. For instance in Asia great emphasis is placed on the formalities of communication such as introductions. In Japan the apparently trivial (in American and European culture) exchange of business cards is a massively important part of business activity. In modern American and European cultures, with heavy emphasis on equality and participation, the position of the person in the organisation is of relatively minor importance; however in high context cultures the position of the person can be extremely important. For instance in the Middle East and Asia there is an expectation that hierarchies should be carefully observed when transacting business. In some Asian countries it can be considered the legal contract is actually exchanged by shaking of hands rather than through precise wording on paper.

The global organisation needs to appreciate that the concept of time can vary throughout the world. In America and Europe time is deemed to be monochronic - that is, schedules and precise timing are extremely important. However in other cultures such as the Middle East time is not considered to be monochronic; in such circumstances time and schedules are deemed to be flexible. A Middle Eastern business person will not consider it to be poor practice to be late for a meeting; as long as the business is transacted within a reasonable time period no offence will be taken.

The importance of understanding these nuances of culture, attitudes, values and behaviour cannot be underestimated. Sometimes these variations can appear, when judged against those based at the national level, to be very strange. An organisation seeking to be global in its perspective must educate its managers to fully appreciate and positively respond to these variations.

Attitude and Culture

For a global organisation to succeed it has to give express attention to developing the right type of attitude in its managers and to developing organisational cultures consistent with its global perspective. In this context it is possible to isolate three types of attitude and culture:

ETHNOCENTRIC

This approach will tend to emphasise the values of the home country. In such circumstances the organisation would automatically seek to transact its business in the language of and with values reflective of its own nation. An example might be a British educational establishment seeking to educate overseas students but using the English language and in the United Kingdom. This is not to be disparaging of such an approach. From the organisation's perspective it is the least expensive and most convenient option. However if that organisation finds itself competing against a more flexible approach, where for instance consideration is given to the home language of the student, it may find itself less favourably positioned in terms of winning contracts.

POLYCENTRIC

The polycentric attitude and culture will be accommodating to the values and customs of the customer's country. Business will be transacted in the manner of the country of the customer. Local managers will be educated in the business values of the community in which they are operating.

GEOCENTRIC

This type of value and culture is based on the assumption that the adoption of purely polycentric approach will present certain problems for the organisation. The polycentric approach may result in managers specialising in transacting business in one country. This specialisation might inhibit the organisation's ability to deploy employees and managers throughout the world in line with its developmental needs. Furthermore the variety exhibited may result in a loose arrangement of subsidiaries or sections. In certain circumstances this looseness may cause the organisation to be uncertain of its organisational mission, its organisational values and its unique features. Some observers suggest that the truly global organisation will develop an approach which, although appreciative of the variety of cultures within which it operates, also embraces a unique organisational perspective. This perspective will allow the organisation to accommodate variety of experience without sacrificing the organisation's own unique attitudes and values.

The distinction between the three approaches in the context of higher education is shown in Figure 16.3.

Domestic	Polycentric
Students come to UK	Students educated in own country
Students educated in English	Students educated in own language
Students educated in British practice	Students educated own practice
All staff located in UK	Staff based in separate countries

Geocentric
Students educated wherever they choose
Students educated in whatever language they choose
Students educated in any practice they choose
Emphasis in curriculum to international dimensions
Staff moved where needed and according to development needs
Unique organisational approach to education - common educational methods used

FIGURE 16.3 *Domestic, Polycentric and Geocentric approaches to Higher Education*

Does the Global Organisation Exist?

The analysis to date suggests that, with the will, an organisation can be transformed from a domestic organisation to a geocentric or global organisation. The latter type of organisation sheds itself of any national values and loyalties. Its market and its focus is global and in no way will this global perspective be threatened or compromised by national considerations. However such an approach might be seen to be unrealistic in practice. It can be argued that there are still strong forces preventing a multinational organisation acquiring truly global characteristics. These forces may be particularly powerful in times of scarcity of resources. At such times it might be that these forces will cause undue loyalty to local, home-based interests. No matter how global the operations of the organisation it is possible that financial ownership may cause it to retain its original national base; no matter how global the operations of a Japanese enterprise its financial ownership may continue to be located in Japan. Hence it might be naive to assume that this geographically-centred ownership will not be reflected in decision making. Given that an organisation is to a substantial extent profits-driven there might be a tendency for decisions to be taken in the interests of those receiving these profits. A slight variation to this theme is the fact that decisions might also be taken which reflect the taxation residence of the supposedly global and geocentric organisation. Even if there is a wide distribution of financial ownership it is likely that there will remain a firm, usually original country based, strategic apex. Under such circumstances it might be equally naive to assume that the home country loyalties will be so easily sacrificed. A common accusation is that the high tech, research-based, future-focused operations of organisations are frequently located in the local national base of the strategic apex.

Summary

It can be concluded that there is an emerging international imperative in the managerial environments of many organisations. This imperative is driven by the reduction of international trade barriers, by ease of access to information, by ease of international travel and maybe by the emergence of an international culture. If an organisation seeks to take advantage of the emerging international market it has to change its perspective in that it has to be increasingly appreciative of variations in values, attitudes, behaviour and business practices. However it must be acknowledged that the assumption of this changed perspective is very difficult and maybe, in its purest form, impossible.

Exercise

In the context of an organisation with which you are familiar determine an approach to facilitate its adoption of a truly international perspective in its operations. Appraise the difficulties it might encounter in the development of such a perspective.

Further Reading

Hall, E. T. (1976) *Beyond Culture*, Anchor Press
Hofstede, G. (1990) *Cultures and Organisations*, McGraw-Hill
Kay, J. (1993) *Foundations of Corporate Success*, Oxford University Press

Kreitner, R. (1995) *Management*, Houghton Miffin
Usunier, J. C. (1993) *International Marketing: A Cultural Approach*, Prentice-Hall International

Chapter seventeen

Organisational Design

L E A R N I N G   O B J E C T I V E S

- Understand the importance of organisational design in the successful management of an organisation

- Identify the various forms of organisational design which might be encountered

- Appreciate the importance of identifying diversity in attempting to map the design of organisations

- Appraise the factors which need to be considered when an organisation plans its design

- Apply the concepts studied in the context of organisations with which you are familiar

- Identify areas where further research is necessary

As has been mentioned in the last chapter, one of the most important determinants of organisational success is the appropriateness of its structure, design or arrangement. Most large organisations employ people with varied skills and expertise. Despite the fact that in previous sections of this book the flexibility of the human resource has been stressed, it must be admitted that one of the most important determinants of, or limitations on, the success of human enterprise within an organisation, is how individuals are grouped within the organisation.

Dawson (1993) defines structure as 'the creation of rules, roles and relationships which, at best, facilitates effective coordination and control, as far as corporate governors are concerned'.

The importance of informal organisational structures has been examined previously but it is an undoubted fact that formal organisational structures to a great extent shape individual and group activity. The fact that person A is institutionally grouped with persons B,C, and D, to a substantial extent determines that his or her communication will be more extensive with these persons than it might be with person E, who will be part of another group or section. Reinforcing this will be the fact that, in most circumstances, persons A,B,C, and D will, by the organisations formal structure, be charged with forms of human enterprise different from those allocated to others. This must not be interpreted as a claim that organisational structures are the only factor shaping individual actions or freedoms but rather that such formal organisational structures are a very important constraint on individual action. Nor should it be claimed that all organisational structures totally constrain or limit human endeavour; rather the realistic claim can be only that formal structures can and often do, to a substantial extent, shape human actions. Thus it is likely that someone grouped into a finance section will devote most of his or her operational activities to financial matters.

When an organisation decides how to arrange its operational activities it is presented with a number of choices. Sometimes the organisation will choose a universal option and all its activities will be similarly arranged; sometimes it will choose different options for different parts of its activities. Sometimes an organisation will arrange its activities in the same way at the different levels of responsibility; sometimes the organisation will choose different options at different levels of responsibility. This diversity of options for organisational design will be explained and illustrated during this chapter. Whilst acknowledging that an examination of activity within a particular enterprise would reveal diversity and hybrid forms of organisational design it is nevertheless necessary to examine each major type of organisational design in its purest form.

Design by Product or Market Segment

In this circumstance the major or only feature of the arrangement of responsibilities is that each individual product is provided by a different group of people. A diagrammatic illustration is provided in Figure 17.1

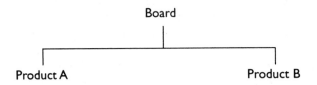

FIGURE 17.1

An example of this form of arrangement would be the existence of a separate housing directorate and a separate social services department under the control of the one United Kingdom local authority. It must be realised that such arrangements can obtain at lower layers of authority; for instance, the social services directorate would be organised into separate sections to administer its different products such as children's service, services for the elderly. In its purest form each product section would provide all the activity required to produce that product, including direct product delivery activities and connected support services. An example in the private sector would be a group arrangement where each subsidiary would operate in different economic sectors with virtually complete autonomy. This form of design affords certain advantages and problems.

ADVANTAGES

a) When the organisational design affords separate and mostly autonomous organisational groupings for each individual product area, both communication with clients and individual product designs should be aided. If the individual decision-making section has only one product and only one client grouping to deal with, then such an arrangement should focus attention on the demands of that product and that client grouping to maximum extent. Thus it is likely that such an organisational design would, if accepted by all the workers, facilitate the development of a task or client culture (see next chapter).

b) It should foster inter-disciplinary communication: all the people working on the production should have the same loyalties and work priorities (ie the production of the product). Both those working in direct delivery positions (eg school canteen workers) and those providing support facilities (eg finance, personnel) work for the same production activity and should develop common or shared purposes. As has already been seen in this text, inter-disciplinary communication is one of the major problems facing any large, complex organisation. This better communication should result in a situation where the support services provided are individually designed to meet the potentially unique needs of the individual production activity.

These advantages can be seen to be extremely important but it must be acknowledged that there are some problems with this form of organisational design.

PROBLEMS

a) The career development of those working in support service areas (eg finance or human resource experts) may be hindered or restricted by the lack of breadth of experience afforded by such a design. At any one time the accountancy experience gained in a school meals section will be restricted to those financial issues concerned with school meals. It could be argued that this problem of career development could be solved by moving those in support services around between product groupings to widen their experience. This is a solution to the problem but it renders the advantage of loyalty to product delivery advantages previously quoted redundant.

b) There may be major common features in the support service needs of the various product groupings. Under such circumstances there may be losses of the economies of scale afforded by larger separate support service departments. An example would be that, in unit terms, it would probably be cheaper to process the wages of those working on several products than to provide for each separate product to have its own wages run.

c) To some extent the professional integrity of certain support services, notably finance, may be sacrificed to the short-term gain of the producer department needs. For instance those involved in the finance discipline may come under pressure to reduce internal controls to accommodate short-term economies. In an organisational design which reflects a more function–centred arrangement those in support services can be protected from such pressures.

Design by Territory or Region

In such a design the main or only criterion in the arrangement of responsibility is geography. Each geographical area is afforded its own separate organisational division. A diagrammatic presentation is given in Figure 17.2

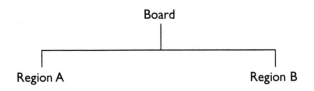

FIGURE 17.2

An example of this form of design would be the regionally based Inspectorate of Education within the Department of Education and Science or, in the private sector context, the different regions of British Steel. In its purest form all those working on the product delivery, whether directly or in support service areas, would work for the same department. Circumstances where there may be compromise arrangements will be examined later in the chapter. Such a form of organisational design has certain attractive features and certain drawbacks.

ADVANTAGES

a) If the different territories are identified in such a way that the different regions embrace differing patterns of client demand, then this should result in more attention being focused on the particular needs of these different client groups. Thus, for instance, certain geographical areas may have different prevailing problems. An examination of any industrialised country would show that the demographic balance of age groups tends to vary across this country. Thus, for instance, if there is found to be a higher proportion of school-aged children in an inner city area then the local authority representing that area should afford high priority in its resource allocation to the serving of the needs of that community. Another local authority area may have a high percentage of elderly residents; in this local authority area the social services activities would need to be emphasised. To some extent, therefore, it is the recognition of geographically varying needs which has dictated that in the United Kingdom local authorities be afforded some freedom in their operational activities.

b) It presents a more accessible communication channel to clients. A client wishing to communicate with the organisation is able to contact it with greater ease; for instance, a neighbourhood office in the local authority housing function allows ease of access to tenants wishing to pay monies or to report problems encountered.

PROBLEMS

a) The problems with the support advice functions identified in the previous option may be encountered also in this arrangement, for example problems of career development, inefficient use of resources, compromise of professional standards.

b) The whole rationale of the arrangement demands that there are geographical differences in client needs. If these differences do not exist then the need for geographical autonomy diminishes. This was at the heart of the argument in the United Kingdom when the National Curriculum was developed in the late 1980s as an attempt to impose national standards on what many saw to be an unnecessarily diverse education system.

c) The problem just examined could result in other difficulties. If the standards of education or health, provided by the regionally organised public sector, vary too much across the country through such a form of organisational design, then the labour mobility in the country could be hindered. Alternatively, if the standard of steel manufactured by the regionally-based steel organisations varied too much, the reputation of the parent organisation would suffer. However, it must be stressed that this potential problem is restricted to a small number of activity areas.

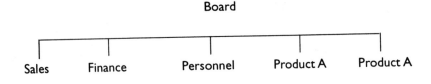

FIGURE 17.3

Design by Function

In this circumstance the organisation arranges its activities by function or by professional specialism. A diagrammatic presentation of this situation is given in Figure 17.3. An example would be an engineering company organised along traditional lines; in such a situation there would be a separate finance department, personnel department, legal department, marketing department and engineering department. Throughout all sectors of economic activity this is the most commonly encountered form of design. It is the form of organisational design recommended by traditional or scientific management theorists such as Weber. It concentrates on the advantages to be obtained by the division of human enterprise within an organisation into small specialist areas. It is best suited to those organisations operating in relatively stable environments and to organisations where the support needs of different products are similar. This form of design affords a number of important potential advantages and problems.

ADVANTAGES

a) It provides an opportunity for many employees, particularly those working in what are recognised to be professional disciplines, to develop their career to maximum effect. For instance, the human resource professional should be able to practise on the full range of human resource activities across all production activity within the organisation.

   The need to satisfy the career development needs of staff, particularly those in support functions, is in reality not an advantage in its own right but a reflection of an organisation with a person culture. The difficulties of undue concentration on such a culture are examined in the next chapter.

b) It should ensure that professional standards in support services are not sacrificed to the short-term needs of production. This will be a function of there being separate responsibilities for the heads of the separate departments. Thus, the integrity of the finance discipline should be protected by a head of finance who is institutionally independent of the heads of production activities. However, it must be recognised that the professional integrity of support services is not an end in its own right; rather the quality and standards of support advice should be determined by the needs of production. This is not to claim that professional integrity should necessarily be sacrificed. Support advice should meet the needs of production in both the long and short term. It is only when there is a conflict between these two time scales that the demands of professional integrity should intrude. For instance, the limiting of internal controls to advance short-term economies may impact negatively on production in the longer term and under such circumstances the demands of professional integrity should intrude.

c) It affords the benefits of specialisation and economies of scale, in both production and in support service activity areas.

PROBLEMS

Under these arrangements there may be a tendency for support service needs of customers to be ignored or not to receive due attention. For instance, the potentially different budgetary demands of different production departments may not be as immediately satisfied as they might be if these support services were located in producer departments. Similarly, this form of design may produce a tendency to ignore the cost of support services. If the support services were located in producer departments there may be an increased tendency to question their cost efficiency and effectiveness; they would be viewed more readily as a cost of production and could be subject to more cost scrutiny. In many ways this is not a problem of organisational design but of lax management practices. To some extent this problem could be overcome by introducing more cost and service consciousness within a centrally provided service department by, for instance, competitive tendering and service level agreements.

Design by Matrix

Under the arrangements of such a design, the authority over people working in an organisation is divided between a functional or professional manager and a product manager. It could be viewed as a hybrid of the functional and product forms of organisational design. In most cases where a matrix design is used an employee will be seconded to work on a variety of projects. The employee would be responsible to the product manager for ensuring that the work done was properly matched to the demands of the particular task; at the same time he or she would be responsible to the functional manager for the professional integrity of his or her work. An example might be found in the higher education service; the functional manager would be the manager of the academic discipline and the product manager would be the person charged with developing and running a particular course within the institution. It may well be that from time to time the product and functional manager are the same person; for instance, in the higher education context the functional manager would be responsible for both teaching standards and research (research being an example of a product).

This is a common form of design in companies where an emphasis is placed on flexibility in work practices and where the production activity revolves around differing products; it is of particular utility where such products are relatively short lived. A diagrammatic representation of this form of design is found in Figure 17.4 This form of design affords several advantages which can be considered to be broadly equivalent to those in both of its constituent forms of design.

	Sales	Engineering	Finance
Product A			
Product B			
Product C			

FIGURE 17.4

ADVANTAGES

a) It should focus the attention of the different disciplines on the demands of production and upon client demands. This should be ensured by the work of the product manager.

b) It should ensure that the advantages of maintaining professional standards are not sacrificed. This should be assured by the work of the functional manager.

c) It should facilitate more flexibility than would obtain under a pure functional organisation. The professional knowledge and skills of the expert can be harnessed to the particular demands of particular tasks. This advantage should be reinforced by the variety of work to which the professional is exposed. Thus it can be seen that this form of design might aid the career development of employees.

d) It should encourage inter-disciplinary communication. The more the different disciplines come together in task meetings, the more they are exposed to each others' needs and perceptions. Furthermore, the need to meet client demands through the use of different skills should encourage the development of a team spirit or an accepted common goal. The importance of developing a team psychology on many occasions has been already examined in this text.

e) For the design to work to maximum extent there is a need for a participatory style of management to be used by the product manager. The benefits to be obtained by optimum involvement of all people working on a task has been examined in depth in a previous section of this book.

f) Where the system works well it should eradicate the conflicting demands, previously identified, of meeting the unique needs of individual products and the need to maintain certain professional standards. Under these circumstances the respective managers and the respective professions should each more readily appreciate the contribution of the other. It can afford to the individual worker both the stimulation of providing a professional standard and also the stimulation of tailoring professional standards to the precise needs of differing production tasks.

The advantages just examined are seen to be very important and matrix organisational designs are being used increasingly throughout many sectors of economic activity; however, the use of a matrix design does present certain potential problems.

PROBLEMS

a) It is a potentially costly form of organisational design; the introduction of the two types of manager increases the numbers of managers. However, in a career development context this could be seen as an advantage.
b) It is a potentially confusing form of organisation; certainly in the first stages of its introduction there will be confusion amongst staff as to who is responsible for which domains of activity.
c) There is the possibility that conflict between the two types of manager could develop. This is a real difficulty since the one will approach the problem from a professional or functional perspective whereas the other will approach the same problem from a task or product perspective. The establishment of effective communication channels between the two groups should help overcome this difficulty. At the same time, it must be admitted that the establishment of effective communication is in itself a very difficult and probably expensive task. Essentially, a matrix organisational design affords both the benefits and disadvantages of the marriage of differing organisational cultures and this will be examined in the next chapter.

The Complexities of the Real World

As has been mentioned previously, the various types of design are rarely encountered in their purest form. In most large, complex organisations different designs are used for different parts or different levels within the organisation. This might be best illustrated by examining an extract from a possible design within a large health enterprise, shown in Figure 17.5. In this situation the health institution can be seen to be divided at the first level of responsibility partly on a product basis with separate departments for community and hospital services, and partly on a functional basis with central support services. The community services department is then sub-divided on a territorial basis into Area A and Area B. The next level of organisation then divides each community health area into different products. This reflects the different solutions needed at different levels in the organisation. The institution's community services department would be responsible for determining the overall community health strategy and priorities of the institution. Within these broad strategies and priorities, the different areas would determine the required action through their special knowledge of the needs of that area. These actions would then be implemented by the district nursing, school health, health visiting sections with their specialist knowledge of the particular needs of their respective client groups. Underpinning this would be the central support services department providing to all levels a functionally based and driven service.

It must be stressed that this is a hypothetical design produced to illustrate the mix of designs which could be encountered. For instance, at the area level the tasks could be effected through a matrix design. Perhaps, to reflect the more complex environment of the real world, we could introduce the complication of working groups spanning all disciplines (matrix design).

It must be emphasised that this is merely an extract from what would

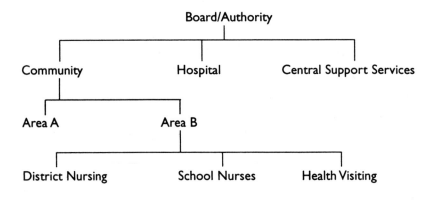

FIGURE 17.5

probably be a much more complex overall organisational design. It may be, for instance, that the hospital department is organised purely on a product basis; whereas the central support services department could be organised purely on a functional basis.

Thus in a large, multi-purpose organisation there may well be different designs adopted for different tasks and at different levels of responsibility within the organisation. The more varied an organisational design, the more likely it is that the individual solutions adopted meet the particular problems of the various levels and activities. However, a complex and varied organisational design is by its nature more likely to demand effective communication between the different parts of the overall structure to eliminate, for instance, any problems caused by overlapping areas of responsibility.

Decentralisation of Decision Making and Management Structures

One very important determinant of the desired organisational design is the extent to which it is necessary or suitable to devolve or decentralise decisions to direct service producers. This is an issue which will vary from organisation to organisation and indeed vary within an organisation. The vast majority of recent management thought has addressed the issue of the desirability of decentralising management decision making wherever possible. However, a rigorous examination of this topic will reveal that the desirability or otherwise of decentralising decision making is a product of a number of interrelated features of the job being examined. The following analysis will be based in part on the work of Mintzberg (1983) and a development of his ideas, where appropriate, into a more comprehensive examination of the subject area. It must be stressed, at this stage, that the conclusion reached from the examination of each individual feature will not necessarily be wholly clear in all cases. An example of this judgement problem is presented well in the first feature examined.

THE COMPLEXITY OF THE ENVIRONMENT

In some ways the more complex the environment the more need there is to devolve decisions to service providers. The environment will be so varied that the standard responses dictated by a centrally-based decision-making system would not be appropriate. Thus, for instance, the curriculum demands of subjects in higher education vary greatly with the subjects being studied and it could be argued that a significant degree of autonomy needs to be given to those with the expert knowledge of each curriculum area. Similarly, the commercial environment faced by different subsidiaries is likely to be so complex that a significant degree of autonomy needs to be afforded to those most familiar with the environment of each individual subsidiary. At the same time there is a greater need for senior centrally-based management to exert some control in a complex environment than there is to exert control over a simple environment. It is probably the case that the balance of the argument dictates that decentralised solutions are best in these circumstances and that the central control exerted is kept to the bare minimum necessary.

THE HOSTILITY OF THE ENVIRONMENT

If the environment is hostile (eg large numbers of consumer complaints or extensive competition) there is a need for the organisation to assume significant control over the situation. This will dictate a more centralised solution to the problem of organisational design since the ultimate responsibility for organisational performance and success will lie with central senior management. Any organisation receiving adverse publicity in the media might be advised to exert more stringent organisational controls over its activities until the adverse criticism is overcome. This argument can be seen to be a powerful centralising force in the usually more competitive environment of the private sector, in that the existence of a competitor could be judged as constituting a hostile environment.

THE DYNAMISM OF THE ENVIRONMENT

If the organisation is facing a rapidly changing environment, any design which slows its response such changes can be seen to be undesirable and in rapidly changing environments the usual desired design solution will be one of decentralisation. However, on some occasions the change can be so substantial that the organisation needs to influence central control to reassert control over the situation. Thus at one and the same time a dynamic environment produces forces driving both centralised and decentralised solutions. The precise judgement to be made will be a product of the particular circumstances of the case in question.

CONSENSUS ON APPROACH

The more consensus there is on the methods of working, the more central solutions can be applied; if there is no consensus on a method of operating there can be no central 'fount of knowledge' on the issue. The absence of such consensus may well be a product of rapidly changing circumstances and it is necessary to appreciate that the various factors outlined may be interdependent.

RISK OF FAILURE

If the risk of failure is great there is a need for the central management of an organisation to exert control over the situation, since the responsibility for ensuring organisational success lies with centrally-based senior management. This is a very important factor in many public service activities. Many people would argue that there will continue to be a need for some degree of central control over public services for this very reason. Naturally this argument can, in its turn, be seen to argue strongly for a degree of central control in a highly competitive private sector environment.

In the real world these factors will not always argue in consistent directions. For instance, the environment within which many computer development companies operate is both complex and hostile. In such a case, the various facets of the environment argue for differing solutions. It is the task of those charged with prescribing the organisational design to assess the relative importance of the competing arguments. In the public service the relative strengths of the competing arguments are often a matter of judgement; furthermore, it must be stressed that these are often matters of political judgements made by party politicians. The design of an organisation can, very often, be seen to be partly a matter of rational argument and partly the result of a subjective political judgement. Such political judgements are not an uncommon feature of decisions affecting organisational design in the private sector.

Outsourcing

An area of management activity which has assumed some prominence recently is outsourcing. This is where an organisation externalises a particular part of its product or service to an outside organisation. This is most commonly undertaken in functional or support activities.

REASONS

There are several possible explanations for the growth of this management activity:

a) The legislative environment – this applies in the many parts of the United Kingdom public service in that such organisations are obliged by statute to put some of their services out to competitive tender. If this tender is won by an external agency the natural outcome is outsourcing. However, it must be admitted that some organisations have assumed this solution without being forced to so do by legislation; hence it is inevitable that these organisations are driven by other, more managerially based, reasons.

b) Competition – organisations may be anxious to test the efficiency of their internal monopolistic providers by liberalising the market and inviting competition.

c) New services – not all support activities are historically based in that some support services emerge through new organisational and legislative environments. A good example of this might be the growth in importance of counselling. As a support service increases in importance the organisation might consider that the internal skills it has in this area may be insufficient for the changed circumstances and, in such a situation, it might seek the help of outside agencies.

d) Enhanced skills – the organisation might be attracted by the reputation of an external agency. This might be seen to be a variant of classifications just examined but it might be considered to be a category in its own right. Even if it were satisfied with the quality of provision of an internal provider and even if it were not anxious to introduce competition, it might seek to gain the unique expertise of an external agency. This is quite commonly evidenced when a number of recently retired experts in a field form a company and market their unique experience and expertise.

e) New perspective – again this might be seen as an illustration of categories already mentioned; however, if the driving force is primarily the seeking of a new perspective or originality in an area presently internally afforded, this will warrant separate analysis. Inevitably it can be seen to be closely linked to the category just considered.

f) Reduce human resource management and other non–production problems – some organisations might find that too much of their attention is directed towards human resource issues and too little towards production issues. Under such circumstances an organisation can eliminate the former problem by contracting with an external agency to provide a service. Under such a contractual arrangement the human resource management problems are assumed by the sub–contractor. Another example of this category might be where the organisation feels far too much attention is being directed to budgetary control issues and far too little attention to production issues.

The extreme extention of this philosophy is the concept of the 'one person firm' where the proprietor of the business sub-contracts for all services he or she cannot directly produce.

g) Refocus – again, in some ways, this could be seen as an example of issues already addressed but it has assumed such importance that it warrants special classification. Under these circumstances the organisation may wish to change its focus or enter new markets. If this is the case it may need special help in established or new support services to penetrate that market. This help will commonly be found in external agencies. An example of this might be circumstances where an organisation has internally provided the marketing function but in attempting to enter new, more specialist, markets it might need the help of external marketing organisations.

PROBLEMS

It can be seen that outsourcing, in most cases, constitutes quite radical managerial change and might encounter the management of change problems addressed elsewhere in this section.

a) In most cases it will involve reduction of staff. These problems are examined in another section of this book. In these circumstances the organisation must strive to maintain the morale and goodwill of remaining staff. Any existing positive team spirit should be maintained and the breaking up of established work groups and work patterns can be seen to be a problem.

b) The change may necessitate restructuring and under such conditions the remaining staff and remaining managers will need to be consulted about the new approaches. This should not suggest that, at the first sign of resistance, the organisation should return to the status quo but that the matter needs to be 'sold not told'.

c) Any restructuring needs imagination and the organisation might very easily enter into outsourcing without making complementary changes in its other management structures.

d) As soon as an organisation has transferred any part of its productive activity to another agency it has lost immediate control over that part of the production process. Any production problems suffered by the sub-contractor will immediately affect the organisation undertaking the contracting. The organisation should seek to introduce financial penalties in its contracts which will enable it to seek alternative sources.

e) When an organisation transfers its support services to an external agency it loses some flexibility. It will be bound by the precise terms of the contracts whereas, if the service were provided internally, minor unforeseen alterations could be easily accommodated. In its contracting the organisation should try to ensure that such minor, irregular, unforeseen alterations can be accommodated immediately − possibly followed by a subsequent contract amendment.

f) In certain cases the organisation might have to provide the external agency with personally or commercially sensitive information and it is necessary to protect this confidential information within the terms of the contract.

g) When an organisation transfers some of its activities to another organisation, this might impact on its corporate image. This issue needs to be thoroughly examined before any organisation undertakes this exercise.

CONCLUSION

The concept of outsourcing is very much a part of the management agenda of many organisations; there are certain circumstances where it can afford net advantages to organisations. However, such organisations must consider any problems and seek to overcome them before entering into any such arrangement.

The Learning Organisation

The concept of the 'learning organisation' is one which has received considerable recent attention. One of the major themes of this text is how organisations undergoing rapid environmental change can arrange for all aspects of their management arrangements to be equipped to positively and successfully adapt to such changing circumstances. This particular issue is focused on the way in which the organisation designs its intelligence-gathering functions. This is of particular importance when organisations encounter environmental change. One major feature of such circumstances is the need to appreciate that environmental change has actually happened. Intelligence gathering is an essential feature of coping with or managing of such change.

Although later parts of this section will emphasise that adapting to change is not entirely a management structural issue, the way in which the organisation manages or arranges its intelligence-gathering activities is important in predicting its likely success in such circumstances. Whilst appreciating that many of the options available to enable an organisation to adapt to circumstances of change will be examined elsewhere in this text, it is important that intelligence gathering is briefly addressed at this stage in the book. There are two major options available for such structural organisation.

CENTRALLY THROUGH A SEPARATE FUNCTIONAL DEPARTMENT

This has the advantage of ensuring that there is a pool of expertise (for example, a research and development department) available which enables the organisation to react to the need to change. Such a form of design should allow a powerful intelligence-gathering function to develop. The specially designated and, probably, specially trained staff should afford the resources necessary to identify the need to change and to sustain the organisation in its reactions to such change.

A major problem with such an approach is that the centrally-located staff may become remote from consumer needs. In addition, the location of such a central department might cause those with the most detailed knowledge of consumer needs to feel alienated. This is reinforced when it is acknowledged that consumer signals are very often first detected by those who have direct contact with customers. In many cases these people will not be dedicated intelligence gatherers but production workers and the intimate knowledge of such potentially invaluable intelligence gatherers will be ignored.

To conclude, therefore, such centralised solutions afford both advantages and problems and this form of centralised design is probably best when the perception of the need to gather intelligence is not well embedded in the organisation.

A DECENTRALISED APPROACH

Here, the major responsibility for intelligence gathering lies with those who produce the product or who interface with the consumer. This has the advantage of establishing ownership or internalisation of the importance of intelligence gathering amongst all employees in the organisation. Also the detailed knowledge of these employees is used to maximum effect. Such an approach is probably suited to a more mature intelligence-gathering process.

However, it is probably ill suited to circumstances where the need to monitor 'need to change signals' is not well recognised in the organisation. Under such circumstances the more promotional environment of centralised solutions could be more effective.

Securing Effective Management Within Departments

Irrespective of the design of an organisation or arrangement of responsibilities between departments within an organisation, the management structures within each department can vary. There are two main options.

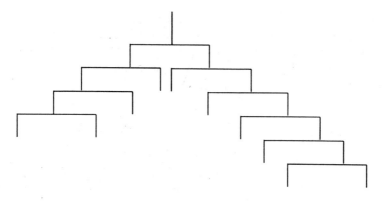

FIGURE 17.6

TALL STRUCTURES

Under this form of inter-departmental structure each manager supervises relatively few subordinates; there is a small span of control (the number of people supervised by one manager). A diagrammatic presentation is given in Figure 17.6. This form of structure has certain advantages and certain problems.

a) It limits the manpower management burdens on the individual manager. The considerable challenge, and probable burden, afforded by such manpower management has been stressed earlier in this book and anything which eliminates the undue burden on the manager can be seen as an advantage to the whole enterprise. However, limiting the area of responsibility of each individual manager affords an expensive form of management. Consequently, an arrangement which obtains more management duties from each individual manager would be less costly in pure financial terms.

b) As there are several levels of management, it affords good promotion and career development possibilities. The importance of the need for organisational attention to be directed towards individuals' growth needs has already been emphasised. This type of management arrangement affords the satisfaction of such growth needs within the routine operational activities of the organisation. However, such an arrangement may inhibit the fulfilment of the growth needs of those lower down the organisation in that, as each manager has relatively little responsibility, there is only a limited need to delegate work. Thus there will be little incentive to develop subordinates and to enrich their jobs.

c) It should at least facilitate, and at best emphasise, vertical communication within the organisation. Despite the acknowledgement of more complex forms of communication, it must be noted that the organisation still needs to ensure good and precise communication channels between management and employees. However, such a form of design makes the communication across the organisation more difficult; for any cross-organisational communication to take place there will be the need to involve many managers. Equally, if there are many layers of hierarchy within an organisation then communication between the top and the bottom of the organisation will be a complex problem in that each layer of hierarchy would be able to impose its own interpretation on the motives and content of the particular communication; there is an increased possibility of corruption of the message sent the more people are involved in the communication exercise.

FLAT STRUCTURES

Under this form of organisation, each manager or supervisor controls relatively large numbers of subordinates; there is a wide span of control. A diagrammatic presentation is given in Figure 17.7. It must be stressed that this is an extract from the organisation chart. Under this arrangement all the second layers of manager might supervise as many people as does the person on the extreme right hand side of the chart. This form of structure in its turn affords to the organisation both advantages and problems.

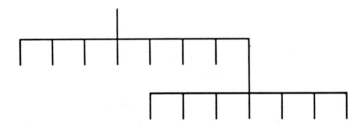

FIGURE 17.7

a) Given that each manager has large areas of responsibility there will be a need to delegate quite extensively to subordinates. Thus there is a greater likelihood that subordinates would be developed and have their growth needs provided by enriched jobs. However, it must be acknowledged that this arrangement keeps to a minimum the number of managers, thus there are limited promotion prospects. The incongruity of developing people for jobs they may never get the chance to occupy must be recognised and those most knowledgeable about the individual enterprise must make the decision as to which factor, the positive or the negative, is the most important within that enterprise.
b) Under this form of arrangement the number of managers is kept to a minimum and the financial costs of management should be reduced.
   However, this form of design places great responsibility and burden on the individual manager. The negative consequences of individual stress have received detailed analysis earlier in this text. The organisation must not make short-term judgements about the need for managerial economies at the expense of loosing the services of managers through stress-related problems.

c) Since there are only a few layers of levels of hierarchy within the department, vertical communication should be facilitated, in that there are fewer layers of hierarchy through which a communication from the top of the organisation to the bottom or vice versa needs to travel.

Given that organisations have the option of choosing one or other of these arrangements, it will be useful examine the factors which the organisation should consider in the design of its internal departmental arrangements.

a) The extent of geographical dispersion of the subordinates – in some ways a large geographical dispersion will strengthen the argument for flat structures in that, if the manager cannot regularly meet the subordinates, he or she will increasingly rely on these subordinates showing initiative. Such initiative is facilitated by flat structures. However, it must also be acknowledged that such infrequent opportunity to meet subordinates demands that managers maintain some effective control over subordinates' actions; under such circumstances, tall structures may facilitate the more necessary managerial control over these dispersed subordinates.

b) The variety of work done by the subordinates – if the employees work in widely varying skill areas an arrangement limiting the numbers of persons for whom a manager should be responsible would be desirable. Tall structures should be used since the more widely varying the activities needing to be supervised, the more need there is to control these activities. However, if the people work in similar skill areas the task of the manager will not be as difficult and flatter structures might suit.

c) The abilities and aspirations of subordinates – if employees are well-educated and trained then they may find the more intrusive style of management found in, and encouraged by, taller organisations inhibiting and demotivating.

d) The culture of the organisation – the importance of this factor is examined in detail in the next chapter.

It must be recognised that these factors are not necessarily mutually supportive; rather the reality may be that some arguments sway towards flatter structures, whilst at the same time other arguments may sway towards taller structures. Under these circumstances an organisation must evaluate the importance of the various factors and make the appropriate decision. Equally, it must be stressed that the arguments may vary radically from department to department and in some organisations there may be a universal style of intra-departmental design; however, in other organisations the desired solution may vary from department to department.

Downsizing

Since the early 1980s the concept of downsizing or, as it is sometimes known, rightsizing has assumed considerable importance in both management theory and practice.

The underlying management principles of the concept have been examined in the immediately preceding part of this chapter; however its recent importance as an economic and management concept warrants specific analysis.

Downsizing was originally advocated by those seeking efficiency improvements. They argued that many traditional Western organisations employed too many people. Technology could be utilised to greater effect and, more importantly in this context, managerial efficiencies could be achieved by reducing the number of managers. In an increasingly competitive environment, it was argued, all organisations had to pay attention to the efficiency of their operations. The proponents of this concept argued that the workers losing their jobs would then be released to work in new organisations and new economic areas. Thus, although there might be short-term social costs, the longer-term consequences of downsizing would be greater economic growth.

The managerial outcome of the philosophy of downsizing is leaner organisation with the managerial structures just examined. Flatter management structures and job enlargement and enrichment can be seen to originate from the management domain. Downsizing, however, can be seen to have its roots in the economic domain. Flatter management structures and the related job enlargement and enrichment have long been advocated for development and motivational reasons. For instance, on 22 May 1996 on BBC Radio 4, Herzberg suggested that downsizing was merely the result of his theories of job enrichment, examined in an earlier chapter, being applied throughout the economy. However, since the early 1980s this advocation has been enhanced by the seeking of efficiency through reducing the workforce and seeking more efficient management structures. If an organisation could achieve efficiency savings and simultaneously extend the responsibilities of managers, the case for downsizing was seen to be very powerful.

Since its inception there has been significant opposition to downsizing – from employee organisations, from those who pointed to the short-term (and maybe longer-term) social costs of reducing workforces, from those theorists who expressed concern about the breaking up of established working groups, and from those who expressed concern about the increased levels of stress which might be found in leaner organisations with more stressful jobs. However, from the early 1980s until 1996 the benefits of downsizing were see to outweigh the short-term problems it created.

Although it is difficult to attach authority to precise dates for the increased potency in the counter arguments to downsizing, from 1996 the claimed benefits of downsizing have become more vigorously and openly questioned. More managers and management theorists began to publicly question the realisation of its claimed benefits. They pointed to the limited increase in economic activity and questioned the extent to which markets operate as efficiently as first claimed; the reality, it was stated, was that the opportunities for unemployed managers and workers to move into new areas of economic activity were limited. Management theorists began to question more openly the motivation effects within organisations. They pointed to higher stress levels and the limited evidence for enhanced motivation. Equally management theorists began to publicly express concern about the loss of skill and the reduced ability to focus on continuity in an organisation which has undertaken downsizing. For instance, in the BBC Radio Programme just mentioned Mintzberg stressed that in many downsizing exercises organisations might not just lose employees but also their most skilled employees. Similarly, he claimed that this loss of expertise might inhibit an organisation's ability to react positively in a competitive environment.

CONCLUSION

Downsizing has been extensively used in many areas of economic activity. Inevitably such extensive use much attest to its validity as an economic and managerial concept. However, it would be remiss to avoid examining the views of those involved in management who have become increasingly suspicious of its universal validity and applicability.

Mintzberg (1983) – Types of Worker and Types of Organisation

An alternative perspective on organisational design might focus on which group of workers assumes dominance in the management process. Mintzberg hypothesises five types of groups of worker in a typical organisation. Figure 17.8 diagrammatically shows the relationship between these types of worker.

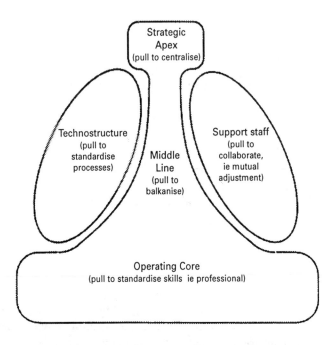

FIGURE 17.8 *Mintzberg's 5 Factors*

a) Strategic Apex – this group composes the senior, strategic managers of the organisation. Their typical function would be to set the overall strategic direction of the organisation.

b) Middle Line – this group would be composed of middle level managers. In a group of companies they would be senior managers of each subsidiary.

c) Operating Core – this group would consist of the production line workers.

d) Technostructure – these workers are concerned with the design of procedures and processes. Examples would be those employees supervising financial or human resource procedures.

e) Support Staff – these employees are typically concerned with affording expert, support advice. Examples of such workers would be those who offer financial or legal advice.

The first three groups of worker are intimately connected through their primary concern with direct service or product delivery. The relationship between these three groups is typically hierarchical. The final two groups tend stand somewhat apart in their organisational roles in that they are typically less intimately concerned with product or service delivery.

Mintzberg further hypothesises five different types of organisation which, respectively, reflect dominance of each type of worker.

a) Simple – shown in Figure 17.9

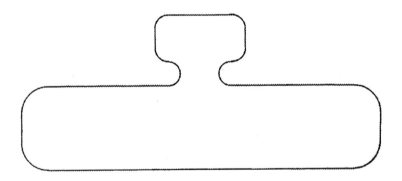

FIGURE 17.9 *Simple structure*

This organisation is dominated by the Strategic Apex. It relies on a single source of power and a single source of intelligence. It suits a simple environment with a good example being a small, owner managed organisation.

b) Machine Bureaucracy – shown in Figure 17.10

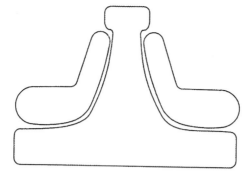

FIGURE 17.10 *Machine bureaucracy*

It is reflective of a somewhat larger organisation than that of the simple model. Work is allocated according to division of labour principles. It is controlled by rules and regulations. It will probably be designed according to functional principles. It is likely to develop hierarchical power bases. An example would be the operation of the Prison Service.

c) Professional Bureaucracy – shown in Figure 17.11

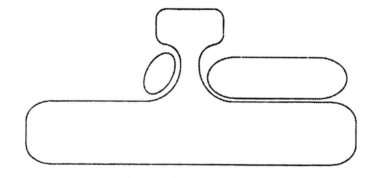

FIGURE 17.11 *Professional bureaucracy*

In this type of organisation the operating core will have significant autonomy. The major aim of such an organisation would be to minimise administration. Support functions, such as finance, would be substantially decentralised. It best suits an environment where major environmental and client variation exists. The primary feature would be that the production workers would be given significant power to determine the pattern of product or service delivery needed for each individual client. It is important to note that this does not mean that the operating core necessarily consists of lower level employees. The distinguishing feature is that they are direct deliverers of goods or services. An example of this approach would be the traditional autonomy given to academics or health professionals. Another example would be the autonomy afforded to partners in professional practices.

d) Division or Diversified - shown in Figure 17.12

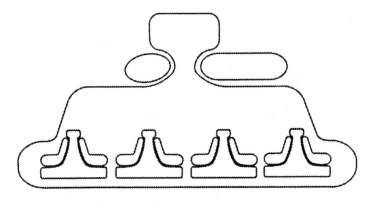

FIGURE 17.12 *Divisional form*

In such an organisation the individual business managers are given considerable freedom to direct resources according to prevailing environmental circumstances. This type of organisation is commonly found where the individual businesses are mutually independent. Middle line workers are particularly forceful in this type of organisation. Examples might be the new managerial approach to education or health.

e) Adhocracy - shown in Figure 17.13

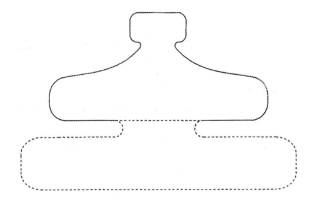

FIGURE 17.13 *Adhocracy*

Such an organisation is dominated by the support structure. It is typified by circumstances where the management of the delivery of the individual product or service is deemed to have primacy. It would tend to be managed according to interdisciplinary project teams. Examples might be found in the construction industry. In such circumstances it might be that the predominant principle of organisational design is that of the matrix. However perhaps the best illustration of this principle is in individual activity areas within organisations. Under these circumstances the support adviser becomes the major focus of decision making. An example might be the evolution of an organisation wide approach to recruitment and selection.

The theory of Mintzberg is particularly interesting since it marries various dimensions of management in that, for instance, it embraces design, culture, communication, processes.

Mintzberg also hypothesises one further approach to managing an organisation which might emerge on rare occasions. He suggests that there are instances where the organisation is imperfectly described by assuming the primacy of one group or other. These instances occur where the primary force in the organisation is its ethical stance. This might be found in a small charitable organisation. It is examined in a later chapter of this section of the text - Ethics and Management.

Recent Developments

Since the early 1990s new approaches to organisational design have emerged. They can be seen as a response to the need for organisations to increase their flexibility in order to respond to rapidly changing circumstances.

STRATEGIC ALLIANCES

There has been an increase in the number of organisations seeking to access new expertise not by developing their own expertise in a particular area but by forming an alliance with another organisation which can afford that expertise. Thus there is emerging a growth in a contracting environment between organisations; under such circumstances they will enter into contracts to jointly provide a product or service. This allows organisations to expand into new markets without being constrained by traditional organisational structures. If the new enterprise proves successful it can be extended; if problems are found the contract can be reconstructed; if it proves unsuccessful the contract can be concluded with minimal negative impact in organisational terms. An excellent example of this was the emergence of Virgin PEPs in the United Kingdom in 1995 where the entrepreneurial Virgin organisation formed a relationship with the traditional-based financial organisation Norwich Union to provide low-cost, easily accessed PEP facilities. Virgin did not have to seek to employ new expertise and similarly Norwich Union did not have to excessively concern itself with managing change; the alliance formed allowed Virgin to afford its expertise in innovation and Norwich Union to afford its expertise in the area of economic activity.

NETWORK ORGANISATIONS

Network organisations have merged from the complementary desires to develop flexibility in organisational design, to empower and develop staff, to develop cross-disciplinary collaboration, to encourage experimentation, to facilitate common values and cultures across disciplines.

First advocated by Toffler and Handy in 1985 they are characterised by flattened organisational designs, with the expansion of project teams. Individuals are encouraged to move outside the traditional source of expertise and begin to relate to other sections in seeking new market opportunities. Such innovation objectives are built into job descriptions and work objectives. The organisational design which complements this more mobile work environment can be seen to be much looser than that connected with more stable work programmes. A useful example might be found in the higher education environment. Traditionally, organisations operating in that environment have organised their staff into subject specialisms. There has been a strong, but admittedly not universal, tendency for courses evolved within this environment to focus on those subject specialisms. However, under this new approach interdisciplinary courses needed in a rapidly changing environment might be facilitated by a looser arrangement which encourages interdisciplinary interaction.

As with the strategic alliances just examined, once the network developed has achieved success it can be consolidated. If the network develops problems it can be refined by, for instance, bringing in new areas of expertise. If the network reaches fruition but cannot be consolidated it can be dissolved. If it fails it can simply be dissolved. The important feature of this approach is that failure must be accepted as an inevitable consequence of the innovatory environment and not something which needs to attract stigma and blame.

Perhaps the most important constituent feature of a network organisation is its culture. The concept of culture is examined in the next chapter. However, in anticipation of the contents of the next chapter, the values which such an organisation will exhibit will be ones which espouse the virtues of innovation.

A network organisation will fail if it is not complemented by staff with the required skills. The nature of such an organisation has been seen to be its cross-disciplinary features. If such cross-disciplinary activity is to develop, staff will need to be skilled communicators with highly refined social, personal and teamworking skills, as well as professional skills.

Finally it should not be seen as a top down solution to cross-disciplinary enterprise but rather a bottom up approach to decision making and innovation. Hence, in design terms, the major problem which might be found is not that of ownership by staff but the releasing of control by senior managers.

Summary

The task of determining a design for an organisation is very often a complex one. Organisational design is only one, albeit important, element of those aspects of the total management task which impact at the organisational level. Large, complex organisations can be designed in different ways. Solutions can take a centralised or decentralised form. The structures adopted in one part of an organisation can and often do vary from those adopted in another part of the organisation. Each form of organisational design has advantages and disadvantages. It is the task of the organisation itself to decide upon the best way to organise or design its activities. Naturally, in making this decision it must consider all the circumstances which obtain within its overall environment. The thorough examination of the topic of organisational design shows that certain forms of design are best suited to circumstances of stability and simplicity. However, when situations of uncertainty or complexity obtain, differing forms of organisational design can assume more attractive features.

Exercise

Choose an organisation or directorate within an organisation. Examine the factors which determine the forms of organisational design it exhibits. Examine an alternative design which might achieve equal or greater degree of organisational success.

Further Reading

Argyris, C. (1964) *Integrating the Individual and the Organisation*, Wiley

Audit Commission (1989) *Managing Services Effectively – Performance Review*, HMSO

Bains Committee (1972) *The New Local Authorities: Management and Structure*, DOE

Beer, S. (1981) *The Heart of the Enterprise*, Wiley

Burns, T. and Stalker, G.M. (1966) *The Management of Innovation*, Tavistock

Child, J. (1984) *Organisations: A Guide to Problems and Practice*, Harper and Row

Curson, C. (ed) (1986) *Flexible Patterns of Work*, IPM

Dawson, S. (1993) *Analysing Organisations*, Macmillan

Drucker, P. (1977) *Management*, Pan

Etzioni, A. (1971) *A Comparative Analysis of Complex Organisations*, Free Press

Garratt, R. (1987) *The Learning Organisation*, Collins

Handy, C. (1991) *Gods of Management: the Changing Work of the Organisation*, Pan

Kay, J. (1993) *Foundations of Corporate Success*, Oxford University Press

Likert, R. (1961) *New Patterns of Management*, McGraw Hill

Mintzberg, H. (1983) *Power In and Around Organisations*, Prentice Hall

Mintzberg, H. (1989) *Mintzberg on Management*, Free Press

Morden, T. (1996) *Principles of Management*, McGraw-Hill

Morgan, G. (1986) *Images of Organisations*, Prentice Hall

Pfeffer, J. (1981) *Power in Organisation*, Pitman

Toffler, A. (1985) *The Adaptive Organisation*, Pan

Torrington, D. and Hall, L. (1987) *The Business of Management*, Prentice Hall

Weber, M. (1947) *Theory of Social and Economic Organisations*, Free Press

Woodward, Joan (1965) *Industrial Organisations*, Oxford

Chapter eighteen

Organisational Culture

L E A R N I N G   O B J E C T I V E S

- **Understand the concept of culture in an organisational context**

- **Appraise the importance of the concept in the organisational context**

- **Identify the range of possibilities available in attempting to classify organisational culture**

- **Assess the advantages and disadvantages of the various types of organisational culture**

- **Identify the factors which need to be considered in determining appropriate culture**

- **Appreciate the need to be aware of diversity in attempting to identify culture in any organisation**

- **Apply the issues addressed in the context of organisations with which you are familiar**

- **Identify areas where further research might be beneficial**

A thorough examination of the way in which individual organisations manage their affairs might result in the recognition of the concept of 'an organisational culture'. The concept of organisational culture is one which has been recognised only over the last few decades. It has grown in importance with the emergence of the contingency approach to organisational design.

A definition of organisational culture might be 'an aggregation of shared values, beliefs and attitudes' (Charles Handy, 1985). Such an aggregation will be more than that of the values, beliefs and attitudes of all employees; rather it will be a reflection of the values, beliefs and attitudes of the organisation itself. It might be best summarised in the often heard statement: 'It might not make much sense to you, but that's the way we do things around here!'

This culture is at best only partly tangible in its nature, in that it is reflected, but not totally described, by managerial structures, processes and priorities. Furthermore, it is probably best illustrated by the actions and attitudes of longer-serving employees since, by the very definition of the term, newer employees may not yet have been fully 'socialised' into these organisational perspectives.

Finally, it would be naive to assume or claim that such organisational practices, priorities and perspectives are entirely 'set in tablets of stone'. A fairer analysis might claim that they are perspectives, priorities and practices which have been evolved within the organisation; as such they can be construed as having, at worst, not caused the organisation to fail and, at best, equipped the organisation to achieve success in its endeavours. With such an assessment it can be seen that organisational cultures can and do adapt and change with circumstances.

It must be recognised that, in many cases, such organisational cultures are well entrenched in the organisation and it would be equally naive to assume that change of organisational culture would be easy to effect. In evaluating this topic it must be recognised that, when the need to change practices is identified, there is a tendency for organisations to begin to effect such change in the more tangible aspects of the management domain. The major thesis of this chapter will be that such changes will be only partially successful at best, and possibly wholly inadequate at worst. The successful organisation needs to appreciate and address its cultural dimensions to achieve wholly satisfactory reactions to rapidly changing circumstances.

In many ways organisational culture can be viewed as a short-term rigidity within the organisation. Values, beliefs and attitudes, particularly when widely held, will not necessarily adapt to changed management structures or changed, imposed work practices.

In most complex, multi-purpose organisations there is likely to be more than one prevailing culture. The reality is that such organisations are so complex that it is highly likely that each section, segment or department may have a different type of culture or display the prevailing culture to a different extent. Given that the view is that organisational culture constitutes a positive response to the evolutionary circumstances of an organisation, and given that in such complex organisations such circumstances are likely to have varied within parts of the organisation, such diversity of culture is almost inevitable. The importance of the diversity of culture and the possible problems it presents will be examined later in the chapter.

Types of Organisational Culture

Given that this topic is, by its very nature, only partly tangible, any attempt to classify or describe individual organisational cultures will be problematic. It is likely that any codification of such cultures is dependent upon the views of the observer or codifier.

Such codifications are likely to emerge not from simple observation of one part of an organisation but by effecting a comparison between different parts of the one organisation or between organisations.

An examination of the British public service might conclude that over the 1980s and early 1990s two distinct organisational cultures could be detected: the public service culture and the entrepreneurial culture. The former would place heavy emphasis on the perceived duty to serve the public; the latter would place greater emphasis on a duty to sell products. These are radically different perspectives on the desired nature of the work task. If accepted, however, this contrast affords an excellent illustration of the importance of organisational culture; only when an organisation accepts the worth of the latter viewpoint will it be in a position to fully adapt to a more commercial environment.

However, for the purposes of the rest of this chapter, the division of culture described will rely substantially but not completely on the work of Charles Handy (1985).

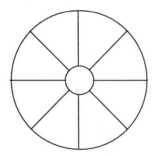

FIGURE 18.1 *The Power Culture*

THE POWER CULTURE

This is reflected in circumstances where power and influence in the organisation are centred on one person or a small group of people (Fig. 18.1). This will probably be reflected in a loose organisational design where much discretion is left to the senior people in the organisation. It will probably be reflected in the type of communication systems where all communication originates from or focuses towards these senior people. It must be emphasised that it is only when such circumstances are widely accepted as inevitable or desirable, that they could be deemed to constitute an organisational culture.

This type of culture is useful in times of crisis where emergency decisions may need to be made. It may also be of use in those organisations with standard and simple production processes. It will be found typically in small family-owned enterprises.

However, as organisations expand and their products become less standard in nature, this type of culture is likely to breed inefficiency and possibly resentment. Under such circumstances, the required expertise needed to make decisions and function effectively is so extensive that no one person can be reasonably expected to make all decisions. In public service organisations, which are usually large and produce non-standard services, such a culture will be appropriate only during times of emergency or during periods where new services are being developed.

THE ROLE CULTURE

This is a very common type of culture observed in mature organisations (Fig. 18.2). It will tend to be reflected in formal functionally-based organisational structures; in addition it may be reflected in the development of standard management and production procedures. It obtains where, for instance, the right of the finance director, and no one else, to determine financial strategy is not questioned. It is reflected in organisations where the standard reaction to human resource problems is to seek the advice of the human relations professional. Perhaps it would be best characterised by the organisation where 'everything has its place'. It is the acceptance or limited questioning of such circumstances, and not the circumstances themselves, which accords them the quality of cultural influences.

It is of particular benefit to large organisations which have seen the need to develop some specialisation in their workforce and to organisations benefiting from a stable environment, in that the best way to react to all circumstances is adequately provided by an examination of history; the code of best practice is readily accessed.

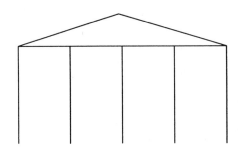

FIGURE 18.2   *The Role Culture*

One of its best illustrations is the United Kingdom public service where, for instance, in central government it is the treasury which has primary responsibility for the management of the economy. Advice on human resource issues in large public service organisations would usually be sought from a centralised personnel or human resource department.

However, as public service organisations find that their environment is changing, such rigid organisational values and perspectives cease to apply to the changed circumstances. More flexible or maybe experimental perspectives or priorities might be seen to be more advantageous. In these circumstances the British public service provides very good evidence of the importance of organisational culture. Many public service institutions have sought employee flexibility and initiative by decentralising decision-making power to direct service providers. However, those organisations which have decentralised their central support departments purely in terms of structural reorganisation have found that often these reorganisations take a long time to produce a benefit as the organisation's culture takes some time to adjust to the changed circumstances. Thus the devolution of financial responsibility to units or trusts in the health service has not been achieved simply by changing the managerial structures; in addition management attention needs to be directed towards change or adaptation of culture.

THE TASK CULTURE

This type of culture is found where maximum attention is devoted to ensuring that the tasks of the organisation are carried out as efficiently and effectively as possible (Fig. 18.3). It is commonly found in organisations with properly functioning matrix organisational structures. It must be stressed that the mere existence of a matrix organisation is not an indication of a task culture. The crucial issue is that the matrix organisation must be completely accepted by all those working within the organlsatlon.

Such a culture is seen to be of particular importance in organisations with non-standard products. In addition, it is seen to be an alternative to the role culture when an organisation which had hitherto benefited from stability suddenly encounters some substantial change in its environment. Thus many public service organisations have imposed matrix organisational designs; however, only those which have fostered the required change in culture have obtained maximum benefit from such organisational redesigns.

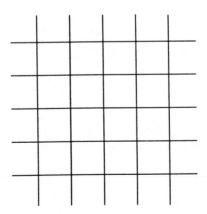

FIGURE 18.3   *The Task Culture*

THE CLIENT CULTURE

This may be seen as a specific type of task culture; alternatively it may be considered that the acceptance of client interests is so firmly embedded in the organisation that it warrants specific mention as a type of culture in its own right. Task culture is more 'paternalistic' in its nature than this type of culture. It is illustrated by the organisation, or more particularly its workforce generally, which sees its primary duty as that of serving client interests and demands. It is often found in organisations which place heavy emphasis on welcoming clients and/or involving them in product design. In many private sector organisations operating in conditions of high profile competition the adoption of this culture has been seen for many years to be a successful strategy. There is a long standing tradition in parts of the retail industry that 'the customer knows best'.

It is in the search for such cultures that the true nature of organisational culture might be revealed. It could be said that the production demands of both the health and education sectors provide an environment for the evolution of such a culture in that the nature of the services is that the individual is afforded education and health care. The production process, therefore, highlights the customer; however, in these areas of productive activity, resistance tends to be encountered if clients try to exert some independence over those providing the service. In both the education and health services, professionals, accustomed to professional autonomy, have not necessarily welcomed changes whereby the consumers are invited to participate in the production process; the concept of parental choice in the British education system of the early 1990s has not been favourably received by all educationalists. Thus the production process itself poorly defines the concept of organisational culture.

THE PERSON CULTURE

This is the type of culture where the primary purpose of the organisation is serving the interests of its employees (Fig. 18.4). Such a culture would place great emphasis on the career development needs of its employees. Much of the criticism of the devolution of support service expertise to operational departments, as a way of enhancing product delivery, focuses on the disruption to career development and this might be interpreted as an indication of the existence of a person culture in such organisations. Such a culture tends to afford satisfaction to the employees and this satisfaction will usually be translated into motivation.

However, the danger with this type of culture is that the needs of the organisation may become subordinate to those of its employees. Thus, although it is relatively well established in the British public service, it must be acknowledged that the more commercial atmosphere of the private sector has tended to prevent the more organisationally negative aspects of this culture developing.

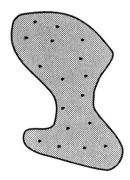

FIGURE 18.4   *The Person Culture*

SUMMARY

These categories of organisational culture should not necessarily be seen as discrete. The reality may be that in any one organisation, or, more specifically, in any one part of an organisation, combinations of such cultures are likely to obtain. Furthermore, such combinations can be reinforcing one of the other. For instance, an element of a person culture can be used as a way of reinforcing motivation to serve client needs, in any attempt to establish a client culture. Similarly, a role culture can be seen to strengthen the career development priorities of a person culture.

THEORY Z

An alternative perspective on culture can be found by examining and evaluating the efficacy of the contrasting predominant cultures in Japan and North America and Europe. William Ouchi (1981) suggested that the predominant cultures in Japan (Theory J) and North America and Europe (Theory A) were radically different. The Japanese experience is based on a parental relationship between the employee and the organisation; the contrasting North American and European culture more clearly distinguishes the separate motives and values of the employer and the employee. The first two columns of Figure 18.5 show the contrasting philosophies exhibited in the two cultures on various features of the organisational environment.

Ouchi considers that the Theory J has many positive features in that it encourages more trust and cooperation between employees and employers; furthermore it facilitates the development of trust between sections and departments. However he suggests that to embrace these positive features a transplantation of Theory J into the North American and European organisational environment would be naive. Rather to obtain full benefit from the Japanese experience a modified version of the Theory - Theory Z - is needed. Theory Z can be seen to be based strongly on Theory J but with some limited features of Theory A introduced. Figure 18.5 in the final column contrasts the consequences of Theories J, A and Z on various aspects of management.

	Theory J (Japanese)	Theory A (American)	Theory Z (Ideal)
Length of employment	lifetime	varies but mainly short	long
Career path	progression and exposure in many areas	specialised in chosen area	less specialised than Theory A
Personnel appraisal	appraisal based on loyalty to firm	appraisal based on performance	primarily loyalty
Promotion Decision Making	slow consensus by many, communication upward, as well as downward	rapid individual by managers	slow consensus by many
Responsibility	collective (as a result of decision making)	individual (as a result of decision making)	individual
Degree of corporate	entire, all aspects of life, including housing, family and schooling	focused on performance only	whole person and all aspects of life

William Ouchi's outline of Theories J, A and Z

FIGURE 18.5

How to Determine the Existing Culture

The fact that organisational culture is intangible in nature has already been acknowledged; consequently, the expectation must be that indirect, rather than direct, signs of detection must be sought. Even though most modern analyses of management acknowledge the existence of culture it must be admitted that it is very difficult in practice to determine or detect the precise nature of this culture. Rather the culture of an organisation tends to be reflected in certain of the organisation's distinctive features.

It could be that the words used in the organisation are reflective of its culture; they can often give some indication of the collective or generally accepted values and attitudes of the organisation. Organisations referring to senior persons in highly respectful tones may be indicating the existence of a power culture; organisations which, in private as well as public, speak of customers in positive terms may well be deemed to have a client culture.

In some ways the style of dress within the organisation may reveal something about its culture; if the dress style is highly formal there may be an indication of power or role cultures. The concept of 'power dressing' is one which has received some attention; some organisations almost demand of their managers that they dress in more 'powerful' ways the higher they progress in the organisation. Often it is possible to predict the seniority of the manager by the apparent cost of his or her suit. Perhaps, more importantly, however, the example of Japanese companies needs to be quoted; these companies commonly ensure that all workers, whatever their managerial importance, wear the same clothes. Undoubtedly this would reflect an attempt to introduce a task culture into the organisation.

The physical layout and environment of the organisation may well be reflective of its culture. Organisations where senior managers have larger and more pleasant offices than junior managers may well be indicating their role or power cultures. Organisations which make a deliberate attempt to provide their customers with a pleasant reception area may be indicating at least the beginnings of a client culture. It must be recognised, however, that such factors as a pleasant customer area will only be accorded culture status if accompanied by welcoming reception staff and a freely afforded willingness to serve customer needs throughout the organisation.

It must be acknowledged that the search for an organisation's culture does not always focus on totally intangible features; established organisational design is highly predictive of organisational cultures. The crucial point to note is that the management structures must be either well established and not resented or, if recently introduced, freely accepted. An organisation which has an effective and accepted matrix organisational design will probably have a task or maybe client culture. Organisations with strong central support service departments will be reflecting their established power or, more likely, role culture.

Similarly, accepted management priorities will be highly predictive of the predominant culture. Organisations which spend large amounts of money on well-furnished customer reception areas may be at least reflecting an attempt to generate a client culture. Organisations which lay great emphasis on developing their staff may be reflecting their person culture. Again, however, these factors must not be examined in a naive way; in the latter case the spending of money on development may be being undertaken so that the organisation would be better placed to develop its products, this probably being an indication of a task culture.

These indicators of culture can be supplemented by questions, both formal and informal, asked of staff; questionnaires can also be a useful means of determining the prevailing organisational culture. External auditors and other external persons who are familiar with the organisation can also be a useful source of advice or knowledge. Finally, the prevailing culture in a similar organisation might be a guide to those kinds of culture which might be found in the organisation under investigation.

What Causes a Particular Culture to Develop in an Organisation?

It must be stressed that organisational cultures are usually a positive feature of the organisational environment; cultures emerge in organisations not by accident, but as a reaction to the prevailing circumstances and equip the organisation to best deal with these circumstances. It is only when the organisation's circumstances change that delay in adapting culture may become a hindrance to organisational performance. Consequently, to progress our understanding of organisational culture it will be necessary to examine those organisational features which help determine the prevailing organisational culture.

a) The ownership of the organisation – in small family concerns there tends to be an element of natural power culture. Most decisions are capable of being made by the owner and most power is centred around the owner. It may be that the small number of employees readily acknowledge the role of the owner in the creation of their jobs and livelihoods. Under such circumstances it may be freely accepted by all participants that the power and influence in the organisation does focus on such central sources. Such arguments are not seen to apply in large publicly-owned institutions in that the fairness of such central exercise of power may not be seen to be so obvious .

b) Size of the organisation – as organisations expand in size there is a natural tendency for power to become diffused. Large organisations tend to develop separate pools of expertise and become suited to a role culture. This is well illustrated in a multi-purpose British local authority where the general assumption is that education matters are the prerogative of the director of education, social services that of the director of social services, finance that of the director of finance. Such an evolution of culture can be seen to be mirrored in the private sector as organisations increase in size and human resource issues become so complex and intertwined that a human resource professional needs to be employed.

c) The nature of the production process – if the organisation provides standard products or services it may lend itself to the effective functioning of a role culture since the tried and tested solutions are best left to those who have most knowledge. However, if the production process is diverse a task culture might be seen to be more appropriate since much more attention has to be directed towards evolving solutions which are driven by the task in hand and, under such circumstances, there will not necessarily be a neatly divided catalogue of expertise.

d) Extent of change in the environment – if the pace of change is relatively slow the role culture might be seen to be an effective type of culture, in that the tried and tested procedures can be effected by experts using rules and regulations as their production tools; however, if the pace of change is rapid a power or task culture might be more effective. Such cultures would tend to focus on speedy reactions to the change or alternatively to the particular demands of the changing tasks.

e) The abilities and expectations of the employees – individuals with limited ability are likely to prefer the security of a power or role culture. Those individuals with little interest in the work situation, similarly, will be content with the ease and security of a power or role culture. However, those individuals who are more able or more interested will tend to feel frustrated by the more rigid values of a power or role culture. They may prefer the more flexible, more varied and probably more challenging environment afforded by a task, client or even person culture (in that they will probably highly value their own growth and development needs).

Summary

These determining factors should not be considered to be discrete; rather the reality is that all of these determining factors will be present in any organisational environment. The appropriate culture can be assessed only after the relative importance of these determining factors is evaluated. For instance, the organisation might be a small family-owned enterprise which employs high calibre staff. Under such circumstances, one set of forces may pull the organisation towards developing a power culture whilst the other set of forces may drive the organisation more towards developing task, client or person cultures.

Changing Organisational Culture

Although the durability of organisational culture must be acknowledged it must be recognised that, as environments change, cultures can, and should, adapt to the new circumstances. Inevitably such change may not be easy to effect but the need to change cannot be ignored. Whilst admitting the difficulty of undertaking such changes there are a number of actions which an organisation can pursue which together might facilitate the desired organisational reaction.

a) Senior management, wishing to encourage new approaches, should present themselves as good role models. For instance, if a more flexible culture is required it would help immensely if the senior managers could exhibit such flexibility. Similarly, if a more customer–focused approach is required, senior managers should be seen to be customer focused.

b) It must be acknowledged that there are difficulties of determining the effectiveness of all reward systems. However it is likely that building in to the reward system incentives for the adoption of such new values will, together with other mechanisms, help engender new collective attitudes and values.

c) Given that senior people can help shape collective values it might be useful to ensure that those who exhibit the new desired values are more readily promoted. Again this could, on its own, be perceived as a crude and devious way of changing culture; however it can be seen, together with other approaches, and sensitively introduced to have some value.

d) When new staff are recruited it might be helpful to try to ensure that only those with these new values are selected.

e) Culture can be seen to be developed by the socialisation process in an organisation. Often this socialisation process is perceived to be informal and substantially outside the control of the organisation. However an effective and informed organisation can, to some extent, influence the socialisation process. At the very least the organisation can so design its induction programme that the new values are emphasised and positively explained.

f) Given that organisational culture is often a product of established group values, the organisation's managers might wish to encourage regular, but productive, inter-group communication and interaction. A common example of this principle would be the creation of multi disciplinary teams to examine problem areas.

g) The senior managers might wish to encourage the assumption of new values by explaining the need to adopt changed values; this might be effected by holding special events to explain the changing circumstances.

h) One additional facility available to senior managers is the generation of a mission statement. Such a statement would hope to express the values, priorities and direction that the organisation wishes to progress. When organisations have such express and published statements values which are not in harmony with such a mission can, at least, be seen to be organisationally dysfunctional.

It must be stressed that each of these actions have to be sensitively undertaken. Each one could, in inappropriate circumstances, seem to be highly threatening and maybe reinforce, rather than change, established cultures. Hence serious consideration must be given to participatory approaches to such attempts to change culture.

Diversity and Patterns of Organisational Culture

The existence of cultural diversity within organisations has already been mentioned. Most organisations are so complex and diverse that the desired culture will vary throughout the different segments of the organisation. A sophisticated management needs to assess that the pattern of its cultures is entirely appropriate; it needs to ensure that the culture that pervades each of its separate tasks and duties is entirely appropriate. One approach to the concept of cultural diversity and patterning of such diversity is that adopted by Charles Handy (1985). Handy suggests that most organisations have four principal types of activity.

a) Steady state – those activities which are concerned with maintaining stability in the organisation (for instance the accounting system, the secretarial system, the wages and salaries system).

b) Innovation – those activities in the organisation which are intended to facilitate change (research and development, market research, corporate planning, efficiency teams).

c) Crisis – this is not a readily categorised set of activities but rather those activities which are undertaken by all sections of an organisation when something goes wrong. Such activities as emergency payments and computer breakdown procedures would fall into this category.

d) Policy – those activities devoted to planning, to the setting of priorities, the establishment of standards.

Handy suggests that most of the activities of an organisation can be categorised neatly into one of these sub-divisions. For each category of action there may be an appropriate culture; the ones he specifies are power for policy and crisis, role for steady state, and task for innovation. The specification of these precise appropriate cultures is not crucial and certainly his specifications can be questioned. The major advantage of such an approach is that the nature of the particular activities can be examined and an appropriate culture determined. His work is diagrammatically shown in Figure 18.6. He recognises that there will be some activities which do not fall neatly into any one category; certain activities may overlap categories. Under such circumstances he suggests that the predominant category is assessed and the appropriate culture or, more realistically, appropriate cultural balance determined.

This is a very important refinement of our understanding of the topic area. What this complication does introduce is the possibility that the actual culture in a particular part of an organisation is not one of the neat divisions or categories previously examined but an amalgamation of two or more cultures. An examination of the real world would suggest that such neat and permanent categories do not exist. The likelihood is that within a well-established role culture an element of a power culture may well exist. Even in an organisation where the role of the finance director is well understood and well entrenched, there will be no reason why a working group might not be introduced which for a particular purpose allows wider access to authority over financial matters. Perhaps the best example is that already mentioned where the routine computer systems would work quite happily within a role culture but where such systems break down the more autocratic style of a power culture would be welcomed. When the breakdown has been rectified the organisation may then freely switch back to its more routine role culture.

The major benefit of Handy's assertions is not the precise conclusions he reaches but the framework it offers as an examination of the desired cultures and, more particularly cultural mixes, in particular segments of particular organisations. Furthermore, such a framework can be used when an organisation finds that its prevailing cultures seem no longer to be appropriate. As such it can form the framework around which a suitable solution can be determined.

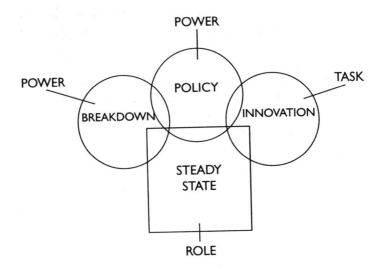

FIGURE 18.6 *Mix of Cultures*
(Source: C. Handy)

Dealing With Cultural Diversity

When organisations exist with different cultures there may be a need to harmonise the diversity caused by such differences. There are times in every organisation when different departments have to liaise or 'meet on common ground'. Under such circumstances the variations in culture should not be allowed to inhibit the desired co-operation. For instance, in a private engineering company there may be a need for the accountant to liaise with the engineering manager. Under such circumstances there is the danger of the varied cultures causing disharmony. There are a variety of potential solutions to this problem.

a) To do nothing and to assume that the common purpose will overcome the potentially different perspectives. This has the advantage of trusting people and giving them maximum control over the tasks they are assigned. It has the additional advantage of minimising change within the organisation; this will be considered in more detail in the next chapter. However, the major point to note is that the management of change is an immense task and, in some ways, one of the strategies which can be used to good effect is to try to limit the disruption caused to the bare minimum necessary to effect the change required. This degree of required change could still be quite extensive. If used as a strategy, however, any organisation would be advised to closely monitor the situation for signs of difficulties.

b) To facilitate cooperation through maximising the occasions upon which these people and cultures meet. This will be best effected if the occasions of such meetings are those which are likely to result in positive outcomes. These successes will create a positive environment for circumstances in the future which may be more challenging to both or all parties.

c) To establish a comprehensive and readily understood set of rules and procedures which may be adopted in the case of any difficulties occurring. This strategy has the advantage of providing a degree of management control over a potentially difficult problem. However, such rules and procedures may be resented and the agreement reached, if any, might prove fragile. This has the additional difficulty of being seen to adopt an immediate negative stance. There is no real reason why the meeting and joint working of cultures should be problematic and any attempt to imply otherwise might be unwise.

d) The appointment of a co-ordinator or co-ordinating department − such a strategy can be seen in the appointment of chief executives in local government and general managers in the health sector. This strategy can provide the advantage of a facility for arbitration. Such solutions introduce yet another potentially different culture into the organisation. In addition the skills needed by such co-ordinators are not easily acquired; if this strategy is adopted the organisation must give great care to the appointment of individuals serving in such capacities. It must be acknowledged, however, that this strategy has been long and successfully adopted in the private sector as the main palliative for cultural diversity. Furthermore, there may well be reasons, beyond the harmonisation of cultures, for the recruitment of such a facility. In fact where managing directors are appointed it is likely that the harmonisation of cultures would feature as a very small item on the job description.

Summary

The management of organisations is not restricted to the problems of managing structures, procedures and processes, people and groups. There is an additional complication in that any organisation can be seen to have a prevailing culture or cultures. However, the detection of an organisational culture is not easy and the reality is that such cultures are indicated by, or reflected in, certain features of an organisations actions or activities. Most large organisations will have a variety of cultures; the likelihood is that this variety is patterned by each major department having its own prevailing culture. This diversity of culture brings further problems for the management of an organisation in that such diversity must not result in organisational disharmony. Organisations can adopt a number of strategies to try to harmonise the different cultures prevailing in their different departments.

Exercise

In the context of the organisation or directorate examined in the exercise in the last chapter, examine the ways in which its culture or cultures could be defined and categorised. Critically assess the factors which contribute to this culture.

Further Reading

Bains Committee (1972) *The New Local Authorities: Management and Structure*, DOE

Beer, S. (1981) *The Heart of the Enterprise*, Wiley

Collins, J. C. and Porras, J. I. (1996) *Built to Last*, Century Business

Curzon, C. (ed) (1986) *Flexible Patterns of Work*, IPM

Dawson, S. (1993) *Analysing Organisations*, Macmillan

Deming, W.E. (1986) *Out of the Crisis*, CUP

Garratt, R. (1987) *The Learning Organisation*, Collins

Handy, C. (1979) *Gods of Management*, Penguin

Handy, C. (1985) *Understanding Organisations*, Penguin

HMSO (1991) Citizen's Charter

Hofstede, G. (1984) *Culture's Consequences*, Sage

Hofstede, G. (1991) *Cultures and Organisations*, McGraw-Hill

Kay, J. (1993) *Foundations of Corporate Success*, Oxford University Press

Mintzberg, H. (1983) *Power In and Around Organisations*, Prentice Hall

Mintzberg, H. (1989) *Mintzberg on Management*, Free Press

Morden, T. (1996), *Principles of Management*, McGraw-Hill

Morgan, G. (1986) *Images of Organisations*, Sage

Porter, M.E. (1985) *Competitive Advantage*, Free Press

Chapter nineteen

Affording Quality

LEARNING OBJECTIVES

- Appreciate the importance of quality in the management of an organisation

- Understand the variety of perspectives which could be applied to the concept

- Identify the importance of the concept at all stages of the management process

- Appreciate the importance of the customer or consumer in this context

- Understand the importance of formal standards in this area

- Examine how organisations could plan for and ensure quality

- Apply the concepts studied to organisations with which you are familiar

- Identify areas where further research might be needed

The importance of quality has increased enormously since the late 1970s. This is not to say that the concept did not exist before that, but it is the formal and public recognition and marketing of quality which characterises the period from the late 1970s.

The concept has become so embedded in United Kingdom and international economic activity that organisations might consider that they have no choice but to publicly embrace the concept. So many competitors will be applying the concept that, if the organisation wishes to remain competitive, it must embrace it as part of its internal environment.

The importance of quality in the organisational and economic environment is such that the British Standards Institute have issued several standards in this area. Broadly the Institute will attach its approval to the product or service if it can be proven to match these standards. Extracts from the most common of these standards is shown in Figure 19.1. Elements of this standard will be examined later in the chapter.

Later in the chapter the concept will be examined in more detail; however, if at this stage it can be accepted that quality embraces both production quality dimensions, user requirement dimensions and marketability dimensions, it might be useful now to examine the reasons for its growth in importance.

---

1 *Direct measurement of quality* - eg length of waiting time, number of errors in calculation, attainment of performance standards

2 *Observation* - eg cleanliness of a street can be observed, with photographs or video tape as evidence, if required

3 *Performance indicators* - where quality cannot be measured directly, performance indicators may be analysed eg non-attendance as an indicator of school quality

4 *Inspection* - an appraisal of a service eg as carried out in schools

5 *Surveys* - users can be invited to record their views or complaints

6 *Self/peer review* - assessment against standards by an individual, perhaps with supporting evidence from colleagues

The following checklist may be useful to you in designing and improving a quality assessment system.

● How will assessment be carried out?

● What records should be kept?

● How will assessment be reported?

● To whom will they be reported?

● What methods will be used to address failure to meet standards?

● How will assessment results be used by the organisation?

● Will performance trends be analysed?

FIGURE 19.1

Reasons for the Apparent Growth in Importance of Quality Issues

To appreciate fully the importance of this topic it is necessary to examine the reasons for its emergence as an issue of concern, or an issue worthy of formal management attention. As with many issues which emerge in the management domain, there are several identifiable reasons for its emergence as an area of concern. This is not to claim that these reasons are necessarily discrete; rather the reality will be that the various factors will, on occasions, have common origins and will furthermore assume a character whereby they reinforce each other.

a) The massive increase in power of the so called 'consumer movement'. This movement began in the United States of America in the 1960s. It focused on the poor quality of mass-manufactured products. The movement quickly found acceptance in the newspaper and media industries. Every major television network in the developed world has a significant number of its programmes devoted to the examination of consumer products. Some of the most popular programmes are those which focus on the poor quality of identified products or services. The movement is now represented in the United Kingdom by several national associations (for example Consumers' Association). All organisations, particularly in times of a highly active press and media industry, will be wary of incurring the wrath of any part of this movement.

b) The recognition of the role that serving the consumer and producing goods which are 'right first time' has to play in the process of motivating the workforce. The best test of whether something has been done well is whether or not those who have paid for a product or those who are meant to benefit are satisfied. The importance of doing something well, and being seen so to do, in the motivation process has been previously documented in this text. Similarly, the motivational problems caused by not doing something well have been established. Further- more, the stigma of a bad reputation is long lasting and demotivating. If management can introduce policies and priorities which recognise such forces it will be well placed to 'tap into' sources of high levels of employee motivation. For instance, in the mid-1980s when British Rail instituted quality improvement programmes in its productive activities it found that, over a time, it began to benefit from lower absentee rates from its staff.

c) The introduction of a more competitive environment – this is particularly important in the more competitive public service environment of the last decade of the twentieth century. Some observers have stated that when most of the public service operated in near monopoly conditions, it was not particularly attentive to customer needs. In the recent past if, in a competitive environment, an organisation is seen not to care about its customer's requirements it will usually find that it does not win the contract. Thus, a finance department in a local authority which finds that it has to contract with other departments for the right to provide it with a financial service will usually negotiate 'service level agreements' whereby the quantity and quality as well as the price of financial services is written into a formal contract.

Equally the introduction of the single market in the European Union has enhanced the competitive environment of many private sector enterprises. However, when an institution has to compete for custom it is necessary to pay much more attention to consumer needs and requirements.

d) Legislation detailing consumer rights – in the public service for instance there has been the emergence of the ombudsman as an investigator of poor quality service delivery. Much United Kingdom public policy during the last few decades has been focused on enhancing consumer rights. The financial cost of producing poor quality products is now, in many cases, prohibitive.

e) The Green factor — that is, the emergence of environmental issues as ones which are worthy of organisational attention and where there is a legislative or moral duty to address. It is very often the case that a good quality product lasts longer than one of poorer quality. Under such circumstances organisations have found that they are strongly encouraged to be mindful of the environmental impact of the management decisions they take. In fact many organisations now, in their publicity and advertising material, focus on the durability and quality of their products as a major positive feature of their productive endeavours.

f) Reduced cost — it has become increasingly recognised that, in the long term, it costs little, if anything, to do the job well. In fact it could be claimed that in the long term it is cheaper to do the job well (even if at a slightly greater cost in the short term). The cost of doing a job badly includes such things as time spent dealing with complaints.

g) It must be accepted that not all the reasons for this apparently new priority area have their origins in organisational enlightenment; the reality is that, in many cases, there is an imposed element in the assumption of this additional management priority. The publication of the Citizen's Charter in July 1991 (this is examined in more detail later in the chapter) has imposed upon many public service institutions the need to embrace issues of quality and customer satisfaction.

What Constitutes Quality

It is true to claim that everyone has some internal concept of quality. These concepts are likely to be categorised by their similarity rather than their diversity. However, if the concept is to be accommodated in management theory, the dissimilarities as well as similarities will have to be examined.

The concept of quality is firmly embedded in the organisational and economic agenda but what exactly constitutes quality is the subject of some debate. To examine the range of opinions on this issue it is necessary to examine four contrasting definitions:

a) 'Quality is Fitness for Purpose': J A Juran — this definition is quite simple; it highlights the importance of fulfilling user requirements. A good example would be a paper drinking cup. It can be seen to have several requirements:

　i) to hold liquid without tainting its taste or constituents. Any cup which was made of materials which chemically reacted with its contents would fail to meet this test of quality.

　ii) to be easy to use; according to this criterion the cup should be capable of being held with ease and capable of being drunk from with ease.

　iii) to maintain the temperature of the drink as would a more traditional container.

　iv) to be safe to use; under this criterion the cup should comply with hygiene requirements.

b) 'Quality is Conformity to Requirements': Philip Crosby — this is again a simple definition. It can be contrasted with Juran's definition in that it focuses more on requirements and the extent to which the product or service conforms with those requirements. It can be seen to be a definition which is much more prescriptive in its nature than that of Juran. The requirements might be externally established and all the organisation then has to do is to conform with those requirements.

c) 'Quality is a predictable degree of uniformity and dependability at low cost and suited to the market': W. Edwards Deming – this definition emphasises the uniformity dimension; hence an organisation which produces one quality product and then fails to deliver to this degree of quality the next time will not be deemed to have quality characteristics. In addition, this definition accommodates cost dimensions. It introduces for the first time Value for Money issues; if a product or service has external quality characteristics but is too expensive, then its quality dimensions can be seen to be limited.

d) 'Quality or Excellence is focusing on and involving the Customer': Tom Peters – this definition reflects the perceived intimate and essential role of the customer or client in the pursuit of quality. Under this approach when, and only when, the organisation has satisfied customer demands will quality be evidenced. It might be well illustrated by examining how an organisation views its customer.

Organisational Views of The Customer

Peters' definition of quality (above) has focused on customer led or driven issues and as such it might be useful to assess the type of reaction to the customer which might be found in an organisation. This can be achieved by the listing of some starkly varied ways in which an organisation views its customers. The views which will be listed may appear to be the extremes of a wide range of possible views. However, the analysis of such extremes may help to illustrate the importance of an organisation's view of its customers.

a) The customer could be viewed as an intruder or could be welcomed as part of the business.

b) The customer could be viewed as someone who is wasting the time of those producing goods and services; an alternative perspective is that the customer is the ultimate provider of wages and salaries.

c) The organisation could treat the customer as if he or she were dependent upon the organisation; alternatively the organisation could be viewed as being dependent on the customer.

Clearly it is the latter set of responses which should be striven for since the alternative approach will lead, at best, to consumer resistance and, at worst, to complete organisational failure.

It must be noted that the definitions of quality do contain many similarities. All definitions would include fitness for purpose and fitness for purpose must accommodate user requirements and cost. Similarly, although Juran merely focuses on fitness for purpose, it could be seen that it also implies predictably and uniformity of standards since a product or service can hardly be seen to be fit for its purpose if its fitness for this purpose is unpredictable.

Perhaps what the different definitions do show is different degrees of emphasis on different characteristics or dimensions of quality. This might be best illustrated in the contrast of emphasis between products and services. Clearly the precise dimension of quality depend on the nature of the industry within which operates. Industrial-based products will contain substantial technological characteristics whereas the service industry will focus more on user requirements and consumer support.

Figure 19.2 graphically show the contrasting emphases.

Quality – The Service Dimension	Quality – The Product Dimension
Accessibility	Durability
Accuracy	Reliability
Customer Focus	Packaging
Price	Price

FIGURE 19.2

Quality in service context

The concept of quality in an industrial or product context has been mentioned earlier in the context of the quality a paper cup. However the concept of quality in a service context is often seen to be more ephemeral. *The Search for Quality* by John Stewart and Kieron Walsh (1989) suggests that quality in the context of a service has three dimensions:

  i) Core Service – the extent to which the service meets the requirements of users;
 ii) Service Relationship – the extent to which the service affords a relationship between provider and user;
iii) Service Surroundings – the extent to which the surroundings enhance the relationship between the two parties.

They examined this in the context of a library:

a) range of books (core)

b) opening hours (core)

c) stacking of books (surroundings)

d) lighting (surroundings)

e) library assistant's interest in library users (relationship)

f) library assistant's knowledge and ability to answer questions (relationship)

An alternative perspective on quality is that afforded by Ernst and Young who assert that there is no one best approach to quality and that the context of the organisation and the product or service dictates the approach which should be adopted. Their findings are show in Figure 19.3.

Improving Quality

The Ernst & Young IQS suggests there is no one best approach to quality. Context determines approach.

A review of 101 quality service companies in the US revealed the following common characteristics:

- a clear vision of superior service, communicated to all employees;
- concrete, regularly measured standards of service quality;
- hiring good people, training them, and empowering them;
- recognising and rewarding service accomplishments.

Examples of Enhanced Quality

It is easy to envisage the improvement in quality of a manufactured product since the product's constituents can be measured against predetermined criteria. However, it must be admitted that in the service sector, particularly in the public service, such quality issues are less easy to identify. All changes in quality do not necessarily involve large change; often, it will entail attention to detail and attention to customer needs.

a) It may constitute a speedier marking of assignments in education – the assumption would be that a quicker feedback to students or pupils would better meet their requirements.

b) Smaller class sizes – the assumption would be that smaller class sizes both provide a better environment for the education of pupils and also meet the wishes of the pupils themselves.

c) Quicker response time in the police service – the assumption would be that from the producer's and consumer's perspectives a better quality service would be afforded.

d) Service level agreements between support and operational departments – this affords a rather different perspective on quality issues in that it focuses on the detailed formal specifications of an agreement between the two parties in the quality debate.

e) Better-designed application forms – the removal of confusing terminology. This is probably a good example of how organisations can effect simple alterations but yet achieve significant improvements in quality. It can be seen to be of immense importance in the public service environment.

f) Better-trained telephonists and reception staff – again this is an issue which is simple to effect and not directly concerned with effecting radical alterations in the production process itself. It affords another example of the importance, in the eyes of the customer, of effecting improvements in the ease of contact between the customer and the organisation. The importance of this point is the stressing of how simple improvements can be deemed, by customers, to constitute significant improvements in the quality of the overall product package delivered.

How to Improve Quality

There are two distinct processes involved in introducing quality or customer satisfaction into an organisation's values and culture. The first concerns the decision about what needs to be done. The second demands that those things which need to be done *are* done. An example of a higher education institution assessing its customers' requirements and preferences is shown in Figure 19.4.

a) Assess customer requirements – in reality this is difficult. Techniques to facilitate such a process are examined in the chapter on Marketing.

b) Examine the extent to which your services meet customer requirements – this may be assessed by such things as market performance, the number and types of complaints.

c) Examine what your competitors or comparable organisations are doing to improve service delivery or quality. In some environments this is easy to achieve; in British local government the external auditor can be a productive source of information. However, in certain environments this information is often denied for reasons of competition. For instance, in the newly privatised water industry, other water companies, with whom information was previously readily shared, are often now seen as competitors and organisations with whom information should not be so readily shared.

d) Establish what can be done to improve service delivery or quality – this may involve the organisation in discussions with both clients and employees. In such circumstances it is necessary that the one is not seen to be a threat to the other. It is difficult to involve clients in discussions without appearing to be too threatening to employees. The overcoming of this difficulty will be considered a little later in this analysis.

e) Monitor and review – there are many examples of improvements being detected when they themselves have been superseded by more effective production methods.

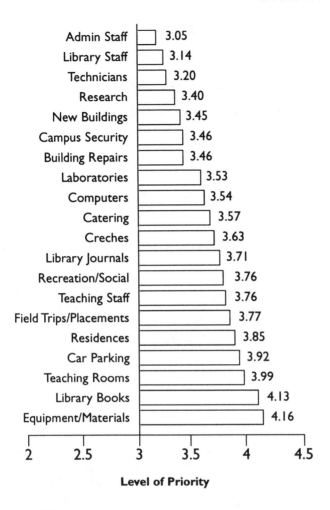

FIGURE 19.4 *Student Survey: Priority of Budget Items*

Improving the Product/Service

One commonly accepted method in this domain has become known as total quality management. This involves the consideration of quality within the perspective of a number of themes and these are summarised in Figure 19.5.

PREVENTION BETTER THAN CURE

ABILITY TO DELIVER

UNIVERSAL GAIN

POSITIVE LEADERSHIP

VIGILANCE

WATCH COSTS

FIGURE 19.5 *Total Quality Management*

PREVENTION

The assumption of this approach to quality assurance is that avoiding poor quality is a much more effective strategy than rectification of poor quality. This involves the adoption of a psychology whereby the organisation itself assures good quality and does not wait to receive complaints; it assumes a proactive role in the determination and assurance of quality.

ABILITY TO DELIVER

This strategy recognises that for quality requirements to be achieved quality aspirations must be capable of being delivered; all staff must be provided with the proper resources and skills necessary to deliver what is expected of them. This approach would emphasise the role played by training and development in the proper delivery of the product. It would also emphasise the importance of everyone in the productive endeavour. In the adoption of this approach the management of the enterprise would need to consider the techniques of employee motivation already mentioned in an earlier section of this book.

EVERYONE GAINS

A major aim of the strategy would be to convince everyone within the organisation that they themselves have something to gain from providing a better quality service. Such gains may focus on job security but an alternative perspective is to stress that everyone within the enterprise is a consumer; the emphasis may focus on them as consumers of the products of other organisations and asking them to reflect on their feelings when they had received poor service. Alternatively, it may focus on their role as 'internal' consumers. This approach would emphasise that in complex organisations every employee in the success of his or her productive endeavours is dependent to a substantial extent on the quality of the service received from others in the organisation. For instance, in the car industry if a worker, charged with polishing a car, receives a car which has poor quality metal then his or her ability to afford a high quality polish is impaired. Similarly, a production manager will need high quality financial information to enable him or her to assess the production costs incurred. Essentially the emphasis is that quality is a team game where everyone depends on each other. Such an approach to quality draws on the benefits to be obtained from a team or group spirit.

THE IMPORTANCE OF POSITIVE LEADERSHIP

Under this approach to quality assurance there is a realisation that such priorities and practices need to be learned and nurtured. This requires astute leadership skills and the probability will be that such skills constitute high profile but unthreatening leadership during times of infancy of the concept but much lower profile facilitating skills in maturity. Essentially the problem will be 'learning when to approach and when to withdraw'.

THE IMPORTANCE OF VIGILANCE

Such a programme is a never-ending exercise and there is no room for complacency. It would be a poor quality programme which assumed that last time's production criteria are entirely appropriate to the next production task. The reality would be that in most enterprises constant vigilance is needed to ensure that there have been no changes in customer expectations and requirements. Essentially this re-emphasises the proactive approach of the exercise.

THE IMPORTANCE OF COST

If the worth of quality is to be assessed and the costs of quality are to be budgeted for, then it is necessary to calculate the net cost or benefit with some degree of precision.

The costs can be determined to be the costs of complying with quality parameters whereas the benefits could be examined as the costs of non-compliance with these parameters.

COMPLIANCE COSTS

These include the costs of determining quality and the costs of assuring quality

NON-COMPLIANCE COSTS/BENEFITS

These include costs of breakdown in production, rectification costs, penalty payments and the loss of custom. Unless the organisation is obliged by statute, only if the benefits exceed the costs should an organisation undertake the assumption of quality improvement. If the costs exceed the benefits then the organisation will have to sacrifice or lower its quality parameters. Alternatively it might assume a longer term strategy and consider that its actions are for longer-term net benefit.

Small or Large Increments in Quality Improvement

In the Japanese environment the concept of 'Kaizen' or continuous improvement is well embedded. The concept is one where everyone involved in the production exercise is charged with and owns continuous small but achievable improvements in quality. Figure 19.6 shows Kaizen Quality Improvement.

In Japan perhaps the most frequent use of Kaizen is the quality circle. Such a circle consists of a group of employees numbering not more than eight charged with effecting improvements in their particular part of their organisation's activities. Such a group or circle will have a number of distinctive features.

a) As few organisational status differences as possible – the group will consist of members from the same level in the organisation.
b) Wherever possible the group will form a natural work group – that is the members should consider themselves to be colleagues linked by their common involvement in the same part of the total production exercise.
c) It should be led by a trained facilitator – this will take the form of encouragement of discussion rather than leading of discussion. It is important to note that this facilitator will be a natural member of the group and that the leadership of such a group is of a low profile nature.
d) They should meet voluntarily – they agree to set aside time to discuss issues. It is important to note that, if this facility is used, time must be set aside in their work programmes to allow the full benefits of such activity to emerge. There will be no purpose in suggesting that such groups meet without affording them time to fulfil this additional duty. Equally, the need for the group to meet must not be seen to

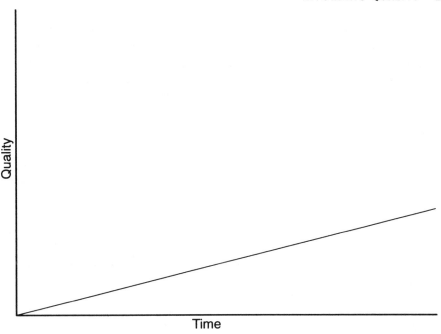

FIGURE 19.6   *Quality Improvement – 'Kaizen' – The Japanese Experience*

be imposed on the group; success will be achieved only if they are convinced of the benefits to be obtained from such meetings. As such it is important to note that quality circles, if deemed appropriate, cannot be simply 'transplanted' into the enterprise; time must be allowed for success to be achieved.

e) They are encouraged to discuss small improvements which can be made rather than large improvements which will prove difficult to make. Under such circumstances it can be seen that quality improvement is a practical concept.

f) They are given resources to put their ideas into effect and more often than not their ideas are accepted by management without question. This removes any threat of loss of motivation caused by frustrated ambition.

Undoubtedly these circles work in Japan. It might be that they can be transferred into other countries with some benefit. However, it must be acknowledged that such 'foreign transplants' rarely achieve the levels of success expected of them; it might be that such ideas might work only in a particular type of environment and that such circles might be a product of the types of organisational culture found in Japan. In Japan the average employee works longer for one organisation than is the case in, for instance, the United Kingdom and in such circumstances it might be that the enthusiasm generated for such ideas in Japan would not translate as easily into the United Kingdom environment. However, it may be that an astute organisational management can create an environment within which such quality circles can succeed in countries other than Japan.

Kaizen is contrasted with the less regular, larger quality improvements emanating from the North American and European quality culture where quality is more commonly researched and nurtured in a central research and development culture. This more radical, less frequent, more centralised perspective is depicted in Figure 19.7 – a traditional North American and European approach.

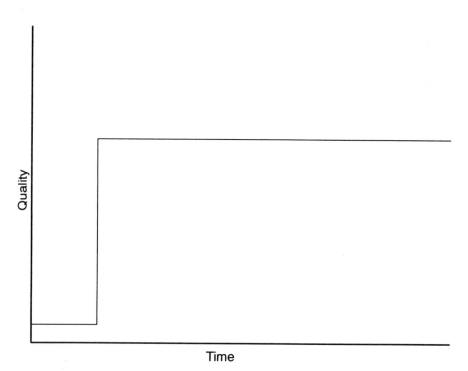

FIGURE 19.7 *Quality Improvement – The Western Experience*

It is very difficult to deny the more positive features of each approach. The more regular, minor steps associated with Kaizen facilitate ownership of quality and a practical approach to the seeking of quality. However the larger, less frequent steps found traditionally in North America and Europe will promote the concept of ensuring product differentiation and the pursuit of a competitive advantage.

Perhaps it is possible and maybe even desirable to retain the advantages of both approaches, whilst introducing no disadvantages, by simply accepting both approaches as valid and pursuing, through different management practices, both approaches. This approach is depicted in Figure 19.8 – hybrid approach to quality improvement.

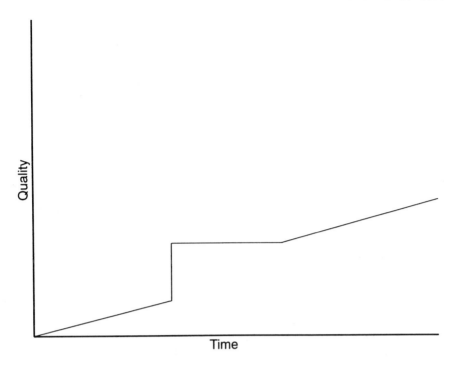

FIGURE 19.8 *Quality Improvement – Hybrid*

The Citizen's Charter

This emphasis on consumer satisfaction within the public service is well evidenced by the Citizens' Charter of the United Kingdom Conservative Government published in July 1991. This Charter was followed by more detailed charters in specific parts of the public service (eg The Patient's Charter in the National Health Service). Under this Charter the consumer interest is deemed to be satisfied in several different ways in the various parts of the public service. The focus of this Charter is to specify the levels of service which customers might expect from the various organisations operating in the public service. Attention will be given to ensuring that the quality of the product or service is clearly stated and that rights of redress are afforded to those customers who find this quality is not afforded to them. These objectives are to be achieved in a wide variety of ways.

a) In some cases further competition will be introduced (for example Post Office delivery service). In such circumstances it is hoped that this will produce a more efficient service for the consumer.

b) In some cases standards expected or targets will be published (for example National Health Service waiting lists, London Underground Standards, Police standards. This specification will highlight those times when this quality of service is not given to the consumer.

c) In some cases the interest of the consumer will be deemed to be represented by privatisation (for example British Rail). The claim is that such privatisation will result in a more efficient consumer service.

d) In some cases the interests of the consumer are to be served by ensuring that an effective system of inspection exists (for example education). This more powerful inspectorate should more readily guarantee that adverse publicity is attracted to poor performance.

e) In some cases the interest of the consumer will be aided by the introduction of systems which afford greater ease in the making of complaints (eg ensuring that staff in Central Government, the National Health Service and Local Government wear badges to enable ease of their identification).

f) In some cases the interests of the consumer are recognised by affording a more convenient service (for example the introduction of fixed appointment times for outpatient treatment).

g) Where regulatory bodies exist their powers are to be increased in order to better serve the interests of the consumer.

Several of these Charter items are restatements of existing government policies. However, some elements of the Charter are innovative in nature. There have been criticisms of this Charter in terms of its details or the fact that it affords no extra resources to organisations to adhere to its contents. However, there has been little or no criticism of the consumer philosophy underpinning its existence. Undoubtedly the most important messages of such an approach are, firstly, the facility it offers to provide a practical example of how quality could be introduced into a public service environment and, secondly, the illustration it affords of the wide variety of actions which can be effected to introduce quality into the delivery of such public service products.

The Management of Quality

It could be considered that the management of quality exists in three phases – these three phases and their interconnection are commonly called the Quality Circle – shown in Figure 19.9.

a) Quality design and specification – quality has to be embedded in the design of a product or service. This involves the assessment of the requirements of the product or service – who is it for and what are their requirements? It involves an assessment of the standards required and the component parts of the product or service. It will embrace an assessment of the desired level of cost and the qualities required of the output. It must be acknowledged that in many cases, with the evolution of products or services rather than their deliberate, conscious specification, this may not be easy.

b) Organising for quality – the mere specifications of design and standards do not of themselves equate to the delivery of quality. Rather processes have to be created which ensure that specifications are achieved. This will involve the examination of systems, structures, procedures and personnel required to guarantee a quality output. Figure 19.10 examines the issues which need addressing at this phase

c) Quality assessment – organisation for quality does not of itself guarantee that quality is being delivered. Organisations will have to assess on a regular basis whether plans are achieving the desired end. This assessment can be carried out by either the producer, the user or a third party. Once this process has been undertaken the organisation can then return to the next cycle of quality management and specify with greater precision its quality design and specification.

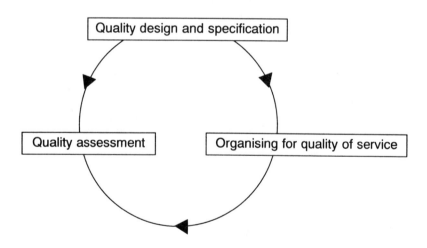

FIGURE 19.9   *The Quality Cycle*

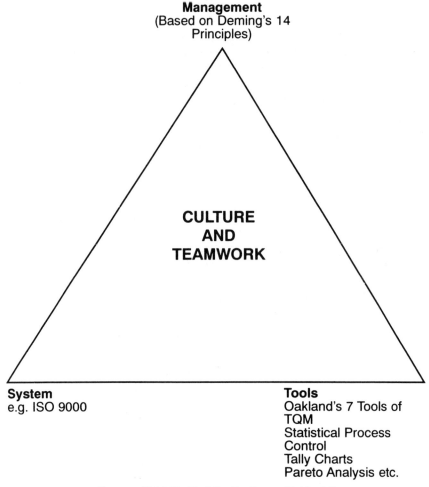

FIGURE 19.10 *The Total Quality System (Oakland, J)*

The Role of Formal Standards

As has already been mentioned, in the United Kingdom the British Standards Institute will afford its approval to organisations which it feels have organised for and adequately managed quality. In this context perhaps the most commonly used and prestigious standard is BS EN ISO 9000 – formerly BS 5750 – Quality Systems. The details of this standard are shown in Figure 19.11. It can be seen to embrace all three phases of the quality cycle just examined.

The Role of Benchmarking

Since the early 1980s the concept of benchmarking has attracted much attention. It has been extensively used in the public service, particularly through the work of the Audit Commission. The recent focus on 'league tables' in education and the National Health Service can be seen to have its origins in this concept. Shell, one of the first proponents of this concept, define benchmarking as: 'The continuous process of measuring products, services and practices against the best competitors or those recognised as market leaders.'

The developments of a quality system that conforms to this standard will involve the following elements:
- establishing a quality programme and policy
- training all staff in quality policy and procedures
- designing the organisation to maximise quality
- ensuring that responsibilities for quality are clear
- developing sampling, testing and inspection procedures
- ensuring the quality of bought-in services and products by sampling, testing and inspection
- planning output, so that customers get what they want when they expect it
- developing appropriate production methods
- monitoring work in progress
- ensuring quality control of output
- corrective action
- creating a documentary record system that enables quality to be demonstrated and managed
- systems for identifying work and materials at each point
- document control, ensuring only current procedures and instructions are in use
- procedures for handling, storage, packing and delivery of products
- building in traceability of work
- control of non-conforming products
- auditing the quality system.

FIGURE 19.11

There are generally considered to be four main levels of comparison which can be used:

a) Internal – under such circumstances the organisation or a third party (eg external auditor) will measure its performance against past achievements.
b) Industry – in this circumstance the organisation or a third party will compare performance against others in the industry.
c) Worldclass – in this situation the comparison will not be limited to the industry concerned (eg health laboratories practices might be compared not just with others in the health sector but with laboratories in all commercial or industrial sectors).
d) Customer – the previous levels of comparison can be seen to emerge from a parental perspective since it is the organisation itself which seeks to define the comparators. However, the final level has as its driving force the customer or client. Under this approach it is the customer who decides what elements of production should be improved and how these improvements could be made. This level of comparison, in its philosophical base, is examined earlier in the chapter where the role of satisfying the customer is specifically addressed.

Whatever the level of comparison the aim will be to compare a wide range of activity with predetermined standards: it may be the final product or service (eg a motor car) or it may part of the product (eg car valeting); it might be a support service (eg finance), or it might be a particular practice (eg discipline in education). Inevitably the purpose will not be to simply make the comparison but to take remedial action.

Under such circumstances it is essential that the comparator is carefully chosen; equally the need to regularly question the legitimacy of the comparison must be noted. If remedial action is needed it is essential that the comparison provides information which allows remedial action to be taken.

Finally, if the organisation is to receive full benefit from the concept, as with other quality issues, it must be owned by all people involved with productive activity. Thus, if benchmarking emerges from top level decision making, its benefits must be effectively 'sold' to all involved. It could be that benchmarking at certain levels could form part of the work of the Quality Circle examined earlier in this chapter.

Summary

In many parts of productive endeavour there may have been a history of paying limited attention to client needs and similarly paying limited attention to the quality dimension. However, as organisations begin to operate in more competitive environments, the issue of satisfying customer needs and delivering good quality cannot be ignored. It might be concluded that unsuccessful organisations are those which do not react to the needs and demands of their customers, who do not anticipate the skills and abilities of their competitors and who do not adapt to changes in technology. Finally, it is possible to introduce programmes which both emphasise the quality dimension and also introduce best practice in management generally.

Exercise

Examine the constituent features of quality. Choose an organisation or product with which you are familiar and examine the ways in which they exhibit the characteristics you have just described.

Further Reading

Adair, J. (1986) *Effective Teambuilding*, Gower
Audit Commission (1989) *Better Financial Management*, Audit Commission
Burns, T. & Stalker, G.M. (1966) *The Management of Innovation*, Tavistock
Connock, S. (1991) *HR Vision: Managing a Quality Workforce*, Institute of Personnel Management
Cummings, T. G. and Worley, C. G. (1993) *Organization Management and Change*, West Publishing
Deming, W.E. (1986) *Out of the Crisis*, CUP
Garratt, R. (1987) *The Learning Organisation*, Collins
HMSO, (1991) Citizen's Charter
Kay, J. (1993) *Foundations of Corporate Success*, Oxford University Press
Morgan, G. (1986) *Images of Organisations*, Sage
Peters, T.J. and Austin, N. (1986) *A Passion for Excellence*, Fontana/Collins
Porter, M.E. (1985) *Competitive Advantage*, Free Press

The Management
of Change

It must be recognised that the major theme of this text is that of management in a rapidly changing environment and hence throughout this chapter reference will be made to other sections of the book which might help embellish our understanding of managing change.

All organisations are increasingly subject to environmental change. As will be seen such changes can come from a variety of sources. Such changes can vary in extent from small to large. In many ways it could be claimed that change is an integral feature of organisational or human existence in that, for instance, the mere introduction of one new customer into a list of several hundred thousand could semantically be deemed to constitute change. At the outset it might help to acknowledge that the subject matter of this chapter addresses not the management of change but the management of substantial change. As will be seen, such substantial change will introduce either opportunities to the organisation, or threats, or, more interestingly and more realistically, a combination of both.

As will be acknowledged in this chapter, many of changes encountered by organisations, and many of the options available to the organisation to cope with or manage these changes, have their counterparts in individual human existence.

As a start to the analysis it might help to examine the variety of changes which might impact on an organisation. Change can originate from many sources. Some change may be imposed upon the organisation; some may be initiated by the organisation. It may immediately place the organisation in a more advantageous position by developing a new and better production process. It may, at first glance, appear to place the organisation in a less advantageous position, for instance, a major section of its activities may decline in market importance.

In some ways, how the organisation reacts and manages change is affected by whether such change is imposed or whether it is internally driven. Similarly, the strategies adopted by the organisation can, to an extent, be seen to be dependent upon whether the change has favourably or unfavourably impacted upon the organisation.

During this chapter it will be recognised that there are some common reactions to change, irrespective of its origins or its impact upon the organisation. It is necessary to examine in some detail the precise natures of change which may impact upon an organisation.

a) Changes in production technology – for example, the development of computer-aided teaching has impacted on the way in which many higher education institutions organise their curriculum activities. Similarly in the private sector with a computer software company, changes in computer hardware technology radically influence and affect the software produced.

b) Changes in information technology – for example, the massive growth in computer packages enabling the organisation to more quickly access sources of information. This is a common and important cause of change in organisations. It is examined separately in a separate chapter of this section and this chapter should be read in conjunction with the chapter on Information Technology.

c) Changes in legislation – this can take two distinct forms:
   i) new demands directly relating to the production process (eg National Curriculum) – this is more likely in the public than private sector;
   ii) new demands less directly relating to the production process (eg new employment legislation).

d) Emergence of competition – for example, the growth in competitive tendering which has impacted considerably upon many public service organisations or the removal of international trade barriers in the private sector

e) Increased or more sophisticated consumer demands – this has been aided by legislation, by the growth in the consumer movement and by changes in the expectations of society. Thus, for instance, all organisations, whether in the public or private sectors, have found that they have had to give much more direct attention to consumer demands and preferences.

f) Changes in the market – a good example of this can be found in the public service where demographic changes have demanded that United Kingdom local authorities direct more attention to the care of the elderly as a result of their increasing numbers.

This is an important and continuous example of the need to change which is examined in a separate chapter of this section. Hence this part of the chapter should be read in conjunction with the chapter on Marketing.

g) Changes in employee expectations – for example, demographic changes (reduced numbers of younger people) whereby some people have suggested that organisations need to give more attention to employee needs, may result in younger employees making greater demands on the organisation.

As a consequence of this demographic change and the increasing need for organisations to encourage innovation, the role of the manager can be seen to be changing from that of proactive decision maker to that of nurturer and facilitator of subordinates' ideas, initiative and actions.

Difficulties Encountered in Organisational Change

Coping with or managing organisational change is often one of the most difficult tasks facing the management of the organisation. To understand fully the potential problems encountered in the management of change it is necessary to examine briefly the reasons why change is often resisted.

a) Change can result in people losing their jobs, in people losing their status and in the dissolution of established working groups. Those who stand to lose, in any way, by the introduction of this change may, quite understandably, place barriers in the way of those wishing to introduce that change.

b) A particular change may result in people being promoted or in people being given more challenging jobs. Unfortunately the ready support of these people in implementing the change cannot be relied upon immediately. Most people gain some form of comfort from the status quo; they have some fear of the unknown. Even those who have something to gain from the introduction of the change have to be reassured and convinced of their future gains.

c) Finally, it is important to note that often organisational change may be caused by some deficiency in present modes of activity. Under these circumstances it would be a naive management which would expect that the immediate reaction of employees to this change will be one of welcome and happy acceptance.

How to Detect the Need to Change

Sometimes organisations receive instructions to change their activities. However, in the organisational domain the need to change is not something which will appear as an instruction on the board agenda. More often the reality is that organisations themselves have to detect the need to change some aspect of their operations.

The difference between good and bad management may, very often, be the ability to detect signals of problems with existing activities at a stage where something can be done about them. In most situations an early detection of the need to change will result in more minor change being necessary than would result from late detection of problems. It must be stressed that minor change should be easier to implement than is radical change; it is often said that 'a stitch in time saves nine'.

Some of these 'need to change' signals are quite obvious; however, many signals are quite subtle in nature and it will require astute and vigilant management to detect them. It cannot be claimed that all such signals necessarily mean that the organisation has to change. However, they are signals of potential difficulties which may require the organisation to change. Undoubtedly, early detection of difficulties is desirable. Furthermore, in most circumstances minor change is preferable to radical change.

a) Complaints from customers/clients. Quite obviously such complaints are indications that something is wrong. For instance, the management of a hospital receiving complaints from patients about the quality of cleanliness would be well advised to investigate the nature of these complaints. It must be stressed that in the United Kingdom public service such complaints could be received through intermediary sources such as an ombudsman, a consumer council or a regulatory body. However, this does not diminish the importance of such signals in the private sector. Any private sector organisation needs to retain its customers to survive; a car repair organisation will soon detect the need to change its practices if it finds repaired cars returned for further inspection. Such returns are usually accompanied by vociferous and, in the long term, more organisationally damaging complaints.

b) Criticism from the press or media. All organisations need to protect their public image. If something happens which causes adverse press or media reaction, the organisation would be well advised to investigate. This is of particular importance in the public arena within which most public service organisations operate. But perhaps the best example of this in recent years has come from the supposedly less public atmosphere of the private sector in the United Kingdom – the investigation of the Maxwell Empire by the press and media.

c) Loss of market position or deteriorating financial performance. In many ways this is the most obvious and most powerful signal that something is wrong. Under normal circumstances all organisations would see the maintenance or enhancement of their market position and the achievement of their financial targets as their most important objectives.

d) Disputes and staffing difficulties. Staff unrest (perhaps characterised by excessive sickness, industrial disputes or high turnover) is a signal that the organisation is not functioning as smoothly as it might. The importance of such signals regarding organisational malfunction has been examined in earlier sections of this text.

How to Implement Change – the Private Life Analogy

To appreciate fully the ways in which organisations might cope with or manage change it might be useful to consider circumstances in our private lives where we have encountered the need to change, to examine our reactions, (both emotional and intellectual), to such changes and to assess what, if any, strategies we employed to deal with them.

An analysis of such personal circumstances will reveal that, just as organisational change is sometimes imposed and sometimes self-driven, so is change experienced in the personal or private domain. Similarly, as with organisational change, personal changes will sometimes favourably impact upon the individual and sometimes unfavourably. To some extent, therefore, the analysis of these individual reactions and strategies for coping must acknowledge this wide variety of individual experiences. Perhaps more interestingly, it could be claimed that, accompanying these admitted variations, is a list of responses which are not affected to any great extent by variations in the nature of such changes.

OCCASIONS OF CHANGE IN PERSONAL CIRCUMSTANCES

The list can be seen to be quite varied, embracing imposed and self-assumed change, embracing favourably disposed and unfavourably disposed changes. Important changes to note are those in marital status, in occupation, and in family composition. Important emotional and intellectual reactions to note are: fear, resentment, welcome, challenge and, perhaps most interesting of all, in many varied circumstances, mixed feelings.

Strategies for coping embrace: anticipation, thinking it through, seeking the advice of personal support systems (eg family, friends), ignoring it and hoping it will go away, fighting it, changing expectations, affording time to deal with the issues raised, accepting the inevitability of the change. It must be noted that many people could relate times in their lives where to accord the term 'coping' to the situation would be a denial of the truth; quite simply many people have encountered changes in their lives with which they have not really coped.

It would be interesting to reflect to what extent the following analysis, relating to the organisational domain, has its counterparts in this personal domain.

Change – the Organisational Perspective

The aim of the management of organisational change could be examined from two distinct viewpoints:

 i) damage limitation;
 ii) maximisation of success.

These two different perspectives will not be specifically addressed in the following analysis, but a rigorous understanding of the analysis will need to acknowledge these two rather different perspectives.

The aim of managing change in an organisational context is portrayed in Figure 20.1: the organisation can be seen as progressing from the present state, through the transitional state (the period or process of the change) to the future desired state. Such a level of analysis is useful in that, as a first step in the understanding of the topic area, it shows the chronological order of the process of change: the organisation moves, or attempts to move, with either the purpose of damage limitation or maximisation of success, from a present situation to a situation which will more accurately describe its aspirations or its anticipated position in the future.

What such an analysis fails to reveal is, firstly, the detail of the process which might be involved in such a successful transition and, secondly, the fact that at the end of any process of change there is a need to effect a period of stabilisation or consolidation (however short this may be).

A more thorough analysis of the organisational reaction might be deemed to be that revealed in Figure 20.2. This shows the movement from the present state to the future desired state through the possible different stages of the transitional state portrayed in Figure 20.1, to the period of stabilisation or consolidation. The actions portrayed in Figure 20.2 may be effected over a wide range of time periods; sometimes the change required permits a long adjustment or transitional period, sometimes the change requires a very speedy response from the organisation. Sometimes the stabilisation period will be of extremely short duration, alternatively this period may be long lived.

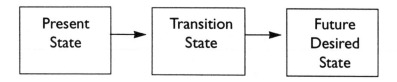

FIGURE 20.1 *Managing Change*

Similarly, the respective importance of the various elements in the process will vary; the circumstances of the change may be such that no really important key influences, other than the driver of the change, will be found. Sometimes the circumstances of the change will reveal a wide range of such key influences.

Sometimes the driver of the change will be able to easily persuade others of the need to change and in such circumstances democratic leadership styles are facilitated; on other occasions the circumstances may be such that an agreement on an desired course of action is problematic and more autocratic leadership styles might be needed.

Activities Involved

There are two separate types of activity involved in managing change.

DIAGNOSIS OF THE EXISTENCE OF A PROBLEM

As has already been acknowledged not all signals of potential problems need result in remedial management action. However, it is the task of management to distinguish between those signals which do and those signals which do not require remedial action (or change). The successful diagnosis of a problem requires the ability to distinguish between the symptom of a problem and the underlying problem. In diagnosing a situation the manager has to access as much information and advice as possible. This does not mean avoiding managerial responsibility but using all available resources. Certainly thought must be given to accessing all advice and information, both external as well as internal to the organisation. Finding out what other managers or organisations have diagnosed in similar situations is one of the skills of the good manager. There is always the danger of 'reinventing the wheel'. In most situations there is much virtue in not hiding the issue since there will be much more damage inflicted if someone feels they have been lied to or denied access to information. Diagnosis certainly requires a thorough understanding of all aspects of the organisation: its production methods, its structures, its management processes, its people, its culture. Successful diagnosis requires an appreciation of the scale of the problem. The required management action will be different if the problem is diagnosed as being of a unique nature than it would if it were diagnosed as being of a recurring nature. Diagnosis requires an understanding of the level at which the problem is located; management action will differ depending on the level in the organisation at which the problem is located.

Good managers will never overreact to a problem. The causes of most problems are simple and simple problems usually require simple solutions. The car mechanic would usually check the plugs first when looking for the cause of a car's problems.

Sometimes the diagnosis will be best executed by involving others but, on many

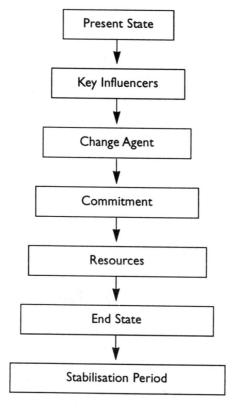

FIGURE 20.2 *How to Manage Change*

occasions, the manager might be advised to step away from the detail of the issue to effect what Turrell (1986) calls a 'helicopter view' whereby the driver of the change (change agent) affords himself or herself an examination of the problem from a wider perspective. The analogy is that the change agent rises above the problem and views the whole scenario from a higher and wider and, hopefully, more objective perspective.

Effecting the Cure

This process begins when the diagnosis has been completed. It is a process where there are many potential pitfalls. The aim of the intervention process will be to remedy the problem or to implement the change. In such circumstances the successful manager would be well advised to know the organisation in all its parts: its people, its culture, its structures, its technologies, its processes. The aim of a successful intervention must be to change as little as possible to overcome the problem or ensure that it will not reoccur in a different guise. The manager must be prepared to meet resistance. Persistence and patience are two very important skills of the successful manager and he must be prepared to achieve success, if necessary, bit by bit. The art of good management requires an appreciation of when to start and when to stop the intervention. As with the diagnosis process, intervention demands the accessing of all sources of information and advice, again both internal and external. Wherever possible, sources of resistance must be won over – usually before the technology is changed. However, it must be stressed that these qualifications must not be seen as weak management; on the contrary the manager has to be prepared to be as bold as necessary. Some situations demand leading from the front, others demand leading from the rear; most, however, demand leading from the middle. Having approached the problem in general terms, it might be useful to examine some of the issues involved in more detail.

FINDING THE KEY INFLUENCERS

When the change agent has completed the diagnostic stage, he or she will have determined both the reasons why the change is necessary and also who needs to be involved in the change.

The technique of 'forcefield analysis' is fundamental to the effective management of change. It is essential that, in major change, thorough environmental analysis is undertaken. Under such an approach all the stakeholders will be examined and their positions on the change assessed. The technique of forcefield analysis allows the analyst to plot these reactions and their interactions. Thus it is important not just to assess the reactions of the individual stakeholders but to assess their interactions. Within this approach it is possible to determine likely movements in opinions when various stakeholders positions have been addressed. For instance, if the views of customers were addressed the view of those employees having to deal with customer complaints might be seen to change in that they might encounter fewer demotivating experiences. The precise state to the forces needs to be reassessed at every stage in the change exercise. Only when the positions of the various stakeholders at each stage of the exercise is analysed will the change be able to be properly managed. Forcefield analysis necessitates that the 'helicopter view' examined in an earlier part of this chapter is adopted.

The technique of forcefield analysis, briefly summarised in Figure 20.3, will enable the change agent to isolate those who are favourably disposed towards change, those who are agnostic towards the need to change and those who would wish to obstruct the change. The persons who are classified as favourably disposed towards the change and who are in a position to help the smooth running of the transitional period are designated 'key influencers'.

GETTING COMMITMENT

Having identified these key influencers, the change agent has to obtain a substantial degree of commitment, at best, or minimise resistance, at worst, amongst all those affected by the change, particularly the key influencers. This may involve coaching the working group towards the desired objective; it may involve democratic or unthreatening autocratic leadership styles. Undoubtedly this commitment will be stronger if all or most of those involved can be persuaded of the inadequacy or inappropriateness of current performance. The change agent has to 'lever' at the pace that the particular task requires or demands.

From present state	To desired state
Forces For Change	Forces Against Change
Public complaints	Staff resistance
Staff dissatisfaction with present methods	Staff apprehension about motives behind the change
Small pockets of support	Pockets of real resistance

FIGURE 20.3 *Force Field Analysis*

GETTING THE RESOURCES

The fact that many changes involve painful decisions by many of those affected has already been acknowledged. Having, probably through great effort, obtained a degree of commitment to the need to change, it is necessary to obtain the resources to put into effect the desired change. The detrimental motivational consequences of not providing adequate resources to effect such change, particularly if there had been resistance to it, would be something to avoid at all costs.

IMPLEMENTING THE CHANGE

The plans should have been drawn up, the commitment obtained and the resources harnessed. The next step is putting into practice the plans just drawn up. Some detail relating to such actions will be addressed in the next part of this chapter. However, an additional point to note is that careful monitoring of progress needs to be effected. In practice, many well conceived plans need to be refined when all the practical problems are revealed. In implementing change Lewin (1951) hypothesised three separate processes

a) Unfreezing existing behaviour old processes, behaviours, values, cultures, designs are commonly well embedded in and strongly favoured by the organisation and its employees. When change is being implemented these old approaches must be eliminated. The use of the word unfreezing clearly indicates how difficult it might be to effect this unlearning process.

b) Determining new behaviour-in addition to unfreezing the old approach new ways of doing things must be found. It might be that some involvement in this search by those affected by the unlearning process might help assuage some of the problems connected with unfreezing.

c) Freezing or embedding new behaviour-given that unfreezing old approaches was difficult it may be seen that a similar degree of difficulty might be encountered in the embedding of the new approaches. The use of the word freezing well reflects the importance of ensuring that the new approaches are owned by all those affected.

Stabilisation period

After any substantial change an astute management would be advised to ensure a period of stabilisation. This period serves a number of purposes.

a) It affords a period for the reviewing of progress – in many cases, even if there has been careful monitoring of the success during the implementation stage, the full consequences and success of the changed circumstances can be assessed only in retrospect.

b) It allows a period of consolidation for the new production methods. Inevitably, changed circumstances need a period of consolidation for all the new requirements to be fully assimilated.

c) It allows a period of recuperation for all those affected. Quite simply it must be accepted that in most circumstances the potentially painful transition needs to be followed by a period, however short, when those who still feel aggrieved or pained can 'lick their wounds'. In most circumstances, following periods of substantial change such stabilisation periods should be as long as possible.

Figure 20.4 shows the strategy employed by Cheshire County Council, a British local authority, in its change of management arrangements in the early 1990s. This figure shows the importance attached to the period of stabilisation. The desired future state was achieved by creating intermediary states, the achievement of each of which created an environment for optimal success of the final change objective.

This chronological approach to managing change can be facilitated by the regular updating of stakeholder positions afforded by forcefield analysis.

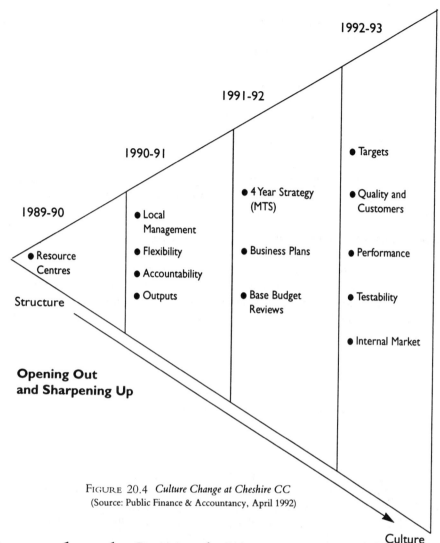

FIGURE 20.4 *Culture Change at Cheshire CC*
(Source: Public Finance & Accountancy, April 1992)

Interrelated Critical Success Factors

In implementing change it is necessary to examine the concept of the critical success factor. This indicates that, in all the behaviours needed to be changed, some are more essential than others. That is, no matter how much is changed, if these essential activities are not changed then failure will ensue. Perhaps the most interesting case to examine is where there are several critical success factors and success will only result when all, not just one or some, factors are addressed. An example might be an ambulance service in need of improving its performance. The service will find that there are three key activities necessary to achieve effective performance.

a) Response time - if a patient is seriously ill or injured the service will have to plan to treat the patient within a specified time period. Unless this is achieved the patient's health may deteriorate to such an extent that successful treatment is unlikely.

b) Appropriate treatment - when the ambulance has arrived success will only be achieved if the ambulance staff are adequately skilled and resourced to stabilise the patient. If this is not afforded an adequate response time is irrelevant. However equally if the ambulance arrives too late the skill of the ambulance crew is similarly irrelevant.

c) Transference to hospital - once the patient is stabilised he or she then has to be transferred to an appropriate hospital to receive the next stage in the treatment programme. Again it is little use stabilising a patient and then not knowing which hospital is able to accept the patient.

It might be useful to note that, in the context of the ambulance service management structure, each one of these critical factors are likely to be the responsibility of different sections of the service. The first might require that ambulances are stationed at key locations rather than at headquarters. Success will result only after careful research. The second is a training issue and the last is a communication problem. Hence it must be noted that the implementation of change can be a complicated and multi-disciplinary process.

Who Should Be the Change Agent?

The assumption up to now in the analysis has been that the driver of the change or the change agent is automatically a senior person in the enterprise. Very often this will be true, since substantial change is often best implemented by someone with both complete knowledge of all facets of the organisation and sufficient power to sustain the change. However, it must be admitted that other legitimate possibilities exist.

AN EXTERNAL AGENT

This is someone outside the organisation. Perhaps the most common example of this would be the management consultant. The use of such consultants has certain very real advantages:

a) usually they have the skills necessary to rigorously examine the problem;

b) the external knowledge they have acquired will allow them to afford the organisation the benefit of learning from others mistakes and successes;

c) they should approach the problem with no preconceived ideas and bring with them the benefits of objectivity;

d) they might be seen as 'neutrals' and, as such, their recommendations might be more acceptable to everyone.

However the use of such consultants has certain dangers:

i) they may be seen by the workers as an unwarranted intrusion into the exercise – someone who 'will cause havoc and then leave us in the mess';
ii) they may lack the intimate knowledge of the particular organisation. In such circumstances their decisions might not be practicable.

THE EMPLOYEE

It must be acknowledged that this constitutes a high risk strategy; however, in certain circumstances the organisation may allow the employee or, perhaps more effectively, a group of employees to act as the change agent. An example of this would be the quality circle examined in the last chapter. This would have the advantage of obtaining more employee commitment to the change but it may lack the desired degree of organisational control over the change required. Under such circumstances the leader would be advised to effect a 'loose/tight' leadership style, allowing the employees the freedom to evolve their own solution whilst at the same time maintaining some control over their actions.

Participation in the Change Process

As change impacts on many people motivational and communication principles, examined in a previous section of this text, suggest that everyone should be involved in the process. It might also be seen that extensive involvement of all affected may delay the adoption of the change and place the organisation in adverse competitive circumstances. It would be useful to examine circumstances where extensive participation is likely to succeed or fail. If participation is used in inappropriate circumstances it may result in disrepute for a concept which in other, more favourable, circumstances might be extremely useful to the organisation.

Child (1983) suggests that participation is likely to succeed best where there is general agreement on the need to change but where the details are open to debate. Under these circumstances there will be a need to allow debate to ensure ownership of the chosen option. However where there is no general agreement on the need to change, rather than waste time debating the need to change, the change agent might be better advised to spend time developing explanations of the need to change which could then, subsequently, be quickly resolved. Finally Child argues that debate will be inhibited if one individual has a monopoly of wisdom and exerts too much power in the debate process. For debate to succeed each participant should feel that he or she has something to offer and that whatever is suggested is likely to be seriously considered.

Individual Differences

The analysis so far seems to suggest that all people are identical in their ability and willingness to accept and adapt to change. Given the diversity of human personality and the diversity of human experiences it might be simplistic to make such an assumption. Ackoff (1986) has hypothesised that individuals can fit into four main categories in terms of their ability or willingness to handle change.

a. Inactivist - this person would be happiest leaving the handling of change to others. he or she might be best characterised by statements such as 'ignore it', 'it will go away' or 'I don't want to know'. In cases where the organisation seeks to obtain major commitment to change it will need to devote special attention to these employees.

b. Reactivist - this person would be predisposed to fight the demands for change. This person might prove to be useful to an organisation when faced with imposed change which it feels it has a chance of overriding. However in cases where the organisation is voluntarily implementing change or where the imposed change cannot be resisted, this type of person will rarely be of use to the organisation. Hence in the latter circumstance the organisation must find ways of winning over or isolating such people.

c. Preactivist - this type of person will be predisposed to be prepared for and predict the need to change. He or she will commonly be found voluntarily gathering intelligence about when and how to change. It may well be that such people are well suited to become Change Agents.

d. Interactivist - this person has similarities to the preactivist but is much more likely to be seen stimulating change. The preactivist will signal the need to change only when necessary but the interactivist will be constantly seeking to change existing activity. The interactivist might be best placed in intelligence gathering activity; however it may be that it would be a brave step to appoint such a person as a change agent since, in many cases, he or she is likely to provoke negative reactions in those less disposed to change. Perhaps the unique role of this person is stimulating, rather than managing, major change.

Common Reasons for Failure

It will be helpful to summarise areas where change has been found to fail. This will help focus the manager's mind on key issues which should be addressed in successfully managing change.

a) Misunderstanding the dynamic nature of change - the assumption that, once change is successfully managed, the manager's responsibilities end. However the reality in many cases is that, once one change has been successfully managed, there is then a need to change elsewhere.

b) Lack of planning – the previous analysis has shown that managing change can be a complex exercise. Such complexity necessitates careful planning to ensure that all involved are informed or that all resources necessary to effect the change are available.

c) No clear vision – in most circumstances the organisation will have a range of options from which it can choose. Only an organisation with a clear vision of where it wants to go will be able to proactively and rationally choose correctly from this range.

d) Goals are too distant – in many circumstances significant changes will be demanded and this may require considerable motivational skills by the change agent. One useful way of sustaining high levels of motivation is allowing those affected to see the positive results of their endeavours. Even though the final desired end state may be some distance away it might be useful to build into the change process some intermediate goals. A very good example of this factor is the introduction of physical environmental improvement in the regeneration of inner cities. The new employment possibilities may be difficult to achieve in the short term but the creation of a more pleasant physical environment might be easier; this might encourage those involved in the more complex task and also might encourage new employers to enter the area.

e) The quick fix – the introduction of intermediate, reinforcing goals should not be confused with this factor. There might be a desire to achieve quick results by accepting a compromise option. Such options should be chosen only if this compromise solution is as effective as the available, more complex, options.

f) Failure to understand the knock-on effects – this is closely related to the quick fix issue just addressed. Perhaps the best analogy might be the repair of cars. It has often been stated that merely mending one part of the engine, without adequate training to understand the impact of this repair on the rest of the engine, is likely to result in failure.

g) Too much or too little involvement – the uses and misuses of participation have already been examined. If the appropriate environmental circumstances are favourable to extensive participation, such participation should be undertaken. However participation should not be pursued at all expense. Participation in the wrong circumstances can, for instance, inhibit creativity and innovation.

h) The choice of the wrong change agent – this has been examined at length previously in this chapter and it might be necessary to merely briefly conclude that the correct choice from the available range of agents must be made.

i) Cultural resistance – some organisations have cultures which facilitate change, others have cultures which do not so readily accommodate change. If an organisation is to be prepared for the rapidly changing managerial environment of the new millennium, it must facilitate the development of change accommodating cultures. Good examples of such counterproductive cultures are blame and fear cultures. If the organisation is to be prepared for regular change, the fear of failure must be eradicated and similarly the hunting down of those who try to adapt positively, but perhaps occasionally fail, must be discouraged.

j) The legacy of previous change - it must be acknowledged that most changes take place in an environment where the organisation is still dealing with the consequences of previous changes. Circumstances where problems encountered with change are not quickly addressed will inhibit the organisation's reaction to subsequent change.

Pilot Studies in the Change Exercise

Many organisations implement change by first trying it out through a pilot study. The pilot study has certain very real advantages as a means of implementing change.

a) It can encourage experimentation but at the same time limit damage if the tried solution turns out to be inappropriate.

b) It can smooth the way for the real change. The good points of the change can be detected and any 'teething problems' can be overcome.

c) It can help spread the adjustment to change over a longer time period. In such circumstances the adjustment to change can feel less painful to all those affected, and the less the pain felt, the less the resistance should be.

However pilot studies can bring with them potential difficulties.

a) Firstly, they can delay the change unnecessarily; a smooth change is to be welcomed but a smooth change implemented too late has no positive features.

b) Secondly, the pilot study can be effectively 'ignored'. Comments like 'Ignore it ! It will go away' are often heard.

c) Finally, it might be seen to be artificial. Comments such as 'forget it! It's not the real thing' can also be heard.

Finally it might be useful to briefly examine facilities examined elsewhere in this text which might facilitate the smooth running of the change process.

a) Change will be facilitated by effective training and development.

b) The uncertainties created by change will be ameliorated by the use of mentoring whereby a protege, the person affected by the change, is guided through the change by a mentor.

c) Team involvement and effective team building can help the individuals affected by the change to adapt positively to the change.

d) Counselling can assuage the more negative consequences of change.

e) Career Planning can help employees react positively to the change by anticipating the change and planning a positive career reaction to the change.

f) Effective market positioning can enable the organisation to proactively respond to changes they might encounter.

g) Creating an atmosphere where all affected by the change feel involved in the management of that change can help avoid the more negative, counterproductive reactions which might be found.

h) Planning information technology can help an organisation react in an organised fashion to a rapidly changing environment.

Summary

It must be recognised that most, if not all, organisations are increasingly subject to change. This change can be as a result of an organisation's own decision; however, more commonly, the change is imposed upon an organisation. Successful organisations have to respond positively to such change. It must be stressed that the successful implementation of change, through whatever agents, is a skill which distinguishes the good from the bad manager. The implementing of substantial change is a potential organisational problem which can, to some extent, be overcome by planning and good management. The major strategy which the manager can use in the planning of such change is careful consideration of the circumstances of the case in hand.

Exercise

Examine an organisation with which you are familiar. Choose two occasions where it has or had to adapt to a changing environment. Critically appraise the ways in which it adapted in those two cases.

Further Reading

Ackoff, R. L. (1986) *Management in Small Doses*, Wiley

Benis, G.W. et al (1976) *The Planning of Change*, Holt, Rinehart and Winston

Broome, A.K. (1990) *Managing Change*, Macmillan

Connock, S. (1991) *HR Vision: Managing a Quality Workforce*, Institute of Personnel Management

Cummings, T. G. and Worley, C. G. (1993) *Organization Management and Change*, West Publishing

Kanter, R.M. (1984) *The Change Masters*, Allen and Unwin

Kay, J. (1993) *Foundations of Corporate Success*, Oxford University Press

Lewin, K. (1951) *Field Theory in Social Science* Harper & Row
Matteson, M.T. and Ivancevich, J.M. (1987) *Controlling Work Stress*, Jossey Bass
Morden, T. (1996) *Principles of Management*, McGraw-Hill
HMSO, (1986) Change and Innovation – a Challenge for the NHS
Plant, R. (1987) *Making Change and Making It Stick*, Fontana
Waterman, R. H. (1987) *The Renewal Factor* Pan

Chapter twenty-one

Ethics and Management

L E A R N I N G   O B J E C T I V E S

- Appreciate what is meant by the term ethics
- Understand the constituent features of ethics
- Appraise the interrelationships between these features
- Identify the importance of legislation in this area
- Assess the extent to which organisations should embrace ethical issues beyond legislative requirements
- Apply the issues examined to organisations with which you are familiar
- Identify areas where further research might be necessary

The study of the role and importance of ethics in the management of organisations has assumed substantial importance in the managerial environment. At various points in this text the difficulties of organisations retaining control over their actions has been attested. In this analysis the subject of ethics and management will be examined from two perspectives:

1. Ensuring management activity serves organisational purposes and benefits;
2. Examining the issue of whether the organisation is pursuing ethical objectives in its relationships with its external environment.

This distinction is of considerable importance since the first could be deemed to be an irrefutable principle of management, whereas the importance of the second is debatable. The extent to which an organisation owes a duty to the outside world to abide by ethical standards is not universally accepted within the practice of management, although it is recognised that some ethical principles have to be adopted by organisations in their relationships with their external environment.

Ensuring Organisational Benefit from All Activity

This issue is examined in detail in the chapter on intrapreneurship. As organisations seek to gain competitive advantage in the various markets in which they operate they seek to afford extensive managerial freedom to those managers who operate in those markets. This spirit and culture of independence can afford real benefits to an organisation. The spirit of entrepreneurship might need to be induced by an organisation: it might need to encourage innovation; it might need to nurture imagination, it might need to financially support emerging innovatory products; and it might wish to facilitate entrepreneurship in its workforce by providing special incentives to employees involved in such ventures. This culture is further facilitated by delegating budgets and encouraging managerial independence.

Such independence and innovatory cultures might introduce elements of danger into the organisational environment. The concepts of organisational and individual properties might be less readily separated. In circumstances of strong centrally controlled managerial environments, individuals are constantly driven to assume organisational values; additionally there is no scope for anything to be undertaken which does not benefit the organisation and the organisation alone. However when managers are freed from such constraints the ease of individual as well as organisational gain is increased. Furthermore, even if no independent gain is suspected, such independence could induce in an organisation excessive variety of approaches to identical aspects of management which might threaten the coordination of the various parts of the organisation.

If real threats to organisational control exist, the organisation will have to impose some controls over the potentially damaging aspects of intrapreneurial independence. A useful way of inducing such internal ethical standards and organisational controls is the creation of codes of practice. Such codes of practice would expound the principles which should be pursued in managerial decisions in an intrapreneurial environment. Below are some questions which might be asked in the preparation of such codes and to determine ethical benchmarks.

1. Are my actions legal?

2. Is my decision balanced – have I considered the interests of all stakeholders in the making of my decision?

3. Would I be happy if someone else made this decision?

4. Can I explain my actions to my superior?

5. Can I explain my decisions to my subordinates?

6. Would I pursue such actions in my relationships with my family?
    If these codes are to have full impact they must be pursued with a substantial

degree of consultation with all those affected. Clear explanations of the need for such codes needs to be given.

Ethical Relationships with the External Environment

There are clear connections between the two categories in that one of the driving forces in pursuing ethical principles in external relationships is affording a positive role model to discourage poor internal ethical standards. However the need to pursue ethical standards in an organisation's relationships with its external environment warrants examination in its own right.

It might be claimed that, with the pressures of an increasingly competitive commercial environment, any arguments as to the legitimacy of such an approach can be seen to increase in strength. There are three separate aspects to this concept: legality, the assumption of social and environmental costs, as well as financial costs in the organisation's economic models, and the pursuance of ethical principles.

LEGALITY

The assumption of legal principles is easiest to justify. Any organisation will incur potentially damaging financial costs if it pursues activity without considering its legality. Equally important, however, is the poor reputation that might ensue; in a competitive commercial environment, an organisation with a poor reputation will not be best placed to succeed.

ASSUMPTION OF SOCIAL AND ENVIRONMENTAL RESPONSIBILITY

This concept assumes that it is difficult to separate the prospects of a business from the prospects of the society in which it operates. Without considering the external social impact of an organisation's actions that organisation will not be able to fully appreciate the full, long-term, internal impact of its decisions. This is a less clear issue to accommodate than legality.

The assumption of such responsibilities can be seen to limit the short-term commercial options available to an organisation. For instance, if an organisation considers increasing its level of activity and then rejects this on the grounds of the increased traffic problems it might cause in the area in which it operates, it has obviously lost this commercial opportunity. Similarly, if an organisation chooses to introduce physical environmental protection projects beyond those required by legislation, this can be seen to increase at least its short-term costs and threaten at least its short-term competitiveness.

It must be admitted that there are ethical arguments surrounding this subject but, at this stage, it is useful to pursue other arguments in favour of such a strategy. In the long-term any organisation will be required to finance any harmful social or physical environmental effects of its actions. As societies finance their social and environmental policies from taxation sources and as organisations contribute to this taxation, such costs will in the longer term impact financially on such organisations. In addition it could be argued that, if these costs do not impact on the organisation but on others, the financing of such costs will decrease the organisation's customers' net disposable income; hence in such circumstances the organisation will be affected, in the longer term, by all the costs of its actions. Within the context of this argument, an organisation might seek to gain a competitive advantage by seeking a reputation as a socially and environmentally responsible organisation. The organisation might seek to provide aid or financial support to local, regional, national or international artistic, social, sporting, environmental or charitable ventures. The driving force might be to secure a market position or it might be driven by purely altruistic motives. Commonly, but not universally, such support is accompanied by publicity for that support.

It might be useful to conclude that many organisations such as McDonalds, place great emphasis on the publication of their social and environmental policies. In addition organisations, such as McDonalds and Pilkington, can sometimes have two separate budgets to help support such ventures. One budget sum will be made available for public ventures and another sum for less public ventures.

PURELY ETHICAL DIMENSIONS

The legitimacy of this category is less readily obvious. It is intimately connected with the other two categories in that legality and the assumption of external costs constitute elements of ethics. However, in the context of this argument, those elements will be excluded. Without the assumption of legality, ethics is predicated on value judgements. It embraces balance, equity, fairness. The questions asked earlier concerning ethical benchmarks, originally examined in the context of internal ethics, can be seen to apply equally to the corporate dimension.

The issue of the legitimacy or utility of such an approach remains to be addressed. In the short term the assumption by the organisation of ethical values might reduce the competitiveness of that organisation. For example, to remain competitive the organisation might wish to take public advantage of a situation where one of its competitors encountered problems. Perhaps an environmental accident in one petroleum company could be publicly exploited by its competitors. However, if the organisation questions its ethical values, it might decide not to exploit this commercial opportunity. It might consider that such an environmental disaster was a consequence of operation in the industry and hence it would not be fair or ethical to exploit this unfortunate event. It might consider that such exploitation might cause it to be subject to retaliatory action at some time in the future. Perhaps the concept of ethics would be better demonstrated if the action were motivated not by fear of retaliation but from a more altruistic perspective illustrated by the statement treat others as you would wish to be treated yourself.

Another factor to consider is that in rapidly changing environments an organisation could benefit from some guidance as to its fundamental principles. Thus it might be that the formulation of its mission and/or corporate objectives might include an ethical dimension.

Finally the organisation might conclude that, in the longer term, there might be a competitive advantage in publicly embracing ethical principles. Such an organisation is likely to gain a high public reputation and this reputation might be exploited by the organisation in obtaining a competitive advantage or niche place in its markets.

Range of Managerial Responses

The analysis has tended to focus on the positive features of such an ethical approach. However, the problems, particularly short-term, have been explored. Under such problematic circumstances it is inevitable that organisations will vary in the extent to which they embrace these issues. Some will emphasise the shorter-term strategies since, without such an approach, the organisation may not have a long term; some will pursue longer-term considerations since they wish to pursue longer-term objectives. Equally organisations will vary in the extent to which they are likely to encounter such issues. Some will operate in economic areas where externalities are limited whereas others will operate in circumstances where externalities predominate.

What cannot be disputed is that the organisation must be prepared to react to such potential complications in ways which are consistent with its environment. The assumption of wider ethical standards by United Biscuits is shown in Figure 21.

> "We compete vigorously, energetically, untiringly but we also compete ethically and honestly. Our competitive success is founded on excellence - of product and service. We have no need to disparage our competitors either directly or by implication or innuendo...
> No-one may attempt improperly to acquire a competitor's trade secrets or other proprietary or confidential information. 'Improper' means are activities such as industrial espionage, hiring competitors' employees to get confidential information, urging competitive personnel or customers to disclose confidential information, or any other approach which is not completely open and above board."
>
> (United Biscuits)

FIGURE 21.1 *External Commitments*

Introducing Ethics into an Organisation's Values

If an organisation has assumed an extensive role for ethics in its core of values, it must examine ways in which ethics can be introduced into its daily routines. There are three possible mutually reinforcing strategies which can be taken by an organisation.

ETHICS TRAINING

If the organisation is to embrace ethics then all people involved in the organisation's activities - possibly including its customers - need to understand the utility of the concept and how it can be evidenced in the policies, decisions and management of the organisation.

ETHICS ADVOCATES

At the policy level it may be that, particularly in the early stages, there needs to be a special examination of all activity to ensure it complies with acceptable ethical standards. Thus the concept of ethics needs special advocates to establish it as a credible and important concept within the organisation.

CODES OF PRACTICE

The concept of ethics, particularly once it has been established, can be continued and nurtured by the establishment of principles in codes of conduct which all employees are required to follow.

Summary

In an increasingly complex managerial environment all organisations have to determine their stance on ethical issues surrounding their managerial decisions. Such factors can intrude into an organisation's internal and external relationships. Legislation sometimes imposes ethical obligations on organisations but the issue of ethics extends beyond mere legality. There are costs associated with the assumption of such obligations but there are also potential benefits to be obtained from such an approach. Any organisation should determine its response to this issue having considered its special circumstances. Having determined its position on this issue managerial decisions should be consistent with such a position.

Exercise

In the context of your chosen organisation examine the ethical issues which might constitute part of its environment. To what extent does the organisation embrace these ethical concerns? Is the organisation's reaction to these issues adequate or sensible? If you consider the organisation's reactions inadequate suggest ways in which its reactions could become more appropriate and effective.

Further Reading

Cannon, T. (1992) *Corporate Responsibility*, Pitman

Gray, R., Owen, D., Maunders, K. (1987) *Corporate Social Responsibility Accounting and Accountability*, Prentice Hall

Frederick, W.C., Post, J.E., Davis, K. (1992) *Corporate Strategy, Public Policy and Ethics*, McGraw-Hill

Harvey, B., Smith, S., Wilkinson, B. (1984) Corporate Social Responsibility, MacMillan

Knox, J. (1985) *An Introduction to Corporate Philanthropy, B.I.M.*

Smith, D. (ed) (1993) Business and the Environment, Paul Chapman

Management Processes

OBJECTIVES

Any organisation, no matter what its structure or design, effects its management duties through the undertaking of certain processes. After reading this chapter the student should be able to understand the range of options available to an organisation in its choice and design of such management processes.

INTRODUCTION

No matter what style of individual management adopted by the manager, no matter what the organisational design, the individual organisation fulfils many of its management obligations through the processes of planning, control and accountability. For a thorough and comprehensive understanding of the total management task it is necessary to examine these processes.

The Process
of Planning

- **Understand the importance of effective planning in the management of any organisation**

- **Identify the various approaches to planning which could be undertaken by an organisation**

- **Appreciate the importance of choosing the right approach**

- **Examine the factors which need to be considered in determining an organisation's approach to planning**

- **Understand the interrelationships between planning and control**

- **Apply the concepts studied to organisations with which you are familiar**

- **Identify areas where further research might be necessary**

Any attempt to manage an organisation must include planning. Without planning the organisation can have no purpose, no rationale upon which to decide how and when its resources should be allocated and no way of determining the extent of success of its operations. This is not to claim that great thought always goes into the planning process. However, an organisation which lays great emphasis on the planning of its activities should be better placed to achieve success. The planning process can typically embrace a number of levels or stages. At this time the assumption will be that each one of these stages or levels involves either a formal document or a formal deliberation or consideration; however, as will be seen later in the chapter, some approaches to the process of planning may not result in formal documentation or deliberation.

a) The corporate objectives or mission statement – for an organisation to be able to plan properly it needs to know what its purpose is; it needs strategic objectives or a mission. However, rarely will an organisation have one objective. Some objectives will be production centred, others will be based upon desired financial performance, others will involve more social objectives (for example environmental issues, employment issues). An organisation operating in the public service is likely to have a more complex set of objectives than would many enterprises operating in the private sector. The likelihood is that there will be more social objectives intruding into its purposes; this does not mean that organisations in the private sector have no social objectives, but merely that the extent of imposed or voluntary social objectives will likely be greater in the public service. Figure 22.1 shows a list of possible objectives for organisations operating in a wide range of economic environments.

Objective	Charity	Hospital	Insurance Company	Car Manufacturer
1. Survive	✔	✔	✔	✔
2. Provide a service	✔	✔	✔	✔
3. To grow	✔		✔	✔
4. To be efficient	✔	✔	✔	✔
5. Make profits			✔	✔

FIGURE 22.1   *Objectives for Various Organisations*

As will be seen later, some enterprises will regularly and rigorously reappraise their objectives, whereas others will hardly ever overtly question their objectives. This statement will usually be based at the organisational rather than operational unit level.

b) Strategic plan — typically this will be medium-term in nature and based upon an organisation's objectives or mission. Depending upon whether the organisation rigorously questions its objectives, the evolution of this plan may involve high-profile, positive activity. However, if the organisation rarely questions its objectives or mission there is a likelihood that such a plan will be based extensively upon that of the last planning period and altered, if at all, only at the margin. This plan will again be based at the organisational rather than operational unit level.

c) Short-term management plan — this will be based upon the strategic plan. This, in its turn may vary radically from one planning period to the next or it may vary hardly at all. The period covered by such a plan would usually, but not necessarily, be one year. Unlike the previously mentioned plans, this plan will usually be based at the level of the operational unit, be it a direct production unit or a support unit.

d) Resource plan/budget — the operational unit will be afforded resources sufficient to enable it to achieve its plans. The nature of this budget will be examined later in this text. It must be acknowledged at this stage that this order of analysis assumes that budgetary allocations are based upon previously planned activity; as will be seen later in the text. However, budgetary constraints may be the primary driving force in the planning process.

e) Individual targets – this short-term management plan will be subdivided into a series of individual or small group targets.

f) Monitoring – the operational unit is then measured against the achievement of its plans, its budget or its targets. As will be seen in the chapter on the Control Process this activity needs to be conducted in due time for remedial action to be taken.

g) Budgetary control – this is the special form of monitoring concerned with the financial consequences of operational activity. It is examined in more detail in the next chapter.

h) Control – the achievement of a plan or, indeed, a set of objectives is not in all cases necessarily an indication of organisational success. An organisation has still to discover whether the achievement of its plans and objectives has made the desired impact on perceived need. This additional problem is likely to be encountered in the less financially motivated parts of the public service. This issue is addressed in more detail in the next chapter.

Approaches to or Philosophies of Planning

Not all organisations approach their planning in the same way. In fact the precise format adopted in the previous analysis is, in most easily understood form, merely one of a number of possible approaches to planning. An organisation can base its planning on the following approaches or philosophies.

THE RATIONAL APPROACH

This is modelled in Figure 22.2 and is the approach which has just been assumed in the immediately preceding analysis. It is the view propounded by the scientific management theorists Weber and Fayol. Under such a system the organisation would identify the problem and set specific and measurable objectives against which it could monitor its actions; in the determination of its plans it would identify all alternative means of fulfilling its objectives, predict all possible consequences and then determine the most appropriate plan. The consequent monitoring and control would be established against the basis of clearly specified objectives, plans and targets. An assessment of the validity, acceptability and practicality of this approach reveals that it would be acceptable only under certain tightly defined circumstances.

FIGURE 22.2 *The Planning Cycle*

It is useful where the organisation is able to adapt, without any restrictions, to changing objectives. Also, it has utility where it is easy to assess all possible outcomes. Finally, there is a much greater incentive to use this approach where the organisation has encountered criticism for its present activities or where there is no consensus on the appropriate required action. Under these circumstances the tried and tested will not suit consumers and a real attempt to seek alternatives, has to be made.

If there are no problems in assessing alternatives, it is an acceptable approach to the planning task in times of a rapidly changing environment or in times of severe organisational failure. However, in many organisations it will not be easy to determine all possible outcomes. In addition, many organisations in the public service and the private sector operate in the type of environment where strong pressure or interest groups prevent an organisation departing too radically from established practice. In many organisations, in times of stability, it could be claimed that existing activity constitutes a tried and tested way of meeting consumer needs and that such a radical reassessment of activities would rarely be appropriate.

THE BOUNDED RATIONALITY APPROACH

This approach was first formally described by the theorist Simon. Like the previous approach it involves the examination of alternative plans and an attempt to assess their respective outcomes.

However, it differs from the rational approach in that it seeks a less radical or extensive range of possible alternatives. Under this approach the fact that not all options can be easily determined is acknowledged; furthermore, there may be rigidity within the organisation (for instance, narrowly defined employee skills), preventing it from deviating too far from existing patterns of activity. As such a more limited model is constructed, that is the one which will suffice ('satisfice'), based upon only those alternatives which are deemed practicable. In many ways it could be seen as a compromised form of the rational approach.

Its benefits and applicability are based upon those of the rational approach. It is an approach which again has more validity when the organisation knows its present activity patterns are no longer appropriate. Equally, it is an approach which can be defended when there is no consensus on what to do. It is particularly useful where the organisation is undergoing change in its environment. Under all these circumstances the tried and tested will not be acceptable.

However, as with the previous approach, it is of limited use where there are powerful pressure or interest groups defending the status quo. It is seen to be a waste of resources if consumer satisfaction exists with existing activity. This approach is probably more realistic than the previous approach in that it does more obviously acknowledge the constraints of existing stores of knowledge; clearly the organisation has to plan and, more particularly, act within certain time constraints, and to expect circumstances to obtain where it would be allowed to delay action while all possible options are considered may be seen, in practice, to be naive.

THE MUDDLING THROUGH OR INCREMENTAL APPROACH

This approach was first formally described by the theorist Lindblom. It states that with limited knowledge, limited time, political resistance to massive change, strong protective pressure groups, producer resistance to change, the best, and certainly most practicable, approach is to base the plans for the future on what was done in the past.

An assessment of the practicality and validity of this approach suggests that it is suited to certain situations. If the organisation has no reason to believe its past activities will not continue to bring success any approach other than this would be both a waste of time and inappropriate. Where the organisation is constrained by powerful internal interest groups or, more importantly, where the organisation's consumers would be resistant to change (however desirable this may be from the viewpoint of the organisation) such an approach can be seen to be the most appropriate. Finally, where the organisation is forced to operate within short time frames in its planning process, it may be that the bold stances of the previous approaches result in radical change for little purpose. For instance, in a United Kingdom local authority there is little sense in undergoing radical change when in four or less years the political balance of the local authority could change and the initially brave decision may be reversed. In times of organisational failure and in times of environmental change such an approach has much less validity.

It can be concluded that the various planning strategies each have circumstances where they are the most appropriate reaction to the prevailing circumstances. It is possible that as circumstances change an organisation may have to change its chosen approach to planning. However, any change to an established approach to planning will constitute a major change and the management of change problems identified in a previous section will be encountered. It must never be claimed, however, that difficulty is a sufficiently powerful excuse when all other factors seem to dictate the need to change.

What Constitutes a Good Planning System?

Despite the fact that organisations can adopt radically different approaches to their planning duties, it must be acknowledged that any system, based on any approach, can be judged as to its success, against a set list of desired characteristics.

a) A strong sense of purpose – although this is not an essential prerequisite of a good plan, if an organisation finds difficulties in establishing its purpose or mission it is not really best placed to take full advantage of a positive planning system.
b) As much certainty as possible – this does not necessarily mean that an organisation operating in uncertain conditions cannot plan, but a stable environment does provide a much more certain atmosphere to facilitate the planning process.
c) Good access to information – for any organisation to successfully plan it needs to access information which will enable it to assess all the required options. In addition, the organisation needs to be able to determine the extent to which its plans are being achieved. This intelligence gathering will be hindered by poor access to information.
d) Commitment – certainly many management tasks fail through inadequate commitment. This commitment is especially important in a task or duty as vital to organisational success as planning. This need to assure commitment will be examined in more detail later in this chapter.
e) Realism – the very uncertainty of the planning environment makes it difficult to predict the future with a real degree of certainty and yet any plan which is based upon seriously unrealistic assumptions is not best placed to succeed. Thus in all its planning obligations the organisation would be best advised to 'keep its feet on the ground'. The financial elements of this realism will be examined specifically later in the chapter.

f) Flexibility – this may appear at first glance to be a strange requirement of a plan given that the very aim of the plan is to ensure that action accords with stated aims. However, the organisational and planning environment may change in ways which were not predicted when the plan was drawn up; under such circumstances it will be detrimental to the good reputation and future success of the planning process to insist that the plan is pursued despite the changed circumstances.

The Importance of Financial Factors

When an organisation undertakes its planning duties it is essential that it pays specific attention to the financial consequences of its plans or the financial constraints within which the plan is to be effected. These financial factors are expressed in a budget. This budget is constructed for the following reasons.

a) So that the organisation can achieve its plans by harnessing the necessary resources. Clearly the organisation will never achieve its plans and objectives if it lacks sufficient money to produce its products.
b) So that the spending and receipt of money can be co-ordinated. The budget enables an organisation to ensure that money is spent only when an organisation can afford to so do and that money is received at times when it is most needed by the organisation; without a budget the organisation's plans would not be capable of being achieved.
c) To highlight the existence of surplus resources. At times when such surplus resources exist, management decisions as to extensions of activity, diversification or utilisation of money by investments can be made. The construction of a budget provides the organisation with a better appreciation of its capacity to plan in certain areas.
d) The associated budgetary control affords one of the more easily measured forms of control. This will be examined in the next chapter.

Involving Employees in the Planning Exercise

The evidence strongly supports the argument that, in most circumstances, there are powerful reasons for obtaining the co-operation and participation of all those people who will be involved in an organisation's operational activities in the preparation of the plan. This should establish the principle of ownership outlined elsewhere in the text; if people who are charged with achieving the plan are actually, to some extent, involved in the preparation of that plan, they can be seen to become more involved and more committed to maintaining the integrity of the plan. Without this involvement, the planning process could be viewed as remote, or even irrelevant. The importance of a task is less readily understood and accepted if that task is seen to be imposed upon potentially unwilling participants. This principle has been examined in more detail in the chapter on Human Motivation.

An Integrated Approach to Planning

An alternative perspective on the planning process is that based upon the work of Rogers in 1990. Figure 22.3 shows the progress of the planning process from needs analysis, through assessment of desired detailed parameters, to the production process, to the control process. The perspective is useful in that it can be seen to embrace the rational, bounded rationality and incremental approaches to the planning process. The model can be seen to be a resolution of potentially conflicting demands or pressures at various stages in the planning process.

a) The needs of the various constituencies are assessed – the pressures on the organisation from internal and external sources are examined. These pressures exert on the organisation a need to act or plan its next course of action. These pressures encompass:
   i) market intelligence information – for instance, whether competitors are going to improve their product or change their market position or whether the organisation has itself decided on the desirability of market repositioning through identifying gaps in the market or the existence of new markets;
   ii) the changing political or legal framework within which the organisation is operating;
   iii) pressures from employees to vary productive activity.
b) Precision in product or service specification – the broad need to act has now been determined and the organisation then rquires to 'put flesh' on its intentions. In this it will be mindful of a number of potentially conflicting pressures:
   i) more precise information regarding customer requirements;
   ii) availability of resources to achieve the desired outcome;
   iii) the cost of achieving the required outcome – the organisation then has to resolve these potentially conflicting pressures which then allows it to progress to the next stage in the planning process.
c) Specification of product or service characteristics. This specification will have to be determined by assessing another set of potentially conflicting pressures:
   i) market expectations;
   ii) internal intelligence;

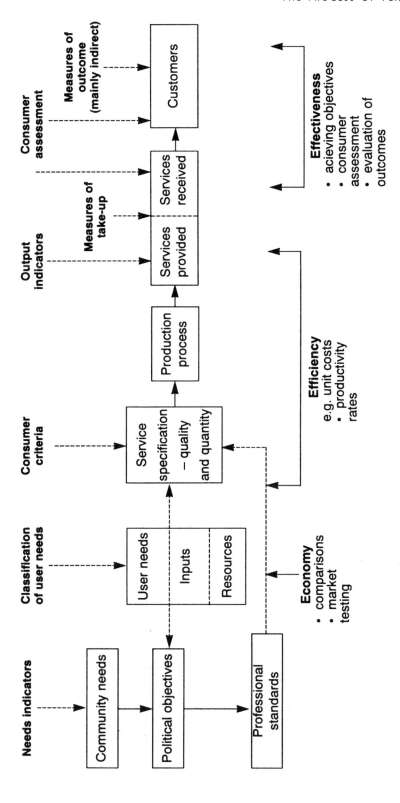

FIGURE 22.3. *The Planning Process*

iii) employee pressure — when it has decided upon its product or service specification it then progresses to the production process.

As can be seen from the Figure this model then extends into control activity. This section of the model will be examined in the next chapter.

Business Planning

Over the past few years, in many organisations in the public service and the private sector, the desire to devolve management decisions to those most directly connected with the production process has seen the emergence of a 'business planning' approach to the planning and associated budgetary process. Under this approach much more emphasis is given to business or financial objectives; much more independence over the way in which objectives are to be achieved is given to those immediately involved with direct service provision. The business plan will have a number of sections:

a) a specification of objectives;
b) an identification of target markets;
c) the specification of production and financial targets;
d) the generation of a marketing plan;
e) the production of an income and expenditure budget;
f) a specification of anticipated sources of finance;
g) the production of a cash budget.

This can be seen to be a 'telescoping' into one document of a wide range of management activities which would, in a functionally-based organisation, be undertaken by different parts or sections of the organisation. It can work only if the organisation has a clear indication of its mission and that of its component parts and if there is a willingness to devolve many decisions to those who implement them. There are a number of potential difficulties with such an approach which need to be overcome.

a) It has been stated that one of the primary purposes of the business planning approach is to establish more commitment amongst operational staff to the achievement of the targets specified in the plan. Hence it is essential that those involved in the production have some significant input into the construction of the plan. This necessitates that those charged with constructing the business plan must have the adequate skills to fulfil all the technical requirements of its production. This is a significant problem given the variety of tasks undertaken. It is necessary, therefore, either to train all those involved in these new skills or to import such expertise into the working group. This importation will bring new complications to the management process and these are examined elsewhere in the text.

b) If the various sections within the organisation each pursue their own objectives and business plans there could emerge within the organisation inconsistency or, worse still, incompatibility of such plans. There will be a need to maintain some separate organisational identity, purpose and integrity; the limits of authority of the corporate institution and that of those involved in the creation of these plans must be clearly understood and accepted. However, it must be recognised that once a degree of independence has been granted to those producing the business plans they must be allowed to pursue their task with minimum interference.

c) The production of a business plan serves no purpose if it is not subject to the same degree of monitoring and control as are traditional budgets and plans. Given the philosophy of devolution, it is essential that such monitoring and control are not resented by those involved in the planning process. This might be best effected by allocating the duties of monitoring and control to those involved in the construction of the plan. The alternative would be to run the danger of being seen to impose external monitoring and control; this might be detrimental to achieving the desired high levels of motivation. However, it must be admitted that such external monitoring and control would at least be effected by those with the required skills. Perhaps if such external activity is to be undertaken it should be low profile and unobtrusive in character.

d) The business plan can focus too much on the short term at the possible expense of the long term. Thus care must be taken to ensure that longer-term strategic objectives are considered within the planning process.

Summary

The planning process is probably the most important process within the organisation. As such, it is essential that the way in which plans are created accords as fully as possible with the philosophies and cultures of the organisation. The necessity to plan involves the necessity to consider financial aspects and consequences. The primary requirements of a plan and budget are that they should be accurate, realistic and compatible with organisational objectives. In most situations, the more involved all employees feel in such processes, the more successful these processes will be. A plan and a budget which is not accepted by those who are charged with its operations is not best placed to succeed.

Exercise

In the context of the organisation examined in the exercise in the last chapter critically appraise its approaches to planning its policies and actions.

Further Reading

Argenti, J. (1968) *Corporate Planning*, Allen and Unwin

Burn, T. and Stalker, G.M. (1968) *The Management of Innovation*, Tavistock

Fayol, H. (1949) *General and Industrial Management*, Pitman

Goldsmith, W. and Clutterbuck, D. (1984) *The Winning Streak*, Weidenfeld and Nicolson

Miles, R.E. and Snow, C.C. (1978) *Organisational Strategy*, McGraw Hill

Mintzberg, H. (1978) *Patterns in Strategy Formulation*, Management Science

Morden, A. R. (1993) *Business Strategy and Planning*, Mcgraw-Hill

Morden, T. (1996), *Principles of Management*, McGraw-Hill

Quinn, J.B. (1980) *Strategies for Change*, Irwin

Rogers, S, (1990) *Performance Management in Local Government*, Longman

Simon, H.A. (1965) *Administrative Behaviour*, Macmillan

Taylor, F.W. (1947) *Scientific Management*, Harper and Row

Townsend, R. (1984) *Further Up the Organisation*, Michael Joseph

Weber, M. (1947) *Theory of Social and Economic Organisation*, Free Press

Woodward, Joan (1965) *Industrial Organisation – Theory and Practice*, OUP

Chapter twenty-three

The Control Process

L E A R N I N G   O B J E C T I V E S

- Understand the importance of effective control in the management of any organisation

- Identify the various approaches to control which could be undertaken by an organisation

- Appreciate the importance of choosing the right approach

- Examine the factors which need to be considered in determining an organisation's approach to control

- Understand the interrelationships between planning, control and accountability

- Apply the concepts studied to organisations with which you are familiar

- Identify areas where further research might be necessary

One of the most important management processes in an organisation is that of control. The assumption is that an organisation must have a reasonably clear view of what it wants to do and as such it will specify objectives and targets. Once it has set its objectives and targets it must determine the extent to which it is meeting these objectives and targets. This is essentially two distinct processes: firstly determining whether stated objectives and targets have been achieved and secondly determining whether the objectives and targets specified were appropriate. The nature of the control process and its place in the total management process is shown in Figure 23.1.

It must not be claimed that the control process is always easy to implement. Indeed, although there are a variety of activities or media which allow the organisation to control its activities, it may well be that such facilities are not readily available in every case; furthermore, it cannot be guaranteed that the messages they give will always be consistent.

a) Simple observation – under this activity the controller, usually the manager, must simply undertake the normal management duty of observation. In many cases this affords the simplest and indeed most valid control messages. For instance, the simple action of visual observation should help detect a poor quality product or impoliteness to customers or consumers. However, in many cases simple observation will not access all the important 'control messages' and other media can and should be accessed.

b) Complaints – under this form of arrangement the controller may assume that the organisation is successful unless there is a complaint. In the United Kingdom public service there are a variety of institutions and complaints media which help the organisation in this aspect of its control processes. In addition to complaints direct from the consumer, the additional facilities of ombudsmen, user councils and regulatory bodies are available in many public service institutions.

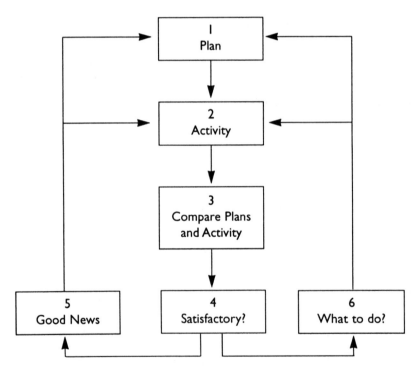

FIGURE 23.1 *The Control Process*

c) Quality control processes – many organisations employ quality control personnel or build quality control tasks into the jobs of production personnel. Most examples of such processes are found in the industrial sectors of economic activity.

d) Client or customer satisfaction questionnaires – it may well be that such quality control measures are not as immediately available in all cases and, as such, more indirect quality assessments such as the customer satisfaction questionnaire may be necessary; only when an organisation determines when it is meeting consumer needs will it be able to express satisfaction with its performance. A good example would be the well established consumer satisfaction questionnaires used by British Rail.

e) Performance appraisal – it must be acknowledged that, to some extent, information on organisational performance can be accessed from the records of the performance of individuals within the organisation. This has been examined in more detail in an earlier section.

f) Budgetary control – obviously the financial performance of an organisation is a crucial element in its overall performance and the fact that an organisation has achieved its budgetary targets must, to some extent, reflect favourably upon the organisation. This can be seen to be of particular importance in those organisations where financial objectives assume primacy.

g) Internal audit – the internal audit section of an organisation is part of the control process of the organisation. Organisations charge such sections with the examination of the systems used in the organisation to achieve production. The examination of such systems is an essential part of the overall control process. The more internal audit involves itself in value for money assessments (examined later in this chapter), the more powerful its role in the overall control process.

h) External audit – the external audit of an organisation is an additional audit control. The more the external audit involves itself in value for money investigations and the publication of performance indicators (for example the audit commission in the United Kingdom public sector) the stronger its place in the overall control process becomes. It must be acknowledged that in the private sector the role of external audit in the total control process is much more limited; however, this does not mean that the importance of external audit in these circumstances should be dismissed.

Value for Money Investigations

In many cases organisations may find that simple assessments of performance are difficult to achieve for the following reasons.

a) Very often objectives are not specified in terms which lend themselves to ready measurement. For instance, it may be difficult to obtain general agreement on the purpose of health care: is it to cure the sick, to prolong life, to improve the quality of life or to prevent ill health?

   The reality is that it is all of these but it is very difficult to attach a level of importance to these differing objectives. In some cases the evaluation of competing objectives involves the making of value judgements. For instance, is the purpose of education to fulfil intellectual growth or to provide a well-educated work force? The two objectives are not necessarily compatible since it is a matter of judgement whether an education in Latin, for instance, is of any use to employers.

In addition, the various objectives may not be in complete harmony, a person's life can be prolonged without any significant improvement in its quality. For instance, in the context of the health sector, the value of five years' remission is compared with a cure which lasts for 20 years but where there is significant pain to be borne.

Finally, even if it is possible to separately identify these objectives, it is very difficult to measure the achievement of such objectives. For instance, in practical terms, it is difficult to determine the stage at which someone is cured.

b) Very often legitimate comparisons are not readily available. The primary measure itself means nothing; it acquires meaning only when it is compared with something. Comparisons may be against predetermined standards, over time or with comparable organisations.

Sometimes there are problems with the making of such comparisons; the potential importance of hidden or quasi-inputs must be considered. In education it has been established that such features as the innate ability of the child, or level of parental interest, are as important determinants of performance as is the quality of teaching. When making comparisons over time, against pre-set standards or with other institutions it is essential that variations in these inputs are discounted before judgement is made. Unfortunately, the innate ability of the child and level of parental interest are not features which automatically lend themselves to universally accepted quantification; for instance, there is disagreement amongst the experts on what constitutes intelligence and as such there are no universally accepted measures of intelligence.

Value for money investigations are attempts to place numerical analysis on performance in such areas of difficulty. They do not overcome all the problems just stated but perhaps, if those problems are viewed as reservations which apply before unduly bold statements of performance are made, value for money measures can be seen as a useful additional tool to partly assess performance in those organisations where simple measures of performance are not readily available. They are measures which attempt to assess levels of performance linked to cost. This cost criterion is particularly important in the public service where public money may be spent in conditions of monopoly or near monopoly. Value for money measures can be classified into six main categories.

ECONOMY

If a budget has been carefully set, a legitimate measure of performance might be the achievement of that budget. This measure will be of particular use where the quantity and quality of the service produced is guaranteed. Under such circumstances the only important measure of performance is the cost of service delivery. The major benefit of this as a measure of performance is that, if quality and quantity can be assured, the measure is precise. In many organisations, whether in the public or private sectors, the major problem with this as a measure of performance is that often this quantity and quality of service cannot be guaranteed. Thus, for instance, the mere paying of money to employ a social worker is no guarantee of service delivery; this can be achieved only when the service itself is examined. Similarly, the mere payment of money to a sales manager in no way guarantees that the sales manager will work in ways which benefit the organisation.

EFFICIENCY

In many organisations there is no direct link between expenditure and output. For instance, the measure of how much money is spent in a school is, in isolation, a very limited assessment of performance. The assessment would be more valid if the number of children educated could be determined; to an extent, the number of children educated for each £3,000 is a better measure of performance than is the amount of money spent. However, this is a complete measure of performance only if the quality of the product can be assured. In the case of education this ready assurance cannot be given since a child can sit in a classroom but not receive any education. However, in some cases quality is readily assured by simple efficiency measures; the obtaining of 100 clients by a sales manager necessarily implies a certain quality of work by that sales manager.

EFFECTIVENESS

In many cases quality or utility of service is not guaranteed by the mere production of a service; the mere placing of a patient in hospital is not a guarantee of good health care. The purpose of hospitalisation is to provide a level of care which could not be afforded in the community. Under these circumstances, for useful judgements about performance to be made, the benefit obtained from expenditure needs to be determined. Effectiveness is the extent to which the organisation's objectives have been achieved, such as the improvement of a patient's health or the level of education achieved by a child. Thus in many cases measures of performance which are restricted to economy or efficiency will be incomplete. This does not mean that measures of effectiveness can be easily achieved and these difficulties have been previously identified. However, the specification of an objective and the assessment of the relative importance of various objectives does allow the organisation to formally review and specify its purposes.

The previous three E's have traditionally been deemed to define all dimensions of organisational performance. However, as the new millennium approaches, the responsibilities of the manager can be seen to be extended. Under this, more expanded agenda, three additional E's can be addressed.

Environmental impact

Organisations are increasingly accountable for the environmental impact of their activities. Thus it could be considered that an organisation's performance should be assessed on this dimension.

Elegance

As organisations exist in an increasingly public environment, some sections of the business community have suggested that organisations should be assessed according to the way in which they conduct their activities. For instance do they build premises which complement and enhance the physical environment within which they operate? In the case of a media organisation, irrespective of its audience share, some favourable judgement would be made if it any of its programmes received awards such as the Golden Rose of Montreux.

Ethicality

This has been examined in a previous section of this text. An organisation which is known to pursue its activities with due ethical standards is likely to receive favourable publicity. Although favourable publicity is no guarantee of future existence and growth, it is not likely to harm the future prospects of any organisation.

Characteristics of an Effective Control System

a) The activity required should be linked to the objectives and plans of the organisation. An activity can be judged only against a robustly argued objective or plan. Activity cannot be validly undertaken unless it is linked to the desired objectives and plans of the organisation.
b) The focus should be on what has been done right and any assessment of what has been done wrong should minimise the extent to which blame is attached. The focus should be on the organisation learning from its experiences, positive as well as negative, not on the allocation of blame. The sole purpose of the process should be to rectify errors not to attribute blame. The control process and the atmosphere within which it is conducted should be acceptable to all involved.
c) That which is expected of employees should be clearly understood. Only when an employee understands what is required of him or her can effective, positive

control be exercised. Similarly there should be no ambiguity over what is expected. Under these circumstances that which is to be assessed should be capable of extensive measurement. Without this measurement criterion there might be wasteful and demotivating debate surrounding the assessment.

d) If there is any area of tolerance, that area should be clearly specified and understood. In practice rarely will all deviations from precise standards be deemed to require remedial action. Thus it is essential for everyone involved in the control process to understand what the degrees or parameters of tolerance are.

e) It would help if the employee felt a degree of ownership over that which is being assessed. This is not an essential feature of a control process but, as has been seen elsewhere in this text, an employee will feel more responsible for something to which he or she is committed

f) If an employee is to be effectively controlled he or she should be able to affect that which is being measured. Thus work should be allocated on the basis of individuals being able to control its outcome.

g) Targets must be realistic – there is little positive purpose to be served by assessing negative performance if positive performance were unlikely to be achieved. Any target expected of an organisation, a part of that organisation, a team or an individual within that organisation, must be capable of being achieved under normal circumstances. Any attempt to imply adverse judgement in circumstances where targets could never be achieved will be demotivating.

h) All those who are subject to control should receive adequate feedback as to their performance and what, if any, remedial action is necessary.

Feedback in the Control Process

Control is not an end in itself; rather the primary aim of control is to improve performance by ensuring that resources are more effectively deployed, and that mistakes are rectified. An essential element in the control process is feedback. If those who are performing are unaware of the extent of achievement of their plans and any problems which might be developing they cannot take the remedial action required. Any feedback system must have a number of characteristics.

a) Timely – the information generated by the control process must be fed back in time for remedial action to be taken.

b) Reliable – the control process is expensive and it is counterproductive to produce unreliable control information.

c) Precise – the information generated should focus on those aspects of performance which need to be addressed. There is a danger that the key information could be 'crowded out' by less relevant information about performance. A common fault found in the control process of many organisations is the presentation of feedback information in too large a quantity. Put quite simply the document or communication is only useful if it is read or listened to.

d) Right recipient – the information should be received by that individual or group of individuals who are both concerned with and able to effect any necessary improvements in performance.

Targets in the Control Process

For a control process to work effectively expectations or targets must exist. No commentary can be made on performance if the required performance is not specified. Any target must have a number of essential features.

a) Relevant – targets must be closely linked to plans and objectives.

b) Understood – targets must focus clearly on essential aspects of performance. Care must be taken to ensure that key issues are not clouded by unnecessary detail. They must be focused upon those issues which are generally accepted as constituting an important part of the production exercise. Thus targets must not be viewed as being imposed upon an organisation by senior management.

c) Wherever possible they must be measurable – there is little point in specifying targets if important areas are left to subjective judgement.

d) Realistic – if remedial action is to be taken if targets are not achieved, and given that control activity is costly, there is little point in specifying targets which are too difficult to achieve. The demotivating effects of not achieving work targets has been addressed in an earlier section of this book.

e) Areas of acceptable tolerances must be clearly specified – in reality not all non-achievements of targets should demand remedial action. In practice there will be certain levels of tolerance which would not necessitate management action. However, if such flexibility exists there is the possibility that needed remedial action does not take place. To overcome this difficulty such tolerances should be tightly specified and clearly understood.

An alternative perspective on the control process is that of Drucker shown in Figure 23.2.

Economic	- Control mechanisms should produce better value for money. In all probability they should be kept to a minimum.
Appropriate	- Control mechanisms should be directed to the high risk areas.
Simple	- The messages obtained from control processes should be capable of being understood.
Timely	- They should produce the information required at a time appropriate to remedial action being taken.
Operational	They should send these pieces of control information to - those capable of effecting remedial action.

FIGURE 23.2 *Drucker's Criteria for Control Effectiveness*

The subject of control can be seen to be complicated by the increasingly diverse nature of organisations. Organisations are increasingly characterised by their internal diversity. Hence the control process which applies in all parts of the organisation should be suited to the needs of those individual and diverse parts and the organisation as a whole. It must be noted, however, that this diversity has on occasion caused an organisation to ensure that the control process is not so diverse that the organisation's corporate identity and values is sacrificed – this is examined in the chapter on Ethics and Management and in the previous section of this text.

Working within these increasingly diverse parts of the organisation is an increasingly diverse workforce. The organisation must appreciate that its workforce exhibits varieties of age, ethnic origin, gender and ability; as such any control process must embrace this variety and must be seen to be acceptable to all parts of the organisation's workforce.

Who Drives the Control Process?

Control systems can be implemented in different ways. Although the various possibilities will be considered in a discrete fashion it may well be that the control strategy adopted in a particular organisation may draw on more than one of the discrete possibilities examined; for instance, in some parts of an enterprise there may be a strong reliance placed on rules and regulations, whereas in a different part of the same enterprise more employee-centred strategies might be adopted. Finally, there can exist control strategies which are amalgamations of two or more strategies, for example where some emphasis is placed on control by rules and regulations but where employees are encouraged to use their initiative where the rules and regulations do not provide the appropriate signals.

PERSONALISED CENTRALISED

Such a strategy exists where the control process is driven by one person or a small number of people, where a small number of people decide when levels and standards of performance are and are not acceptable. This is a useful strategy in small owner-managed enterprises where the power in the organisation is centrally rooted. Such a strategy may fail to win the maximum cooperation of the rest of the employees of the enterprise. The larger the enterprise the more essential this cooperation becomes. In addition, the more educated the workers the more such a strategy might be resented.

BUREAUCRATIC

This form of strategy can be seen to exist where rules and regulations form the basis for the control systems. Given the communication problems in large, multi-purpose enterprises, such an approach will create the certainty and specification needed. However, care must be taken to ensure that such rules and regulations are entirely appropriate. In times of rapid environmental change if this approach is maintained the rules and regulations will need to be regularly updated. In addition, it must be recognised that employees are not passive partners in the exercise and may resent the rigidity of such an environment for control; they may continue to apply the rules and regulations as stated when they have long recognised their inapplicability.

CULTURAL/EMPLOYEE CENTRED

With this approach the employees themselves drive and implement the control process. It must be seen that this creates an environment highly conducive to employee cooperation; however, it may remove organisational control. It is particularly suited to organisations where employees feel a strong personal identity with the work of the organisation. It may be illustrated by Japanese companies where the workers develop strong loyalties to the organisation. In the United Kingdom it might be best illustrated in professional groups (eg the health service). Undoubtedly most enterprises will benefit from this approach to the control exercise. However, where it does obtain the organisation would be well advised to complement this approach with other, more formal, control strategies.

An Integrated Approach to Control and Planning

In concluding this chapter it is useful to examine an alternative model of control. Figure 22.3 in the last chapter shows how control can be seen to be a natural progression from planning. The part of the model intimately concerned with planning has been considered in the last chapter. It is now necessary to focus on those sections of the model which are concerned with control.

1. The simple examination of the resources used by the production process will provide a measure of economy.
2. The immediate outcome of the production process will be the production of products or services. These when compared with the resources deployed will enable the organisation to assess the efficiency of its operations.
3. The model allows us to differentiate between those products or services which are provided and those which are taken up by customers. This enables the organisation to assess the extent to which it is satisfying customer demands or needs. This could be deemed to constitute a measure of effectiveness.
4. There will then be the assessment of outcomes – that is whether, or to what extent, productive endeavour was worthwhile. At this stage it is possible to assess the value of the organisation's activities. For instance, is the organisation and/or the customer better placed after its programme of actions than it was before it undertook its productive endeavours?
5. Finally, the model embraces the feedback loop to the next stage of planning where the organisation learns from its experiences and plans the next cycle with more precise intelligence.

Summary

The process of control is of immense importance to an organisation. Without an effective control process an organisation will not be able to rectify its mistakes or improve its production performance. There are several activities which any organisation undertakes which together compose its control process. The design and operation of a control process and strategy is something which demands careful organisational thought and attention. Undoubtedly, any control process should have its formal components but the full benefits of any control exercise are observed only when all those affected fully understand and accept all its component features.

Exercise

In the context of your chosen organisation examine and criticise the ways in which it exerts and exercises control over its policies and actions and those of its staff.

Further Reading

Audit Commission (1989) *Managing Services Effectively – Performance Review*, HMSO

Audit Commission (1989) *Better Financial Management*, HMSO

Burns, T. and Stalker, G.M. (1968) *The Management of Innovation*, Tavistock

Cummings, T. G. and Worley, C. G. (1993) Organization Management and Change, West Publishing

Drucker, P. (1977) *Management*, Pan

Fayol, H. (1949) *General and Industrial Management*, Pitman

Goldsmith, W. and Clutterbuck, D. (1984) *The Winning Streak*, Weidenfeld and Nicolson

Miles, R.E. and Snow, C.C. (1978) *Organisational Strategy*, McGraw

Mintzberg, H. (1978) *Patterns in Strategy Formulation*, Management Science

Morden, A. R. (1993) *Business Strategy and Planning*, McGraw-Hill

Morden, T. (1996), *Principles of Management*, McGraw-Hill

Randell, G.A., Packard, P., Slater, J. (1984) *Staff Appraisal*, IPM

Rogers, S, (1990), *Performance Management in Local Government*, Longman

Simon, H.A. (1965) *Administrative Behaviour*, Macmillan

Taylor, F.W. (1947) *Scientific Management*, Harper and Row

Townsend, R. (1984) *Further Up the Organisation*, Michael Joseph

Weber, M. (1947) *Theory of Social and Economic Organisation*, Free Press

Woodward, Joan (1965) *Industrial Organisation – Theory and Practice*, OUP

24

Chapter twenty-four

The Process of
Accountability

LEARNING OBJECTIVES

- Understand the importance of effective accountability in the management of any organisation

- Identify the various approaches to accountability which could be undertaken by an organisation

- Appreciate the importance of choosing the right approach

- Appreciate the importance of legislation in this area

- Examine the factors which need to be considered in determining an organisation's approach to accountability

- Understand the interrelationships between accountability and control

- Apply the concepts studied to organisations with which you are familiar

- Appreciate the particular significance of concept to public service organisations

- Identify areas where further research might be necessary

Whilst the accountability process is by no means restricted to the public sector environment, it must be accepted that the public sector provides an excellent illustration of both the need for, and exercise of, such a process; in this chapter many, but not all, examples quoted will come from the public service environment. The term 'accountability' is one of the most frequently-used terms in the management of organisations. The main problem is that it is one of the most imprecisely used terms. Very often the interested observer can conclude only that it means what the person using the term wishes it to mean.

The accountability process can be viewed from the perspective of the organisation itself or from the perspective of individuals within the organisation; the organisation itself will be accountable for its policies and actions and individuals within the organisation will be accountable for their performance.

On some occasions it is used in a way which implies that there is a need to justify policies or actions. If this definition is adopted, the individual or organisation needs to convince others of the validity of such policies and actions. On other occasions the term seems to imply that there is a need to simply account for or record what is done. Under this second definition merely reporting what was done would seem to be sufficient in fulfilling any accountability obligations. On still other occasions it can be used in a context which suggests that the duty is an amalgam of the previous two; the necessity to be in some way responsive to or mindful of the needs and wishes of others. Under this definition, from the organisational perspective, as long as the organisation is seen to be aware of the wishes of others, it has discharged satisfactorily its accountability obligations.

Why Does an Individual or Organisation Need to be Accountable?

It might be that examining the issue from the viewpoint of why an organisation or individual needs to be accountable provides a more productive area for investigation than asking what is meant precisely by the term 'accountability'. There are several reasons why an organisation or individual needs to be, in some way, accountable for its actions.

a) Firstly, from the organisational perspective, other people have given the organisation money; it is necessary in the economic exchange for the organisation to account for the spending of that money. This it can do by delivering (to that person's satisfaction) the good or service for which the money was paid. Thus, in many ways, the customer is a very active participant in the accountability process. Similarly, from the individual perspective, each employee is financially rewarded by the organisation and as such the organisation can reasonably expect to hold him or her accountable for his or her actions.

b) The organisation's or individual's actions may impact upon others, sometimes in indirect ways. In the organisational context, a chemical company's factory will impact upon the physical environment making the company in some way accountable for its actions to those living nearby. Similarly, in the individual context, each employee's work will impact on others within the organisation (upon internal clients or upon work colleagues) and those individuals can reasonably expect him or her to be accountable to them.

c) Sometimes others vest power in the organisation or the individual. In the British organisational context, Parliament may grant to a public service organisation the right to provide services; thus it is argued that the organisation must be accountable to Parliament in the same way that a child is accountable to its parents. The extension into the individual environment is based upon the employee/ employer relationship being viewed from the parent/child perspective.

d) Sometimes the organisation will exist for the specific purpose of providing goods and services which would otherwise be the responsibility of the clients themselves; the organisation must be accountable to its clients for providing at least as good a quality of product or service as they would have provided for themselves. Thus a school must be accountable to the parents of pupils for the quality of education afforded.

e) Reinforcing the previous argument, it must be admitted that sometimes authority is given to an organisation or individual because of supposed expertise in a particular area. Under such circumstances it will be necessary to be held to account for this use of expert knowledge. For example, a doctor will need to account to his or her patients for professional judgements.

Although it must be acknowledged that these reasons do not apply to the same extent to all organisations, nevertheless they do apply to all organisations, particularly to public service organisations. However, in the public service sector there are additional reasons why organisations need to be accountable for their policies and actions.

a) Taxation funding – much of the public service is funded in whole or in the main from taxation sources. Under such circumstances the income contributor is denied the choice as to whether or not to pay for the service provided; an elderly person might feel that the education service needs to account for its actions since he or she is an income contributor but does not benefit directly from the service.

b) Monopoly power – much of the public service benefits from a monopoly position. It must be emphasised that, as competition is increasing in such areas, the importance of this point is diminishing. Nevertheless there are still huge sections of the public service which benefit from monopoly or near monopoly power (particularly in the short term, for example, once a contract has been won in an environment of competitive tendering). Thus, in many cases in Britain, consumers have to use the local authority refuse collection service since it will have no real competitor during the period of its contract.

c) Political factors – even though the points made previously are legitimate, it must be accepted that it is a political reality that the democratic process itself would demand accountability in the public service even if the previously mentioned points did not exist. It is difficult to envisage a situation where elections were completely abolished no matter how competitive the environment within which public service organisations work.

How is Accountability Achieved?

Having assessed the need for accountability, at both the organisational and individual level, it may prove productive to examine the process from the perspective of the methods employed to achieve accountability. A rigorous examination of this topic proves there are many ways in which an organisation, or an individual within the organisation, can be held accountable for policies and actions. This is not to claim that all organisations apply all methods, nor indeed that they are equally important in all organisations.

a) Election – in the public sector sometimes the organisation has to account to the electorate. Here the electorate examines the policies and actions of those in power in the organisation and decide whether to re-elect them or to elect others. In the case of elections in the private sector the electorate is the registered shareholders; however, in those public sector organisations subject to direct election, the electorate is more widely specified. The election could be seen as the most powerful of all methods of accountability, but it suffers from a number of problems.

   i) In many cases electoral turnouts are poor, particularly in private sector elections, local authority elections and European Parliament elections.

   ii) Often votes are cast on non-organisational issues, for instance in many cases in the United Kingdom people vote in local authority elections on national not local issues.

b) Annual reports – most organisations are obliged by law to publish annual reports which record their financial transactions and, increasingly, record their achievements. This is a method of accountability which is much more detailed in its nature than the election in that the annual report will examine in some detail the performance of the organisation. As such it is a very useful method of accountability; unfortunately it suffers from one major problem: reports are not read widely.

c) External audit – most organisations are obliged to have their financial records subject to external audit. This is a detailed scrutiny of the legitimacy of the financial records and, in the case of many United Kingdom public service organisations, an examination of the operational performance of the organisation. This point has been addressed also in the last chapter. It can be a particularly sophisticated method of accountability. However, it suffers from the problem of limited publicity; even in the case of the public service an adverse external audit report could not really be claimed to capture the imagination to the same extent as an election.

d) Scrutiny by other agencies – these include, in the United Kingdom public service, the Monopolies and Mergers Commission, user councils, controlling/regulatory agency, parliamentary select committees, government departments. Such scrutinies are not confined to, but are seen to be more important in, the public service. For instance, government departments may monitor the performance of such organisations through requiring them to complete questionnaires, or by sending inspectors to examine standards of service provision (eg education inspectors). Some public service organisations are subject to investigation by a formal user council, notably the public corporation sector. All organisations, particularly those operating in the public service, are potentially subject to parliamentary examination through select committees. All organisations can be examined, at the request of a government minister, by the Monopolies and Mergers Commission. Many of the newly privatised public service organisations are scrutinised by specially appointed regulatory bodies (for example Ogas in the gas industry). Such scrutiny, where it happens, can be seen to be a particularly powerful, detailed method of accountability.

e) Judicial – all organisations may have to account through the judicial process for their actions. Such examination may take the form of, for instance, courts or ombudsmen. These investigations tend to be extremely rigorous and, when they occur, judicial accountability is a very powerful method of accountability.

f) Public/open – this embraces a wide variation of methods of accountability. It is seen to be of particular importance in the public service, although its applicability is by no means restricted to that sector of economic activity. It consists of such things as being seen to cooperate with the press and media, liaison with interest and pressure groups, holding public meetings.

g) Market choice – when organisations operate in conditions of competition they are accountable through the market. It could be claimed that all the external methods of accountability are, in part, substitutes for this method of accountability.

h) Internal – all the methods just examined can be seen to be external in nature (that is the organisation being accountable to the outside world). However, organisations also have to ensure that people or groupings of people working in the organisation are accountable one to another. Such managerial techniques as budgetary control, internal audit, performance appraisal all combine to produce the internal methods of accountability.

Barriers to Accountability

No matter how sophisticated the accountability process within an organisation there are always potential barriers to its effective operation. Such barriers need to be specified since only when they have been identified can an organisation begin to overcome them.

a) Monopoly power – one of the most important barriers is the denial of proper consumer choice. If monopoly power obtains, the consumer is denied effective choice in the purchase of products and services. It is the absence of consumer choice which forces many public service organisations to seek more complex methods of accountability.

b) Information barriers – any system of accountability needs reasonably accurate information to work effectively. However, it would be untrue to claim that all information is readily accessible; most organisations may find that they have information barriers, both for the purposes of internal and external accountability obligations. It may be that within any organisation there are people who deliberately deny information to others or who deliberately distort this information. Such denial or distortion of information may be caused by fear, suspicion, uncertainty, ambiguity, bias or lack of understanding. An organisation must ensure that such problems are overcome before it can claim that its systems of accountability are completely effective.

c) Time barriers – many methods of accountability require that the organisation allocates sufficient time to ensure they work effectively. The major problem is that accountability itself does not produce a good or service. Every minute spent on accountability removes a minute from the direct production process. This complaint is often heard from workers and managers during a period of crisis. Thus methods of accountability will work effectively only when they are seen to be important and have been afforded their legitimate status by all levels of management.

d) Conflict with autonomy – it has been seen that autonomy is a major source of motivation and stimulation in any organisation. However, every question asked takes away some autonomy. It has often been claimed that the obligations of accountability in the public service have been a barrier to innovation. The reality is that there is a place for both innovation and effective accountability in the public service since, without a degree of innovation, the value for money objectives of accountability will not be achieved. It is essential, therefore, that accountability is not seen as a threat to a person's autonomy. This can only really be achieved if the concept of accountability is seen to be important by all people working in the organisation. Such acceptance is best achieved by discussion rather than confrontation. It requires that those responsible for the accountability process are prepared to listen to the views and fears of others. It demands mutual trust and respect between the producers and those responsible for ensuring that the accountability process operates effectively.

Summary

Although accountability is by no means confined to the public sector environment, much of the variety of the accountability process will be found in that environment. The search for a precise definition of the term might be elusive but it might be seen to encompass a degree of responsiveness, together with an element of justification, in addition to an element of answering. There are many methods of achieving accountability. Each method adds to the total accountability process but each method on its own has certain deficiencies. It can be seen that the various methods of accountability reinforce each other. There are real barriers to the effective working of the accountability process but a vigilant management can ensure that these barriers are overcome or at least are minimised.

Exercise

Examine what is meant by the term accountability. Compare and contrast the ways in which I.C.I., the police service and another organisation with which you are familiar exercise and fulfil their accountability obligations.

Further Reading

Audit Commission (1989) *Better Financial Management*, HMSO
Audit Commission (1989) *Managing Services Effectively – Performance Review*, HMSO
Beer, S. (1981) *The Heart of the Enterprise*, Wiley
Citizen's Charter (1991), HMSO
Drucker, P. (1977) *Management*, Pan
Harvey-Jones, J. (1990) *Making It Happen*, Guild
National Audit Office (1986) *The Financial Management Initiative*, HMSO

Co-ordination

L E A R N I N G   O B J E C T I V E S

- Appreciate the need for co-ordination
- Understand the range of co-ordinating mechanisms available
- Appraise the effectiveness of these mechanisms
- Apply the issues raised to organisations with which you are familiar

---

As organisations develop and expand their activities, the range of work undertaken and types of worker employed are likely to similarly develop and expand. Under such circumstances the organisation might find that its various and increasingly diverse constituent parts may result in inconsistency in approach, policy making and resource allocation. The organisation is then faced with the responsibility of ensuring that all its activities, its goals and the work of all its employees are mutually compatible. Thus in managing the organisation the professional managers are charged with the extra duty of coordination. This is not to suggest that coordination issues are unimportant in small, simple organisations but as organisations grow and diversify the concept of coordination becomes more obvious and immediate.

The problem of coordination is well illustrated in multi-purpose, public service organisations such as local authorities. In these organisations the various activities tend to be driven by the need to adhere to statutory requirements. Commonly the public service dimension is replacing a previously charitable involvement. Under these circumstances the typical reaction of a the local authority is to employ highly skilled professional people to fulfil each individual statutory requirement and to appoint a separate committee of councillors to oversee the work of these professionals. Undoubtedly this style of management has benefits in that it tends to breed exceptional commitment to the work undertaken - both at employee and councillor level. The one observed problem with this approach is the limited co-ordination it engenders. Such highly committed individuals can tend to pursue their responsibilities with such vigour that they become oblivious to the other activities and obligations of the local authority. The problem is further exacerbated by the traditional approach of local authorities to promote employees on the basis of their technical, rather than managerial, skills. This professional culture was further reinforced by the fact that councillors were rarely allowed to move between committees and once appointed to a committee they were encouraged to serve for long periods on that committee, developing very strong loyalties to the service concerned. During the 1960's and 1970s local authorities began to address and rectify this co-ordination problem. The approach they adopted in the facilitation of their new co-ordination responsibilities will be examined later in the chapter.

The issue of co-ordination is further highlighted by the possible problems of three highly fashionable aspects of modern management - delegation, decentralisation and intrapreneurship. The issues of delegation and decentralisation and their associated problems have been analysed earlier in this text. The subject of intrapreneurship is examined later in the text. However, not withstanding the advantages of such innovations, the possible problems revolve around the potential excessive diversity of decisions taken.

The organisation, at the strategic level, is charged with ensuring a consistency in, and an organisationally distinctive approach to, the varied decisions taken by individuals operating in the less rigid managerial environment of the late 1990s.

Facilitating Co-ordination - Mintzberg (1989)

Mintzberg suggests that co-ordination can be developed through a variety of managerial responses and initiatives. These responses range from people issues, to procedures, to cultural dimensions. His analysis is diagrammatically shown in Figure 25.1.

Mutual Adjustment

Under this approach the various segments of the organisation are encouraged to meet and interact on a regular basis. The intention would be for this regular interaction to facilitate mutual respect, mutual learning and possible increased harmony of response. The classic example of such an approach is the creation of a multi-disciplinary team to explore a new area of activity. The team would be reflective of the various disparate sections and traditions in the organisation. As long as the team membership is carefully selected, mindful not just of technical skills but also the team skills espoused by Belbin (considered earlier in this text), effective team working should result. The well-managed organisation would ensure that this increased interaction spread benefits beyond the task in hand. When well managed, the team approach can

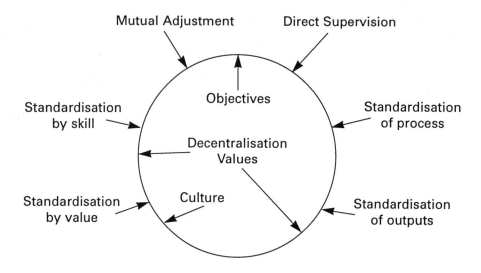

FIGURE 25.1 *Mintzberg and Co-ordination*

facilitate increased co-ordination in that it will encourage increased internal communication. Furthermore the increased mutual respect engendered will render future disputes about resource allocation less likely. The benefits of increased interaction can be consolidated and embedded by regular meetings of various disciplines to examine issues of mutual concern. The Bains Committee (1972), The New Local Authorities: Management and Structure, recommended this in the context of the local authority. Employees at common levels in the organisation but working in different sections (directors, deputy directors, section heads) would meet on a regular basis to examine problems they had encountered in the work environment. The idea is that the exploration of such problems in this widened arena might reveal the commonality of experiences and engender a true team spirit in the overall work of the organisation.

DIRECT SUPERVISION

If the work of disparate sections results in excessive variation one way of overcoming this would be to appoint an individual charged with the specific duty of overseeing the work of these disparate sections. The Bains Committee Report recommended the appointment of a chief executive whose primary responsibility would be to ensure that the work of the various departments were properly co-ordinated.

STANDARDISATION OF PROCESS

If all activity were to undergo an identical or similar process it may be that the work of the organisation would be more reflective of effective co-ordination. Again this approach is shown in the Bains Committee report which recommended the institution of a policy and resources committee. All new projects would have to be vetted by this committee. Under such an approach an intelligence system is created which more rigorously monitors the work of the various sections of the organisation. A good example of this approach is the concept of franchising: the intention is for several organisations to be involved in the delivery of a standard service. In such circumstances processes and procedures are carefully and rigorously monitored by the franchising organisation.

STANDARDISATION OF OUTPUT

This would be particularly useful where the major co-ordination problem is the variation in output of a similar product from different production locations. The aim would be to establish a set of common specifications which would apply to all products or services no matter where they are manufactured or provided. This is an approach which has assumed significant importance in the 1990s. Many organisations have established procedures or standards which hare adhered to in the delivery of a service or the manufacture of a product. The external approach to vetting of quality and the conveying of approval by the British Standards Institute can be seen to be reflective of this approach. Similarly the publication of performance indicators in the United Kingdom public services is intended to develop an overall improvement in and standardisation of the performance of similar organisations. If the relative performance of various organisations is published there is a pressure for the output of the perceived poor performers to more readily conform to the results of the perceived good performers.

STANDARDISATION BY SKILL

This is appropriate when the problem is excessive variation in the delivery of one product or service. Under such an approach standardisation and co-ordination would be achieved by ensuring that all producers employ resources of a common standard. Common raw materials can be specified but perhaps the most difficulty would be in ensuring that the employees involved in delivery have common skill levels. Although the major feature of Franchising is Standardisation by Procedure, franchising can also be seen to be reflective of this approach. In many franchising operations the skill level and required training of the employees working in the franchised operations is carefully specified and controlled.

STANDARDISATION BY VALUE

This is particularly appropriate where the aim is to enhance the co-ordination of the work of different sections or different professions. The role of the previous approaches cannot be ignored but in this context only when the varied employees have common values will the work of the organisation be truly coordinated. An example might be found in the work of a hospital: in such an organisation the employees will come from such varied backgrounds as medical, nursing, scientific, paramedical, human resource, finance, I.T. The values of these various professions are not necessarily identical and only when the organisation ensures some commonality of value will true co-ordination obtain.

Co-ordination – a Managerial Approach

The work of Mintzberg is extremely useful in isolating the range of co-ordination options available to an organisation. The question remains how to ensure that an organisation establishes managerial procedures and practices which will facilitate such approaches. Inevitably the managerial approach of any organisation will be firmly rooted in the particular environmental circumstances of that organisation. However it might be useful to examine an approach which might form the basis of managerial reaction in many organisations.

a) Develop a mission – a mission will help give the organisation a long term purpose and a set of collective values. The mission will help the organisation appraise its options and monitor its activities. Only when actions are consistent with the express mission will success be deemed to obtain. It must be stressed that only when the mission is collectively developed will the desired dimension of ownership be developed.

b) Establish guidelines – once the mission has been created the organisation might be advised to establish guidelines which are reflective of the mission. Any action taken by any employee will then have to be in accordance with these guidelines and hence the desired level of consistency will be ensured. Only when these guidelines are collectively owned will they produce the required results.

c) Ensure regular reporting – the strategic apex of the organisation needs to be regularly appraised of the achievement of the various parts of the organisation. Co-ordination is not effected by a mission or by guidelines but by the adherence to this mission and these guidelines. Care must be taken to ensure that this level of control is not perceived to be imposed on those actually providing the product or service.

d) Ensure regular meetings and questioning – the desired degree of commitment can be facilitated by allowing all those involved to attend meetings and discuss problems they are encountering. As long as an atmosphere of cooperation is created, these meetings should ensure that the organisation's standards continue to be appropriate.

e) Ensure a corporate identity – the concept of a mission and collective dimension can be reinforced if the organisation gives express attention to the development of a corporate identity. The various employees should understand that they are all working towards collective goals and that they all rely on each other. Perhaps such an approach is best evidenced in organisations where uniforms are worn. Pupils at school are encouraged to develop this corporate identity by wearing a school uniform. Members of an army regiment wear the badge of that regiment. In most areas of economic endeavour, however, the crude uniform/badge approach is more problematic. In cultures where such a uniform culture has not obtained the introduction of a uniform regime might be seen to be crude and ineffectual. What is important is the existence of the corporate identity rather than the way it is exhibited. Perhaps a compromise approach is seen in the more common recent development in many organisations of prominently reinforcing the organisation's corporate identity in ensuring prominent placing of the organisation's name and logo throughout the premises. It must be stressed that this could be seen to be trivialising the work of the organisation and that it is not the physical presence of the corporate logo but the collective awareness of the corporate identity which is important.

Summary

The work of the organisation is varied and this very variety creates an additional duty of the manager. The manager must ensure that this variety does not result in excessively disparate approaches and actions within the organisation. Co-ordination can be effected through a number of mechanisms. However it is probably in the mix of these mechanisms rather than the choice of one or other that the key to organisational success lies.

Exercise

In the context of an organisation with which you are familiar outline the co-ordination problems it encounters. Examine ways in which the co-ordination of its activities could be improved.

Further Reading

Bains Committee (1972) 'The New Local Authorities: Management and Structure', DOE

Handy, C. B. (1985) *Understanding Organisation*, Penguin

Mintzberg, H. (1983) *Power In and Around Organisations*, Prentice Hall
Mintzberg H (1989) *Mintzberg on Management*, Free Press
Morden, T. (1996) *Principles of Management*, McGraw-Hill
Toffler, A. (1985) *The Adaptive Organisation*, Pan

Management Functions

OBJECTIVES

Although the text has so far emphasised the variety of the management experience, it must be recognised that management in most enterprises addresses a number of common, management functions. After reading this section the student should have a better appreciation of the nature of and the management problems associated with the more common and hence more important of these functions.

INTRODUCTION

No matter what the context of the organisation a number of readily detected functions will be undertaken within that organisation. For instance the organisation will need to control its financial operations, it will need to market its activities, it will need to control and manage its information technology. An examination of the nature of these functions and an analysis of any special managerial problems associated with the management of these functions will combine with the previous sections of this text to effect a complete appreciation of the total management task.

Chapter twenty-six

Finance

L E A R N I N G   O B J E C T I V E S

- Appreciate the range of financial issues involved in managing an organisation

- Understand the role played by the director of finance

- Assess the budgeting and budgetary control processes

- Appraise the options available for structuring the finance function

- Apply the issues considered to an organisation with which you are familiar

---

One very important, and arguably the most important, dimension of the management of an organisation is that of finance. This dimension embraces a wide variety of activities: how it collects its income; how it controls its expenditure; how it schedules the receipt of income and the payment of expenditure; how it finances its activities; how it secures its assets; and how it accounts for its activities.

Many organisations effect these activities through a designated financial director. Although later in this chapter alternative means of discharging these financial obligations will be examined, the assumption at this stage in the analysis will be that these obligations are discharged by such a designated director through a specifically created directorate.

Range of Functions Provided by the Finance Discipline

Any finance directorate has a number of potential duties and responsibilities. It might be useful to examine in a little detail some of the more important of such potential duties and responsibilities.

COLLECTION OF INCOME

It might be useful for the organisation to locate its income collection activities in a finance directorate which has both the skills and desire to effectively execute this function. Income collection necessitates not just the receipt of such income but also the responsibility for properly accounting for such income. The finance director will be the individual, within the organisation, most skilled in this respect. There will also be an increased likelihood that physical security will also assume greater importance to someone who has the specific responsibility for all financial matters.

For any organisation to achieve success it needs income. Hence the securing of the collection of income is one of the most important, if not the most important, duties of the organisation. As such, any decision about how this income is to be collected can be seen to be an issue of great importance to the organisation.

PAYMENT TO CREDITORS

Many organisations choose to arrange for any payments to their creditors to be made through a central finance department. This affords the benefits of ensuring that due regard is paid to ascertaining the legitimacy of the expenditure. It has the additional facility of ensuring adequate security over such potentially valuable assets as the cheque book. Locating such functions in one central directorate affords economies of scale in the payment operation.

PAYMENT OF SALARIES AND WAGES

No matter how much attention is paid to the more glamorous aspects of management, an organisation still needs to direct attention to its more routine but fundamentally important duties. High on this list of duties must be the payment of its workforce. Most organisations find net benefits in centrally locating the wage and salary payment systems. The benefits of economies of scale and due care and attention are not least amongst these perceived net benefits.

FINANCIAL STRATEGY

An extremely important aspect of any organisation is that it plans for its growth and activities in financial terms. No organisation can function without a ready source of finance. Organisations will find that usually there are a number of alternative sources of finance, ranging from stocks and shares, through loans (long and short term), through grants to financing from internal sources. Such a wide range of alternatives inevitably means that the organisation needs to carefully choose, from amongst this range, the most appropriate sources of finance. This will require detailed knowledge not just about the organisation but also about the technicalities of such sources of finance. Even in those organisations where other financial issues are delegated to operational departments, control over financial strategy is often centrally located.

Control over insurance

Most organisations will own substantial assets. These may range from large physical assets, through information technology assets, to its human resource assets. It is an inevitable consequence of organisational activity that these assets need to be insured against such potential difficulties as loss, damage or poor workmanship. Insurance options range from internal sources, through large external block policies to smaller individual external policies. The decision about the appropriate insurance strategy requires specialist insurance or financial knowledge and lends itself to execution by a centralised and specialist finance directorate.

Control over accounting and audit arrangements

It is a requirement of organisational existence that all income and expenditure is duly accounted for. This will require both the accurate classification of such income and expenditure and its subsequent vetting for legitimacy. This subsequent vetting is known as 'internal auditing'. Although in the area of accounting a role could be seen for operational department activity, demands of accuracy and consistency may dictate that such responsibilities are located in a centrally-sited directorate with the required technical skills.

Budgeting

The previous activities undertaken within a finance directorate are extremely important; however, particularly in a large organisation, the activities of budgeting and budgetary control can be seen to be essential.

A budget is a quantitative financial plan of the activity to be undertaken during a specified period in order to achieve the objectives set for that period. That is it is closely linked to and, in some ways, consequent upon the setting of objectives. It is expressed in financial terms and is analysed in high specific quantitative terms; the latter point is extremely important if and when the budget is flexed (see later in this chapter).

Budgetary periods can vary - typically from five years to one month. However the usual detailed budget is constructed for the financial year. The rest of this analysis will assume a yearly budgetary cycle.

The budget can be located at organisational or section level. The organisational, or master, budget summarises the objectives, plans and their financial expression for all sections – production or direct service provision, human resource management, sales, marketing, legal, estates, finance. The budget of the section reflects that master budget as it impacts on the specific section.

Naturally the economic environment of organisations is likely to vary and it might be expected that the approach to budgeting might similarly change. An organisation operating in circumstances where income is market or output driven commonly projects the income it wishes to raise during the period. Expenditure projections, then, will be based upon that which will facilitate the achievement of that income. An organisation, such as many public service organisations, might consider that its income is fixed; its budget, then, will be driven by the need to obtain maximum impact or value for money from that fixed income.

A budget can be deemed to be fixed or flexed. A fixed budget will assume that all income and all expenditure is stable and incapable of alteration. This is the typical approach of an organisation with fixed income. However an organisation's budget might be considered to reflect its level of activity. If the organisation sells more products or services than it budgeted for, then the level of expenditure might have to change. Given that the organisation usually wishes to maximise its income, it would be organisationally dysfunctional to assume that expenditure has to conform with fixed projections. In these circumstances the organisation's expenditure has to be classified as to whether it is fixed, variable or semi variable in nature. If the expenditure is deemed to be fixed in nature it should not increase, or indeed decrease, if income or level of activity changes. An example might be the premises costs or the strategic apex costs. If the organisation finds its expenditure in this area increasing it cannot be explained by variations in level of activity. If a cost is variable in nature it will vary with different levels of activity. An example might be raw materials costs where, the more finished goods are sold, the more raw materials are consumed. In this case the objective of expenditure control must be to ensure that any variation in cost is reflective of the variation in the level of activity. A cost which is semi-variable in nature should be reflective of its fixed and variable elements - an example is telephone charges where the rental element is fixed and the calls element varies with calls made.

Finally it must be realised that it is not the budget itself which it important; rather it is the fact that the budget will be adhered to which is crucial in the effective management control of the organisation and the effective organisation should ensure that its budgets are deemed to be important. The modern approach to ensuring such importance is to try to encourage ownership of the budgets by allowing extensive involvement of those operating the budgets in the construction of such budgets. This involvement is commonly known as participatory budgeting.

BUDGETARY CONTROL

The importance of achieving budgetary targets has just been attested. All income and expenditure should be compared on a regular basis with the budget to ensure that proper management control is effected. Although the period at which this comparison is made can vary it is essential that any undue deviations are recognised and that remedial action can be taken to resurrect the primacy of the budget; the common period for detailed budget and actual comparisons is monthly - the argument is that a month is long enough to ensure that the pattern detected is legitimate but also short enough to allow remedial action to be taken.

As has already been mentioned, care must be taken to ensure that only truly deviant patterns necessitate remedial action. If the variations from budget can be explained by variation in level of activity then no action is necessary. The technique of standard costing breaks costs down into their price and usage constituents. As such, when the technique is applied, attention should be directed only towards the relevant deviant feature – for example excessive price, excessive usage. It must be stressed that budgetary control is not purely a policing activity; there will be important lessons to be learned from this exercise which will result in better budgeting in the future. Figure 26.1 shows the interrelationship between the planning and control elements. An example of this might be that the problem detected by the control process lies not with performance but with an unrealistic budget being set in the first place.

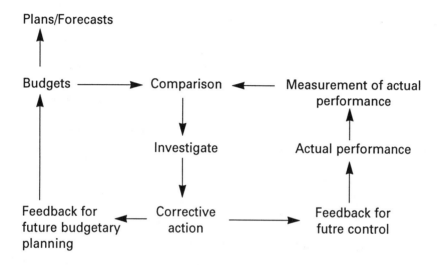

FIGURE 26.1 *Budgetary Control*

Management of Finance Functions

Despite the analysis just undertaken, over the past few years there has been a tendency to decentralise many of the finance functions to operational directorates or departments. Therefore, it is necessary to examine those features of the organisation which determine the desired structure or arrangement of its financial responsibilities.

Many of the issues involved in the way in which the finance department is structured have been examined in detail in the section on the Organisational Domain. However, it might prove useful to illustrate many of these principles in the context of the finance department. The finance department is a very good example of a traditionally centralised function, embracing both support functions and production functions in its own right. The finance function encompasses both the financial advice functions associated with a support service and functions such as income collection and salaries and wages, both of which could be deemed to be production functions in their own right.

Since the finance department encompasses this variety of functions and since in many organisations the finance function is one which, in a historical context, has been traditionally organised as a separate, centralised department, the study of this function affords a very effective illustration of the various options in organisational design.

General organisational design issues

The desired structure or design is a product of several contingent features.

a) Size – the larger the finance section the more need there will be for formal approaches to the problem of organisational design such as reliance on rules and regulations. The larger the section the more problems are created by span of control issues and the more a tiered or tall structure becomes desirable. Organisational design is a complex issue and the circumstances which have just be outlined might be seen as strongly supporting the radically different solution of the decentralisation of the finance function to operational departments.

b) Diversity of functions – the more operational activities there are within the organisation which are intended to be served by the finance function, the more likely decentralisation of such a function might be desirable. However, it has been previously acknowledged that high diversity of functions could be deemed to necessitate strong organisational and central control and direction. Under such circumstances it might be that centralising the finance function affords this desired central control and direction.

c) Whether the finance department embraces any specialist non–finance functions (eg computer services) – if such services are provided from within the finance department then the appropriate solutions for these services may vary from those from within the mainstream finance functions. Thus, whatever the solutions determined for the finance functions, separate analysis will be needed for the other functions.

d) The established culture in the organisation – the importance of established organisational culture has been examined previously in this text and, despite the logic of the arguments to the contrary, a role culture might cause the finance functions of the organisation to be concentrated in a central department.

e) The demands of legislation – it is important to note that, particularly in the public service, an organisation may not have a free hand in determining the centralisation or otherwise of its finance functions. For instance, legislation may demand the existence of an independent internal audit function. Although this does not preclude devolution of this function it does make it more unlikely.

f) Geographical spread of clients – if the clients of the finance function are widely dispersed there is a stronger argument for devolution than if all the clients are in geographical proximity. Such a wide dispersal of clients would make the necessary liaison with clients much more difficult in a centralised finance department.

A MATRIX ORGANISATIONAL STRUCTURE

The analysis so far has indicated that there are two major alternatives – centralisation and decentralisation. However, it must be stressed that one major alternative exists which might, under certain circumstances, be deemed to embrace many of the advantages of both centralised and decentralised solutions. Under this approach the financial expertise becomes a part of the production team. The finance department may itself provide certain production functions (eg income collection, payments) whilst the more advisory functions of the finance discipline might be undertaken by seconding the finance person to a separate production team. This is examined in much more detail elsewhere in the text. Briefly, it has the advantages of centralisation, ensuring the benefits of professional integrity and reasonably common treatment, whilst introducing the flexibility and consumer serving advantages of decentralisation.

Organisation of Work Within the Finance Directorate

Even assuming that a finance directorate exists with significant areas of responsibility, the work of that directorate can be organised in several different ways. There is no right or wrong solution to the problem of this organisation; rather the appropriate solution is a function of the points already considered in the section on the organisational domain.

FUNCTIONAL CENTRALISATION

Under this approach there will be a separate section for each function, for instance, salaries and wages, accountancy. This separate section would serve all clients throughout the organisation. Figure 26.2 shows an diagrammatic illustration of such an organisation.

FIGURE 26.2 *Functional Organisation of a Finance Department*

The advantages of this form of organisation include the following.

a) The development of specialisation within each functional specialism is facilitated. This allows those working in the organisation to focus all their attention on particular specialisms (foe example auditing).
b) There is equal treatment of all clients. A common approach and common standards will be developed.
c) Economies of scale through the specialisation of the workforce will be likely.

Powerful though these advantages are there are also likely to be disadvantages with this form of organisation.

a) The service given to individual clients may not suit the individual needs of that client. The problems of adopting general solutions to specific problems has been examined elsewhere in this text.
b) There may develop a remote rather than friendly relationship between the client and the finance staff. The importance of this cooperation between members of different disciplines cannot be underestimated.

A SERVICE-BASED STRUCTURE

This exists where there is a separate section within the finance directorate dealing with all financial issues for each individual client. This is shown in diagrammatic form in Figure 26.3

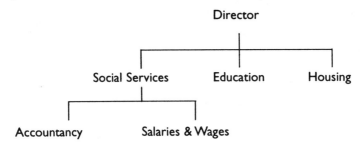

FIGURE 26.3 *Service-based Organisation of a Finance Department*

The advantages of this form of organisation include the following.

a) The client's individual needs are likely to be more immediately satisfied. The advice and information afforded should be tailored to suit the needs of the individual client.
b) There will be a degree of convenience afforded to the client in that all the financial problems which are encountered will be handled by one, readily identifiable, group of staff.

There are, however, certain problems with this approach.

a) The career development of the finance staff may be disrupted or not best served.

It must be admitted that this is a major problem only if a degree of person culture exists within the organisation, that is, if the organisation deems the career development of its staff to be a major priority. Nevertheless, the potent motivational consequences of being seen to be mindful of staff needs cannot be underestimated.

b) There is a possible loss of economies of scale under this, less extensive production process. The number of employees whose pay is processed by an education payroll section is less than that which would be processed by a local authority-wide salaries and wages section. Similarly, in the private sector the administrative cost of each operational department paying its own bills would normally limit the degree of decentralisation of this function.

c) There is the possibility that the wishes of the client may assume too much priority and that, for instance, professional standards will be sacrificed. Finance staff may come under more pressure 'to break the rules'.

d) The benefits of the common approach to similar problems may be lost because different people will deal with the resolution of these problems.

e) The fact that one section fulfils all finance functions for the one client may weaken internal control and, in particular, internal check. There would be an increased opportunity for fraudulent activity if, for instance, one person both ordered and authorised the payment for a particular item. Under more functionally-based structures such activities would be undertaken by different individuals and the work of one individual would act as an automatic check on the work of the other individual.

GEOGRAPHICAL ORGANISATION

This is shown in Figure 26.4. Under this arrangement the finance department would continue to exist as a separate management entity but for reasons of client convenience there would be local finance offices undertaking some or most of the normal finance duties.

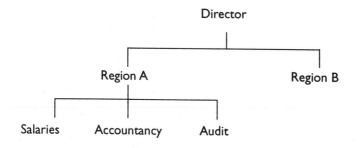

FIGURE 26.4 *Geographical Organisation of a Finance Department*

The advantages of this type of organisation include the following.

a) Ease of client contact will be facilitated and a closer and better relationship with clients should develop.
b) The assumption would be that clients in different geographical areas have potentially different needs and this form of organisation should enable the finance function to better appreciate the needs of individual clients.
c) This improved local knowledge and closer connection with clients should enable the organisation to more speedily and more effectively react to the needs of a changing environment. The precise importance of this point is examined elsewhere in the book.

The advantages of local or partially local organisation are powerful but such a form of decentralisation does present problems.

a) Assets are less easily protected. The incidence of theft in such local bases is greater than in more centralised ones.
b) This problem can be exacerbated if commercially or personally sensitive information is stolen.
c) It is probably more costly in terms of accommodation.
d) The staff may feel they have divided loyalty – to local needs and to professional demands.
e) The staff located in remote sites may feel isolated from the central department. This may have detrimental motivational consequences.
f) The benefits of a common approach to similar problems across geographical areas may be lost as different staff will deal with these problems.

Summary

The finance function is one of immense importance to any organisation. Without effective and secure financial systems no organisation can achieve success. The examination of the management arrangements of the finance function provides a very useful illustration of many of the general points of organisational design. The finance function can be highly centralised or alternatively it can be highly decentralised. In practice, it is possible to action different degrees of decentralisation for different parts of the finance function. It is not easy to design an ideal management structure for the finance function; rather the appropriate arrangements for a particular organisation are a product of the potentially unique circumstances which obtain within that organisation.

Exercise

Critically appraise the budgeting and budgetary processes of an organisation with which you are familiar.

Further Reading

Audit Commission (1989) *Better Financial Management*, HMSO

Audit Commission (1989) *Managing Services Effectively – Performance Review*, HMSO

Beer, S. (1981) *The Heart of the Enterprise*, Wiley

Cummings, T. G. and Worley, C. G. (1993): *Organization Management and Change*, West Publishing

Curson, C. (ed) (1986) *Flexible Patterns of Work*, IPM

Drucker, P. (1977) *Management*, Pan

Mintzberg, H. (1983) *Power In and Around Organisations*, Prentice Hall

Morden, A. R. (1993) *Business Strategy and Planning*, McGraw-Hill

Morden, T. (1996), *Principles of Management*, McGraw-Hill

National Audit Office (1986) *The Financial Management Initiative*, HMSO

Thorne, P. (1989) *The New General Manager*, McGraw Hill

Chapter twenty-seven

Information
Technology

L E A R N I N G   O B J E C T I V E S

- Understand the importance of the information technology function in the effective management of an organisation

- Appreciate the various options available in designing the function

- Appraise the advantages and problems which might accrue from the decentralisation of this function

- Identify the factors which should be considered in the construction of a strategy in this area

- Apply the issues addressed in the context of organisations with which you are familiar

- Identify areas where further research might be needed

The 1980s and 1990s have witnessed a radical change in the use of information technology within organisations. Prior to this period the nature of the technology itself, computer configurations being large and somewhat inflexible, directed the uses of such technology to organisation-wide and mainly procedural or routine issues.

Common uses of information technology were: the payment of salaries and wages, the payment of creditors, the organisation's main accounting and budgetary control systems.

Information technology was seen as a complex subject which could be understood only by those with specialist knowledge; any application of information technology tended to be controlled by specialists working within a dedicated central department or directorate.

This technology was not sufficiently flexible to allow individual sections of organisations to adapt systems to their special needs. Thus, in many ways, information technology could be seen to be a strong centralising force in that remote production sections would rely on such centrally determined and designed systems to afford support and information.

However, recent changes in the management of information technology have been driven by the development of smaller, more flexible machines and related systems. Increasingly, the technology can serve not just organisational purposes but also, through this increased flexibility, the purposes or interests of individual segments of the organisation. Information technology, and more specifically its potential uses, is now more readily understood by those other than computer professionals. As such, many organisations have witnessed demands from operational departments to be allowed to purchase cheap but powerful and flexible machines and related systems from their own budgets; furthermore, expectations have been aroused that such technology need not be driven or used by computer experts but can now be controlled and used by those closest to the production process. Even if such radical changes have not obtained, there has been an increasing awareness of the flexibility afforded by new technology and increasing demands for sectional rather than organisationally based systems to be developed.

Thus it can be concluded that information technology can now be viewed as a strong decentralising force within organisations.

Such developments and specifically the facility of flexibility have afforded many benefits to organisations but that same flexibility has introduced a new set of management problems for organisations. In the following chapter these advantages and problems will be examined and ways of overcoming them will be discussed.

Advantages of Information Technology

Information technology affords many advantages to the operation of an organisation.

a) It facilitates speed of operation – if information can be accessed more quickly the organisation is better placed to react to its consumer needs.

b) It facilitates adaptability and innovation – the fact that most organisations are being increasingly required to adapt to a changing environment has been seen elsewhere in this text. In many cases this adaptation demands a degree of creativity and innovation. Information technology often affords the capability to manipulate information in such a way that experimentation and innovation are aided.

c) It can help the improvement of the quality of the product. The more easily information can be accessed the easier it will be to develop product improvement. The benefits of focusing on product improvement have been examined in a previous section.

d) It can facilitate better communication – for any organisation to work effectively good systems of communication are necessary. Information technology can offer quicker, more flexible, more sophisticated, more accurate and more precise information.

e) It can help to improve motivation – it can introduce a new, more challenging dimension to the production process. Its very newness and the challenge it affords can be viewed as a potentially strong motivating force within the organisation.

Problems Caused by Information Technology

The real advantages of the introduction of information technology have just been discussed and these are powerful advantages. However, an examination of the real world reveals that such flexibility and adaptability can, whilst removing the disadvantages of rigidity, also introduce new types of managerial difficulties. In fact one of the most frequent organisational problems encountered in the late twentieth century is that of management by information technology rather than by managers; for some reason or other, the organisation fails to adequately manage or control its information technology. There are several reasons why such management problems may happen.

a) Information technology is an ever improving product. In addition it is an area where purchasers have limited knowledge. Some companies dealing in this area employ high-profile sales strategies. Under such circumstances the ignorant purchaser may find him or herself being pressurised into buying sophisticated 'gold plated' information technology which is beyond his or her needs. Unfortunately, the more sophisticated the product, the higher its cost.

b) When individual sections within an organisation purchase their own information technology, hardware and software problems of internal communication may arise; it is sometimes found that the technology purchased is not compatible with that purchased by other sections. Given that one of the major benefits of information technology is supposed to be better internal communication, this can be seen to be a serious difficulty.

c) Employee resistance – the problems of managing information technology are not restricted merely to purchasing strategy. Many of the long lasting problems caused by the introduction of information technology centre around the human domain of the total management task. A commonly evidenced reaction is that new technology is feared and fear in itself can breed resistance. However, some aspects of this fear are often well founded in that the introduction of information technology can cause difficulties for employees.

   i) New technology can disturb established procedures. Given that there is a degree of comfort afforded by the known, many employees will find such disturbance at best inconvenient and at worst distressing.

ii) New technology can lead to the break up of established groups. Most employees find great comfort and reassurance in their membership of such groups and any change will be at best inconvenient and at worst distressing.

iii) New technology can result in loss of jobs. The very nature of such technology is that it is supposed to provide a more efficient way of accessing information. Many large organisations employ large numbers of people in their information-gathering functions. Thus the price of increased efficiency may well be the loss of jobs. This is a very important point to consider since the loss of jobs can result in resentment even amongst those remaining in employment.

d) Information technology may result in wider or easier access to confidential or commercially sensitive information. This is of particular importance in the public service. It must not be assumed that wider access to all information is necessarily desirable; such information may contain items of a personal nature which are confidential, for example, certain information contained in school records. In such cases the public service organisation may be under a statutory duty to restrict such information to those who have signed legally binding documents to keep it confidential. Thus widening the access to such records can be seen to be detrimental to the effective management of the organisation. Similarly, the commercial sensitivity of much information generated in the private sector may be a barrier to the over ambitious widening of access to information

e) The disbenefits of decentralisation – information technology facilitates the manipulation of data to produce information. Under such circumstances the staff manipulating the data could do so incorrectly. For instance, medical staff, without financial expertise, could produce financial information which was incorrect or incomplete. The same problem might be encountered in the private sector in financial projections made by, for instance, engineers. There is always a danger that because information is given, no matter by whom, this information is always deemed to be correct.

How to Choose an Information Technology System

Many of the managerial problems created by such information technology purchases can be overcome by careful analysis by the organisation's senior management. The organisation itself must develop a managerial strategy to control or drive its information technology. This strategy can be seen to be a product of the particular circumstances of the organisation. A number of questions can help to illustrate these circumstances.

a) Why is the information technology being changed? Only after asking and answering this question is the organisation in a position to begin to acquire new technology. For instance, if the organisation is experiencing real problems with its existing configurations and systems it has some real and positive incentive to change; furthermore, the type of technology to acquire will be indicated. However, it may be that the organisation finds that the pressures for change originate not from any rigorously examined sources but from the desire 'to follow fashion'. Any changes based on these more flimsy principles may fail.

b) What technology is needed? Having established the reasons for change the organisation then has to determine what its needs are. When it decides to purchase a particular package it must be mindful of its precise needs. Any technology which does not, in any significant terms, meet these needs should be viewed with suspicion.

c) How much money is available? An organisation must examine the availability of resources before it can begin to seek improvements to its existing information systems. Any improvements must be assessed as to their cost implications before they are accepted. Such a discipline imposes a degree of organisational control over well-intentioned but misguided enthusiasm.

d) What is available? An organisation has to consider that what it needs may not necessarily be available in the precise form needed or at a price it can afford. Thus it must ascertain what can be delivered and at what price. The radical changes predicted from such developments have already been examined. For the organisation to properly control these radical changes it must be aware of all or most of the potential alternatives available.

e) What criteria to adopt in the selection? This is a very important question. Factors such as the importance of the initiative, of cost, of delivery timing and who to involve in the acquisition decision are all important. The relative importance of these factors will depend upon the particular circumstances obtaining in the organisation at the particular time; a prepared organisation should be a good organisation.

f) Where are the origins of the initiative? If the initiative originated from senior management it is likely to meet more resistance from employees than if the initiative emerged from the employees themselves. However, if the initiative has come from lower levels in the organisation it should be the subject of careful, but probably low-profile, organisational scrutiny. The importance of keeping such scrutiny low-profile should not be underestimated. These well-intentioned, organisational controls could be so easily viewed in negative terms; as such the benefits of employee initiative and flexibility, addressed elsewhere in this text, may be denied the organisation.

g) What problems have occurred in the organisation previously? Many potential problems can be avoided by learning from past experience. Past experiences may not focus on the introduction of technology; however, it is almost certain that some reasonably similar event has occurred in the past. If this event occurred recently there may be more to be learnt than if it occurred some time ago since the employees involved may no longer work for the organisation. This element of the strategy is very important in that it quite graphically illustrates the fact that the problems of managing information technology are, in many ways, merely extensions of more fundamental management problems and, as such, are addressed successfully by utilising long-established, good management practices.

h) Which elements of information lend themselves to such technology? The answering of the previous questions should have produced more information surrounding the driving forces behind the pressures for change. In all probability such information will reveal that there are areas where such technology can be successfully introduced and areas where it is not suited. The answering of this question may isolate those pieces of information which are, for instance, deemed to be confidential. Under such circumstances, either the information should be kept in a manual form or special controls may need to be placed on access to such information if it is to be kept in any other form.

i) Who should be responsible for generating this information? The problems of non-experts naively assuming that information technology makes the expert redundant has already been emphasised. This does not mean that experts are the only people who should produce the information; however, it does mean that the integrity and authority of information needs to be established. This factor will be examined in more detail later in this chapter.

j) What is the age structure and ability of the organisation's workforce? There is a tendency for older employees to be more resistant to changes than younger employees. This does not mean that older employees will not adapt to changes – in fact some older employees may not be resistant; however, it is likely that more management attention and time will be needed to reassure such employees.

Similarly there is a tendency for less able employees to be more resistant to such changes. Again this does not mean that there will be an inevitable reaction by such employees but that there is a greater likelihood of such reactions. Such resistance can be overcome but more management attention and time will probably be needed. Again, a prepared and vigilant management is a good management.

Thus it can be concluded that, in the light of these potential problems, an organisation needs to have carefully documented procedures for the purchase and use of such technology. The management of an organisation should be particularly aware of the need to train staff in the use of such technology; in addition they need to be aware of the possible need to introduce such developments only after due negotiation and reassurance. An organisation needs to control its information technology rather than be controlled by that same technology.

Managing Information Technology

Essentially the management of information technology embraces two distinct issues:

a) Who should manage the means of generation of information (hardware)?

b) Who should manage the information once produced?

These questions are essentially those of the desirability of centralisation or decentralisation; that is, they lend themselves to centralised or decentralised solutions. Centralised solutions would locate the hardware and ownership of information at a central base (eg an information technology department); this is the traditional functional management arrangement or design shown in Figure 27.1.

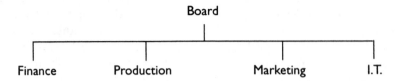

FIGURE 27.1   *A Centralised Technology Function*

Wholly decentralised solutions would allow production units to buy and manage their own information technology resources and to have unrestricted control over the information so produced. This would be the product-based arrangement or design shown in Figure 27.2.

Naturally there might be situations where the technology is centralised but the control of information is decentralised. In addition, the technology could be decentralised but then the information so produced would have to be sent to a central base.

As with many organisational design issues, a matrix form of design could be of use to the organisation in its development and utilisation of information technology. This is shown in Figure 27.3.

The answers to these questions are dependent upon such things as the particular needs of the organisation, its culture, and the extent of its information technology maturity. The more centralised the solution the more rigid the control but the less likely the advantages of experimentation and speed. The detailed consideration of the structural alternatives has been examined in an earlier section of this text.

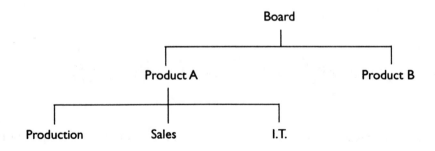

FIGURE 27.2   *A Product-based Information Technology Function*

The Need for an Information Resource Manager

It might now be useful to examine in a little more detail the particular managerial problems created by the generation of information. Some organisations have tried to overcome some of these problems by appointing an information resource manager. This individual could be charged with the responsibility of generating of any information within an organisation. He or she may be further charged with the holding of any information within the organisation, wherever it was generated. Any advantages or benefits obtained from such an appointment can be seen to be a product of the precise duties ascribed to that individual.

The rest of the analysis will assume that the individual is charged with both tasks. The appointment of such a person, with such widely defined duties, can bring certain advantages or, alternatively, overcome certain potential problems.

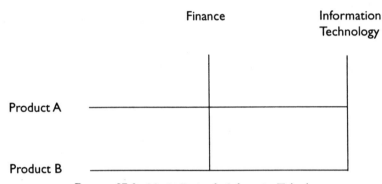

FIGURE 27.3   *Matrix Design for Information Technology*

a) If the information generated (particularly concerning clients) is sensitive, the appointment should guarantee greater confidentiality of information. This confidentiality could be either of a personal or commercial nature.
b) If end users cannot be trusted to properly use or catalogue information, such a post should facilitate better use of the information.
c) If there is a need to carefully catalogue the existing sources and types of information, a manager can effectively discharge this obligation.
d) If there is concern about the generation of superfluous information or duplication of information, the appointment of such an individual can help overcome these concerns. This will be of particular importance in parts of the

public service where, for instance, both the education and social services departments of a local authority might be producing information about a child. Similar problems will be encountered in the private sector where the information requirements of different departments might have a degree of commonality.

e) If there is concern that information is not sufficiently capable of transportation (that is, the information produced by one person or section needs to be used by another person or section but the second user finds difficulty in understanding the information) the appointment of a manager might overcome the difficulties; under these circumstances the information resource manager will be charged with the specification of information requirements and hence the overcoming of such communication difficulties.

However, the appointment of such a manager can bring problems.

a) It may prove difficult to find someone with the appropriate skills. Certainly there is no established profession which might be generally accepted as having the required skills. Perhaps an obvious potential profession is that of librarianship but the changed environment of business management might present barriers to the immediately successful use of members of this profession in this capacity.

b) Those who directly produce goods and services may see this person as yet another level of unneeded management.

c) The existence of such a person may stifle creativity and innovation and this may lead to loss of motivation.

d) The appointment of such an individual costs money. This does not mean that the individual should not be appointed, but it does mean that value for money needs to be obtained.

Summary

The introduction of information technology can facilitate a better environment for the management of an organisation. However, it can create major problems for the management of an organisation. These problems can be overcome, but only with careful and vigilant management practice and planning. It is very interesting to note that many of the management issues related to information technology are merely examples of more deep-rooted and more general issues of management.

Exercise

Critically examine the information technology strategy of an organisation with which you are familiar.

Further Reading

Cummings, T. G. and Worley, C. G. (1993) *Organization Management and Change*, West Publishing

Curson, C. (ed) (1986) *Flexible Patterns of Work*, IPM

Kay, J. (1993) *Foundations of Corporate Success*, Oxford University Press

Long, R.J. (1983) *New Office Information Technology*, Croom Helm

Mintzberg, H. (1983) *Power In and Around Organisations*, Prentice Hall

Morden, A. R. (1993) *Business Strategy and Planning*, McGraw-Hill

Morden, T. (1996) *Principles of Management*, McGraw-Hill

Peters, T.J. and Austin, N. (1986) *A Passion for Excellence*, Fontana/Collins

Porter, M.E. (1985) *Competitive Advantage*, Free Press

Toffler, A. (1981) *The Third Wave*, Pan

Whistler, T.L. (1970) *Information Technology and Organisational Change*, Wadsworth

28

Marketing

L E A R N I N G   O B J E C T I V E S

- **Understand the importance of the marketing function in the effective management of an organisation**

- **Appreciate the importance of the concepts of the 4 Ps in determining an acceptable marketing strategy**

- **Appraise the interrelationships between the 4 Ps**

- **Identify the factors which should be considered in the construction of a strategy in this area**

- **Apply the issues addressed in the context of organisation with which you are familiar**

- **Identify areas where further research might be needed**

The marketing function is best examined by boldly and accurately stating at the beginning of the chapter that every organisation has a market; and furthermore that it is not the existence or otherwise of a market which distinguishes one organisation from another but the nature of the market the organisation faces. Some organisations sell their products to their market; others do not actually sell their products but receive their funding from taxation sources. Those which sell their products do so in circumstances of open competition while others operate in monopoly conditions.

It must be admitted that the acknowledgement of a market does not necessarily mean that organisations will necessarily see their primary duty as being the serving of market needs and preferences. However, the existence of competition makes an organisation more aware of the need to serve its market.

The Organisation and the Needs of its Market

There are a number of ways in which an organisation can respond to its market. It is how the organisation chooses to react to its market which can, to a substantial extent, determine its success. An example of the various approaches being used to serve a target market is shown in Figure 28.1.

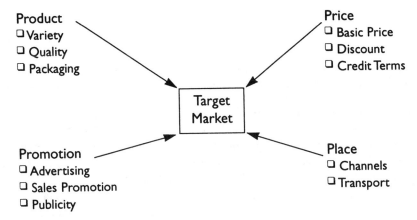

Product
❑ Variety
❑ Quality
❑ Packaging

Price
❑ Basic Price
❑ Discount
❑ Credit Terms

Target Market

Promotion
❑ Advertising
❑ Sales Promotion
❑ Publicity

Place
❑ Channels
❑ Transport

FIGURE 28.1 *The Marketing Mix*

BY PRODUCT

This approach obtains where an organisation reacts to its market by focusing on its products. It determines what quality and what range of products are required to serve its market needs. This approach focuses on three issues.

a) What types of product to provide (the range of goods and services produced) – this approach assumes that the market's and hence the organisation's needs are best served by providing a range of products from which individual clients can choose. In many ways this approach has its roots in the psychology of 'hedging bets'; if one activity fails at least the organisation has other activities on which it can rely.

b) What quality of product to provide – in this case the assumption would be that consumer needs are best served by ensuring that the product quality is correct. An example would be the quality assurance procedures developed in the early 1990s in the United Kingdom public service environment. Similarly, in the same period in the United Kingdom in the private sector many advertisements focus increasingly on the quality of the product advertised. This is best suited to an environment where the product is less well-established and mass produced.

c) What production methods to employ to meet market needs − under these circumstances the organisation considers its primary duty to be that of serving consumer needs by concentrating on production efficiency. This is suitable where the product is well-established, carefully specified and where the environment is stable. The best examples of this kind of approach would be in the private sector; however, an example from the public service in Britain might be the water supply industry. This is the most common focus of attention in the mass manufacturing segments of the private sector.

BY PLACE

This approach exists where the organisation focuses its attention on how to deliver the product to the consumer. It is essentially a decision about two distinct issues.

a) To whom the products should be sold or offered − the choice might be that rather than selling its products direct to the final user, the organisation might wish to place its products through intermediaries such as agents or wholesalers. The major alternative would be to afford the product direct to the final consumer; a good example of this would be direct mail selling.

b) How the products are delivered to customers − having decided who the customer for a particular product shall be, the organisation then has to make a decision about how that product shall be delivered to that customer; examples might be house-to-house sales, or through warehouses, or by retail outlets. Under this approach, in its purest form, the various means of distribution are under the direct control of the producer of the good.

BY PROMOTION

This situation obtains when an organisation concentrates its attention on the selling of the product. The concept of selling is not one which is well entrenched in the public service in general and as such the best examples are found in the private sector. However, this does not mean that this approach has no validity in the public sector environment but, even where this approach could be used (for example public corporations), alternative approaches such as product orientation tend to predominate. Perhaps the best example of this approach is the heavy emphasis on advertising and sales in the double glazing industry. The focus of attention is on how to persuade the customer to use the predetermined product, afforded through the predetermined channels. An example in the public sector might be that a particular political party decides what its policies (products) are going to be, it then has to decide how to promote a feeling of attraction for those policies in the electorate. Essentially it embraces two main issues.

a) Advertising – in this scenario the decision has been made that, for a market to be properly served, it needs to be aware of the product afforded. This necessitates a decision being taken on what the advertisement is going to say (the message) and what medium should be used to transmit the message. The range of messages is quite extensive, from detailed analyses of the strengths of a particular product to a simple association of the product with a particular environment. An example of the latter strategy would be the association of a particular product with a sporting environment through sponsorship of the sports event.

b) Publicity – in many ways this can be seen as similar to advertising. However, it is mentioned separately for two reasons. Firstly, the private sector environment would distinguish between pure direct, paid for, advertising and the seeking of publicity for the product. The public relations activities of a private sector organisation would usually be institutionally separated from its advertising activities. However, the second reason for the making of this distinction is that the pure publicising of a product's availability affords a useful example of this approach to marketing in a public sector environment. A taxation-funded public sector organisation would not be meeting the needs of its market if it afforded a high quality service which was used by only a tiny fraction of those it was meant to serve.

Promotion can be further subdivided into a number of categories. The organisation has a range of options from which it can choose its promotion strategy. The reality is that most organisations will choose a number of these options; the success of a promotion strategy can then be seen in the mix of options it chooses. This mix is commonly known as the promotion mix. The various options can be identified as follows.

a) Advertising – the organisation has to determine the media in which it wishes to advertise. Options range through local, national and international press, professional or trade journals, local and national radio and the increasingly important Internet. Having chosen the media the organisation then has to choose its advertising theme. This can range from simply choosing the words used to examining innovative themes to attract the targeted market.

b) Sponsorship – this has been immensely controversial in 1997 with the tobacco industry sponsorship of Formula One. This example classically illustrates the purpose of sponsorship: the aim is to sponsor a worthy product or service but, in so doing, promote the organisation. The aim is to positively promote the organisation with those attracted to the sponsored product or service. In deciding which product or service to sponsor the organisation would choose those which are complementary to and reinforce its own image and mission. An example might be the Coca Cola Corporation which perceives itself to operate at the global level and seeks to sponsor soccer throughout the world.

c) Sales promotion – this is commonly undertaken in the retail industry with offers such as discounts on goods in supermarkets. In this particular promotional activity great care is take to be consistent with the pricing strategy of the organisation.

d) Public relations – this is examined in some depth later in the chapter but, briefly, the aim is to ensure that the organisation is constantly communicating proactively with both internal and external stakeholders.

e) Personal selling – this is a very common form of promotion in the car industry. However as the concept of networking develops in the communication domain more and more use is made of this option in law, accountancy, education and health. In such cases these organisations seek custom through ensuring efficient and effective personal contact with their existing or potential customers.

The Advertising Dimension can be further broken down into a number of constituent elements. Over a period the advertising of a product or service can be seen to have different purposes. The various purposes of the advertising campaign and the likely effect of the various stages of the campaign is shown in Figure 28.2. Initially the aim might be to simply make potential customers aware of the product. When this awareness has been established it is likely that the organisation undertaking its advertising campaign would then want to establish some form of customer interest in the product or service. Only when this interest has been established can the advertising organisation seek to establish a real desire by potential customers for the product or service. After the desire has been created the advertising organisation is then charged with translating the desire into action – that is the customer is encouraged to purchase or consume the product or service. In a highly competitive environment it is considered unlikely that one campaign can achieve all the required objectives. Rather, given the various stages of advertising just considered, it is probable that the various stages will have to be undertaken with different types of advert and possibly different themes.

Buyer Awareness	Promotional Task	Advertising Effect
Awareness	Establish Buyer Awareness	Inform potential customers about the product or service
Interest	Create buyer interest	Stimulate interest in the product
Desire	Create desire	Induce a favourable attitude, especially in relation to competing products
Action	Sell the product	Induce a purchase by stressing the immediate desirability of the product

FIGURE 28.2 *Levels of Advertising*

BY PRICE

Under this approach the market's needs are deemed to be best served by focusing on the price of the product. It is important that this is identified as a separate marketing strategy. An organisation can attempt to serve its market's needs through the medium of assuring a high quality, and possibly high cost, product or by affording a low cost, and maybe low quality, product.

Although the various approaches have been considered in isolation the reality in most organisations will be that there will be a mix of approaches: the marketing mix. As such the success of an organisation's endeavours is not a product of which approach it has adopted but of the respective importance it attaches to the various approaches. In many ways the various elements of the marketing mix can feed off one another; for example, any message portrayed in serving of market requirements by advertising (promotion) might focus on product quality (product) as opposed to price (price).

   The use of these approaches to show various ways of achieving a single objective, increasing sales, is illustrated in Figure 28.3.

Ideas	Marketing mix
❏ Widen variety	Product
❏ Improve quality	Product
❏ Advertise	Promotion
❏ Increase salesforce	Promotion/Place
❏ Cut prices	Price
❏ Increased access to credit	Price
❏ Open more retail outlets	Place

FIGURE 28.3 *Ways to Increase Sales of Cars*

Marketing in a Service Context

Modern marketers feel that the four Ps approach to marketing is too firmly rooted in the Industrial context. They consider that the four Ps inadequately define the options available in a Service rather than an industrial context. Under such circumstances it its considered that three additional Ps should be introduced and examined along with the previous Ps of product, price, place and promotion:

a) People - in a service context much of the quality of the product might be seen to lie in the trust established between the customer and the person representing the organisation. In the 1990s many organisations have so structured their work allocations that individual customers are allocated an individual member of staff to deal with all their relationships. This is well illustrated when we consider how we relate to a firm of solicitors - we simply ask to speak to the solicitor who is dealing with our case.

b) Physical evidence - there are two separate elements to this feature. Firstly there is the constant awareness of the organisation's connection with the service delivered. This might be illustrated by simple features such as written communication being undertaken on organisational letter-headed paper. A further illustration might be ensuring that the organisation's name and/or logo is strategically placed around the premises or vehicles. The second dimension is ambience - the customer should be afforded a physical environment which is welcoming. Garages in the late twentieth century have pleasant reception areas. Similarly hospitals now have pleasant reception areas with ready access to shops and refreshment areas.

c) Process - the effectiveness of service delivery will be enhanced by ensuring that the service process is customer friendly. In many cases such effectiveness of service delivery will be facilitated by ensuring ease of contact between the customer and the organisation. One way of ensuring such ease of contact will be introducing an appointments system.

Paternal or Consumer-Led Marketing?

An alternative perspective on the marketing function is to examine the extent to which the consumer is invited to participate in the strategies or approaches just outlined. The examples which have been quoted have assumed that it is the organisation itself which makes the real decisions as to quality, prices and distribution outlets. This will be entitled the 'paternal approach'. It cannot be denied that ultimately the organisation itself has the ultimate duty to make such decisions.

However, it would be the most commonly held belief or philosophy of the marketing function that the customer has a major role to play in the making of these marketing decisions. This can be entitled the 'market orientation'. Under this approach the emphasis is placed upon the determination of consumer needs and then the subsequent meeting of them. In many ways this is a more effective way of meeting market needs. It is useful where the organisation is facing a changing environment and has little knowledge with which to make the important marketing decisions; it is particularly useful where the organisation operates in a competitive environment, since the serving of customer needs is one of the more obvious ways of achieving organisational success. It is an approach which obtains more legitimacy where individual needs vary from consumer to consumer. Although this approach is established in many parts of the private sector, it is an approach which has gained more acceptance in the United Kingdom public service only since the 1980s and early

1990s when the demands of statute have been reduced. Under such circumstances the organisation cannot resort to statute as an indication of consumer needs; instead, more attention is given to the ascertainment of consumer needs. In many ways this can be either indicative or facilitative of a client culture (examined in a previous section).

Relationship Marketing

The approach to marketing explained to date focuses exclusively on the marketing of a product or service. However the subject of marketing can be extended to embrace a wider segment of the total management process. The techniques of marketing might be extended beyond the examination of customer markets. The concept of relationship marketing envisages the use of marketing techniques in six separate markets:

a) Customer markets – this has already been examined in some detail.
b) Internal markets – this suggests that organisations' effectiveness is affected by the ease with which their various sections liaise and cooperate with each other. It could be that internal communication or staff attitudes could be facilitated by using the seven Ps of marketing already discussed. For instance cooperation could be encouraged by ensuring personal contacts between the two sections debating changes to established processes.
c. Recruitment markets – in the late 1990s many successful organisations have commented that they have found difficulty recruiting appropriately skilled staff. In such circumstances they have had to focus on how they might more successfully operate in this specified market. They might have to pay more (price), develop developmental programmes such as mentoring (people) or improve their recruitment literature (promotion).
d. Supplier markets – successful organisations such as Marks and Spencer have long realised that their success depends on ensuring an effective supply chain. In ensuring this effectiveness organisations might have to focus on price, people, process relationships with their suppliers.
e. Influence markets – in ensuring effective external communication organisations might be advised to direct their attention to using marketing techniques in influence markets. Organisations need to ensure good relationships with those people or groups able to influence their progress. Examples might be relationships with government organisations or pressure groups. In such cases attention might be given to process, people or promotion issues.
f) Referral markets – many organisations do not have direct contact with customers. Sometimes new customers might be afforded by referral processes. Examples of access to new customers through such intermediaries might be referrals from solicitors, general practitioners, social workers, bank managers. In such circumstances organisations might be advised to give attention to facilitating such relationships by price, promotion, process, place issues.

Public Relations

Public relations is commonly seen as closely linked to marketing. It has traditionally perceived to be synonymous merely with the external communication of an organisation. However, if a more expansive view is taken of the public as in relationship marketing, the domain of public relations can be seen to be similarly expanded. In this extended role it can be seen to have a number of purposes:

a) To encourage good publicity – if the organisation is to achieve good publicity, the media have to be made aware of good, positive stories. The public relations section will commonly liaise on a regular basis with the media to promote good publicity.
b) To offset bad publicity – inevitably organisations do encounter problems and the well prepared organisation will be able to respond positively to explain their position in such difficult times.
c) To influence key people or institutions public relations has a much more proactive role in that it is able to keep the organisation well-positioned in its relationship with key people or institutions such as politicians, and community groups.
d) To communicate directly with stakeholders – many large organisations feel that it is helpful to take a proactive role in its relationships with various stakeholders. The opinion is that, if these stakeholders are to receive information about the organisation, it would be much more productive to receive that information directly from the organisation. A good example of this form of public relations would be the news letter.
e) To link the organisation with its stakeholders – the networking with these stakeholders extends beyond merely communication in that, when properly effected, productive links can be established between the two parties, thus engendering positive atmosphere for future relationships.

Hence effective public relations can be shown to establish positive relationships with the range of stakeholders - customers and consumers, workforce, suppliers, local community, financial community, and policy makers.

The Management of the Marketing Function

Having acknowledged the need for marketing it is now necessary to examine how it can be carried out, structured or managed. The full details on the options available are examined in the previous section of this book. A central marketing department will ensure that the new concept is promoted by a separate power source and a central separate functional department may be useful in the infancy of the marketing discipline. An example of this still most common form of marketing design is shown in Figure 28.4.

However, the assumption of customer-led philosophies might be that those closer to the customers might have a major role to play in the marketing exercise. As such, centralised solutions and designs might produce too much organisational rigidity and the argument for a devolved marketing function or a matrix mode of operation might be attractive. The organisation might be torn between two competing desires: the need to maintain the integrity of and promote the marketing function and the need to obtain the advice and support of those closer to the customer. In such circumstances the marketing function could be executed by a matrix organisational design.

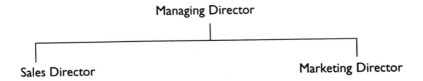

FIGURE 28.4 *A Centralised Marketing Function*

The Product Life Cycle

It is an essential feature of good management in general, and good marketing in particular, to appreciate that in the overwhelming majority of cases every product has a fixed life span. When this product life span is examined it can be seen to be very similar to that of a human being; the product moves from birth, through growth, to maturity, old age and eventually death. This is diagrammatically shown in Figure 28.5. In the home utilities sector an example of a product in infancy might be a robotic house cleaner, a product reaching maturity might be a dish washer, whilst one in relative decline might be the automatic clothes washer. A good management will be that which is constantly aware of this fixed life span, which is mindful of the particular place in this life span of the individual product and which, most importantly, takes the most appropriate decisions based on this knowledge.

This is not to claim that life span of a particular product is easy to determine. It may be that sales statistics or, to use a public sector equivalent, usage, might help in this determination. Such an analysis is shown in Figure 28.6. In this scenario it can be seen that in the vast majority of cases an increasing sales or usage volume will place the product in its early stages of its life cycle; a levelling-off of sales or usage would place the product in its mature period; and a decreasing sales or usage volume would place

Birth

Infancy

Maturity

Old Age/Decline

Death

FIGURE 28.5 *Product Life Cycle*

the product in its declining period. During a period of infancy, resources need to be channelled into the development of the product in order to maximise benefit; during the period of maturity the organisation will need to think carefully about refining or replacing the product in the medium term; when the product reaches its period of decline the organisation needs, if it has not already done so, to develop an alternative product with maximum haste.

Product Portfolios

Although commonly the product life cycle is seen as a development of the concept of the product portfolio, this analysis will treat the two concepts as complementary. The concept of the product portfolio can be viewed as introducing an extra real life element into the analysis and introduces three additional factors into the equation.

a) The organisation will be making more than one product and each product will be competing against the others for its share of a finite resource base.
b) Most organisations would not wish to make only one product, rather they usually wish to spread their activities over a number of products.
c) A range of products can, and probably does, constitute a sensible financial strategy since not only does it spread the risk but also the money from one product can provide the funds necessary to finance the development of another.

The most commonly acknowledged form of product portfolio analysis is that evolved by the Boston Consulting Group. The work is diagrammatically shown in Figure 28.7. The analysis is explained in the form of a matrix which plots each product or business activity in relation to two factors: market growth rate and market share.

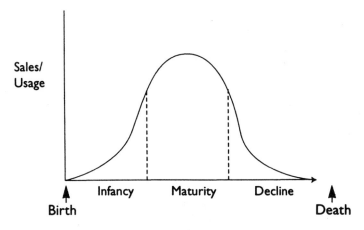

FIGURE 28.6 *Sales as a Projection of Life Cycle*

		Company Market Share	
		High	Low
Growth Rate of the Product	High	I Stars	2 Problem children
	Low	3 Cash cows	4 Dogs

FIGURE 28.7 *Product Portfolio Analysis*

'Stars' are products where the market is growing fast and where the organisation's market position suggests favourable development in the future. 'Cash Cows' typically are products which have reached maturity but where decline is not predicted in the imminent future. As such they require little development money. It is usually the 'Cash Cow' which provides the development funds for the 'Star' or the 'Problem Child'. 'Problem Children' are products where successful development could be predicted but only by the injection of substantial resources, most commonly on advertising, publicity or nurturing potential customers and perhaps at the expense of money being devoted to other products. 'Dogs' are the products where serious consideration to discontinuation should be given. However, it may be that the 'Dog' provides the foothold in the market necessary to develop the 'Star' or 'Problem Child'.

Thus it can be seen that the concepts of product life cycles and product portfolios, when taken together, can provide an analytical framework within which an organisation can design and plan its desired product range and product quantities.

Summary

The acknowledgement of the existence of a market and the need for the organisation to devote its attention to the serving of the needs of that market has been long-established in the private sector. The concept of the market has grown in importance over the past few years in the wider public service. There are several ways in which the organisation can attempt to serve the needs of its market. It is likely that those approaches which allow the customer to participate in the marketing function will hold some attractions as organisations, both in the public and private sectors, encounter rapidly changing environments.

Exercise

In the context of your organisation or an organisation with which you are familiar appraise the marketing strategy and policies.

Further Reading

Christopher, M., McDonald, M., Wills, G. (1980) *Introducing Marketing*, Pan
Colwell, D. (1984) *The Marketing of Services*, Heinemann
Cummings, T. G. and Worley, C. G. (1993) *Organization Management and Change*, West Publishing
Garratt, R. (1987) *The Learning Organisation*, Collins
Kay, J. (1993) *Foundations of Corporate Success*, Oxford University Press
Kotler, P. (1987) *Marketing Management*, Prentice Hall
Mintzberg, H. (1983) *Power In and Around Organisations*, Prentice Hall
Morden, A. R. (1993) *Business Strategy and Planning*, Mcgraw-Hill
Morden, T. (1996) *Principles of Management*, McGraw-Hill

Oldcorn, R. *Management,* Pan
Palazzini, F. S. (1988) *Coca-Cola Superstar,* Barrons
Porter, M.E. (1985) *Competitive Advantage,* Free Press
Wilkie, W.L. (1986) *Consumer Behaviour,* Wiley

Project
Management

L E A R N I N G   O B J E C T I V E S

- Outline the special environmental circumstances obtaining in the management of a project

- Understand the managerial features of a project

- Examine the management problems obtaining at each stage of a project

- Assess the importance of teamwork in the management of a project

- Evaluate the role of network analysis in the management of a project

- Appreciate the issues examined in the context of an organisation with which you are familiar

---

A Project can be considered to consist of a defined set of activities undertaken within a defined time period and with carefully prescribed end results. An example would be the installation of a new information technology system or the building of a new hospital.

In some ways it is true to claim that management is management and that the principles involved in managing a project will be very little, if at all, different from the principles of general management examined throughout this text. However the reality is that there are some unique features of a project which in their turn produce distinctive contingent features of the management task.

A project covers a specific, finite time period and the duty of the project manager is confined to that specific time period. It means, for instance, that when such a manager tries to motivate his or her team members there will be a more limited time period to effect this motivation.

The project is more likely than normal management processes to involve extensive interdisciplinary work. Thus the project manager is more likely than his or her normal management counterpart to be charged with developing interdisciplinary cooperation.

The work of the project manager focuses constantly on teamwork. This is not to claim that teamwork is not part of the work of all managers but to emphasise the primacy of managing teams in the project management environment.

In many permanent managerial environments the manager will be able to flex his or her resources around a multiplicity of tasks and objectives. However this flexibility will be denied the project manager. The manager of a project has to manage within fixed budgetary constraints. The more permanent manager is commonly able to explore different production or delivery methods in his or her search for value for money. This flexibility is also denied the project manager.

Although all managers work to tight time schedules the manager of a project is the most tied to specified time schedules. The project manager has to deliver the product or service by a specific date or financial penalties will usually be invoked. It must be admitted that this is sometimes the managerial environment of all managers but the rigidity of time is much more common in the project environment.

However in some ways the managerial environment of the project manager is simpler than that of his or her more permanent counterparts. A project has a specified objective and outcome and the manager will not need to devote undue attention to the exploration of alternative objectives and outcomes.

In short the managerial environment faced by the project manager is one with a tighter and more rigidly defined agenda. Hence the style of management adopted in this environment will have to be reflective of this environment.

The Essential Ingredients of a Project

A project can be deemed to consist of four fundamental ingredients. These are diagrammatically shown in Figure 29.1.

COST

Each project, be it internally or externally managed, will have a strict expenditure budget. Occasionally additional funds will have to be sought but any increase will have to be approved outside the project management structure.

SCHEDULE

A project will have to be completed within a fixed time period. Extensions can be sought but such extensions will have to be approved outside the project management structure. Schedules are not merely confined to the completed project. Almost universally the project will consist of interlinked activities which have to be undertaken in a fixed pattern. In such circumstances fixed time periods will have to be given to each separate activity. Sometimes the management task is further complicated by the fact that work can be undertaken on these separate tasks independently but the next stage can only be started when all preceding stages are completed. The work has to be so scheduled that these individual, independent activities are completed at around the same time. Any undue delay in one activity will result in a delay for the whole project.

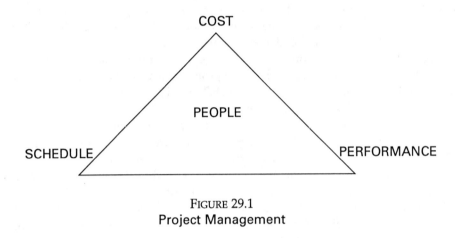

FIGURE 29.1
Project Management

PERFORMANCE

When the project is undertaken it has to be completed according to specified standards and qualities. The whole essence of the project and the management of that project then has to be to ensure that such standards are guaranteed. In other more routine activities perhaps, even if standards are specified, subsequent remedial action can be taken but in the case of the project failure to meet specified standards is synonymous with complete managerial failure.

PEOPLE

The people have to be carefully chosen and they have to be prepared in such a way that they perform to maximum effect within a limited time period. This can be seen to be crucially important in the service sector where the skills of the people involved can, in some ways, be seen to be part of the finished project itself. An example of this might be the design of a new information system. If the people designing this system cannot adequately explain this system and nurture the clients through their learning period the project will be deemed to be a failure.

Choosing a Team

Given that projects are commonly undertaken by a collection of individuals from different disciplines, working together as a team for a specified and limited time period, much of the success of the project can be seen to lie in the choice of the team members. Skills involved in team management have been examined earlier in this text, in Chapter 8. Briefly the manager must give attention not just to the acquisition of sufficient technical skills but must use team members in such a way that they function in a mutually compatible fashion (Belbin (1981)). Similarly the manager must ensure that proper team dynamics are facilitated and that the various stages of team formation are encouraged (Hackman (1987)).

Defining Parameters - Including Time and Cost

The manager of the project may be presented with already negotiated parameters. However in many cases the manager will be intimately involved in the negotiation of the project. He or she will have to ensure that the various activities within the project are adequately scheduled. The technique of network analysis helps a manager properly schedule a project. Figure 29.2 shows the nature of such a network. The circles define events, that is completed activities, and the lines show activities. Events

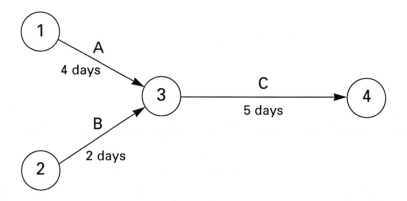

FIGURE 29.2 *A Project Network*

1 and 2 occur independently of each other. Event 3 occurs only when activities A and B have been undertaken. Event 4 occurs only when Activity C has ben added to Event 3. Activity A will take four days, Activity B will take two days, Activity C will take five days. The total length of the project could be the sum of the days involved, that is 11 days; however as Activities A and B can take place simultaneously the total length of the project can be telescoped into nine days, that is Activity A and Activity C.

The technique of network analysis will allow the manager to see if it its possible to direct fewer resources into Activity A and slightly more into Activity B. Under such circumstances it might be that the total length of the project can be further telescoped. Figure 29.3 shows the possible result of such rearrangement of resources.

Network analysis is a technique of potentially considerable, but legitimate, complexity. The technical details will not be examined in any further detail in this text. However further analysis can assess the number of people who need to be involved in each exercise and can further assess the cost effectiveness of reducing time on any project.

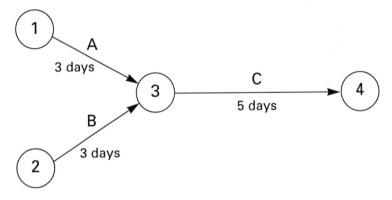

FIGURE 29.3 *The Telescoped Network*

Harnessing Resources

The manager of the project may be intimately involved in the procurement of resources sufficient to effectively execute the project. Such procurement can involve determining sources of supply of materials; it can involve the acquisition and training of staff. As such the work of the project manager can be seen to encompass much of the work of the more permanent manager. In fact in the human domain the work of the project manager is probably more difficult than that of his or her more permanent counterparts in that such managerial activity is telescoped into a shorter, fixed, time period.

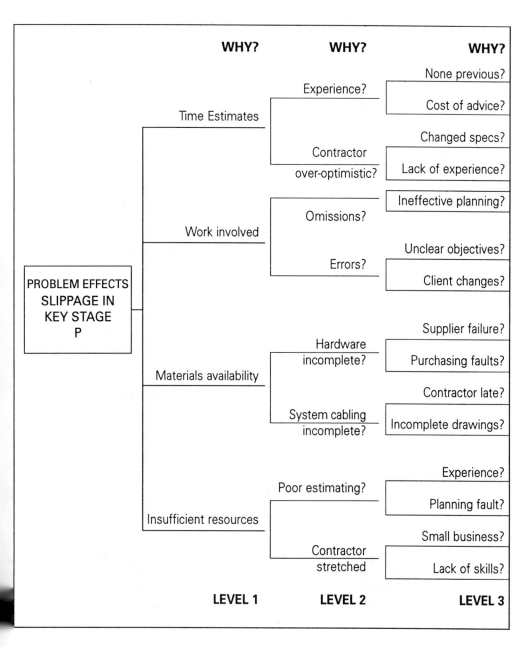

FIGURE 29.4 *The WHY - WHY diagram*

Executing, Monitoring and Controlling

Once all negotiations have been undertaken and once all resources have been guaranteed the manager then has to oversee the completion of the project. Schedules have to be adhered to, team members have to be managed, costs have to be controlled. The technique of network analysis will allow the manager to monitor the achievement of time and cost targets and to determine the extent to which remedial action might be necessary and which remedial actions are and are not feasible. The more the project changes in its structure and its scheduling the more employees need to be kept informed of the nature of any changes occurring. Techniques of team briefing will allow the manager to ensure that all employees are aware of their duties in a potentially rapidly changing environment.

In analysing the remedial action undertaken the manager can employ the technique of 'Why, Why' shown in Figure 29.4; this technique allows the manager to explore in a comprehensive fashion the causes of any problems. It can further isolate the interrelationships between problems. The rigorous analysis of the causes of problems will allow the manager to determine the nature of the remedial action necessary. Figure 29.5 shows the total activity involved in problem solving and the nature of any remedial action plans necessary. Planned and actual activities are compared; variations are analysed and action plans to effect remedial action are constructed.

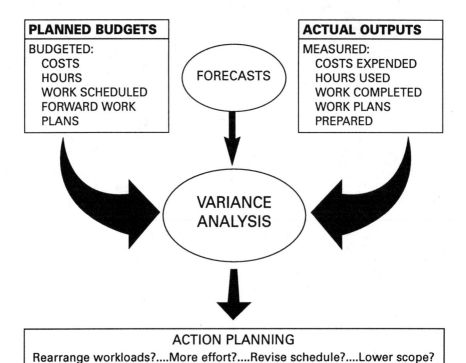

FIGURE 29.5 *Problem solving*

Reviewing

In certain cases, particularly where the manager and the team members may be involved in future projects, it may be useful to review the operation of the project once it is completed. A good example of such review is in the police service where routinely the team members are involved in a debriefing exercise where a completed project is analysed and any strengths and weaknesses are identified. Strengths will be embedded in future similar activity; weaknesses will be analysed and alternatives vigorously sought.

The Adhocracy

The analysis in this chapter to date might suggest that a project manager will be a manager for a relatively short time period. The skills required of a good manager are so scarce that organisations simply continue to rotate the individuals they determine have these skills from project to project. Furthermore in some cases the very managerial environment of the organisation might be deemed to be that of project management. This has been examined in Chapter 17 as Mintzberg's Adhocracy. In such a circumstance the whole organisation revolves around the management of a continuous succession of projects. Examples might be found in the construction and information technology software industries.

Summary

Sometimes the manager has to manage a project. In managing this project the manager will have to rely on his or her general management skills. However there are some distinctive features of a project and the dedicated project manager will have to be capable of managing within this unique management environment.

Exercise

Using an example of a project with which you are familiar, critically appraise its management, highlighting areas where you consider improvement could have been made.

Further Reading

Belbin, R.M. (1981) *Management Teams*, Heinemann
Fraser, A. and Neville, S. (1993) *Teambuilding*, The Industrial Society
Harvey-Jones, J. (1990) *Making It Happen*, Guild
Young, T.L. (1997) *Implementing Projects*, The Industrial Society
Young, T.L. (1993) *Planning Projects*, The Industrial Society

Chapter thirty

Energy Management

LEARNING OBJECTIVES

- Understand the various aspects of energy management

- Appraise the extent to which energy management improves the management of the organisation

- Appreciate the issues involved in the energy management process

- Analyse the interrelationships between these issues

- Outline the skills required of the energy manager

- Apply the principles studied to an organisation with which you are familiar

---

Since the 1970s the relatively high price increases in energy have caused many organisations to give more overt attention to the management of their energy usage. This period has been matched by a more acute awareness of the environmental impact of pursuing a policy of unlimited use of energy. Although, as a part of general resource management, the concept of managing energy has always been part of the managerial agenda of most organisations, the profile of this management activity has increased considerably.

The mission of energy management is to ensure the efficient and effective management of energy in order to meet the organisation's objectives. The managing of energy can be effected through decentralised options by allowing all operational managers to be responsible for managing the energy they consume. However, as the management of energy as a high-profile discipline is in its infancy stage, the appointment of dedicated specialists in this area could be seen to be the wisest option; under these circumstances the concept of energy management could at least be profiled and nurtured as one of worth to the organisation. Many large organisations have appointed dedicated energy managers to oversee the management of this increasingly politically and environmentally sensitive and expensive resource. As the awareness of energy issues increases and as the ownership of managing energy expands, the dedicated energy manager can delegate more and more of the routine energy management issues to operational managers.

Components of Energy Management

Figure 30.1 shows that there are four key components of energy management – advising on energy strategy, promoting energy efficiency, nurturing energy efficiency and procuring energy. In exercising his or her responsibilities the manager will be responsible for these key components. The components are, to an extent, discrete sets of activities; however, in many ways, they develop from each other and together compose an integrated managerial response to the problem of effectively managing energy. The effective execution of one of the components facilitates the development of the other components.

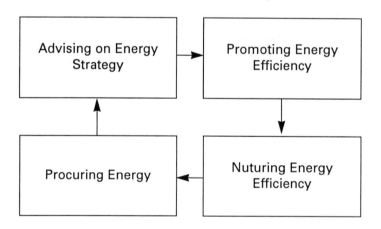

FIGURE 30.1 *Components of Energy Management*

Advising on Energy Strategy

This can be seen as the first logical set of responsibilities. Only when the organisation has an effective energy strategy can it begin to manage its energy resources. This general activity can be viewed as a set of interlinked activities.

Discovery

The first factor to examine is the organisation's current commitment to energy management. If the organisation is, at the very least, conscious of its energy consumption the dedicated manager will be well placed to establish an energy strategy. However if the organisation does not currently seem to place great emphasis on monitoring its energy consumption the manager will have to devote much more attention to persuading those involved of the desirability of an energy strategy. It may help at this stage to emphasise the statutory obligations of the organisation in for instance monitoring environmental impact. In the case of an organisation with limited commitment to this aspect of management, the energy manager might be advised to conduct an energy audit. Such an audit carefully analyses the consumption of energy throughout the organisation. It seeks to assess areas where improvements need to be made. In a specialised type of audit many large organisations have assembled specialist audit teams to conduct investigations. Organisations which sell energy commonly provide such an audit facility; however, even though the organisation might have to avail itself of this option, the subjective nature of such results must be appreciated. No matter how the audit is conducted the results would help illustrate to those needing to be convinced of the benefits of adopting a more proactive approach to energy management. The responsible manager will have to discover the areas where energy is consumed and the patterns of that energy consumption.

Determining areas for improvement

Having examined the patterns of energy consumption the manager then has to establish whether there are any areas for improvement. The manager will have to examine all available alternatives. This may consist simply of economy measures such as switching lighting on only when it is needed. It may require accessing external sources of knowledge about alternative ways of generating energy. Frequently, in the case of an organisation with limited knowledge or appreciation of energy management, sources of information about alternatives lie outside the organisation. Sometimes the specialist energy manager will be able to appraise the various options without seeking the advice of energy consumers. However sometimes in appraising these options he or she will have to seek the advice of those using the energy about issues concerning practical implementation.

Advising on improvements to be made

When the manager has appraised the options and evolved a suggested strategy this has to be sold to the corporate management or strategic apex of the organisation. Thus the energy manager has to be skilled in the formal communication and selling aspects of leadership examined earlier in this text. As some aspects of the strategy may involve substantial change from existing patterns of activity the manager must be capable of explaining and reassuring those who might question the efficacy of the strategy.

CREATING SYSTEMS WHICH MEASURE THE CONSUMPTION OF ENERGY

Once the energy strategy has been created, it has to be put into effect. This will require that an effective energy usage information system is established. Only when the organisation is able to monitor its energy consumption will it be able to effectively manage its newly assumed responsibilities in this area. This new information system might be perceived by energy consumers as an intrusion into their freedom to manage their own activities. In such circumstances the specialist energy manager will have to be skilled in relating to and reassuring other disciplines.

DETERMINING BENCHMARKS

Only when the organisation has established effective comparisons of energy consumption can it claim to be properly managing its energy consumption. Thus benchmarks will have to be established against which the organisation can compare its activity. These benchmarks might consist of previous performance; however, more commonly, they will consist of external comparisons. Frequently, effective energy management requires knowledge of comparator organisations. Such comparisons are often provided by energy providers or by professional groups.

Promoting Energy Efficiency

Once an energy strategy is in place the manager has to ensure that the strategy is implemented. The first stage in this processes is making all people in the organisation aware of the importance of energy management. In many ways the two components can be seen to be inextricably linked in that only when energy efficiency is effectively promoted will a strategy be approved. This promoting responsibility can be examined within the framework previously examined in the chapter on Marketing.

AWARENESS

Energy consumers have to be made aware of their energy consumption and of alternatives to their current patterns of consumption. Here the energy manager might create this awareness by developing a poster campaign whereby posters are placed in appropriate locations around the organisation.

INTEREST

Once consumers are aware of the concept of energy management they have to be attracted to seek more information. This might be effected by a series of meetings on energy management or by distributing pamphlets explaining what this new management discipline involves.

DESIRE

When energy consumers are interested in this new responsibility their interest has to be translated into seeking their approval of the new concept. The manager now has to effectively sell the concept of energy management. The real benefits have to be explained to each individual consumer. Information gathered from the energy audit may be useful in this context.

ACTION

Positive attraction and desire will then have to be transformed into action; consumers will have to implement the new procedures. During this period the dedicated manager will have to regularly liaise with consumers about practical ways of implementing the now approved energy strategy.

Nurturing Energy Efficiency

Once the concept of energy management has been established in an organisation the responsible manager then has to ensure that the concept is effectively managed and that any initial problems are overcome. This nurturing duty is closely allied to the translation of desire into action just examined and requires skills beyond those of creating an awareness and interest in that this awareness and interest have to be transformed into effective management practices.

ESTABLISHING PLANS

The energy manager has to work with consumers to create properly researched and considered plans to put into effect the agreed strategy.

ESTABLISHING PRACTICES

Plans in themselves are not action in that these plans have to be supported by routine practices which will ensure that energy consumption is a real priority of the organisation's day-to-day operational activity.

ESTABLISHING SUPPORTING INFORMATION SYSTEMS

The manager will have already created an acceptance of new monitoring information systems. There will now be a need to design and support these new information systems. If there is a need to obtain the cooperation of energy consumers (in for instance filling in forms) this cooperation must be actively sought. The energy manager will have to be vigilant to ensure that any teething problems with these new systems are quickly detected and overcome.

EMBEDDING A CULTURE OF CONTINUOUS IMPROVEMENT

Plans, practices and information systems are essential to the nurturing of an energy strategy; however the effective nurturing of the energy strategy also depends greatly upon a new energy conscious culture being established. The issues involved in embedding a culture have been examined in an earlier section of this book. However it must be repeated in this chapter that the dedicated energy manager is, in no small part, responsible for embedding this new set of collective priorities.

Procuring Energy

The issue of energy management does not rely solely on the efficient and effective use of existing sources of energy a major part of the energy manager's responsibilities will consist of ensuring that the organisation acquires its energy supplies from the best supplier.

GATHERING INFORMATION

The energy manager will have to gather information about alternative sources of energy. This is an extremely important area of energy management and the last few years of the old millennium are characterised by the increasing numbers of energy suppliers.

CHOICE OF BEST OPTION

Having gathered the information the manager then has to either advise on or actually chose the best option. If the latter is the case the manager may have to seek specialist financial assistance in his or her appraisal.

NEGOTIATING SUPPLY

When the best option has been determined the manager will then have to begin negotiations with the chosen supplier. The unique needs of the organisation will have to be accommodated in these discussions. The manager has to ensure that the suppliers' offer work in ways which reflect the best interests of the organisation. In these discussions features reflective of the special needs of the organisation may have to be negotiated.

ESTABLISHING THE CONTRACT

Once the negotiations are complete legal contracts have to be drawn up. In effecting this part of his or her responsibilities the energy manager may have to seek specialist legal advice and help.

Skills Required of the Energy Manager

The analysis has revealed that there are many features of energy management. The energy manager will have to undertake a wide range of duties and, as such, the skills required of the manager will be varied. Firstly energy management impacts upon all sections of the organisation and the dedicated energy manager will have to be able to communicate with many different disciplines. The energy manager's work involves extensive contact with the strategic apex of the organisation and he or she will have to be capable of appreciating strategic level decisions. The manager will need skills of persuasion and negotiation. Particularly in its infancy, the relatively new concept needs to be positively portrayed and the manager will need selling skills. Some of the work of the energy manager can be considered to be analogous to that of a project manager and as such the manager will need project management skills. Finally it must be acknowledged that energy management is a team, not an individual, activity and thus the manager must have effective teambuilding skills.

Summary

Energy management, as a dedicated high-profile activity, is a recent addition to the agenda of organisational management. In its infancy stage many organisations have resolved to appoint specialist dedicated managers to oversee these newly assumed responsibilities. The work of the manager can be divided into separate, but interrelated, activities. The skills required of the manager embrace most, if not all, of the repertoire of skills required of all of the operational and support managers in the rest of the organisation.

Exercise

From the perspective of an organisation with which you are familiar examine the duties of an actual or potential energy manager. Determine the practical problems he or she is likely to encounter in fulfilling these duties.

Further Reading

Belbin, R.M. (1981) *Management Teams*, Heinemann
Boutall, T. (1995) *The Good Energy Manager's Guide*, MCI
Frazer, A. and Neville, S. (1993) *Teambuilding*, The Industrial Society
Harvey-Jones, J. (1990) *Making It Happen*, Guild
Young, T.L. (1997) *Implementing Projects*, The Industrial Society

Entrepreneurship and Small Medium Sized Enterprises

OBJECTIVES

This section seeks to examine management in the context of smaller organisations. These types of organisation constitute a large proportion of the United Kingdom economy and management in this environment is worthy of separate analysis. After reading this section you should be aware of any individual qualities required of a manager in this environment, of any structures which tend to predominate, of any organisational cultures which are found, and of any special communication methods chosen.

Recently some management theorists have expressed concern that management theory has evolved through the study of large organisations and that the managerial characteristics of smaller organisations are so different from those of larger, corporate organisations that they do not fit into traditional analysis of management theory. This section will show that, although there are some very interesting special features of the management of smaller organisations, large elements of their management practices can be explained within the theory of the management of larger organisations.

INTRODUCTION

An emerging feature of the United Kingdom economy is its heavy reliance on small or medium-sized organisations to employ its workforce and to produce goods and services. These enterprises are commonly headed by a special category of manager – the entrepreneur. In this section the individual characteristics of the entrepreneur will be examined in terms of type, personality type, and modes of operation. The section will also examine the ways in which these small and medium-sized enterprises function in terms of structure, organisational culture, and communication patterns. This section will address the concept of entrepreneurship within an organisation – commonly called – intrapreneurship.

31

Entrepreneurial Characteristics

L E A R N I N G   O B J E C T I V E S

- **Identify Entrepreneurs**

- **Appreciate the wide range of Entrepreneurial characteristics which are encountered**

- **Understand the interrelationships between these characteristics**

- **Apply the factors studied to entrepreneurs with whom you are familiar**

- **Identify areas where further research is necessary**

In this book the concept of entrepreneurship will be examined from a modern perspective. However it must be acknowledged that the concept of entrepreneurial activity has been in existence for several millennia. Many peoples, such as the Phoenicans, expanded the markets for their products by trading on the oceans of the world. Other peoples, such as the Romans, sought to expand their sphere of political, social and economic activity by seeking to conquer other countries. Later in the fifteenth century European countries expanded their sphere of control by exploration of America, Africa and the Far East. In the seventeenth and eighteenth centuries large sections of Europe were subject to substantial economic change – the Industrial Revolution. This revolution was heavily reliant on individuals (mill owners, iron foundry operators) driving through economic changes – mill owners, iron foundry operators. Slightly later in this period large sections of the United States were economically developed again through individual, rather than corporate, activity.

All of these activities constitute features of entrepreneurship in that, at the very least, they involve risk taking. When entrepreneurship in its modern guise is examined it will be seen that it involves substantive features common with these historical analogies.

Types of Entrepreneur

The concept of entrepreneurship is based on studies of individuals and their activities and individual characteristics. As might be expected from such a methodology entrepreneurship is characterised as much by its diversity as its commonality. A simple overview of Richard Branson and Bill Gates will reveal them to be quite different people. The one exhibits more extrovert behaviour whereas the other is perceived to be a somewhat more introverted person. The one does not rely heavily on his own technical skills, whereas the other bases his business activities in areas surrounding his own technical skills. Inevitably individual people have their individual features and any attempt to impose external parameters on their skills, behaviours or motives is fraught with difficulty. Nevertheless it is useful to identify separate types of entrepreneurial activity. Again it must be admitted that an analysis of an individual entrepreneur will not necessarily fit perfectly with the chosen parameters. Equally an individual entrepreneur may well fit into more than one parameter or exhibit different characteristics during different periods of his or her career. A good example of this would be the entrepreneur who seeks to develop his or her own enterprise and then go public (see 'going public' in the following analysis).

These classifications conceptually are quite varied; in some cases they can be seen to be motivation, in other cases they can be seen to be simple behaviour patterns, in other cases they can be seen to be classifications of economic activity. What they have in common is their utility in classifying different types of entrepreneur or entrepreneurial characteristics.

SOLOIST

This type of entrepreneur turns his or her skill and interest into a livelihood. They seek to become self employed and employ their skills within a business context. Bill Gates might be seen to be an excellent example of this category of entrepreneur.

KEY PARTNER

This type of entrepreneur is separated from the Soloist in that he or she seeks to have the support and help - physical, emotional or financial of another person. Thus the concept of partnership does, in certain ways, fit into the entrepreneurial environment.

GROUPER

Such an entrepreneur will seek to work along with others rather than pursue precisely individual objectives. This form of motivation does admittedly have features in common with corporatist, rather than entrepreneurial, activity. However if this type of individual has significant control over the group's activity he can be admitted into the entrepreneurial category. An example of such people might be those who seek employment in cooperatives.

PROFESSIONAL

This type of entrepreneur has characteristics very similar to the soloist in that his entrepreneurial behaviour is based around acquired technical skills. However these technical skills are based around established professional skills (for example doctors, accountants, lawyers). In some ways many of these people might be surprised to find themselves described as entrepreneurs; the self-employment features might be deemed to be merely their established professional career path. However all of these professionals might have found employment in corporate organisations and hence their behaviour does, to some extent, warrant the classification of entrepreneurship.

INVENTOR

This class of entrepreneur will typically be driven by the desire to develop a personally researched product. As will be seen later in this section, this type of entrepreneur could be easily motivated by either push or pull motivation. An example of this classification might be Sir Clive Sinclair with his hi-tech entrepreneurial businesses.

HI-TECH

In many ways this can be seen to be a sub-category of the immediately preceding point; however it is so important in the modern managerial environment that it warrants a category in its own right. This type of entrepreneur will typically seek to exploit his or her appreciation of new technology to develop a new product or to redesign an existing product. Perhaps one of the best examples of this would be Bill Gates and his Microsoft I.T. Range.

WORKFORCE

This is a very common and traditional type of entrepreneur who will work in an existing area of economic activity and seek to develop his or her own enterprise by organising the workforce. A good example of this type of entrepreneur would be a person with a trade skill but who seeks to expand his or her area of control over a wider range of skills (for example a small builder).

INITIATOR

This type of entrepreneur will be commonly seen setting up businesses and then selling them possibly moving into a new sphere of economic activity for his or her next purchase.

CONCEPT MULTIPLIER

This type of entrepreneur will identify an area of economic activity which can be multiplied and exploit this opportunity. Undoubtedly many of the best examples of this form of activity are found in the area of franchising. This class of entrepreneur will be seen entering into franchising operations from both the perspective of the franchiser and the franchisee

ACQUIRER

This type of person will acquire an existing business and seek to pursue his or her career through this mode. The examples of such people are legion. For instance small, local retail outlets are regularly sold to new proprietors.

TURN ABOUT

This is probably a sub-category of the acquirer; however it is so commonly evidenced that it probably warrants separate classification. It would be distinguished from the previous point in that the motives for acquisition embrace desires for expansion rather than consolidation. It must be admitted that these two categories are usually jointly rather than separately evidenced. When someone acquires an existing business, that person commonly consolidates many activities whilst at the same time striving to improve other areas of business activity.

VALUE MANIPULATOR

This person will be driven by the desire to buy and sell assets at a profit. Clearly this is closely connected with the immediately preceding category but the distinction would be that the turn about person might be motivated by the challenge of rectifying problems whereas this type of person would be motivated by the challenge of identifying areas where economic gain would be found. Again it can be readily seen that hybrids of these categories could easily exist – that is someone who would welcome the challenge of rectifying a business but would equally be driven by desire for profit.

SPECULATOR

This category is only marginally different from the value manipulator; the primary distinction is that the Value Manipulator would carefully scrutinise businesses for their likely profit whereas this type of person would be primarily driven by the challenge of the speculation. Again it must be admitted that in practice it is difficult to distinguish between the two. For instance how carefully does a gambler examine the odds and the background to a speculation? However it must be equally admitted that many people who operate in these areas would make a careful and precise distinction between the two areas of motivation.

CAPITAL AGGREGATOR

This classification is very similar to the speculator in that the primary activity is buying and selling at a profit. However the former person might be driven by the challenge of seeking areas where profits might be found whereas the capital aggregator gains most satisfaction from economic gain. Again it must be admitted that in practice it is very difficult to distinguish between the two motives in any entrepreneur.

NURTURER

This category of entrepreneur would gain satisfaction from starting an enterprise and overseeing its expansion into a larger economic activity. An example of this type of person would be the creators of the Woolworth empire of the early twentieth century.

CONGLOMERATOR

This type of person would be challenged by the size of the enterprises he or she operated and also by the diversity of economic areas controlled. Such a person would gain satisfaction from expanding an area of economic activity whilst also overseeing diversification. Examples of this can be found in the Hanson Trust and Virgin empires.

PARENTAL

This type of entrepreneur would be seen to be perpetuating a family business. Examples of this type of person are many but good examples might be found in the farming community. This type of entrepreneur could then pursue different motives such as nurturer or turn about.

GOING PUBLIC

This is most commonly found in conjunction with other categories and is probably best evidenced at a particular period in the career of an entrepreneur. For instance a soloist or an inventor might develop the business and then seek to pursue economic gain or expansion by offering shares in the business to the general public.

ALTERNATIVE

Examples of such entrepreneurs can be found throughout history. However recent social environments have provided equally good examples. These entrepreneurs can be seen to be developing businesses based upon cultures alternative to those generally accepted in the society in which they live. An excellent example of this would be found with the emergence of the Body Shop where the primary motivation was to produce products which matched a Green or environmentally friendly philosophy.

ETHNIC MINORITY

This classification can be seen to be closely connected with the alternative classification. Examples can be found throughout history but again more recent examples provide equally beneficial illustrations. In this case the primary motive would be to serve the demands of an ethnic minority. Examples might be music or food preferences of ethnic minorities. This is afforded as a separate category but the primary motivation for its creation could be found in previous categories: for instance the primary motivation might be financial or social. Interestingly examples can be found of these businesses finding markets beyond the original motivation. Ethnic minority music or food can sometimes find markets beyond those ethnic minorities.

COMMITTED MANAGER

The final two categories might be aggregations of previously analysed points but they afford such an interesting contrast that they might usefully be specifically mentioned. People might find extensive motivation in the desire to manage most or all of the activities they oversee. This might originate in a need to be in control or it might originate from the stimulation of management in its own right – the rest of this text shows how management and being in control are not synonymous concepts. This motivation can be seen in the concept of intrapreneurship examined later in this section.

LIFESTYLE

A person might be driven in his or her business activity by an image of a desired lifestyle. The business might be seen as a way of providing or complementing a lifestyle founded on wealth, control, or freedom. In many ways the most interesting examples are those entrepreneurs who reinforce this desire in a conscious marketing policy. Richard Branson has publicly admitted his interest in challenging ventures but it is interesting to note the extent to which his highly public activities (ballooning or trans-atlantic speedboating) are carefully complemented by his company's brand name and logo.

Summary

It can be seen that entrepreneurs are as much categorised by variation as by similarity. Individual entrepreneurs can be driven by different motives, can be seen to operate in radically different areas of economic activity, and can pursue different strategies. The categories examined in this chapter should be considered as discrete; however the student of entrepreneurship should be aware of amalgamations of these categories within individual entrepreneurs. Finally individual entrepreneurs might be seen to be pursuing different strategies at different times in their career.

Exercise

Choose an entrepreneur and, either by examining the individual or by examining his or her biographical details, assess the extent to which his or her career can be accommodated in the issues addressed in this chapter.

Further Reading

Chell, E., Haworth, J., and Brearley, S. (1991) *The Entrepreneurial Personality*, Routledge
Cope, N. (1995) 'Trying to Prove the Knockers Wrong', *Financial Times* 10th July
Cox, N. (1995) 'Entrepreneur of Old Still Alive and Well', *Independent* 30th August
Deakins, D. (1996) *Entrepreneurship and Small Firms*, McGraw Hill
McClelland, D.C. (1961) *The Achieving Society*, Van Nostrand
'Portrait of an Entrepreneur' (1996) *Management Today* (Feb)

Chapter thirty - two

Factors
Facilitating
Entrepreneurship

LEARNING OBJECTIVES

- **Identify entrepreneurs**

- **Identify the factors which contribute to entrepreneurial success**

- **Understand the interrelationships between these factors**

- **Apply the factors studied to entrepreneurs with whom you are familiar**

- **Identify areas where further research is necessary**

The last chapter examined the variety of entrepreneurial characteristics. Part of that analysis focused on entrepreneurial motivation. This chapter will focus more specifically on what causes or helps an entrepreneur to enter this sphere of economic and managerial activity. As in the previous analysis it must be seen that motivation in this area is commonly complex and people enter into entrepreneurial activity for more than one reason. Sometimes the decision will be a conscious decision on other occasions less conscious motives are involved. However any analysis of this area which did not attempt to scrutinise causal factors in entrepreneurship would be incomplete and flawed. In the first part of this chapter, three possible causal factors will be examined:

1. The skills required in the entrepreneur.

2. The personality characteristics present in the entrepreneur.

3. The economic and social conditions necessary to establish entrepreneurship.

Each of these causal factors will be examined in the next part of the chapter.

Skills

The previous chapter has acknowledged that some entrepreneurs base their careers in areas where they have specific technical knowledge and to this extent this causal factor must have credibility. However, given that most people have technical skills and few people emerge as entrepreneurs, it is necessary to look for skills beyond those which are purely technical. Equally technical skills as the primary requirement for entrepreneurship could never be an acceptable explanation for those entrepreneurs who base their careers around sectors of the economy where they have no technical knowledge.

It might be useful to examine two special skills, other than pure technical knowledge, which have been hypothesised as major causal factors for entrepreneurial success – innovation and risk taking:

INNOVATION

This can clearly be seen to be a quality required of some entrepreneurs; the problem, however, depends on the extent of its importance. An example of a theory emphasising this as an essential quality is that provided by Curran and Stanworth (1989). In this context innovation is characterised by product or service differentiation – that is something which distinguishes it from other products or services in the market. It is difficult to pronounce on the acceptability of such a theory. It is likely that, as a contributory factor, it is difficult to dismiss but, as an exclusive factor, it might prove somewhat more difficult to prove.

RISK TAKING

Risk, it must be noted, is not synonymous with uncertainty. The former can be calculated but the latter remains by its very origins unpredictable. According to such theories the entrepreneur is distinguished from other people, such as managers, by his or her willingness to assume responsibility for the risk that something will fail. Ray (1993) identified risk as an important but not exclusive quality of the entrepreneur.

It must be admitted that these two skills could be seen to be personality based and hence indistinguishable from personality theories. However it is equally possible that people could acquire these skills and exhibit them as behaviour patterns unconnected with their personality. Later in the analysis it will be shown that, although these are two important skills required of the entrepreneur, there are other equally acceptable contributory factors to entrepreneurial success.

Personality

It is probable that personality-based characteristics are those which are most clearly associated with entrepreneurs in popular literature. Certainly the case for innovation and risk taking is powerful and many theorists would include such features as elements of personality. However, as has already been mentioned in the previous chapter, entrepreneurs seem quite a varied group, embracing the seemingly disparate characters of Richard Branson and Bill Gates. This does not exclude the possibility that this disparate group have some common personality characteristics or traits. Thus the nature of personality in entrepreneurship needs to be examined.

McClelland (1961) hypothesised the Entrepreneurial Personality characterised by:

i) Proactivity: showing initiative and assertiveness;

ii) Achievement orientation: the need to strive for success;

iii) Commitment to others.

Much subsequent attention focused on the achievement orientation characteristic as exemplifying the strive for excellence and constant improvement. The work of McClelland was extended by Meredith et al (1982) who suggested the following personality traits:

i) self-confidence

ii) risk-taking ability

iii) flexibility

iv) need for achievement

v) desire for independence

It must be admitted that these characteristics do seem to embrace or possibly account for most entrepreneurial activity. However this personality based theory is still not fully accepted as a full explanation of entrepreneurship in that the range of traits is very wide; they may, for instance, embrace large sections of society and yet entrepreneurs are less liberally distributed. Additionally the emphasis has been on a range of entrepreneurial personality traits with little attempt to isolate the importance of each.

There is some doubt as to whether these are innate personality traits or whether they constitute learnt behaviour patterns. If the latter is the legitimate interpretation it might suggest that the ability to learn from ones experiences is the crucial factor; if this were true it would firmly return the balance to the skills explanatory classification. Timmons (1985) suggested that the innate personality features of the entrepreneur are:

i) high energy;

ii) emotional stability;

iii)   creativity;

iv)   conceptual ability;

v)   vision;

vi)   high profile leadership qualities.

This theory extends the range of theories focusing on personality issues. However the continual problem is that there is little evidence to prove their innate nature; rather the counter argument still remains that such qualities can be learnt.

With the conclusions still uncertain, it is necessary to examine the final type of theory – that entrepreneurial activity is substantially affected by environmental issues; to fully explain entrepreneurship, the environment necessary to facilitate its development needs to be examined.

Economic and Social Environment

As has been mentioned, these theories concentrate on circumstances which will encourage entrepreneurship. This class of theory is especially important in that, if it has some validity, it is the one area that society can control; if society wishes entrepreneurship to flourish, it can at least create environments conducive to entrepreneurship.

Timmons (1985) acknowledged the contribution of cultural issues isolating as an example the different attitudes to failure obtaining in the United States of America and in the United Kingdom. In the former culture failure is deemed to be a learning experience and carries with it little social stigma; however in the United Kingdom Timmons suggests that a more favourable judgement is less likely to obtain and, for instance, access to capital in future may not be as guaranteed.

It is becoming increasingly recognised that, in the development of any business, the ability to insure against risks is an important factor. This area has only just begun to be explored. However Deakins (1993) suggested that the limited insurance taken out by high-technology, smaller firms (possibly indicating less ready access to insurance) seemed to inhibit the success of entrepreneurship in this area.

There has recently been increasing attention to the subject of female entrepreneurship. As such research is in its infancy, it is difficult to use this research to support or reject the environmental theory category. Goffee and Scase (1987) point to differing characteristics in male and female entrepreneurs. It may be that these are innate variations, however the possibility still remains that differences are due to culture.

Studies of differences based on race are similarly in their infancy. Studies by Deakins et al (1992) show that Afro-Caribbean entrepreneurs found greater difficulty in accessing support from banks. The causes of this difference are still not resolved and there may not be any reluctance on behalf of banks to finance such ventures.

However the findings, at present, might be seen to at least not disprove the environmental influence theory in that limited access to such finance could inhibit the success of such ventures.

Recent attention has been directed to regional variations in the creation of entrepreneurial businesses. In the United Kingdom there are wide differences in this regard across the various regions. Figure 32.1 shows the extent of this difference. It is difficult to attribute causes to such variations; for instance it could be that entrepreneurial characteristics are unevenly spread throughout the United Kingdom. However the much more popular explanation focuses on differences in regional environment. Keeble and Walker (1993) suggest that the most important causes of these variations are:

Region	Number of new firms (000)	Formation Rate[1]
South-East	850	100.3
South-West	190	99.7
East Anglia	79	95.8
East Midlands	140	79.3
Wales	93	77.5
West Midlands	180	72.1
Yorks and Humberside	158	70.3
North-West	207	68.7
Northern Ireland	39	61.1
Scotland	134	55.4
North	77	55.3
UK	2,147	81.4

Note 1: Per 1000 civilian labour force, 1981
Source: Keeble and Walker (12)

FIGURE 32.1 *Regional variation in new firm formation rates 1980-90*

i) local population growth;

ii) capital availability;

iii) available professional and managerial expertise.

Deakins (1995) pointed to the much larger creation of high technology firms since 1990 in the West Midlands compared with Scotland. He attests that this is consistent with the variations in access to liquidity suggested by Evans and Jovanivic (1989); the higher home ownership rate in the West Midlands compared with Scotland is seen as a greater source of security for loans.

Importance of Skill, Personality, and Environment

The possible contributions of each factor have been examined. Each appears to have some contribution to make to the expanding store of knowledge in this area. Perhaps the most useful conclusion to make would be that each has a role and, rather than rejecting any category, explanations or descriptions accommodating all in a modified contingency approach might prove successful in the medium term. When such evidence has been collected in the longer term more definitive theories might evolve.

Push and Pull Factors

An alternative perspective is one which distinguishes between push and pull factors; a distinction could be made between those factors which pull the entrepreneur into this area of activity and those which push him or her into action. Pull factors are those which are internal to the entrepreneur – they explain some inner need of the person. Push factors are external to the entrepreneur – they explain the external environment which caused the individual to pursue the path chosen.

PULL FACTORS

From the previous chapter it can be seen that there is a range of internal driving forces in the creation of the entrepreneur. Commonly evidenced qualities include the fact that they are risk takers, able to tolerate stress, with a significant degree of confidence in their own ability, with a welcoming for a degree of independence and with a considerable degree of mental energy and perseverance. However these are merely personal characteristics and undoubtedly will be evidenced in people other than entrepreneurs and clearly factors other than those outlined need to be present.

  i) Entrepreneurs commonly have a strong desire for independence in their working lives – Bolton Report 1971 – The Committee of Enquiry into Small Firms.
 ii) A desire to exploit a commercial opportunity is quite common in entrepreneurs
iii) A strong desire to make use in their working lives of a hobby or a previous experience is also evidenced.
 iv) Entrepeneurs have an above average desire to utilise financial incentives.

Push Factors

It is quite usual for these internal driving forces to be reinforced by external events. Entrepreneurs commonly express the fact that they feel they were partly pushed into independent occupation.

Many entrepreneurs move into their career when their initial employment was removed by redundancy. Although this can be evidenced in several types of entrepreneurial activity, it is particularly evidenced in entrepreneurial activity closely connected with hobbies or experience.

Problems encountered in previous corporate employment. Some entrepreneurs identify frustration with their previous working environment or problems with their superiors as a strong driving force to seeking independent employment.

This approach would seem to complement the earlier part of this chapter in focusing both on innate qualities and on environmental factors in the creation of entrepreneurship.

Summary

The factors which cause a person to enter into an entrepreneurial career or those which facilitate the career of the entrepreneur are many. When the complete perspective of entrepreneurship is examined it is impossible to attach primacy to either the skills required of an entrepreneur, to the personality requirements of the entrepreneur or to the economic conditions which allow entrepreneurship to flourish. Rather the picture which emerges is one which must recognise the contribution of all three key factors in the creation of entrepreneurship. An alternative perspective is one which examines the factors contributing to entrepreneurship and distinguishes between those which give the entrepreneur the personal qualities required and those which encourage the entrepreneur to utilise those qualities. From this perspective it is again impossible to attach primacy to either category; the picture which emerges is again one which recognises the contribution made by each category.

Exercise

In the context of your chosen entrepreneur examine the factors which have contributed to his or her success. Assess the extent to which internal or external features are responsible for this success.

Further Reading

Chell, E., Haworth, J., and Brearley, S. (1991) *The Entrepreneurial Personality*, Routledge

Cope, N. (1995) 'Trying to Prove the Knockers Wrong', *Financial Times* 10th July

Cox, N. (1995) 'Entrepreneur of Old Still Alive and Well', *Independent* 30th August

Deakins, D. (1996) *Entrepreneurship and Small Firms*, McGraw Hill

Drucker, P. (1977) *Management*, Pan

McClelland, D.C. (1961) *The Achieving Society*, Van Nostrand

Goffee, R. and Scase, R. (1987) *Patterns of Business Proprietorship among Women in Britain*, Croom Helm

Timmons, J.A. (1985) *New Venture Creation: A Guide to Entrepreneurship*, Irwin

Small Medium Enterprises

LEARNING OBJECTIVES

- Identify small medium enterprises (SMEs)

- Identify the factors which contribute to SME success

- Understand the interrelationships between these factors

- Identify the importance of SMEs in modern economic activity

- Appraise the extent to which SMEs have unique managerial characteristics

- Appraise the extent to which they exhibit managerial characteristics found in larger, corporate organisations

- Apply the factors studied to SMEs with which you are familiar

- Identify areas where further research is necessary

Definition

Much attention has recently focused on SMEs. Inevitably there will be debate about what constitutes a small and medium organisation. The following classifications are those which are most commonly accepted:

i) self employed - 1 employee

ii) micro business – between 1 and 20 employees

iii) small business – between 20 and 60 employees

iv) medium business – between 60 and 199 employees (European Union definition) between 60 and 499 employees (United Kingdom Department of Trade and Industry definition) Clearly the last classification and its two variable upper parameters affords an area of uncertainty. It is difficult to determine the most appropriate upper parameter; however in interpreting the points made in this text readers should assume that hypothesised characteristics are relatively less likely to obtain towards the upper range of the United Kingdom definition.

Importance of SMEs

These types of organisation are important for both economic, social and managerial reasons.

ECONOMIC

As shown in Figure 33.1 SMEs account for 66% of employment. Their entry into markets also ensures competition with the consequent hypothesised improvements in efficiency and quality.

SOCIAL

SMEs protect society from domination by large conglomerates. They ensure alternative sources of supply. This advantage also transfers into the employment market and the ease of emergence of these types of organisation provides competition in the employment market. Hence employees have alternative employment prospects to those which might be afforded by the large corporate entities.

An additional advantage is that they might be seen to be closer to their consumers and hence more responsive to consumer needs. The interface between this increased responsiveness and innovation is examined later in this chapter.

In an economic and social environment which increasingly recognises the importance of the Green dimension, such firms might, and commonly do, differentiate their product lines to accommodate environmental protection issues. This is most obviously evidenced in the alternative entrepreneurial category examined in a previous chapter of this section.

Firm size and share of employment UK 1979-89 (*totals may be different due to rounding)

Firm size	1979 No. (000)	1979 Share of employ-ment %	1986 No. (000)	1986 Share of employ-ment %	1989 No. (000)	1989 Share of employ-ment %
1-10	1597	19.2	2308	27.8	2802	28.6
11-19	109	7.6	84	6.0	92	6.0
20-49	46	6.9	56	8.2	57	7.6
50-99	16	5.3	16	5.8	18	5.8
100-199	15	10.2	9	7.4	9	7.2
200-499	5	8.1	5	9.5	6	10.6
500+	4	42.8	3	35.1	3	34.2
Totals	**1791***	**100***	**2481***	**100***	**2988***	**100***

Source: Employment Gazette (modified) February 1992 and other editions. Crown Copyright © Reproduced with th permission of the controller of HMSO.

FIGURE 33.1 *Growing importance of SME's*

MANAGERIAL

Figure 33.2 shows that 94% of economic entities can be classified as SMEs and thus any analysis which fails to examine the specific managerial features of 94% of organisations could be substantially flawed. Although it must be admitted that SMEs will vary in their managerial and leadership features, it is probable that they more readily exhibit entrepreneurial characteristics than do larger, more corporate organisations. This will be examined in more detail later in this chapter. At this stage it might be useful to examine the findings of the Bolton Committee of Enquiry on Small Firms 1971 They have certain characteristics:

a. they tend to be a mirror of their owner;

b. they tend to be independently, rather than corporately, owned;

c. they tend to have small, rather than large, shares of the markets in which they operate;

These characteristics are the consequence of the following factors:

i) Small businesses are a natural outlet for enterprising individuals;

ii) They constitute the most efficient size of organisation in many markets;

iii) They afford specialist supplies to larger organisations;

iv) They tend to be the most effective suppliers to specialist markets;

v) They tend to facilitate innovation;

vi) They nurture emerging industries;

vii) They act as useful competition in freeing markets.

Size distribution of firms based on turnover 1989			
Turnover(£000)	**Number of firms (000)**	**% share**	**Cumulative % share**
0-14	1046	35	35
15-49	939	31.4	66.4
50-99	345	11.6	78
100-249	339	11.3	89.3
250-499	139	4.6	93.9
500-999	82	2.7	96.6
1000-2499	56	1.9	98.5
2500-4999	20	0.7	99.2
5000-9999	11	0.4	99.6
10,000+	12	0.4	100
Totals	**2989**	**100**	

Source: Employment Gazette (modified). Crown Copyright ©
Reproduced with th permission of the controller of HMSO.

FIGURE 33.2 *Importance of SME's*

Why Growth in Importance

SMEs have increased in importance to the United Kingdom economy. Figure 33.1 shows the growth in their importance between 1979 and 1989. This expansion has caused such organisations to be the subject of increasing attention. Approximately 1,000 new organisations are created in the United Kingdom very week. It would be helpful, at this stage, to examine the causes of this increasing attention and importance.

a) In many Western economies unemployment has increased – this causes an increased importance to the push factors hypothesised in the last chapter.

b) In Western economies it has been the service sector which has increased in importance at the expense of the industrial sector. In the United Kingdom the service sector accounts for approximately 70% of gross domestic product. The service sector, with its more obvious need to focus on customer needs and preferences, tends to be populated by smaller organisations.

c) In the United Kingdom since the mid–1980s there has been a greater emphasis on sub–contracting whereby organisations tend to focus their managerial attention on their core activities and buy in support services. The tendency has been for smaller organisations to assume these responsibilities. Even where large service organisations have assumed these responsibilities their managerial processes have been more geared to devolution of responsibility and empowerment examined elsewhere in this text.

d) Complementing these dynamics in the private sector have been decentralising dynamics in the traditional United Kingdom public sector. Large public sector organisations have been disaggregated into smaller organisations. An example would be the emergence of agencies to replace many executive responsibilities of central government departments. Perhaps more important however are the managerial changes in public sector organisations. The National Health Service and Education have been substantially decentralised in their management. In the National Health service smaller providing organisations have emerged. In the Education Sector many of the responsibilities of Local Education Authorities have now been assumed by smaller governing bodies based in each school. The reason for this disaggregation and decentralisation has been the publicly expressed desire to introduce more innovation, more customer responsiveness.

In addition the United Kingdom public sector affords an excellent example of organisations limiting their operational responsibilities and replacing their role as enabling rather than operational organisations. This has led to the concept of contracting-out or competitive tendering. In this emerging environment many public service activities are subject to competitive tendering and subsequent competition. This has resulted, in the main, in the emergence of small organisations providing public services. In certain instances, where national groupings have been successful (for example refuse collection) managerial structures and processes giving freedom to individual contract managers has been quite common; this approach to management, although not immediately creating small organisations, has created a managerial environment similar to that of small organisations. This point will be examined in more depth in the next chapter.

e) Small organisations have also emerged through the growth in what has become known as the enterprise culture whereby many Western governments have tried to stimulate entrepreneurship through such mechanisms as tax incentives and reductions of barriers to entry into existing markets.

f) The emerging social environments stimulating industries such as health foods, health and exercise clubs, and health promotion groups has facilitated the emergence of small organisations in new markets or in markets previous populated by large organisations.

Innovation

In the context of this subject area the issue of SMEs and innovation requires specific analysis. Much of the detail on the concept of innovation is covered in another section of this text. Innovation is not merely invention but also involves the development of the product from the idea through to production. More importantly, however, it must be acknowledged that innovation also embraces older products in new markets, new marketing strategies, new technology, and new packaging.

For many years SMEs have been prominently connected with nnovation; this connection is illustrated in Figure 33.4 which shows the causes of innovation as hypothesised by Drucker.

Sources of Innovation - Peter Drucker

A. Unexpected Success - e.g. development of computer for scientific purposes but expansion into wider markets
B. Unexpected Failure - e.g. baked potatoes were originally sold with a side salad these proved unpopular so to use up the stock they were sold with fillings and these proved enormously successful
C. Production Demands - e.g. the need for cheaper, more efficient production methods
D. Demographics - changes in such - e.g. increasing numbers of elderly people in the market
E. Changes in Values - e.g. health foods
F. New Technology - e.g. television, information technology.

It might be interesting to examine the causes of the close connection between SMEs and innovation. SMEs are more closely associated with opportunistic entrepreneurial activity. Their communication patterns – which will be examined later in this chapter, are less rigid, more informal, speedier thus enabling them to react more quickly to perceived opportunities. Their smaller size tends to ensure that they are more closely associated with their markets and hence can more readily accommodate changes in customer preferences. However it must be seen that SMEs do have difficulties in achieving maximum success in the field of innovation in that they may not have the financial and management resources to fully develop or market the full development of new products or services.

Structures

The principles of organisational design are addressed elsewhere in this text. However at this stage it is useful to summarise the organisational design features which will be facilitated by smaller organisations.

Inevitably SMEs are varied organisations and the difference in size between two and 499 employees can show that it is difficult to make unqualified statements about their organisational design.

Certainly expanding SMEs might have to develop their organisational structures away from unstructured organic designs into more structured bureaucratic, inorganic designs. However when contrasted with much larger organisations they can be seen to be more flexible in their use of employee experience and expertise, less bound by functional divisions, less prone to vertical communication patterns, more prone to horizontal communication, using the more complex, extended communication patterns.

Organisational Cultures

The principles of organisational and sub–organisational culture are examined in other sections of this book. However again it is useful to examine the types of culture which might more readily be associated with SME's.

As suggested in the immediately preceding analysis it is unlikely that there will be universally evidenced organisational cultures in the SME environment. However it is likely that the less bureaucratic structures which will tend to predominate will be matched by less rigid cultures. If Handy's classifications (examined in another section of this book) are used it might be seen that the smaller size of such organisations facilitates the less rigid task culture as opposed to the more rigid role culture commonly associated with larger organisations. Other cultural classifications which might be seen to be clearly facilitated by the SME environment are client or risk. The closeness to the client and the increased focus on risk in such organisations has been examined previously in this section.

Communication and Marketing

The principles of communication and marketing are examined in other sections of the book. However the special features of communication within and marketing of SME's is worthy of separate analysis.

As mentioned earlier, inevitably SMEs are varied organisations and the difference in size between two and 499 employees can show that it is difficult to make unqualified statements about such communication patterns or marketing strategies. However smaller organisations tend to be less rigid and less hierarchical. They also tend to be subject to more flexible organisational designs. As such there will tend to be less emphasis placed on formal communication and somewhat more emphasis placed on informal communication patterns. The more limited focus on formal communication will tend to limit emphasis placed on vertical communication; certainly where it does exist vertical communication is likely to be more informal and this informality should encourage much more two way communication.

The less rigid organisational designs with somewhat less focus on functions will mean that horizontal communication should be much more productively pursued.

When the organisation focuses on external communications it must be admitted that size will inevitably restrict the budget available for such communication. Under such circumstances such organisations will have to strive to develop more informal external communication patterns. Although it is difficult to make unqualified judgements, SMEs are more closely associated with networking in their external communication. Smaller organisations tend to make much more use of established relationships and utilise such relationships in their pursuance of new markets or new contracts.

This focus on the informality of networking also extends to and, in fact, is probably best evidenced in the marketing activity. Restricted budgets mean that rarely can SMEs compete with the professionally produced marketing and advertising of larger, corporate organisations. To compensate for this they can be seen to make extensive use of networking in the pursuance of their marketing objectives.

Summary

SMEs are an increasingly important part of modern economic activity. They are the repository of great innovative strength. Although SMEs are quite varied in nature there is a strong tendency for them to exercise flexible design structures and processes; they tend to exhibit the more flexible types of organisational culture. Communication patterns and marketing strategies tend to mirror their flexible nature. In many ways they constitute managerial qualities ideally suited to the fast changing environment in which many organisations operate.

Exercise

Choose, either from personal knowledge or from your general reading, a small or medium-sized enterprise. Examine the constituent features of the organisation and assess the extent to which it exhibits characteristics similar to those explored in this chapter.

Further Reading

Dawson, T. (1998) *Principles and Practice of Modern Management*, Tudor
Deakins, D. (1996) *Entrepreneurship and Small Firms*, McGraw Hill
Drucker, P. (1977) *Management*, Pan

Evans, D. and Jovanivic, B. (1989) 'A Model of Entrepreneurial Choice' *Journal of Political Economy* , vol 97, no.4 pp 808-27

Handy, C. (1985) *Understanding Organisations*, Penguin

HM Government (1971) *Committee of Inquiry on Small Firms* (Bolton Report), HMSO

Ward, R. and Jenkins, R. (eds) (1984) *Ethnic Communities in Britain*, Cambridge

34

Intrapreneurship

L E A R N I N G   O B J E C T I V E S

- Identify intrapreneurs and strategic business units (SBUs)

- Identify the factors which contribute to intrapreneurial and SBU success

- Understand the interrelationships between these factors

- Identify the importance of SBUs in modern economic activity

- Appraise the extent to which SBUs have unique managerial characteristics

- Appraise the extent to which they exhibit managerial characteristics found in their larger, corporate, parental organisations

- Examine the dangers of excessive intrapreneurial activity

- Assess how a parental organisation can obtain the benefits of Intrapreneurship whilst avoiding its dangers

- Apply the factors studied to SBUs with which you are familiar

- Identify areas where further research is necessary

Within this section of the text it is useful to examine the concept of intrapreneurship. The need for all organisations to maintain the flexibility to adapt to rapidly changing environments has been examined elsewhere in this book. All organisations, large and small, are operating in a much more obviously competitive environment than that which has traditionally obtained. Under such circumstances organisations, large and small, have to ensure that their market position is adequately consolidated and, perhaps more importantly, seek to prepare themselves for the need to operate in different environments if circumstances so dictate.

In this changing, more dynamic environment, the concept of intrapreneurship has emerged. This is loosely the use of Entrepreneurial activity within larger, corporate organisations.

Characteristics

Unlike entrepreneurship the features which compose intrapreneurship are more consistent when one organisation is compared with another. Typically an identifiable operational area of a corporate organisation will be given a large degree of managerial freedom to pursue its business objectives both in terms of being given delegated budgets and delegated powers over management practices. These intrapreneurial sections are frequently known as strategic business units - SBUs. They may be located at the functional level, for example a finance directorate in a large public service organisation or they may be located at the production level for example a refuse collection directorate of a local authority. In the former case the finance directorate might be allowed to enter into individual contracts with internal clients to provide the finance function in the larger organisation. The precise services requested would be specified and the price of that service would similarly be specified. In certain circumstances the directorate (or SBU) might be allowed to enter into contracts with outside organisations to increase its net income. In the latter case the business would be given strategic operational objectives by the local authority but given wide managerial freedom in deciding how to deliver to those broad objectives. Sometimes both types of SBU might have to compete with other agencies for the right to deliver the service to its clients.

Why SBUs Emerged

The fundamental reason for the creation of this concept has been the striving for managerial efficiency and effectiveness. In the case of the public service this changed environment has, to a degree, been imposed by legislation; however some such organisations have voluntarily assumed this changed environment. The primary driving force throughout all sectors of economic activity has been the increased competitive environment in which the organisations operate. Under these changed economic circumstances organisations have had to closely scrutinise their efficiency. They have to consider, for instance, whether they are achieving maximum value for money from the way they provide their functional activities. The organisation might decide to require its finance activities to enter into competition with outside agencies for the right to provide the service which had hitherto been guaranteed. Contractual obligations might be introduced whereby the precise services expected by clients would be specified and the price received from these services would similarly be specified

In the case of SBU's being created at the production level the driving philosophy is rather different. In this case the business will operate in a competitive environment and the emerging conviction is that to operate in this way the business needs to be afforded more freedom within market conditions rather than organisational constraints. For instance they might want to remunerate staff according to market conditions rather than according to organisational policies. It might want managerial freedom to purchase support services from outside the organisation rather than have to rely on the monopolistic provision afforded by other sections of the organisation.

Both types of SBU have one additional feature - the fact that their managers have to adopt entrepreneurial qualities and styles. They need to more fully involve themselves in the total management process than is usually the case in more function-based larger corporate organisations.

Structures

As with SMEs, which were examined in the previous chapter, it is difficult to hypothesise a precise organisational design that will be followed in all cases. Clearly the design of each organisation needs to be determined by the precise environmental conditions obtaining within each individual SBU. Nevertheless there are some fairly commonly observed design features:

a) There will be a substantial degree of decentralisation - decisions will be taken closer to the production function. This will enable the SBU to develop rapid responses to changes in consumer or client preferences.

b) There will be great emphasis placed on intelligence gathering close to production activity rather than through centrally managed research activity.

c) The more inflexible function-based organisational designs will be kept to a minimum. Rather task-based designs, probably formal but at the very least informal, will emerge.

d) The organisations,through giving autonomy to individual managers, will be flatter in format.

Organisational Cultures

As with all organisations intrapreneurial entities are not described exclusively by their structures; rather it is necessary to examine their collective values and priorities or organisational culture. Again it must be admitted that it is difficult to make statements in this area which will apply to all intrapreneurially based organisations. However the predominant cultural forces will be similar to those evidenced by SME's.

The need for flexibility will render Handy's role culture, found in many large organisations, counter-productive. Their flexible nature will dictate that task cultures (examined in another section of this text) will tend to emerge.

Clearly their intended close relationships with clients or customers suggests that other classifications such as client culture will be productive. Similarly the need to experiment with new processes and new pricing structures will help facilitate the emergence of a risk culture.

Communication Patterns

If the SBU is to obtain benefit from closeness to the customer and intelligence gathering from those closest to the customer its internal communication patterns should reflect some flexibility. Clearly any focus on vertical internal communication should emphasise the need for such communication to be two-way with at least as much emphasis on upwards communication as on downwards communication. However the more complex patterns examined in depth in the chapter of this book on communication must predominate. Circular communication, wheel communication and all channel communication, respecting the contribution of all participants, will be found extensively evidenced either in formal or in informal format. In the SBU, with its close focus on the customer, heavy emphasis will be placed on external communication. Customer liaison will be seen to be an obvious priority. The entrepreneurial features will inevitably advocate effective marketing of the services they have to offer. The functionally based SBU will give specific attention to networking with its internal customers in fulfilling its marketing obligations.

The Corporate Dimension

The analysis of SBUs would be incomplete if it were claimed that the concept of the SBU had been universally welcomed. Undoubtedly the increased customer focus, the greater emphasis placed on experimentation and the more task-oriented design structures have been broadly successful.

However the very independence created has caused some problems for some large, corporate organisations. One major quality of a large organisation is its facility to introduce consistency of approach and consistent standards across all its activities. The dissection of a larger organisation into several SBUs could be seen to be a threat to this quality. The striving for innovation could cause wide diversity of approach across the organisation's various activities. This does not mean that such experimentation should be abandoned; nor, indeed, should it be seen to be an advocating of rigid business practices. However if the diversity in practices within the one organisation is seen to be excessive the organisation must then resurrect organisational control.

The problem can also be viewed from the perspective of the ownership organisation. In smaller organisations there is a greater tendency for the people who make the managerial decisions to also be the owners and any managerial deficiencies will impact on no one other than those making the decisions. In larger, corporate organisations it is much more likely that the managers are not the owners of the enterprise and any deviant actions by managers are likely to impact not just on the people tasking the decisions but also on the owners. Thus there might be a need for a wider form of accountability to be introduced in these circumstances. This point can be seen to especially apply to the public sector where public not private money is spent. Thus in the public sector any loss of money through devolved management powers is likely to be at least embarrassing and maybe unacceptable.

Through a variety of such problems, the 1990s evidenced the emergence of the concept of corporate governance. Many such organisations have sought to impose some corporate standards and controls over their disparate activities. Much attention has been directed to the creation of audit committees as the primary example of corporate governance. However the creation of such committees could be seen in the wider context of organisations seeking to retain the benefits of SBU's without sacrificing organisational standards and principles.

Summary

The concept of entrepreneurship and smaller business units is not restricted to smaller organisations. Many larger organisations have also embraced the benefits of experimentation and proximity to the customer. They have created the concept of the strategic business unit whereby the corporate organisation has experimented with management practices giving greater independence in structures, processes and cultures to their various constituent parts. However if the larger corporate organisation commits itself to the SBU concept it needs to ensure that it retains all the benefits of this approach without sacrificing organisational standards and organisational integrity.

Exercise

Either from your personal knowledge or from research choose an intrapreneur and/or a strategic business unit. Assess the extent to which your chosen organisation and/or individual reflect characteristics examined in this chapter.

Further Reading

Chell, E., Haworth, J., and Brearley, S. (1991) *The Entrepreneurial Personality*, Routledge

Cadbury, A. (1992) Committee on Financial Aspects of Corporate Governance, Gee and Co

Dawson, T. (1998) *Principles and Practice of Modern Management*, Tudor

Deakins, D. (1996) *Entrepreneurship and Small Firms*, McGraw Hill

Drucker, P. (1977) *Management*, Pan

Handy, C. (1985) *Understanding Organisations*, Penguin

McClelland, D.C. (1961) *The Achieving Society*, Van Nostrand

Index